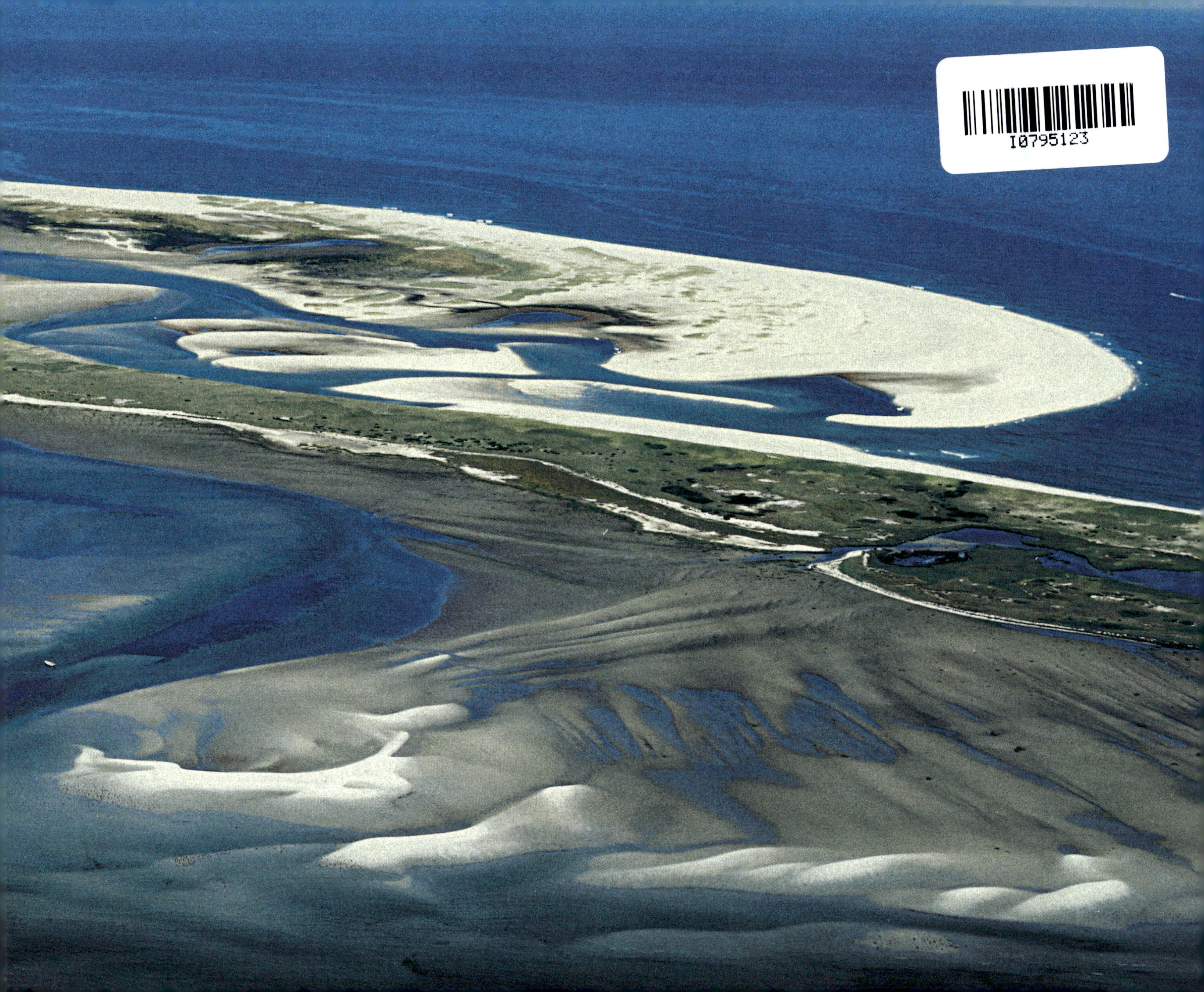

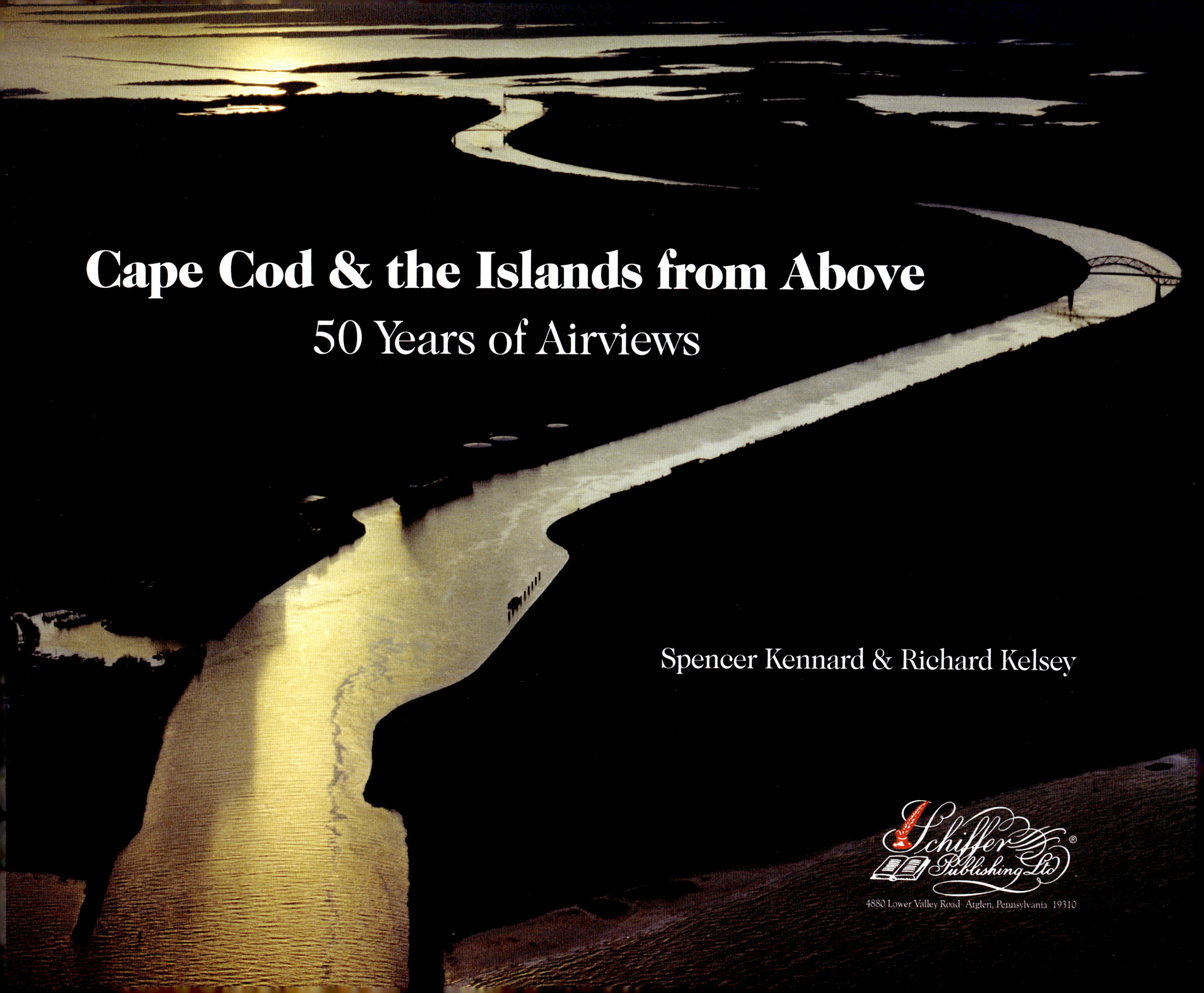

Cape Cod & the Islands from Above

50 Years of Airviews

Spencer Kennard & Richard Kelsey

Schiffer Publishing Ltd

4880 Lower Valley Road Atglen, Pennsylvania 19310

Dedication

This book is presented in memory of
Richard Cooper Kelsey
the ultimate sky-king
and **Spencer Kennard, Jr.**
my spiritual inspiration.

And it is dedicated to
Elizabeth
who thankfully has both feet on the ground.

Acknowledgments

Many of the Airviews seen here would not have been possible without the expert flying of our pilots, so here is a giant "thank you" to all of them. Also, we tip our hats to Tom Gillis for his early guidance. And a big thanks goes to Doug Congdon-Martin and all those at Schiffer Books.

Copyright © 2008 by Spencer Kennard

Library of Congress Control Number: 2008926127

All rights reserved. No part of this work may be reproduced or used in any form or by any means—graphic, electronic, or mechanical, including photocopying or information storage and retrieval systems—without written permission from the publisher.

The scanning, uploading and distribution of this book or any part thereof via the Internet or via any other means without the permission of the publisher is illegal and punishable by law. Please purchase only authorized editions and do not participate in or encourage the electronic piracy of copyrighted materials.

"Schiffer," "Schiffer Publishing Ltd. & Design," and the "Design of pen and ink well" are registered trademarks of Schiffer Publishing Ltd.

Covers and book designed by: Bruce Waters
Type set in Caslon 224

ISBN: 978- 0-7643-3043-8

Printed in China

Schiffer Books are available at special discounts for bulk purchases for sales promotions or premiums. Special editions, including personalized covers, corporate imprints, and excerpts can be created in large quantities for special needs. For more information contact the publisher:

Published by Schiffer Publishing Ltd.
4880 Lower Valley Road
Atglen, PA 19310
Phone: (610) 593-1777; Fax: (610) 593-2002
E-mail: Info@schifferbooks.com

For the largest selection of fine reference books on this and related subjects, please visit our web site at **www.schifferbooks.com**
We are always looking for people to write books on new and related subjects. If you have an idea for a book please contact us at the above address.

This book may be purchased from the publisher.
Include $3.95 for shipping.
Please try your bookstore first.
You may write for a free catalog.

In Europe, Schiffer books are distributed by
Bushwood Books
6 Marksbury Ave.
Kew Gardens
Surrey TW9 4JF England
Phone: 44 (0) 20 8392-8585; Fax: 44 (0) 20 8392-9876
E-mail: info@bushwoodbooks.co.uk
Website: www.bushwoodbooks.co.uk
Free postage in the U.K., Europe; air mail at cost.

Contents

Introduction 4

1. Nantucket & Martha's Vineyard 5

2. Bourne, Falmouth, Mashpee, & Sandwich 25

3. Barnstable, Hyannis, Yarmouth, & Dennis 48

4. Harwich, Brewster, & Chatham 77

5. Orleans, Eastham, Wellfleet, Truro, & Provincetown 108

6. Abstracts 130

7. Things You See While Flying 140

Information about the photographs 160

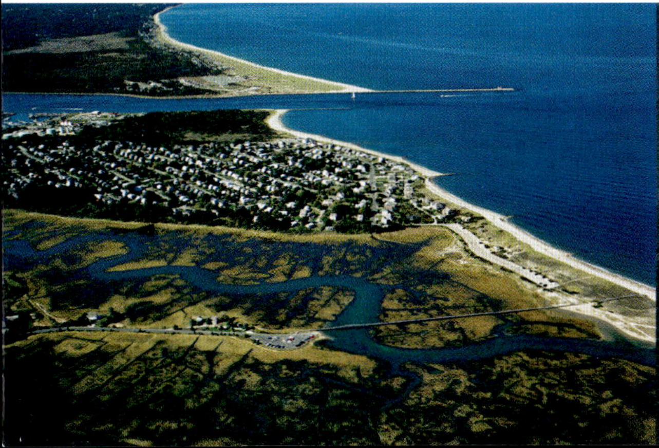
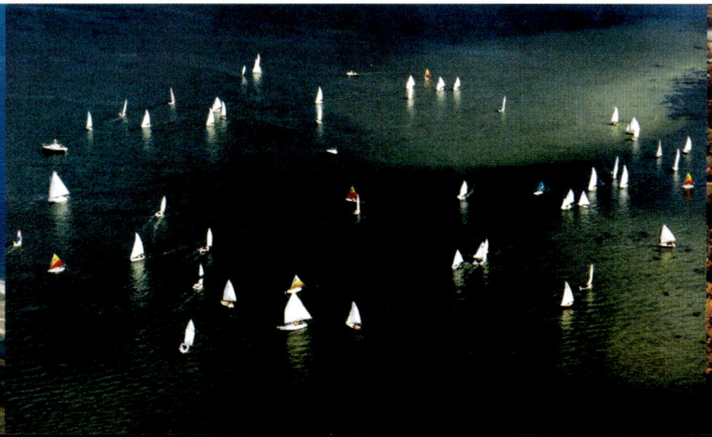
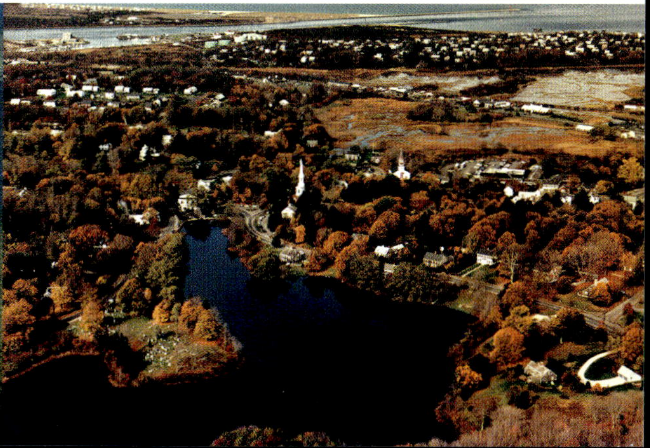

Introduction

Greetings, and welcome aboard as a co-pilot on a journey around Cape Cod and the islands of Nantucket and Martha's Vineyard. This region is definitely one of the greatest outdoor studios on our planet. Starting this visual tour would not have been possible without my mentor, Richard "Dick" Cooper Kelsey, a photographer *extraordinaire*, both on the ground and in the air. Dick was a friend to everyone, and he created dazzling images through a variety of cameras. He had the natural talent of capturing his subjects combined with the love of flying; his Airviews are to be treasured.

The Kelsey-Kennard archives of Airviews span more than 60 years. They capture the natural beauty, environmental changes, as well as the growth of Cape Cod, from the 1950s to the present. Having literally thousands of negatives to choose from, I felt this picture book should have a time-machine approach, to allow us to look both back and down, and see the most recent developments. Many of these are being reproduced for the first time since they were originally taken. They are part nostalgia, part history, and part "Wow!" Please enjoy this celebration with Airviews that expose Cape Cod as one of the greatest sandbars one could ever live on!

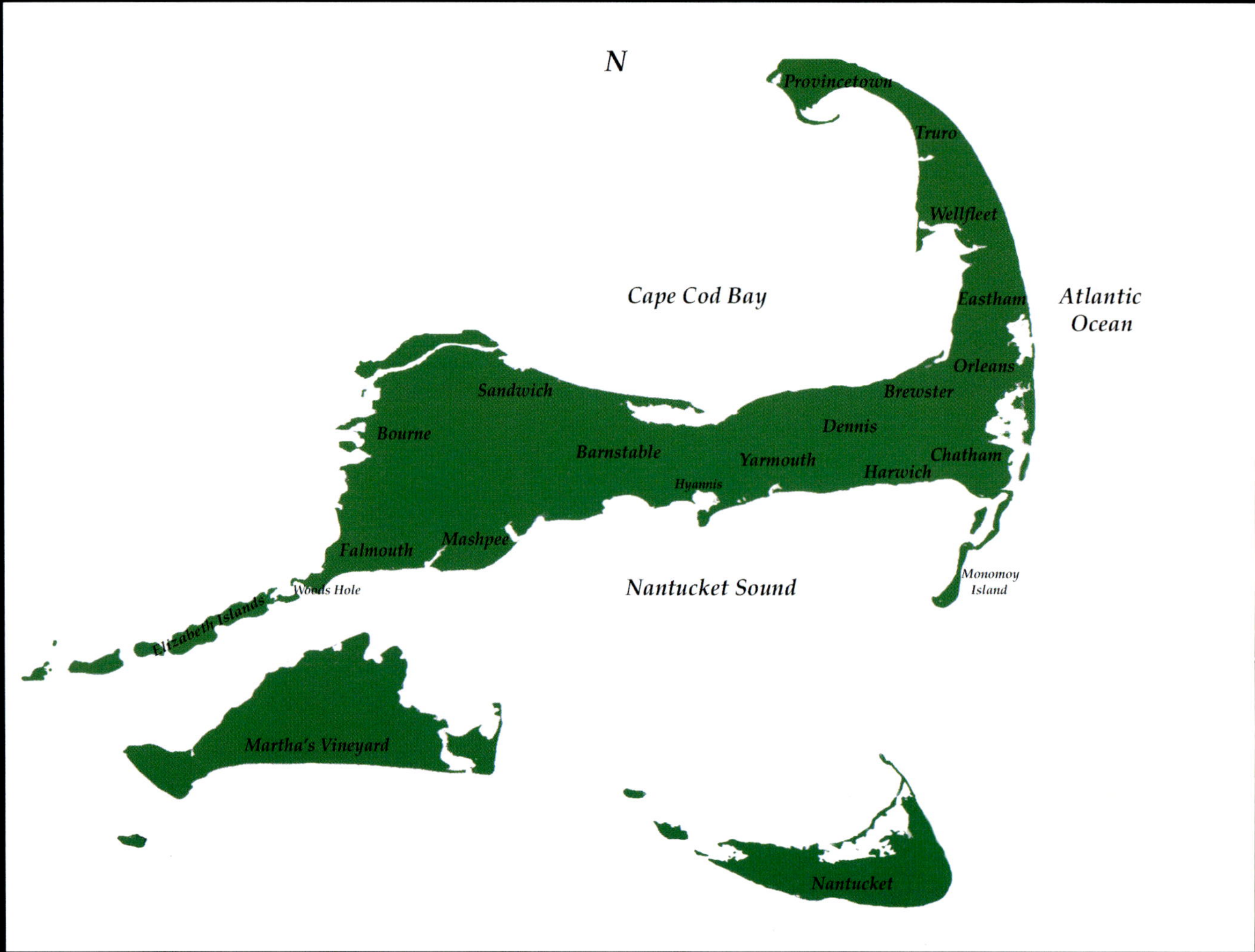

Chapter 1
Nantucket & Martha's Vineyard

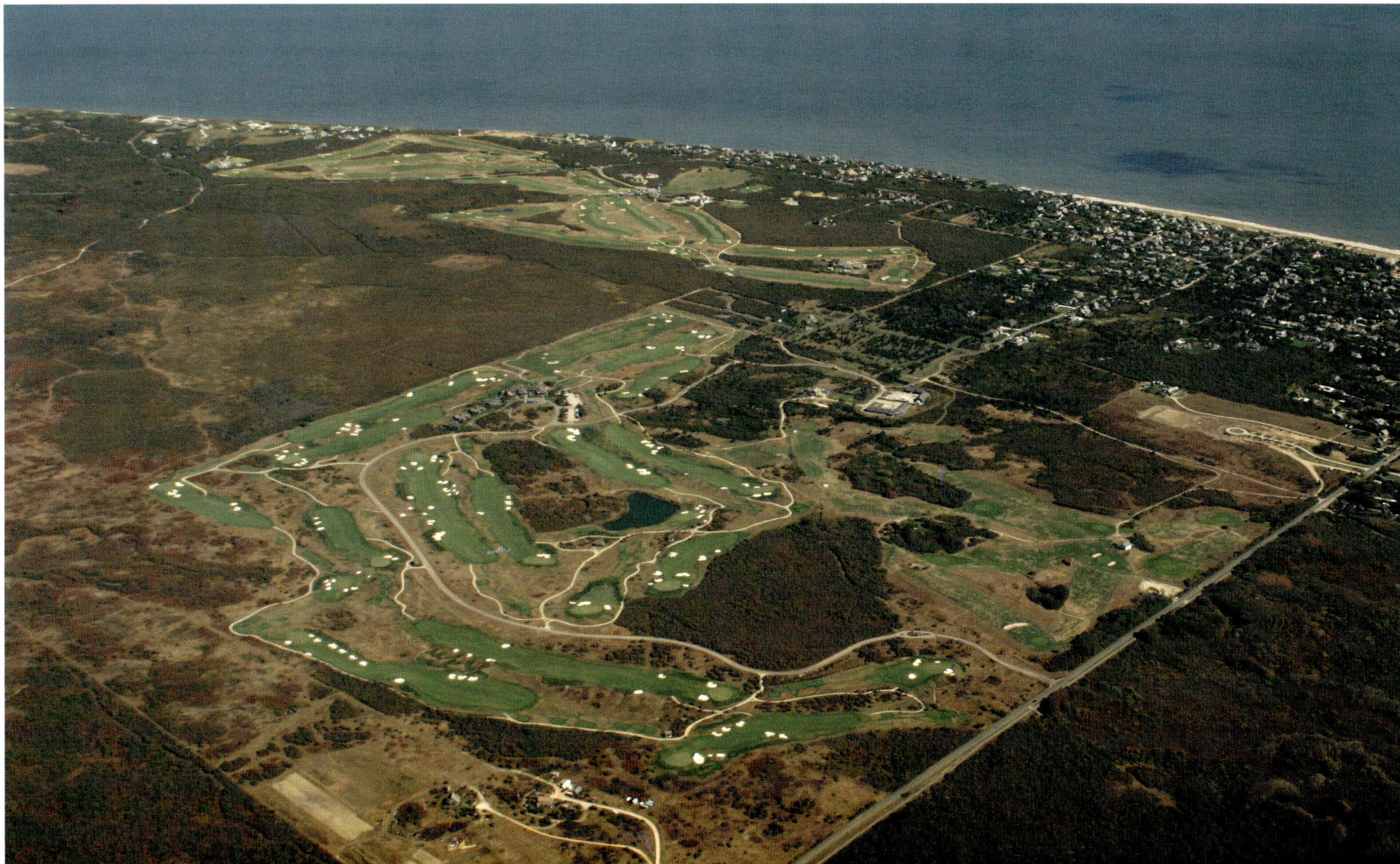

Siasconset golf course.

A high Airview looking southwest across the island of Nantucket.

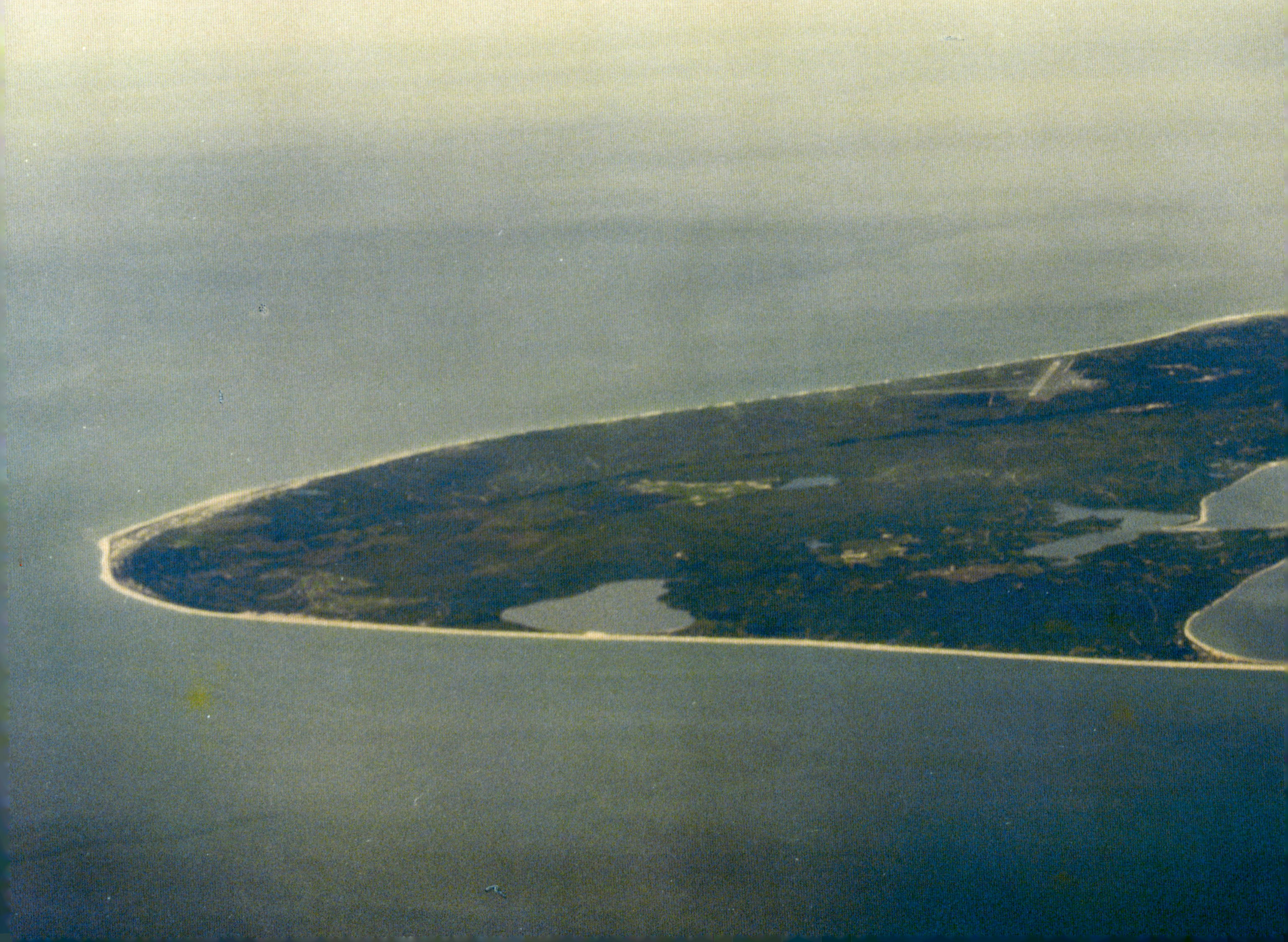

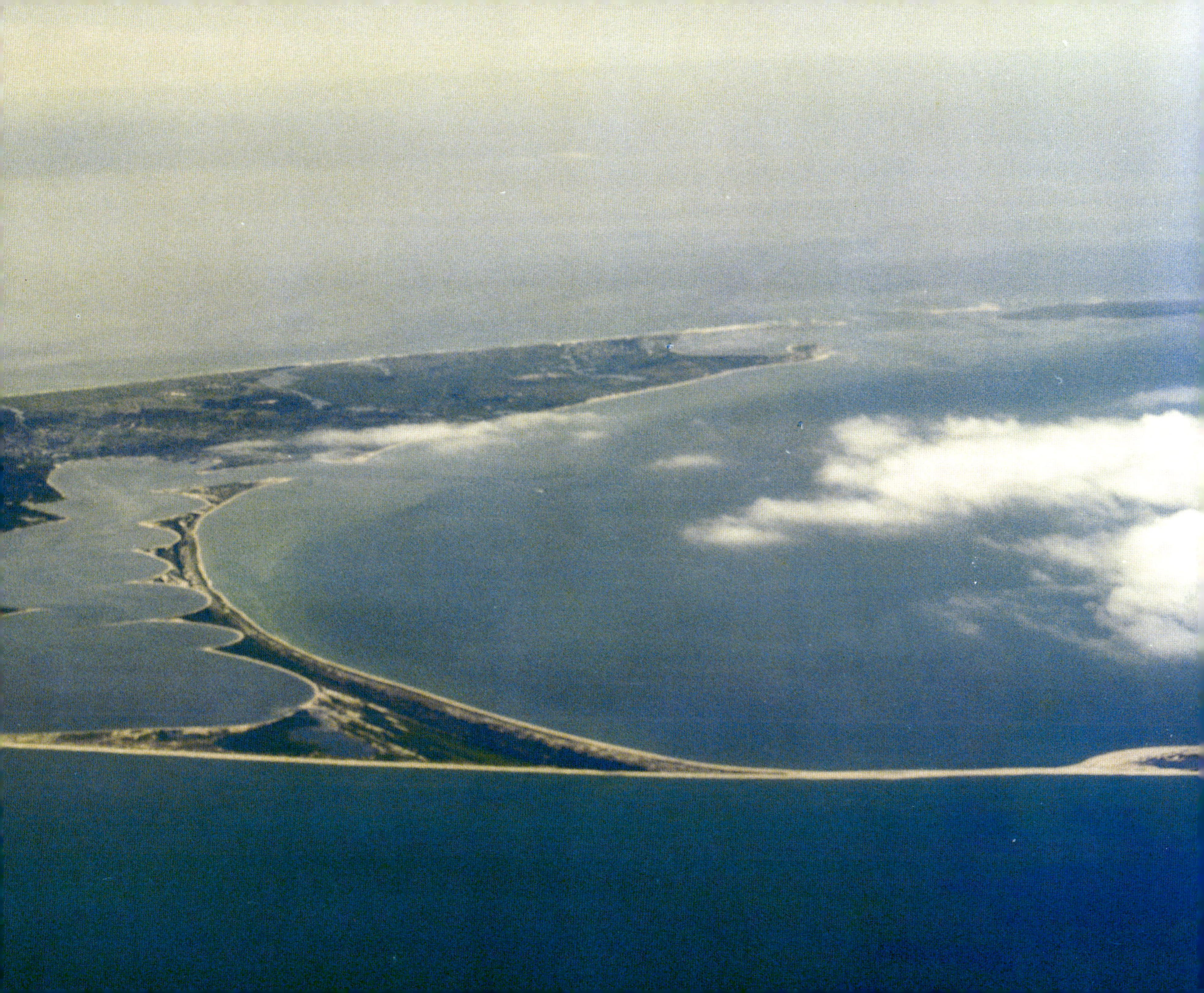

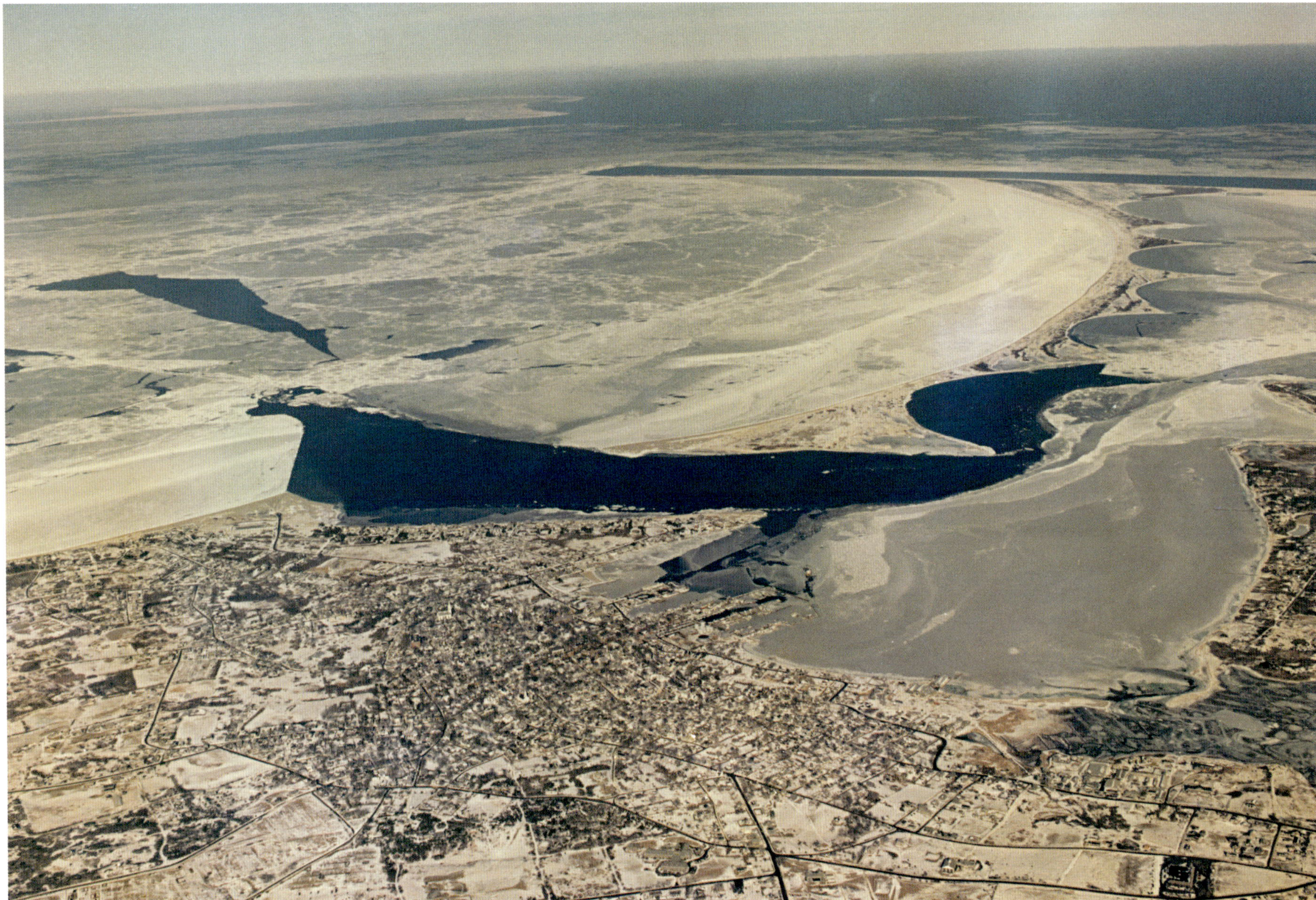

Nantucket Harbor and Sound iced over in January, 1977.

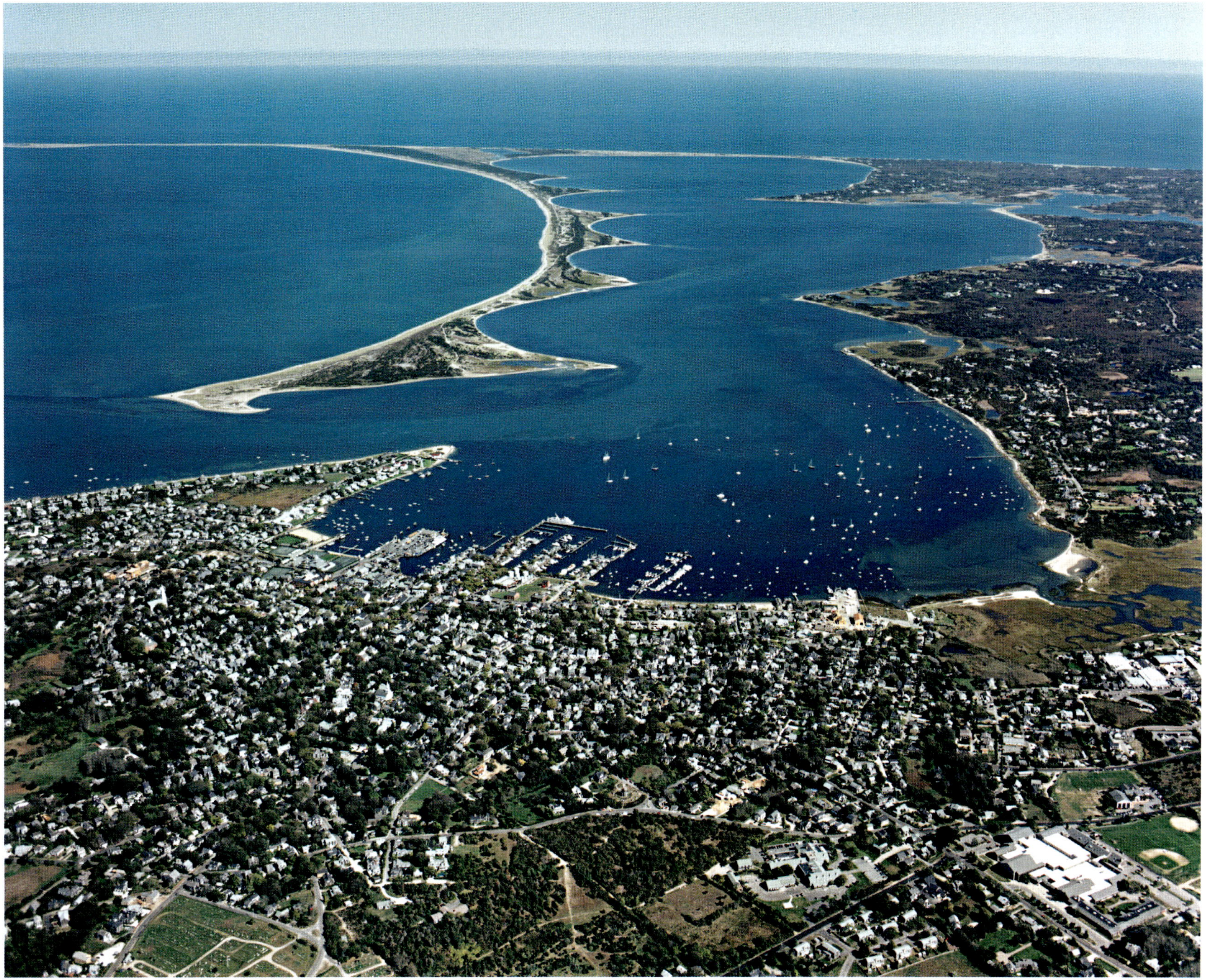

The harbor looking much more appealing for boating.

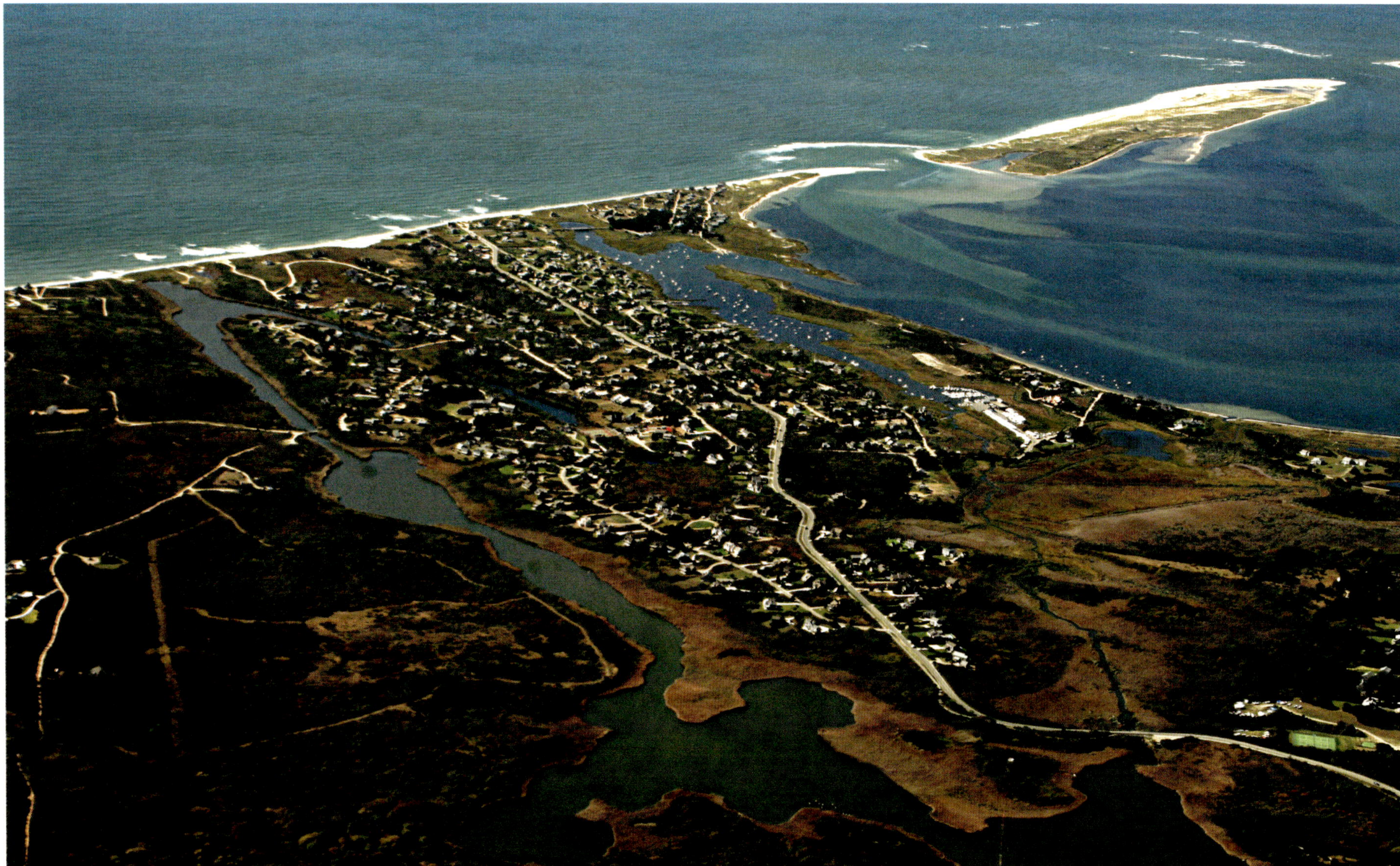

Madaket lies on the western end of the island.

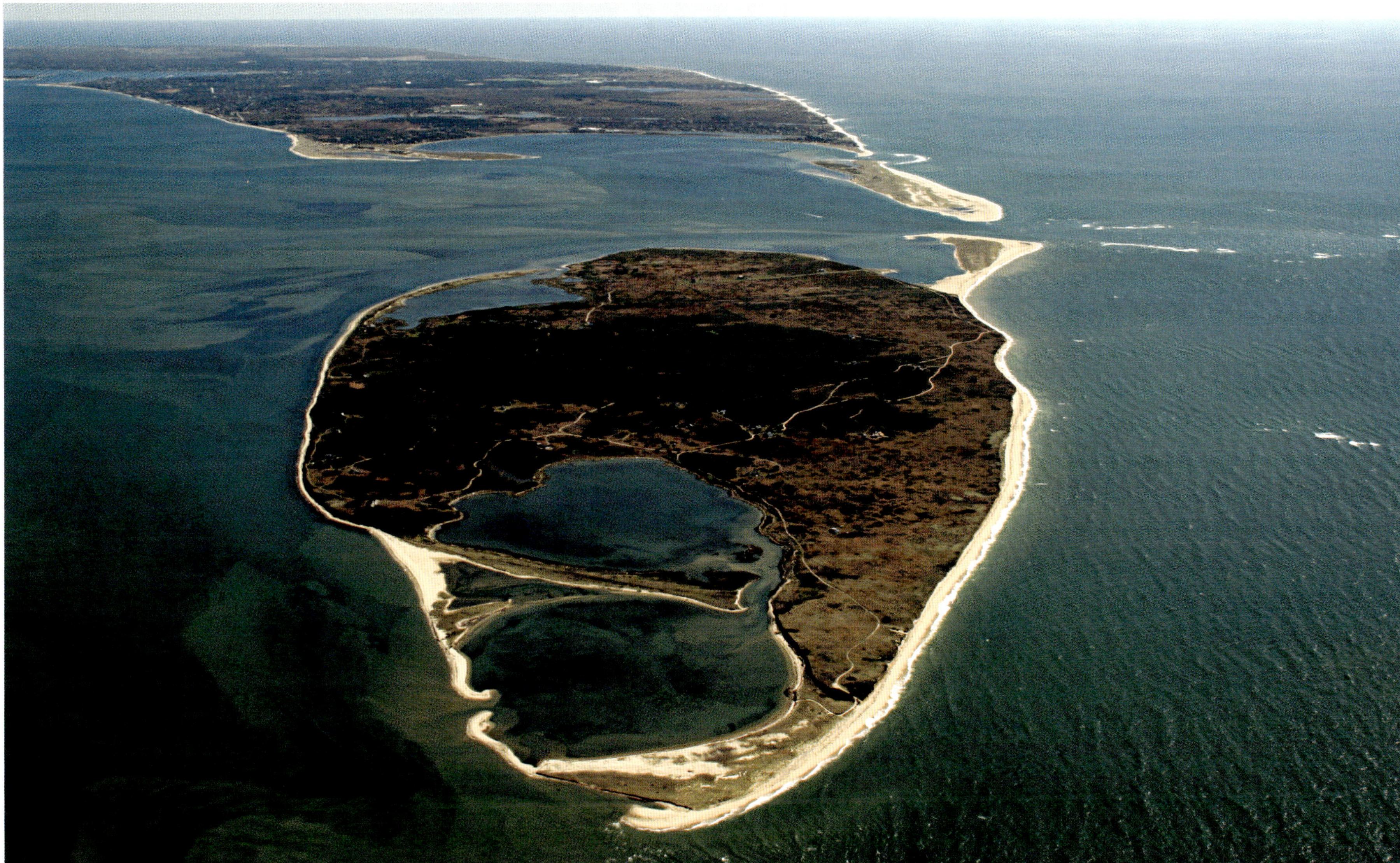

Tuckernauk Island with Nantucket in the background.

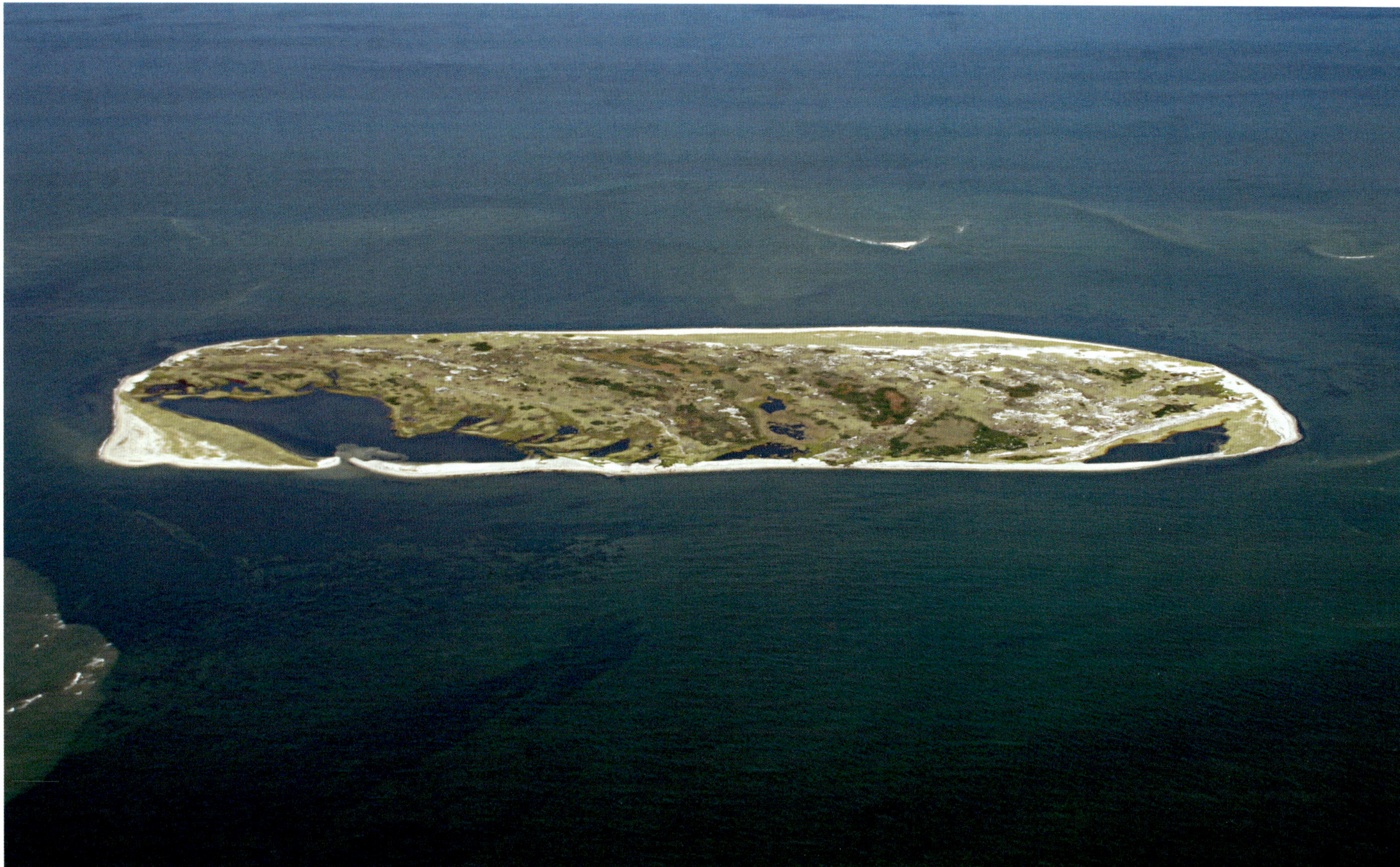

Muskeget Island.

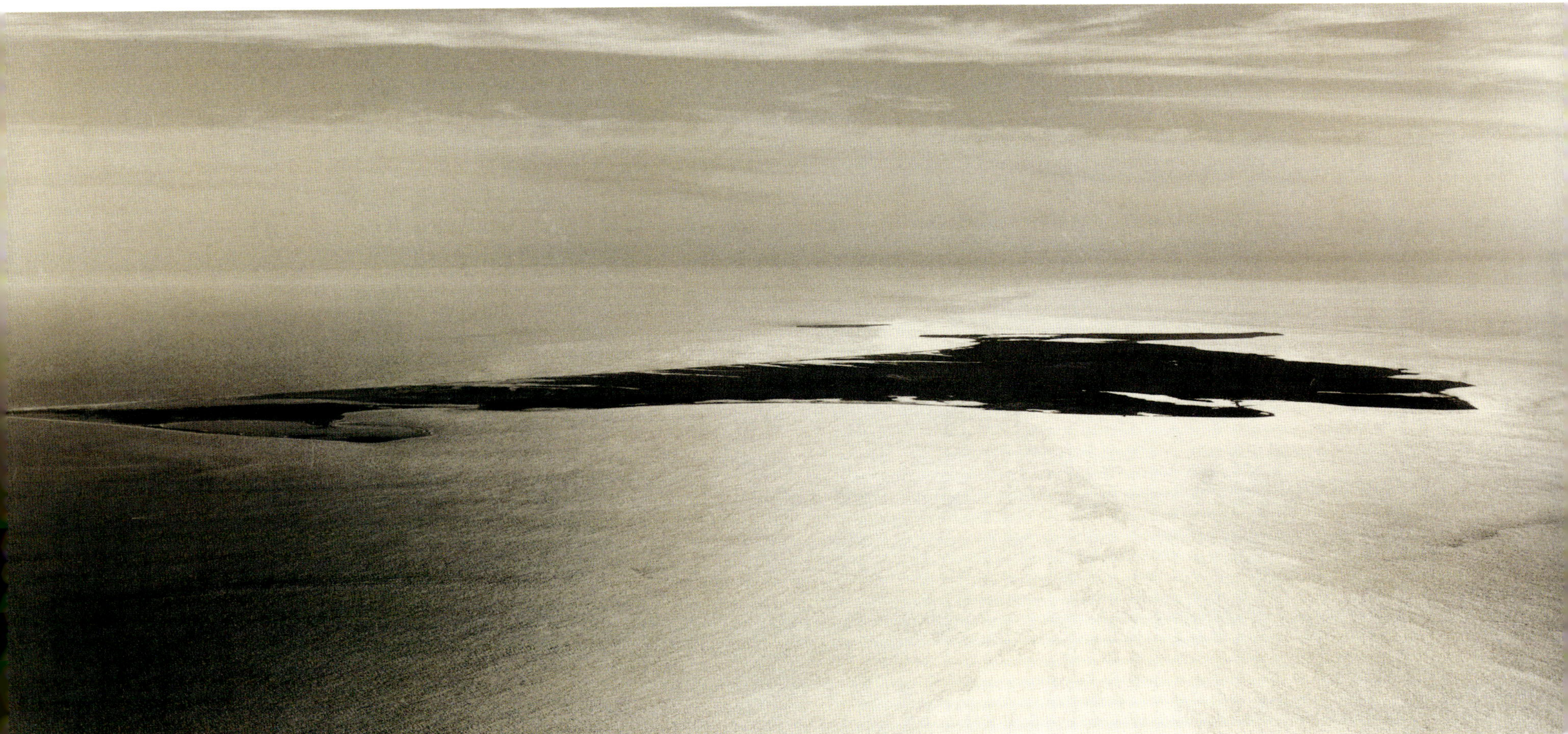

Martha's Vineyard silhouette.

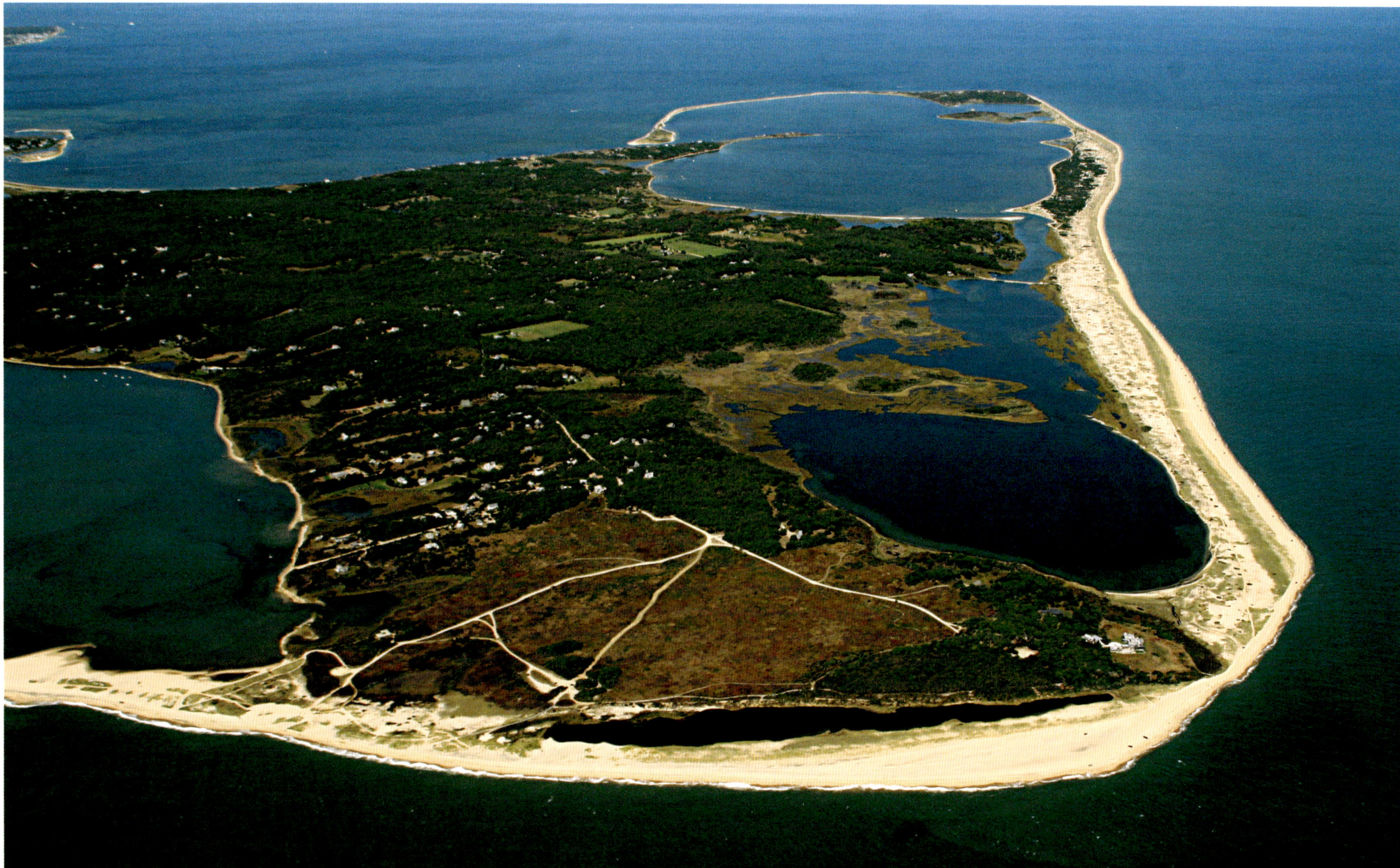

Chappaquiddick Island.

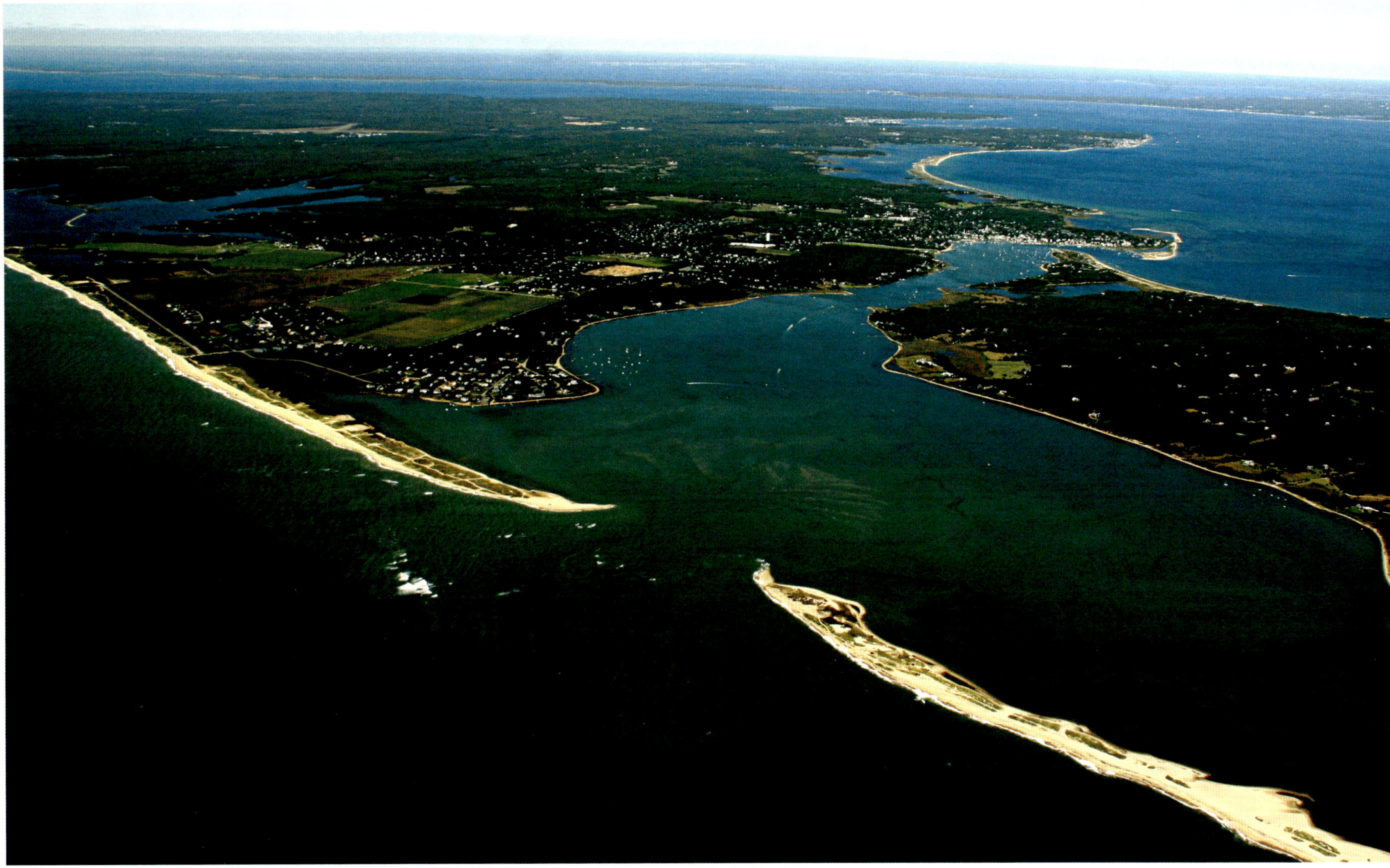

Katama Bay.

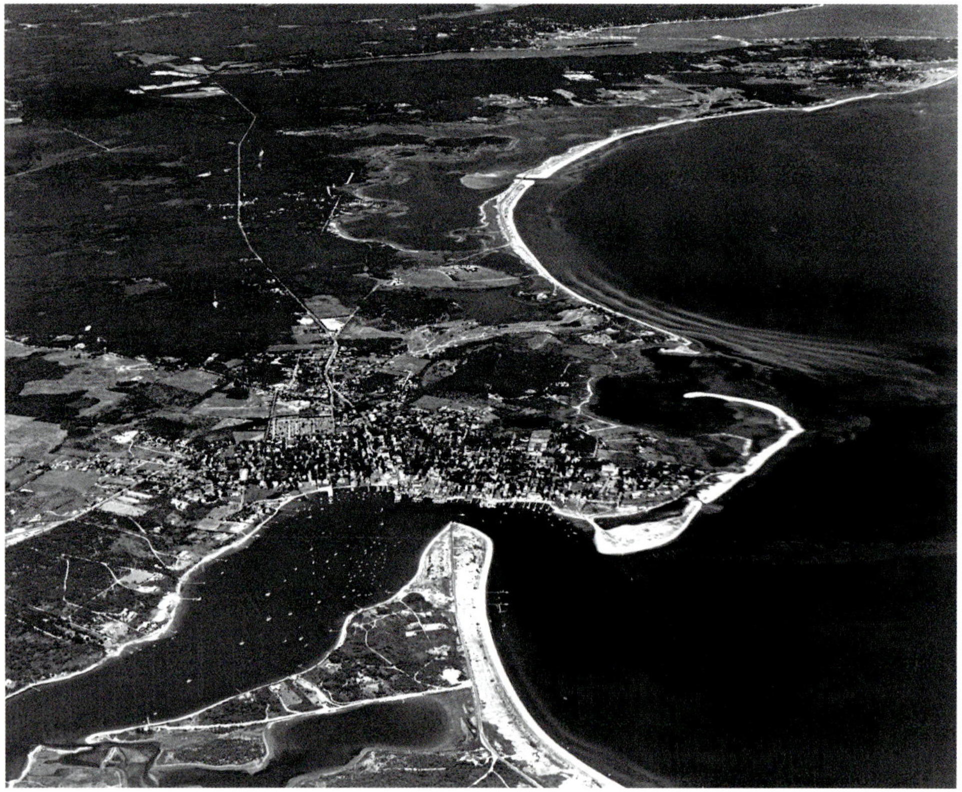

Edgartown looking northwest towards Oak Bluffs in 1966 and 41 years later.

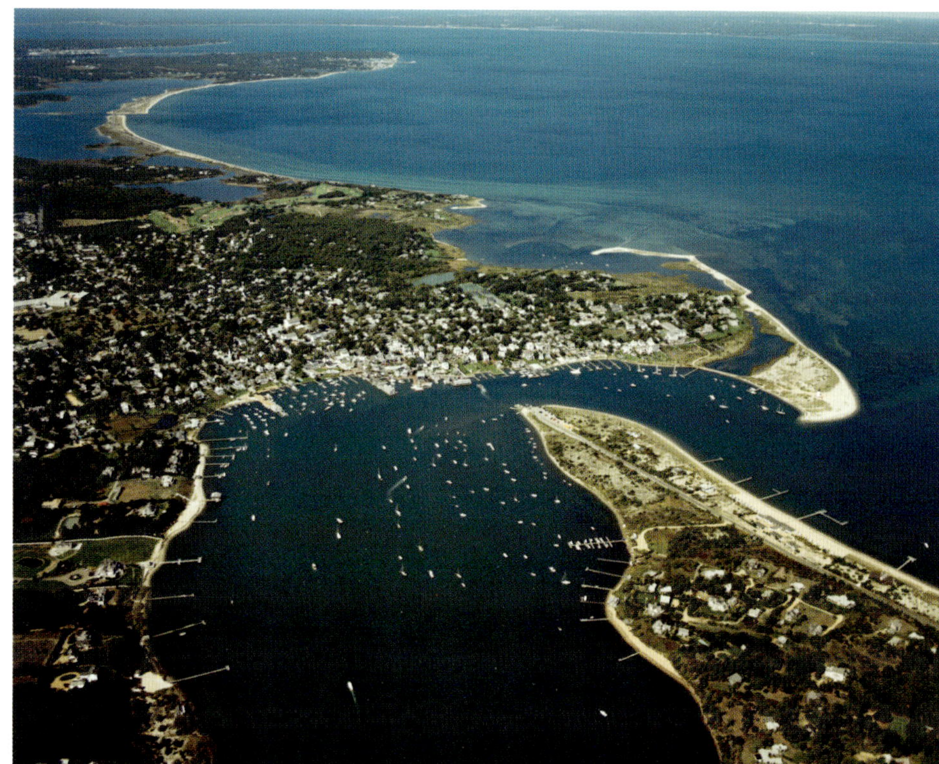

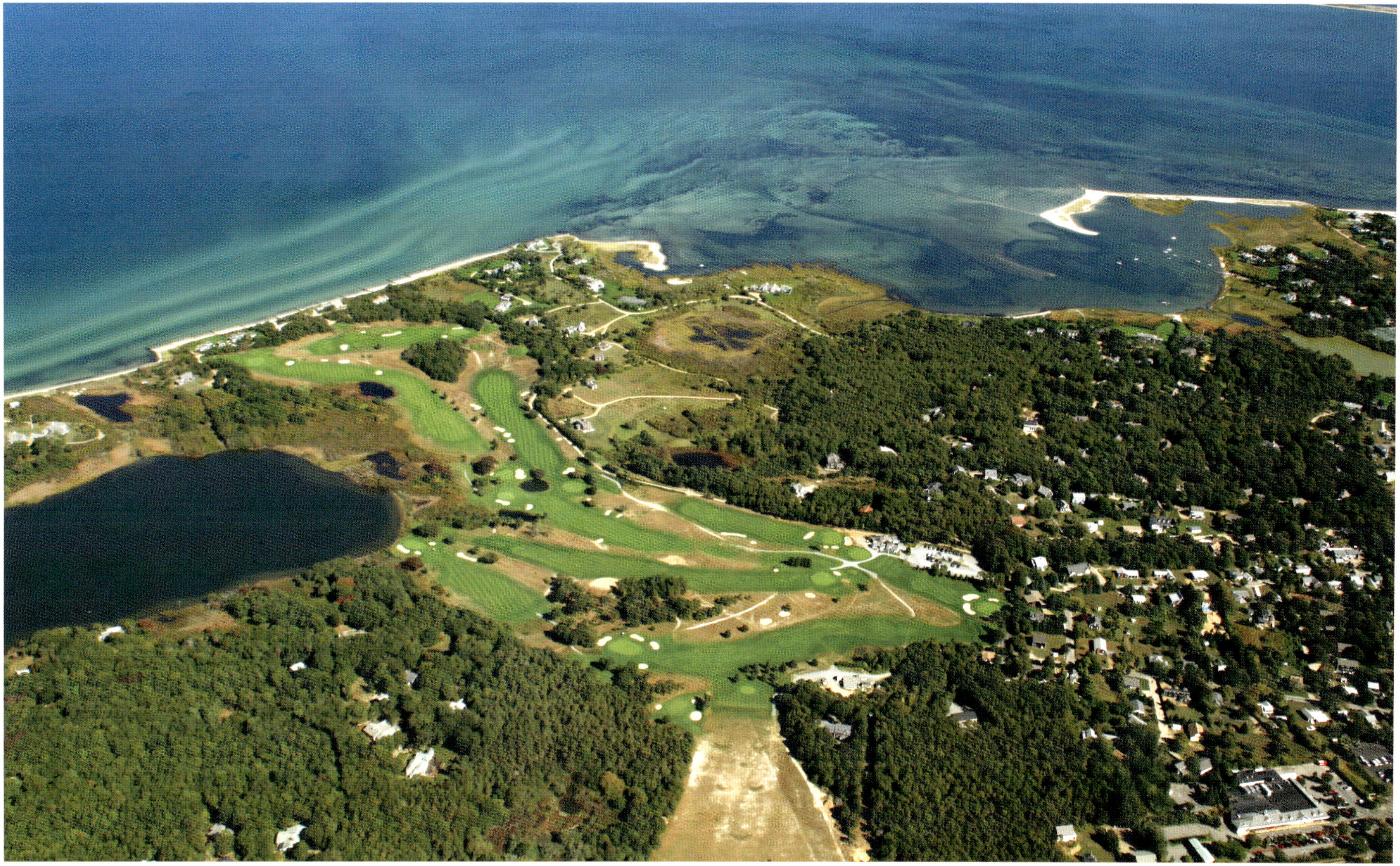

Edgartown golf course.

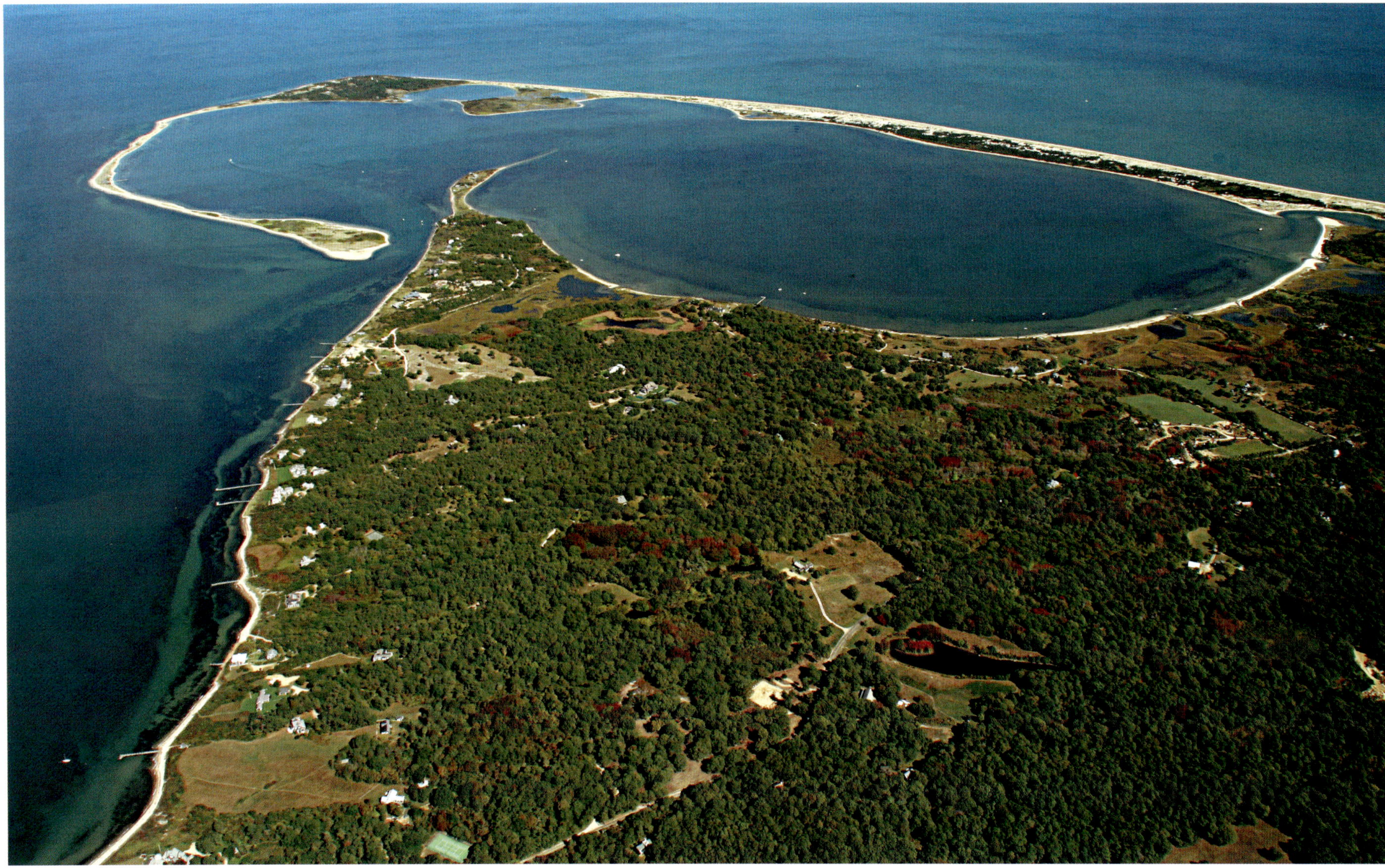

Cape Poge Bay.

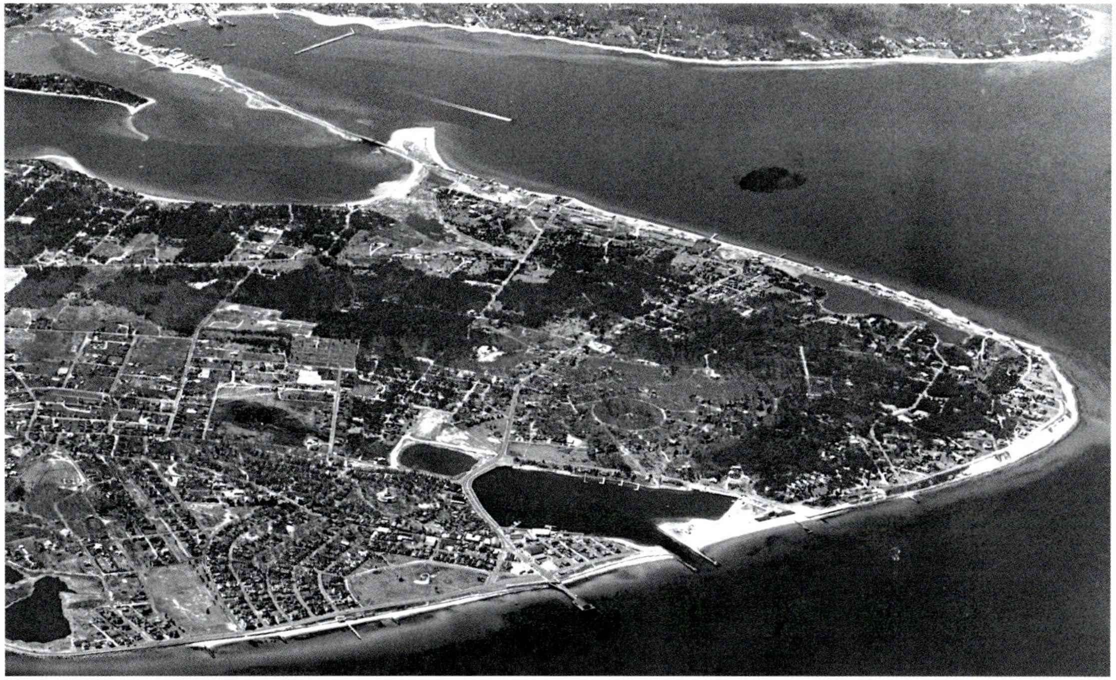

Oak Bluffs and Lake Anthony looking west toward Vineyard Haven in 1966 and 41 years later.

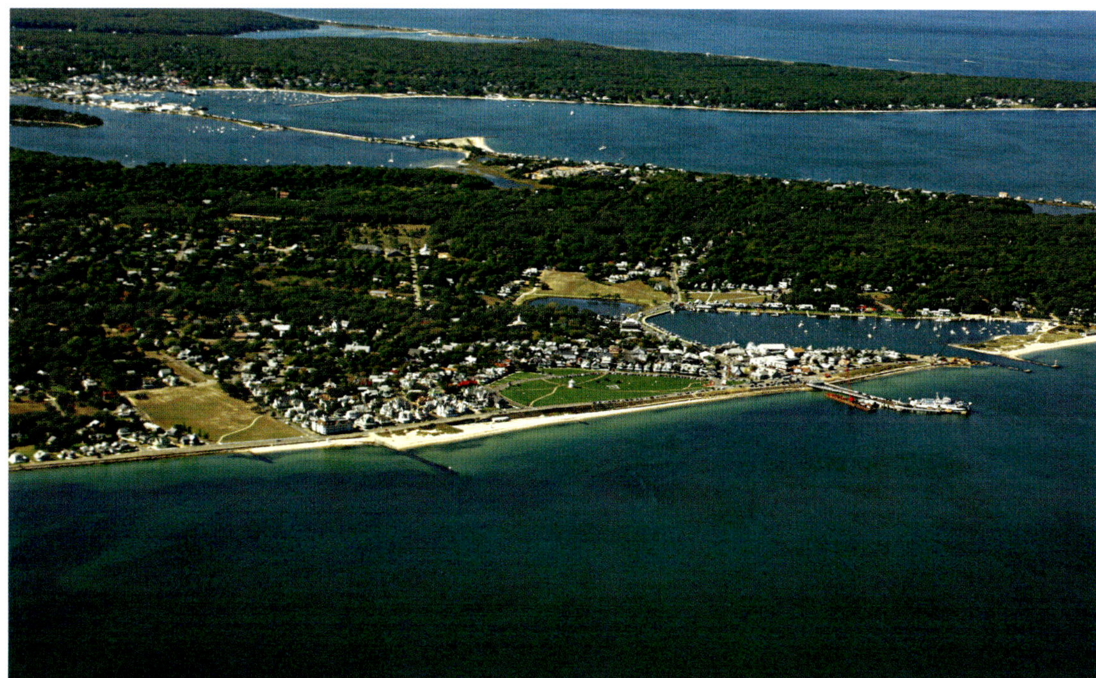

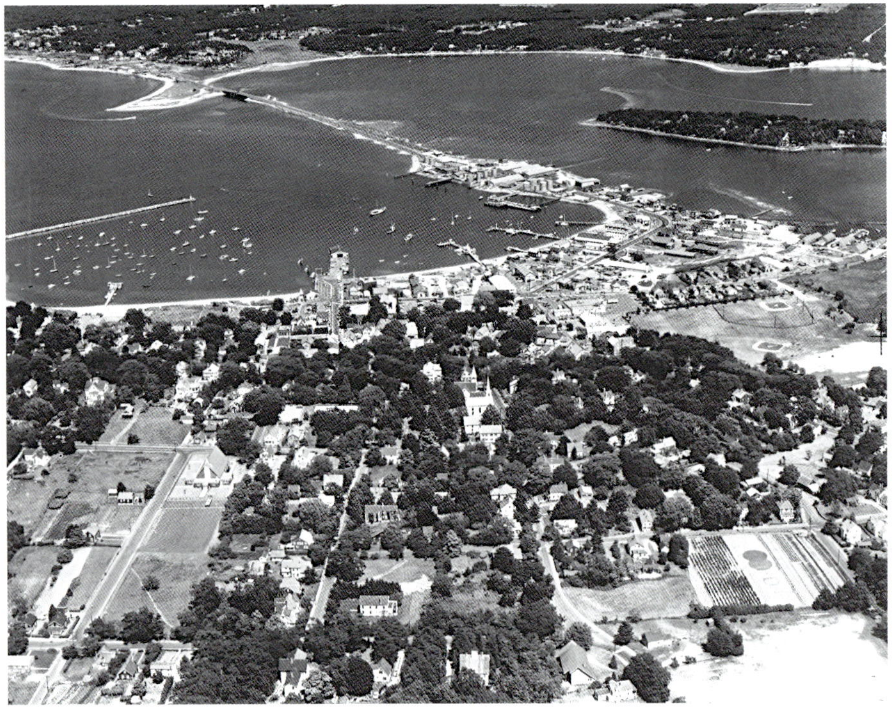

Vineyard Haven and Harbor in Tisbury, as seen in 1966 and 2007.

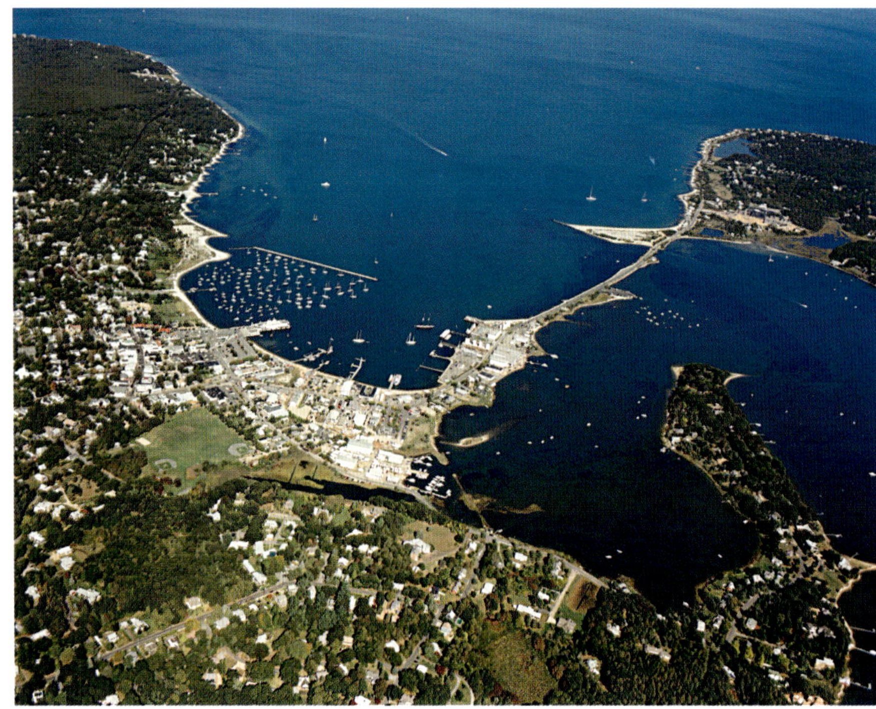

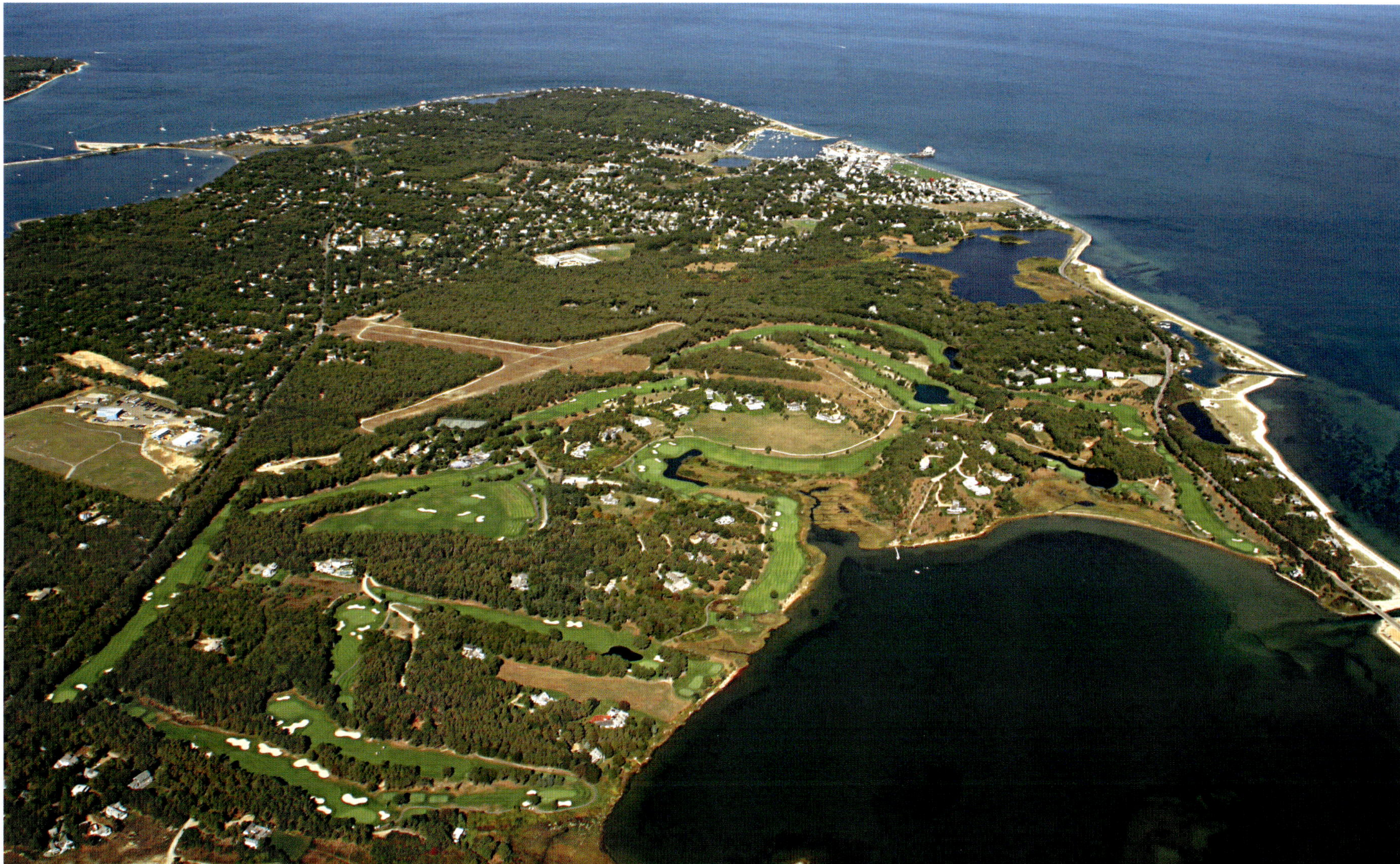

Farm Neck golf course and Trade Wind Airfield are
two landmarks visible from the air in Oak Bluffs.

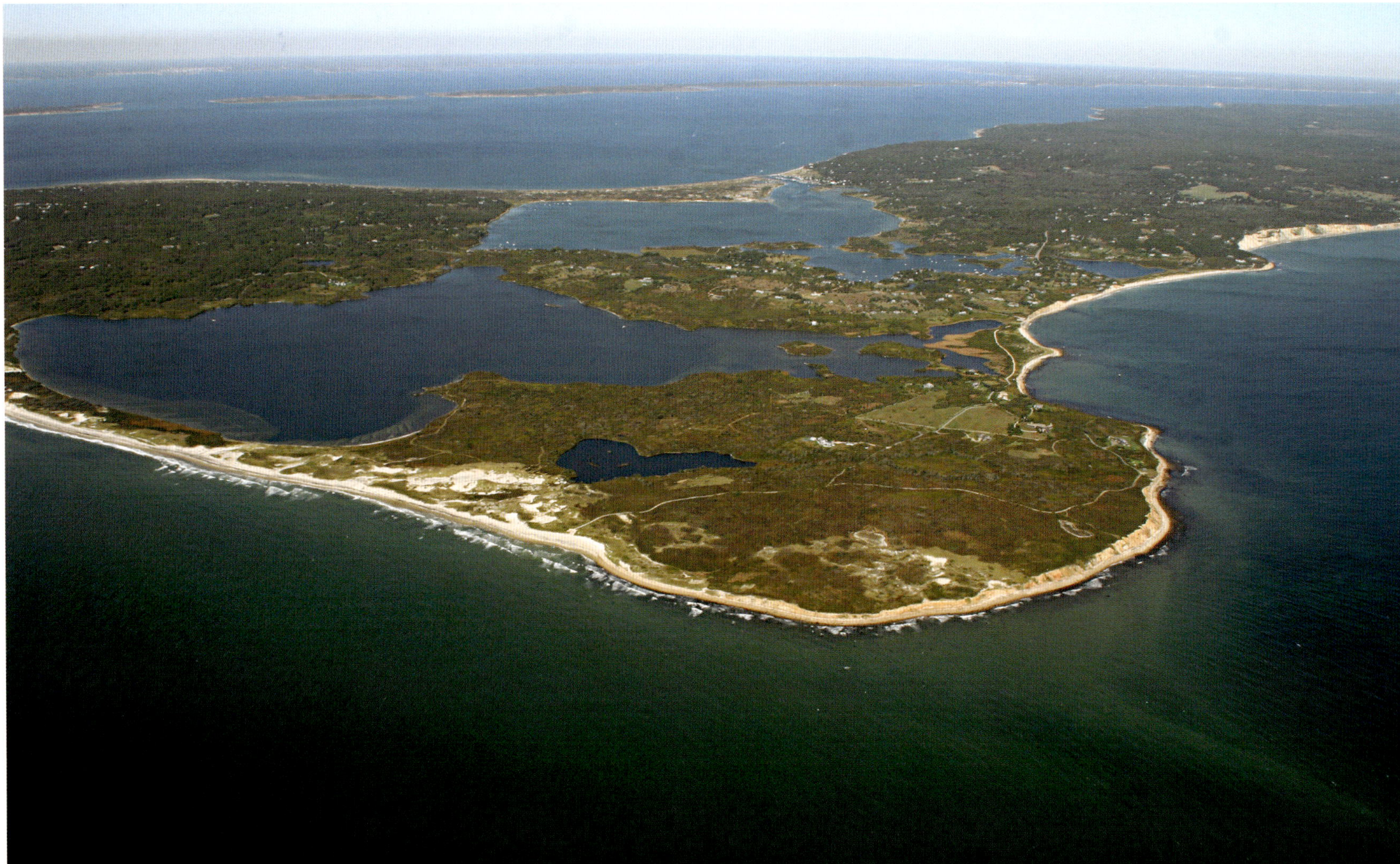

Squibnocket looking northeast to Menemsha and Chilmark.

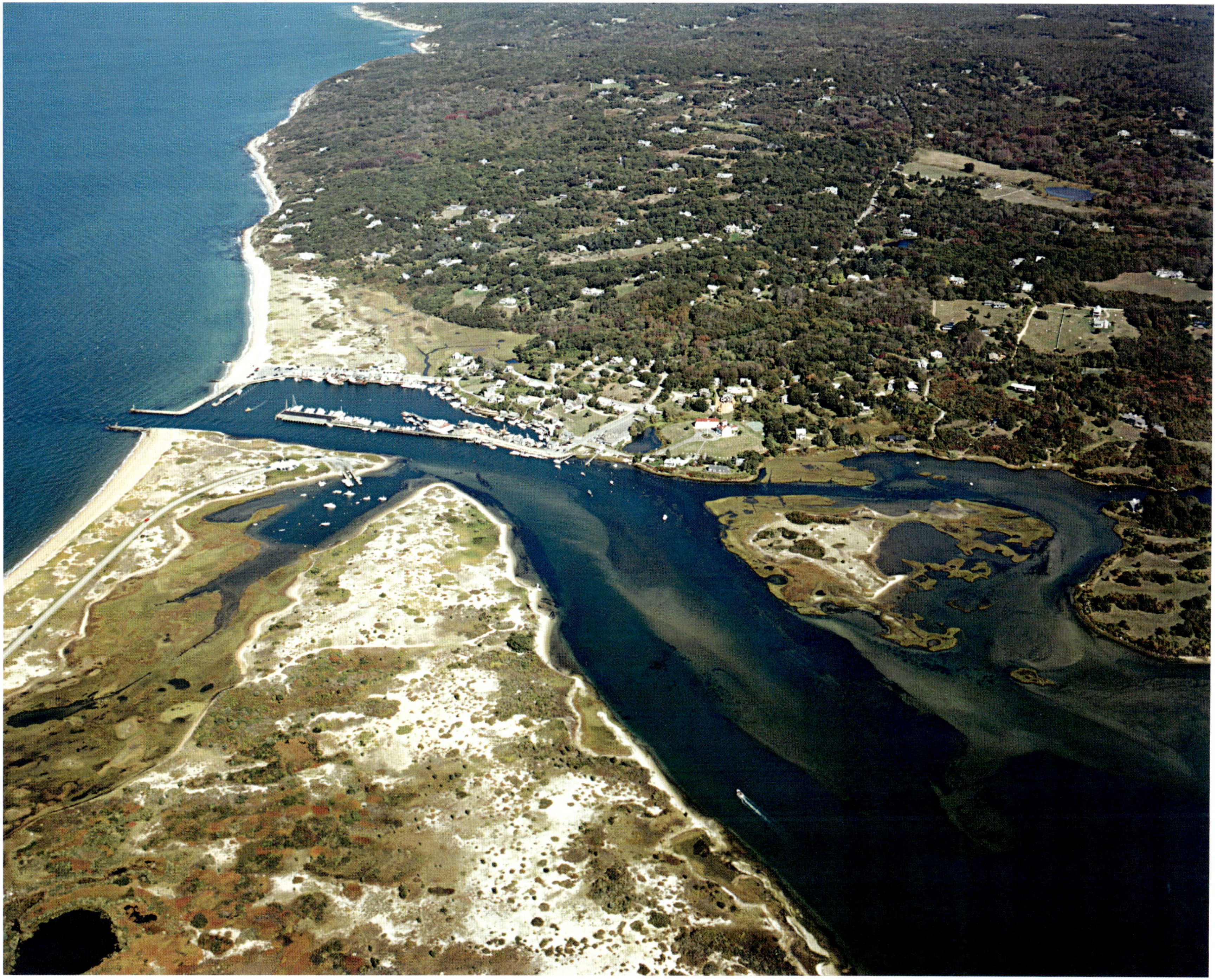

Menemsha Inlet with the Coast Guard Station.

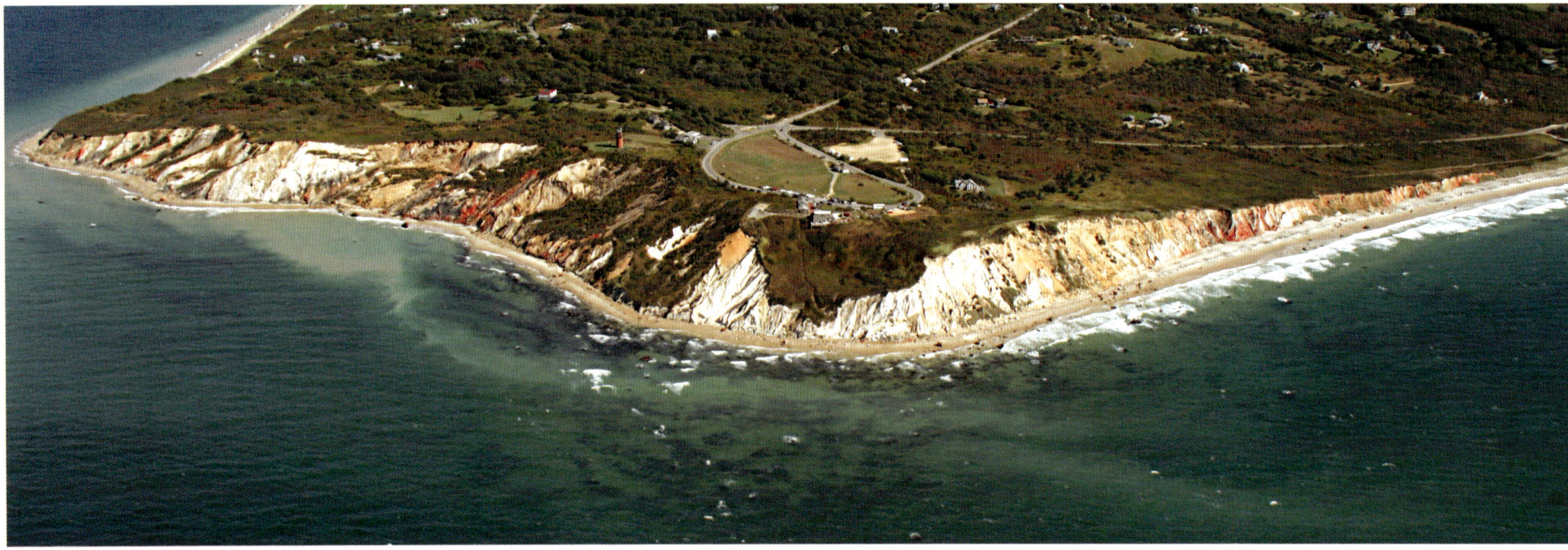

The colorful cliffs of Gay Head.

Chapter 2

Bourne, Falmouth, Mashpee, & Sandwich

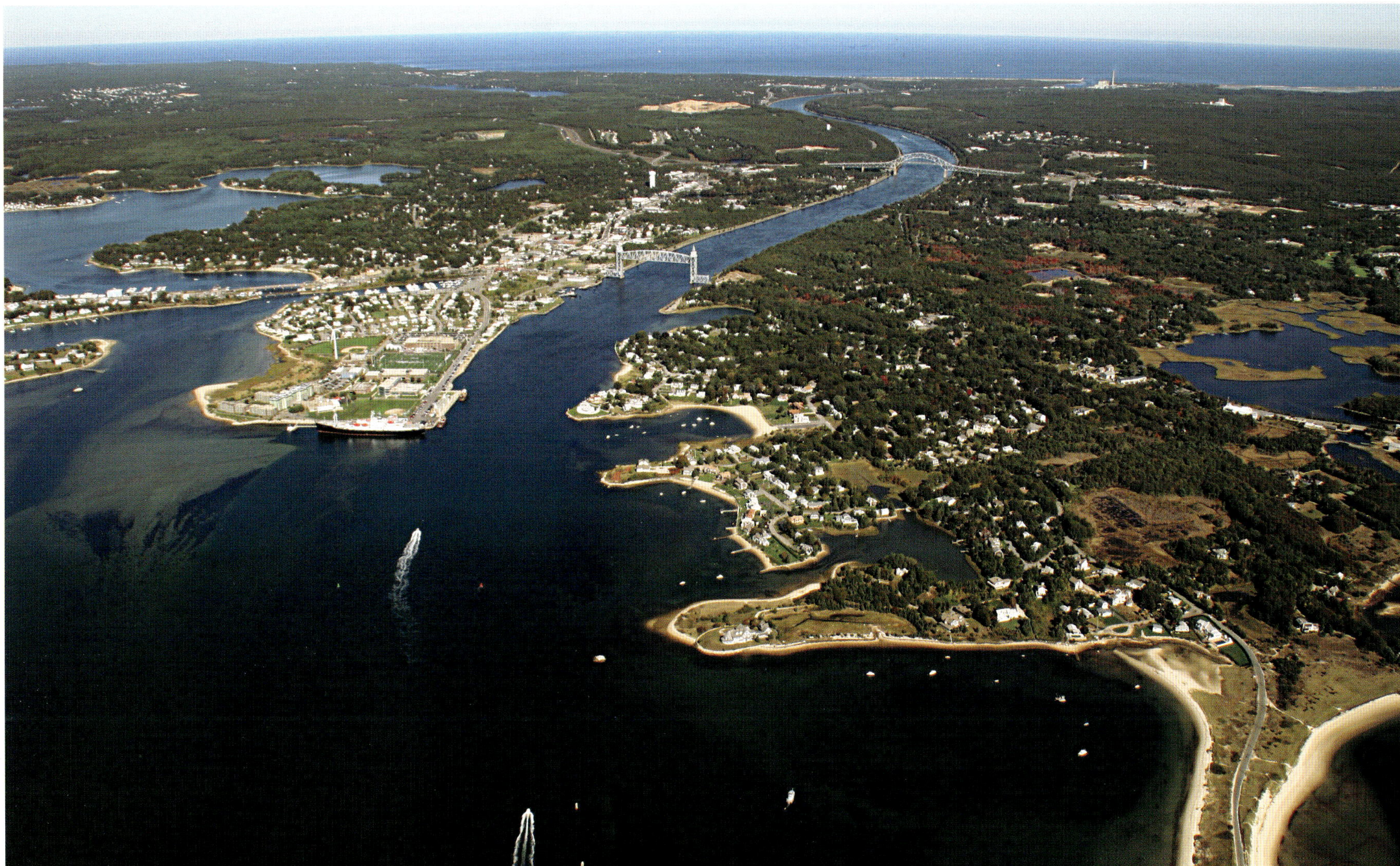

The Cape Cod Canal, with Massachusetts Maritime Academy on the left, winding its way to Cape Cod Bay.

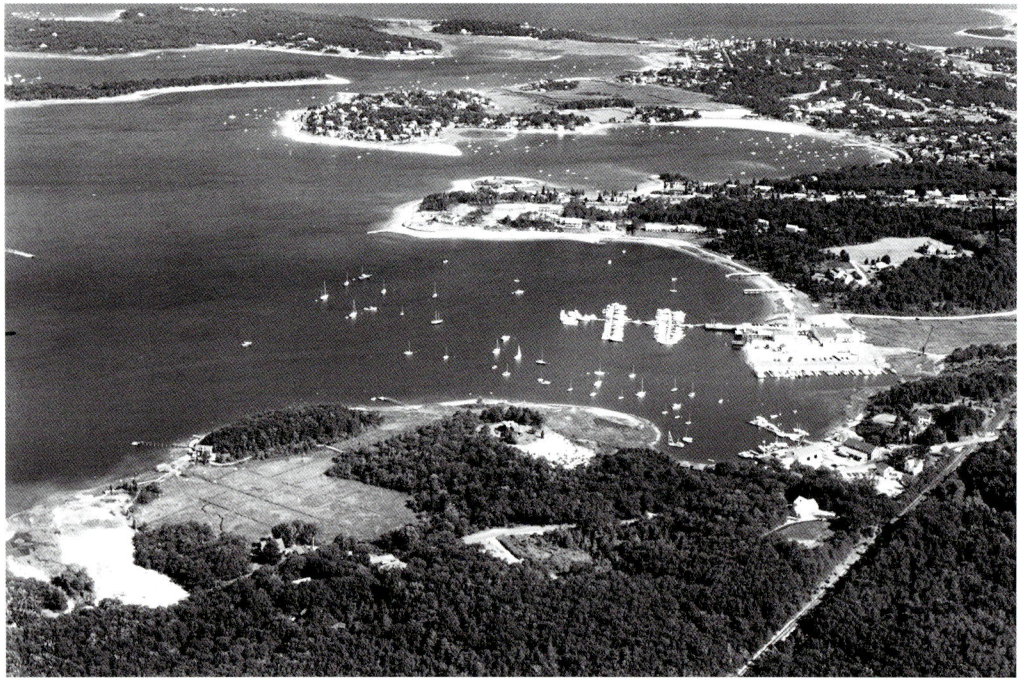

Kingsman Marina in 1969
and 38 years later.

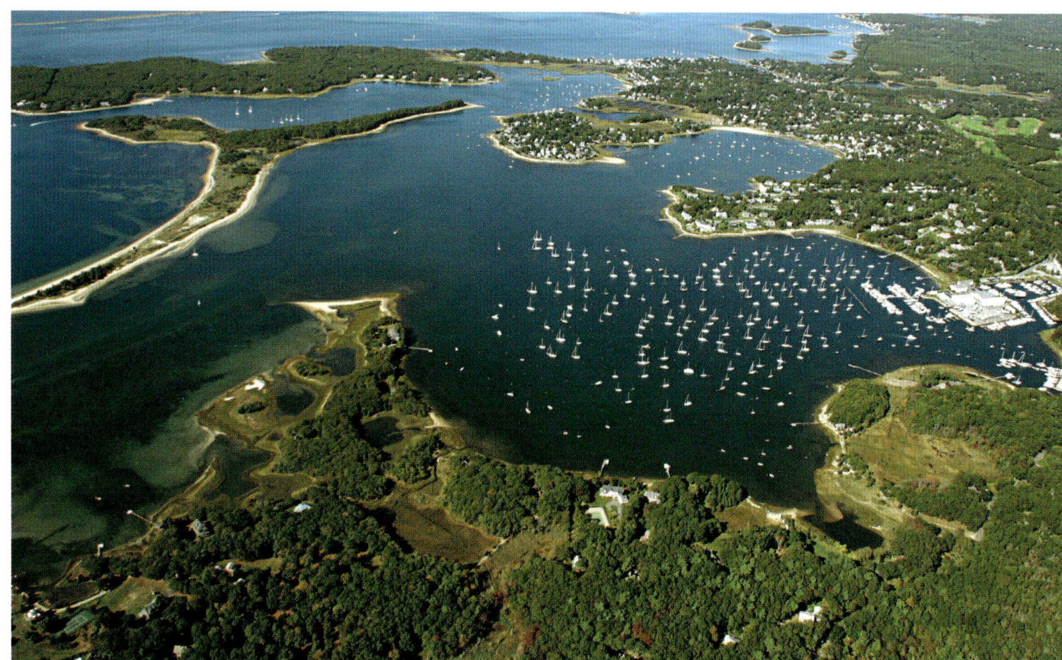

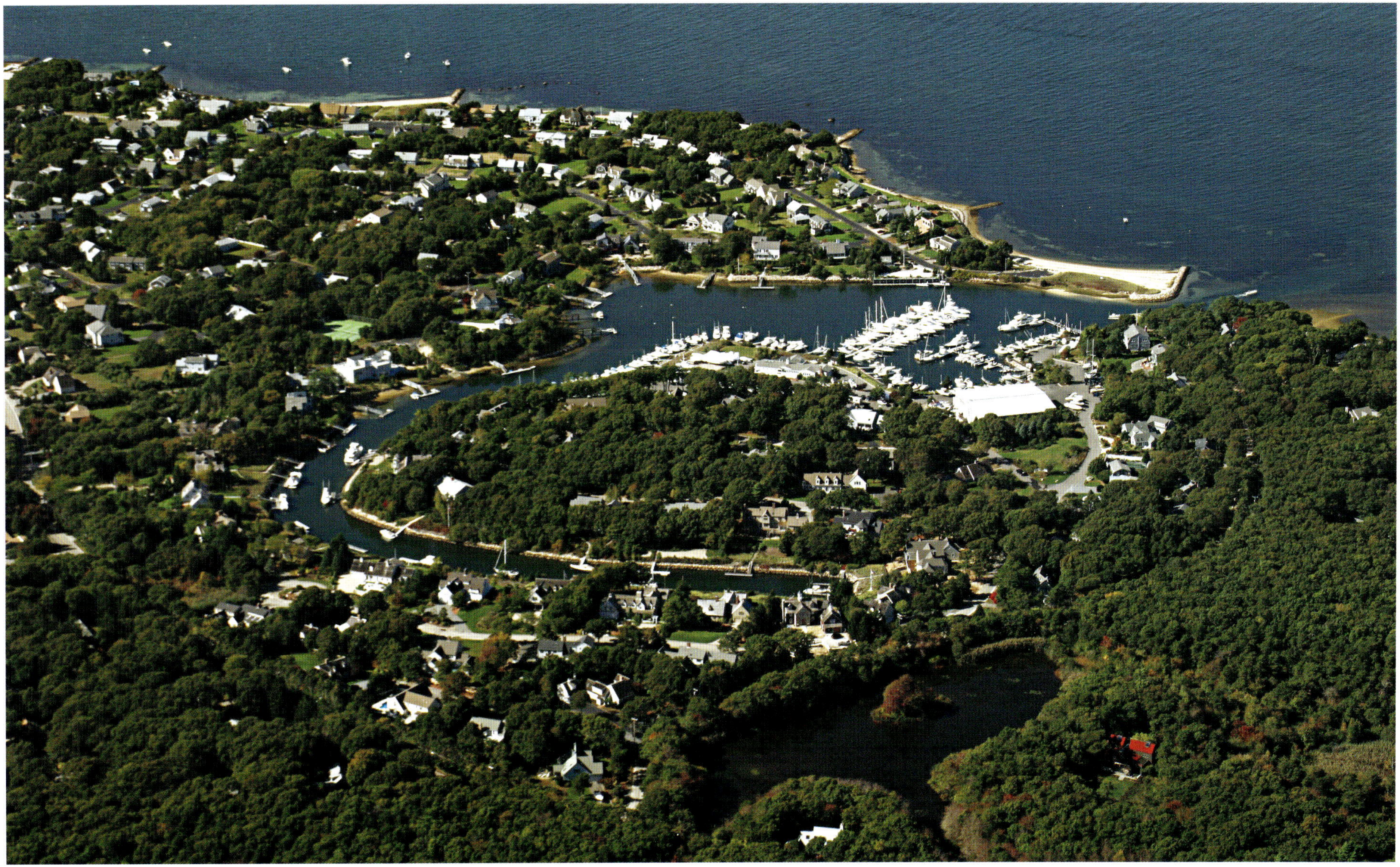

The unique shape of Fiddlers Cove.

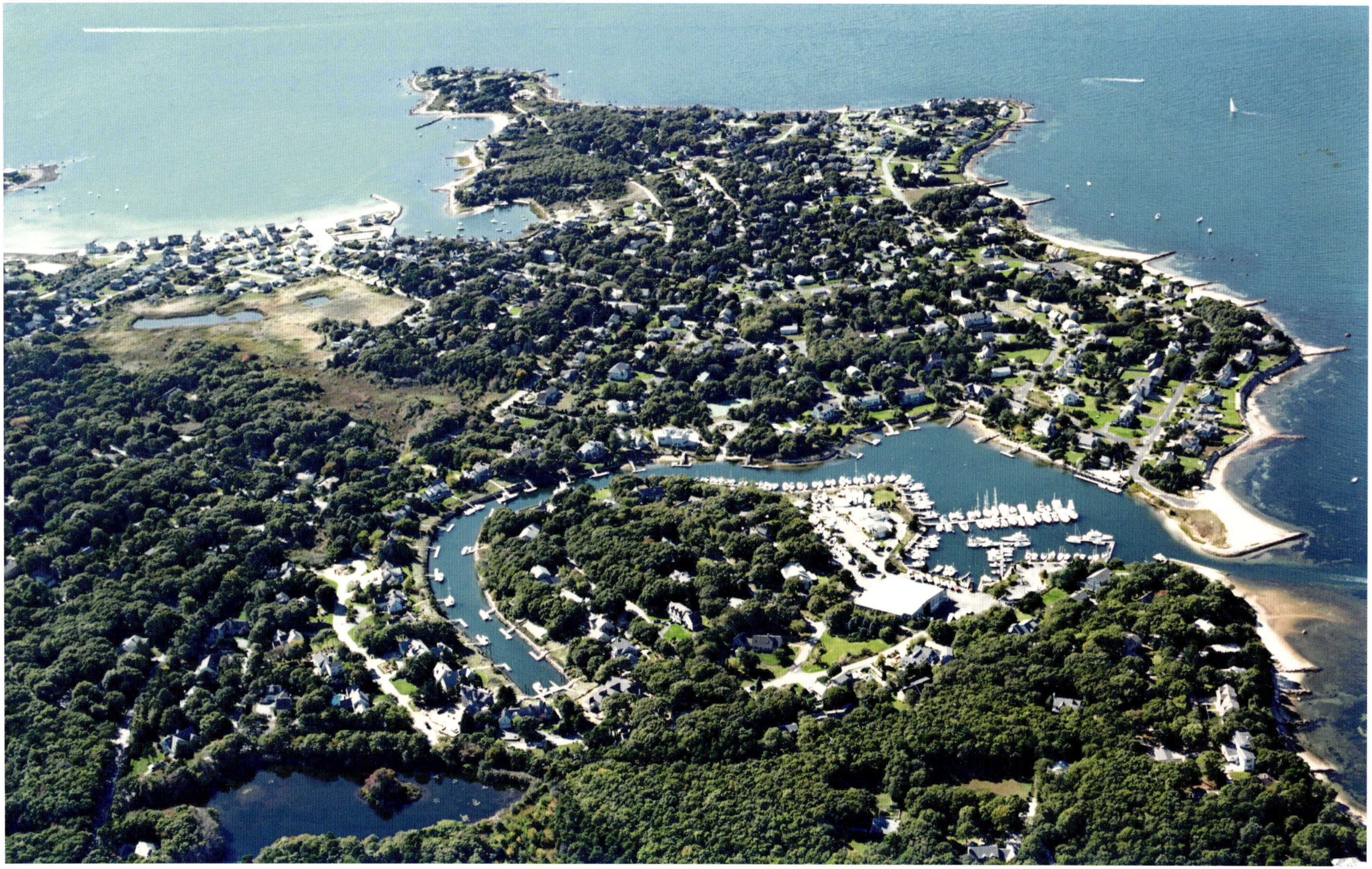

Fiddlers Cove to Nyes Neck.

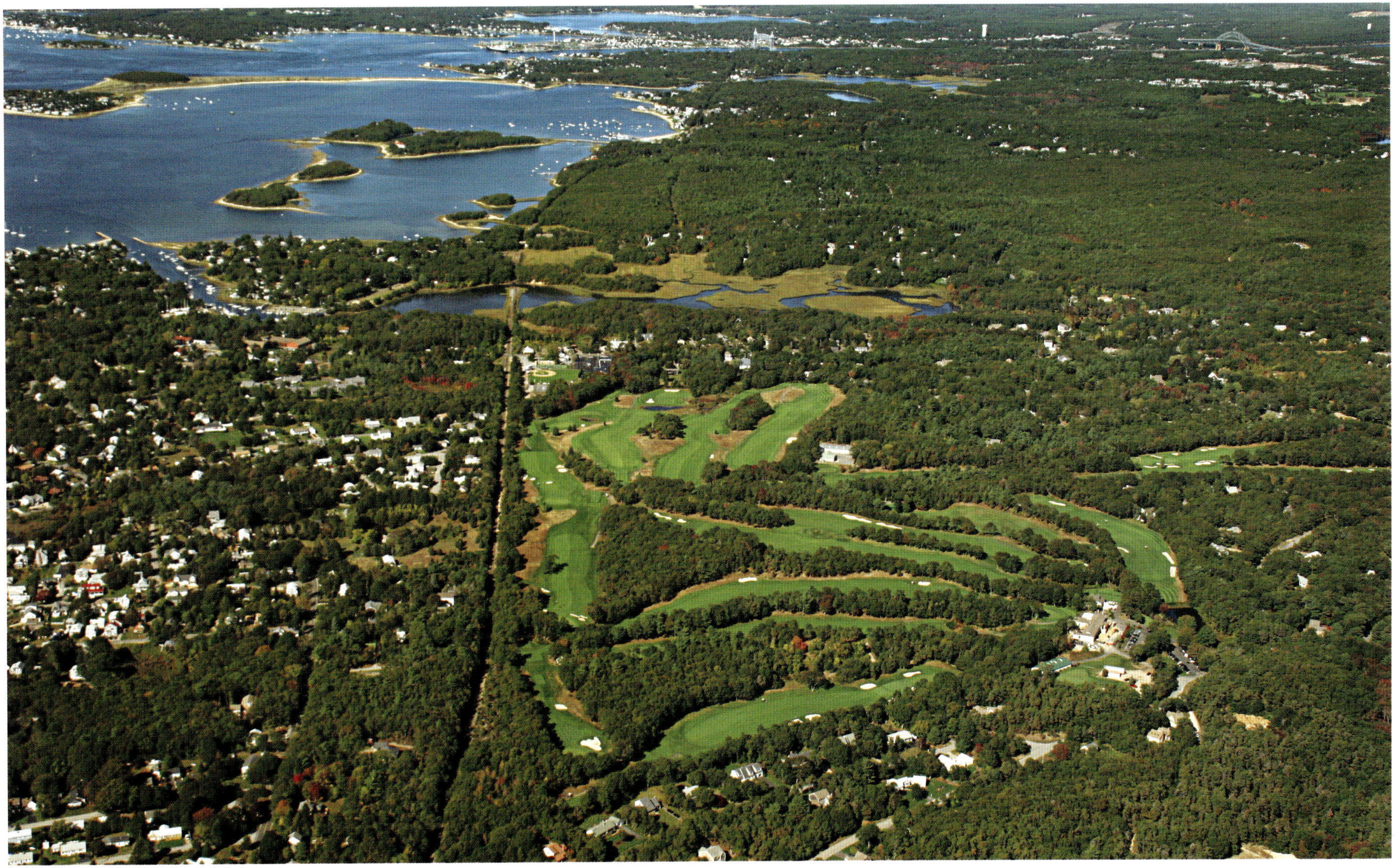

Pocasset golf course.

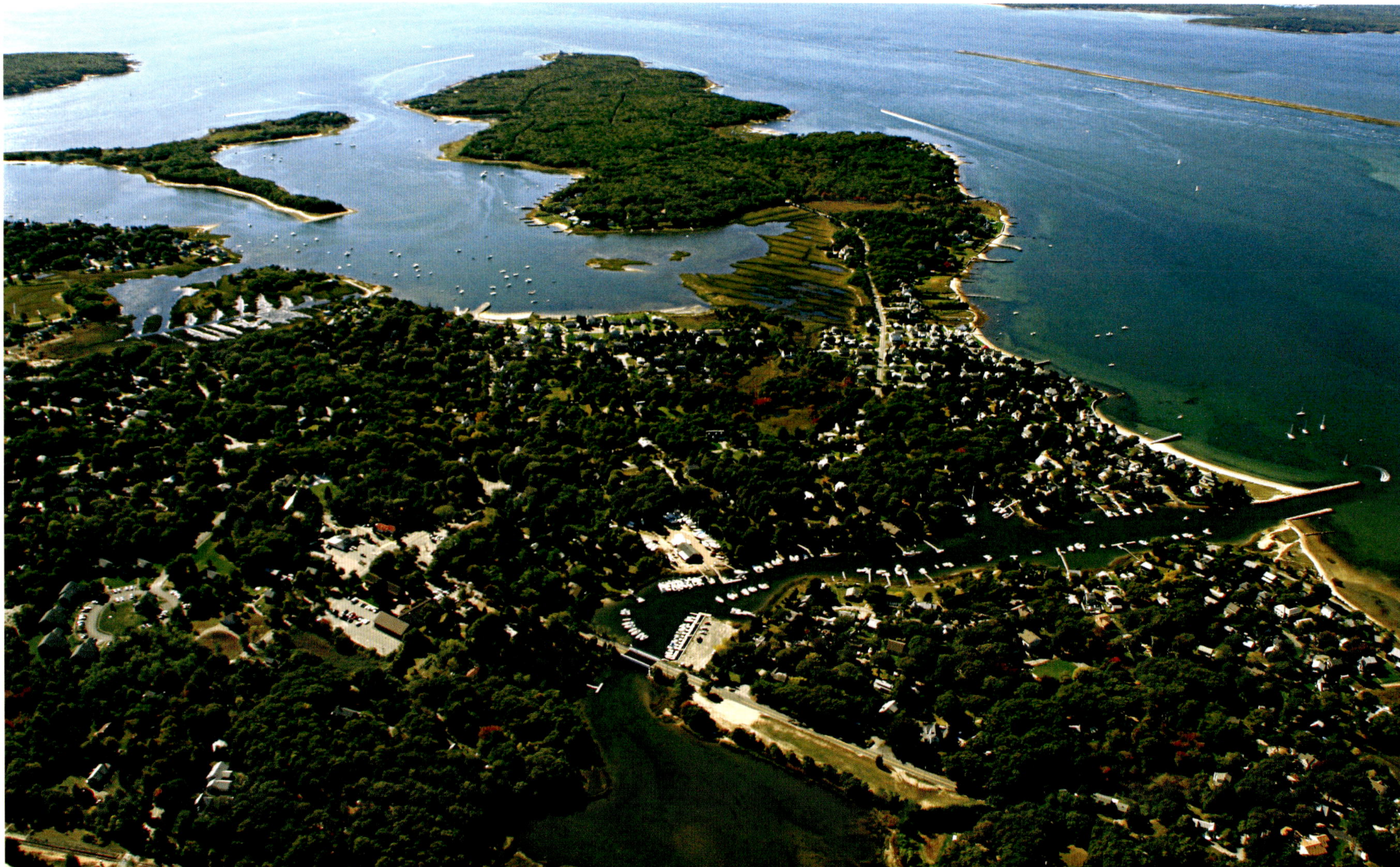

Pocasset River out to Wings Neck.

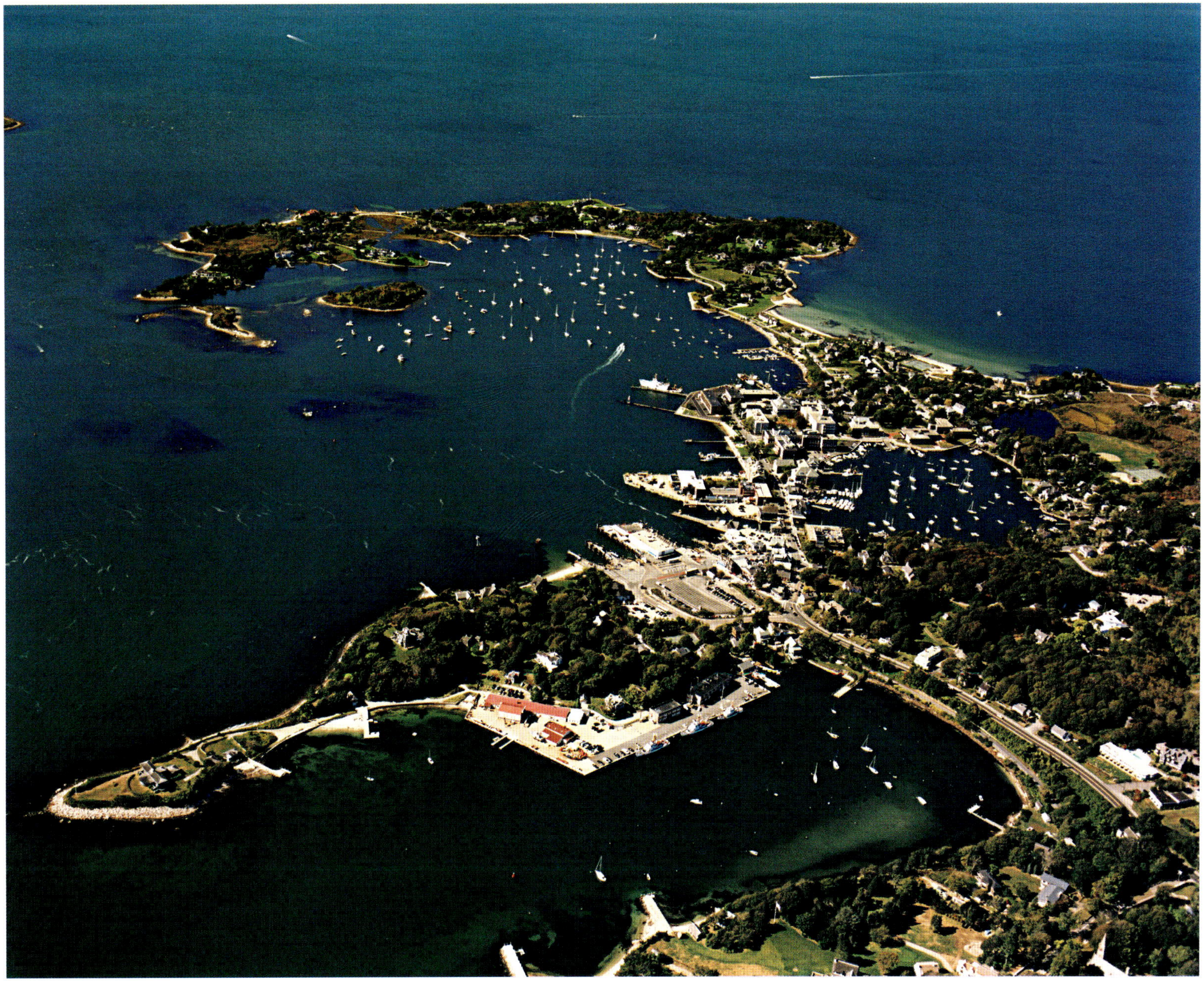

Little Harbor to Penzance Point.

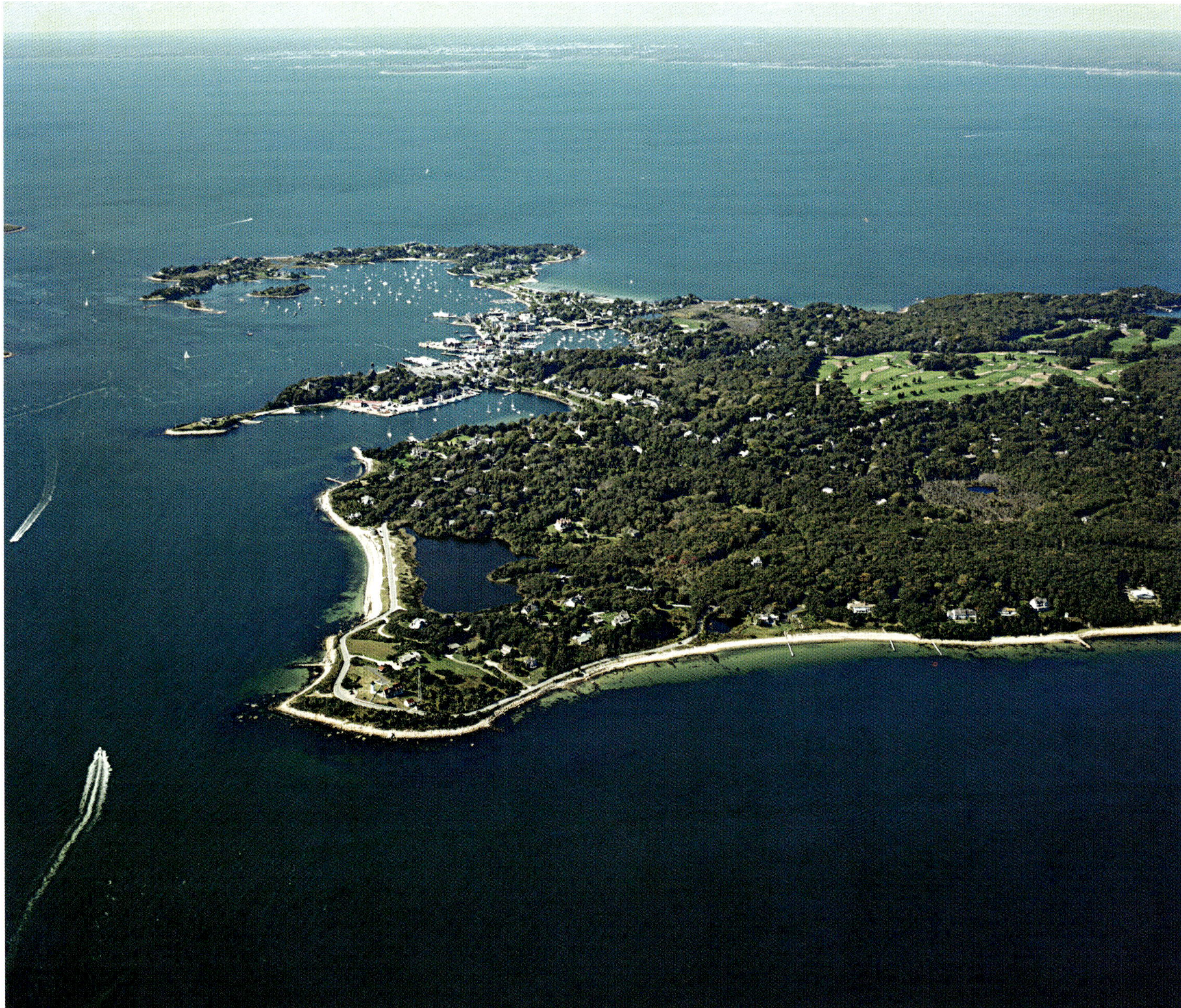

Nobska Point Lighthouse looking west.

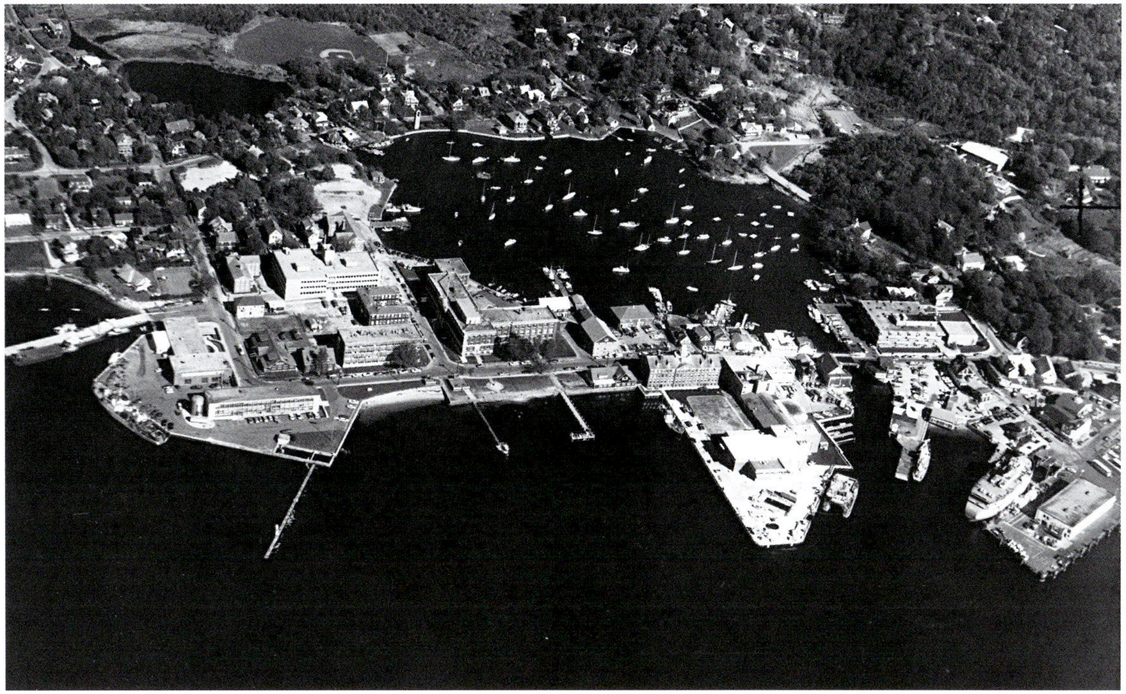

Woods Hole Oceanographic Institute in 1969 and 2007.

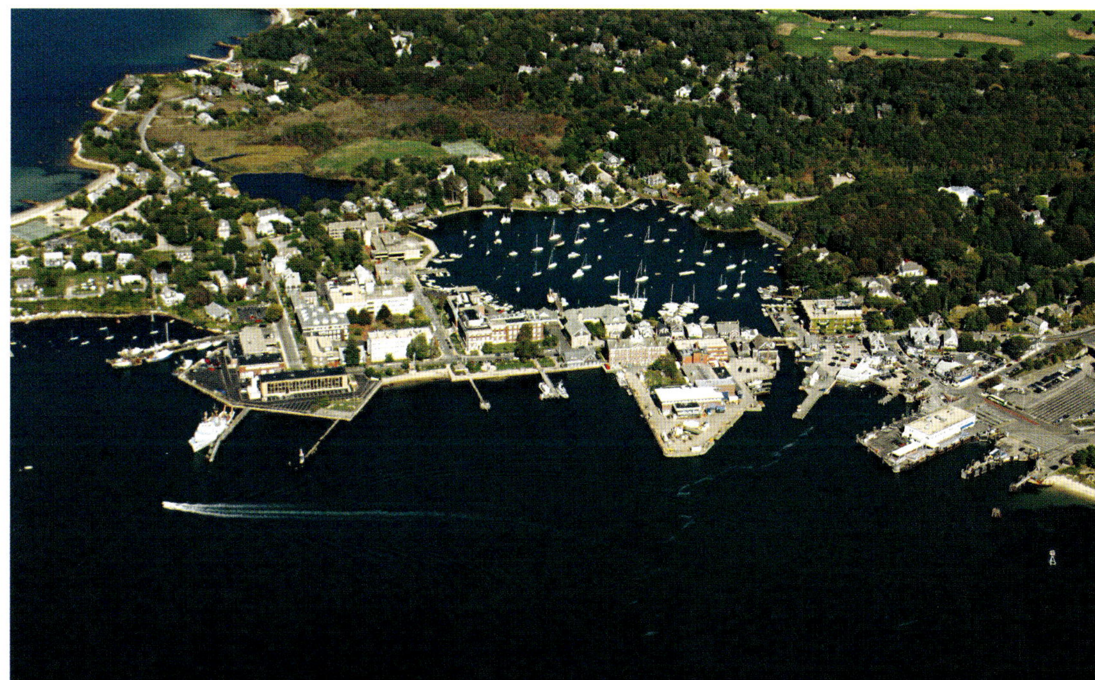

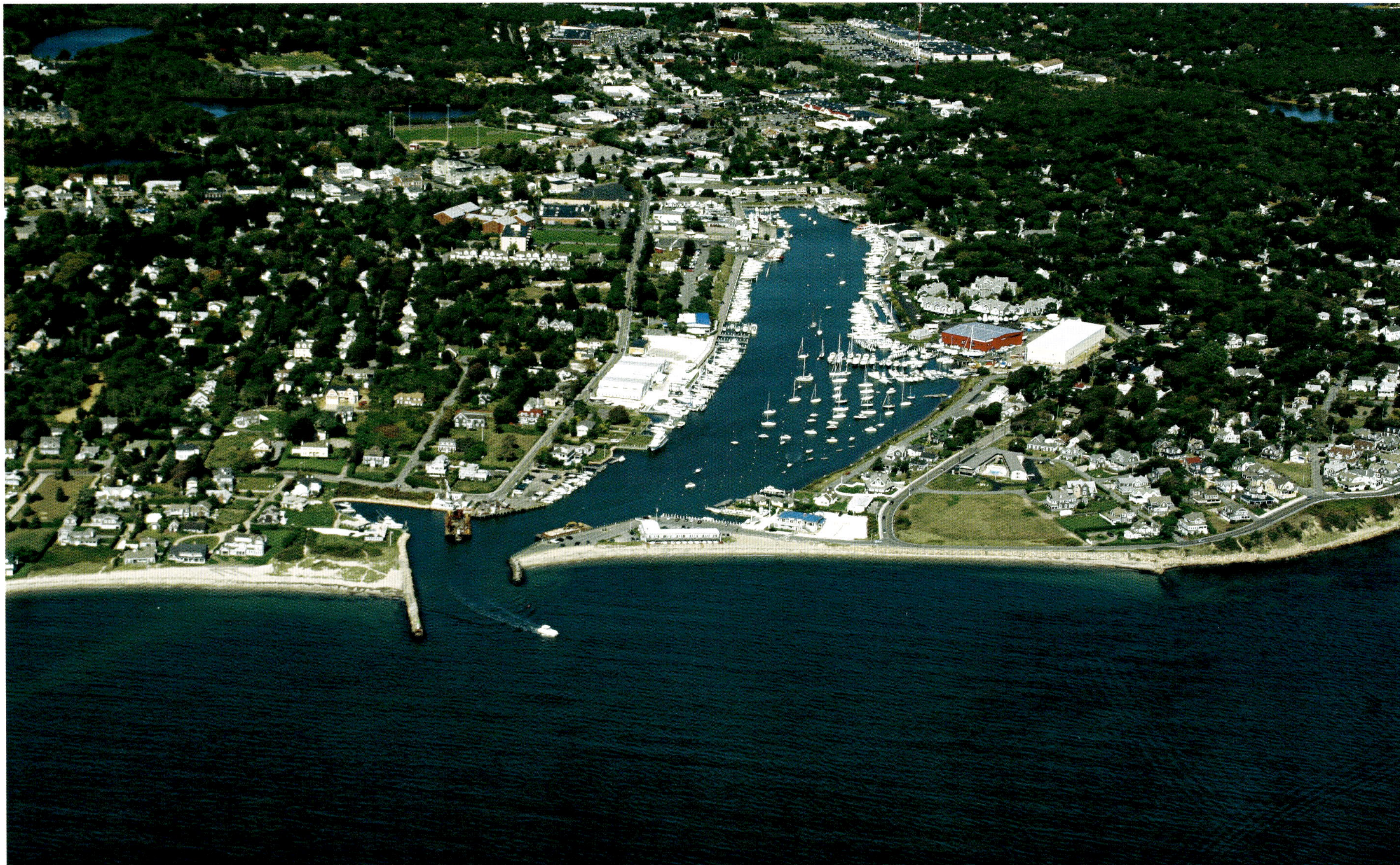

Falmouth Harbor.

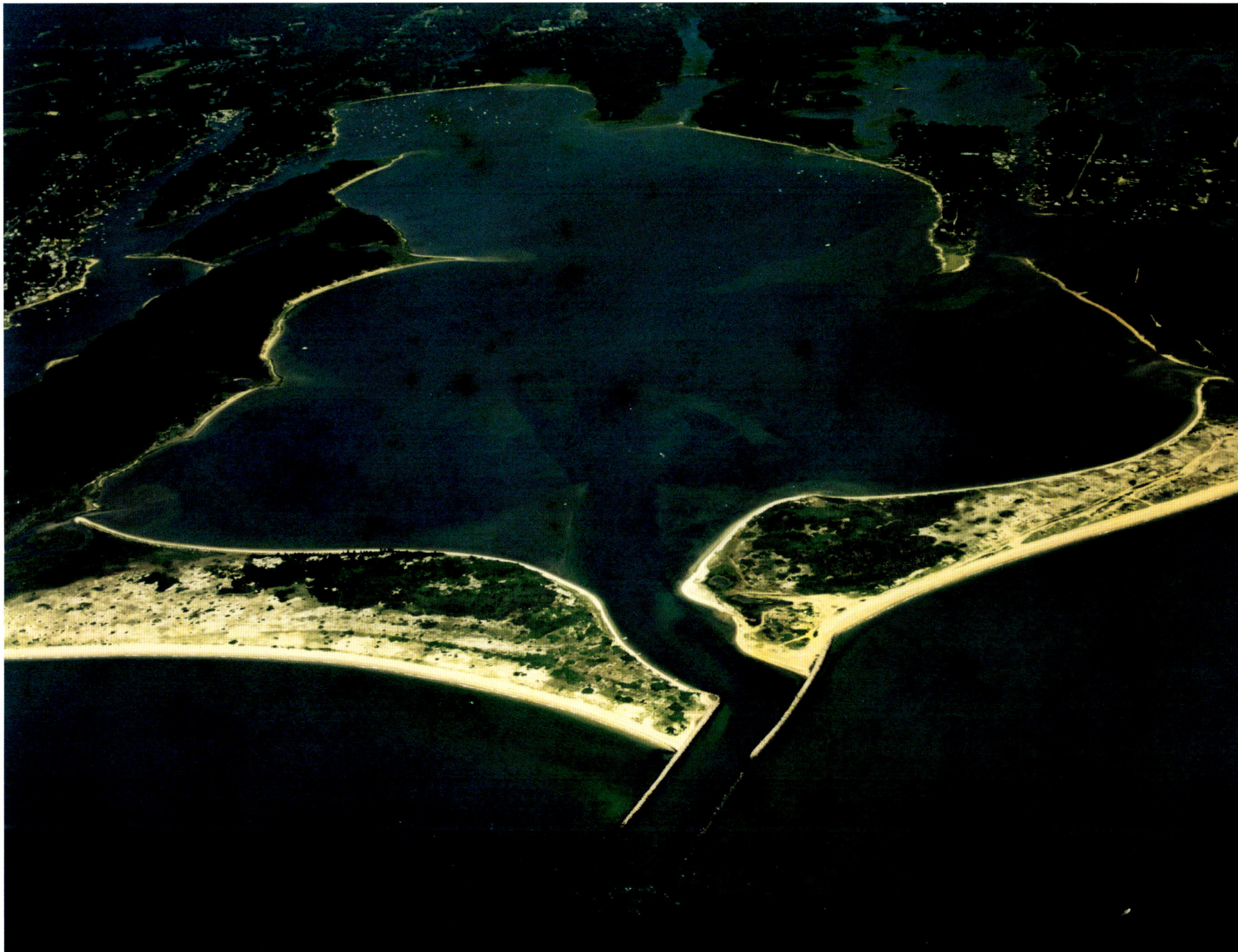

Waquoit Bay.

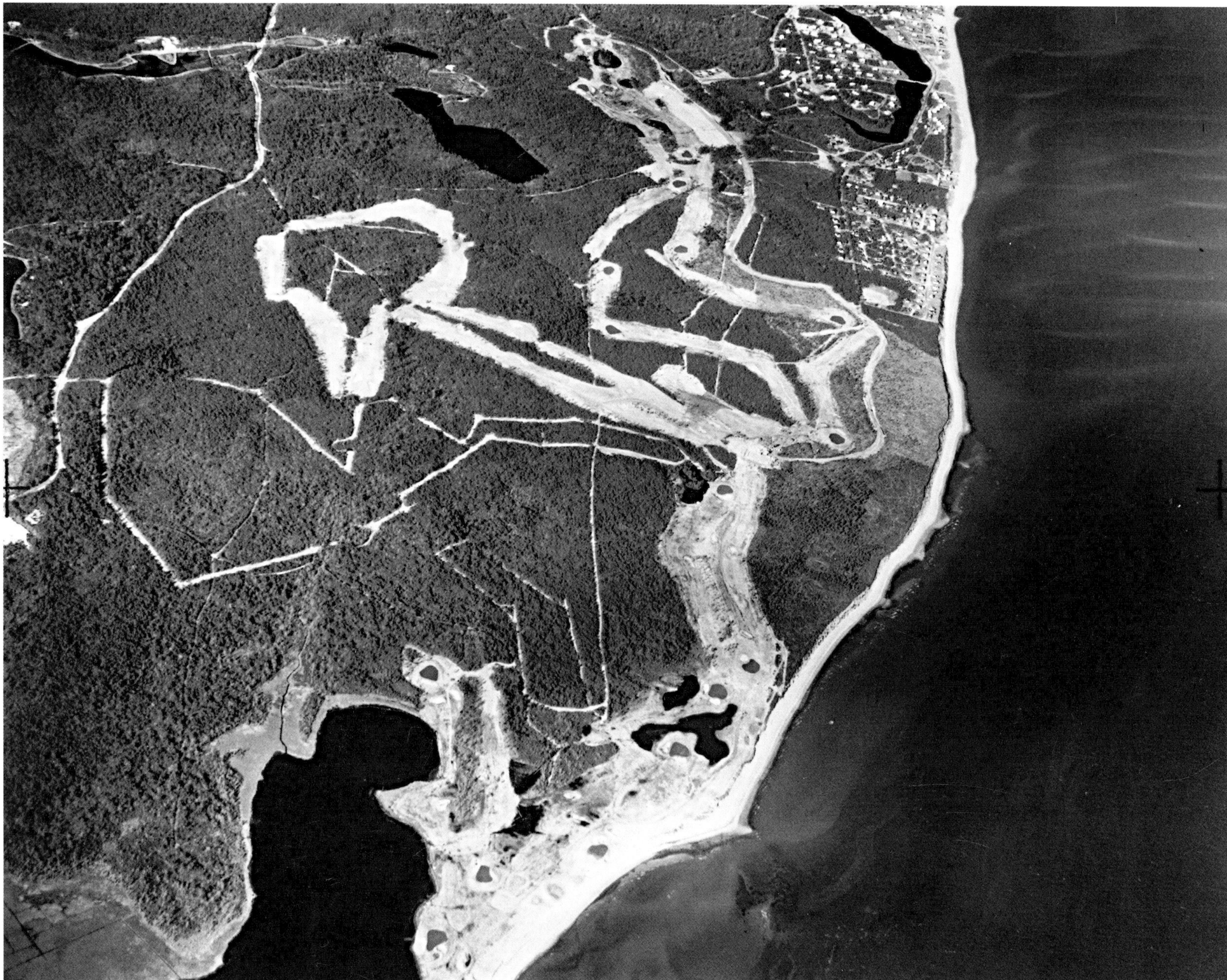

New Seabury, the early stages in 1964 and 39 years later. {opposite}

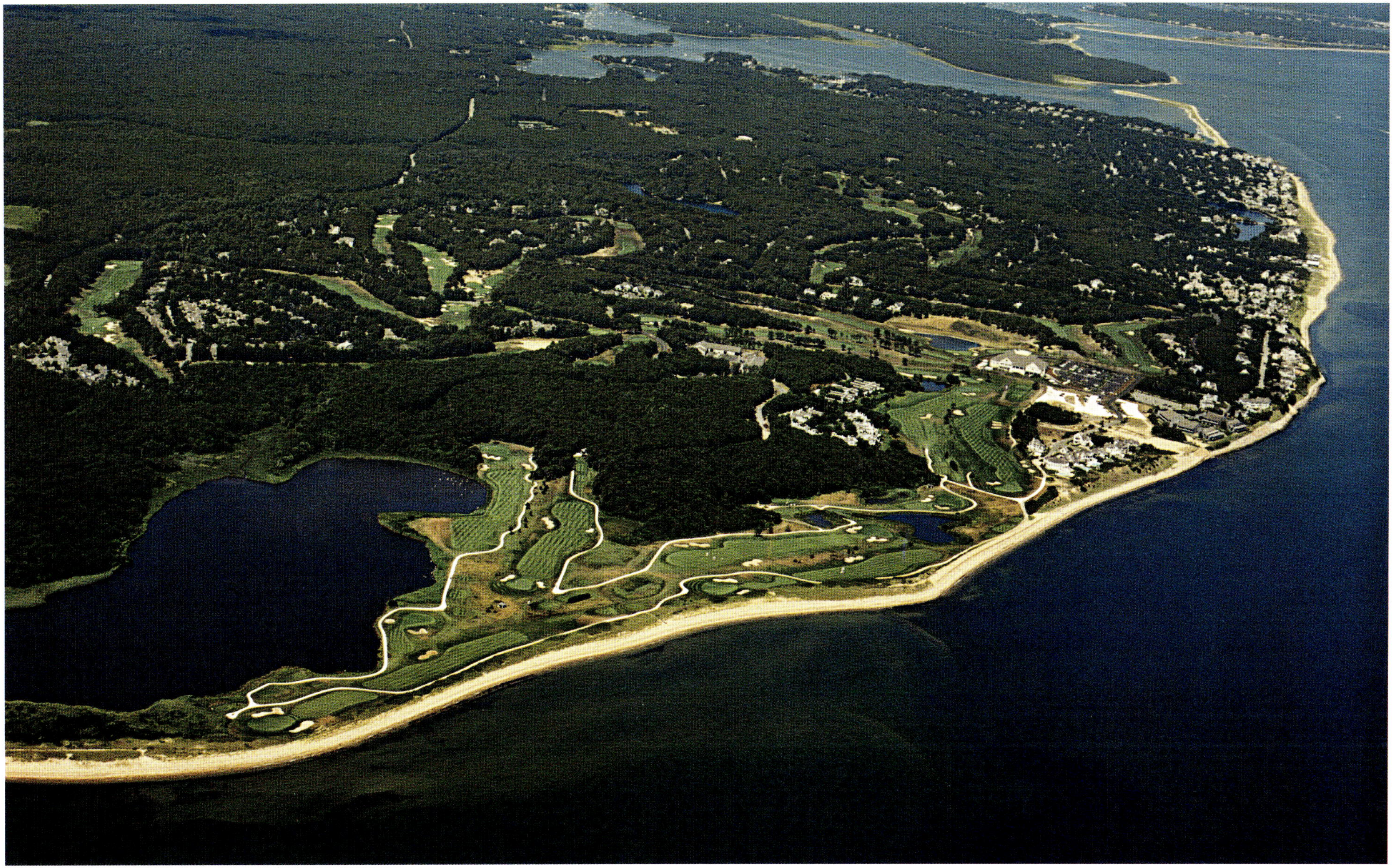

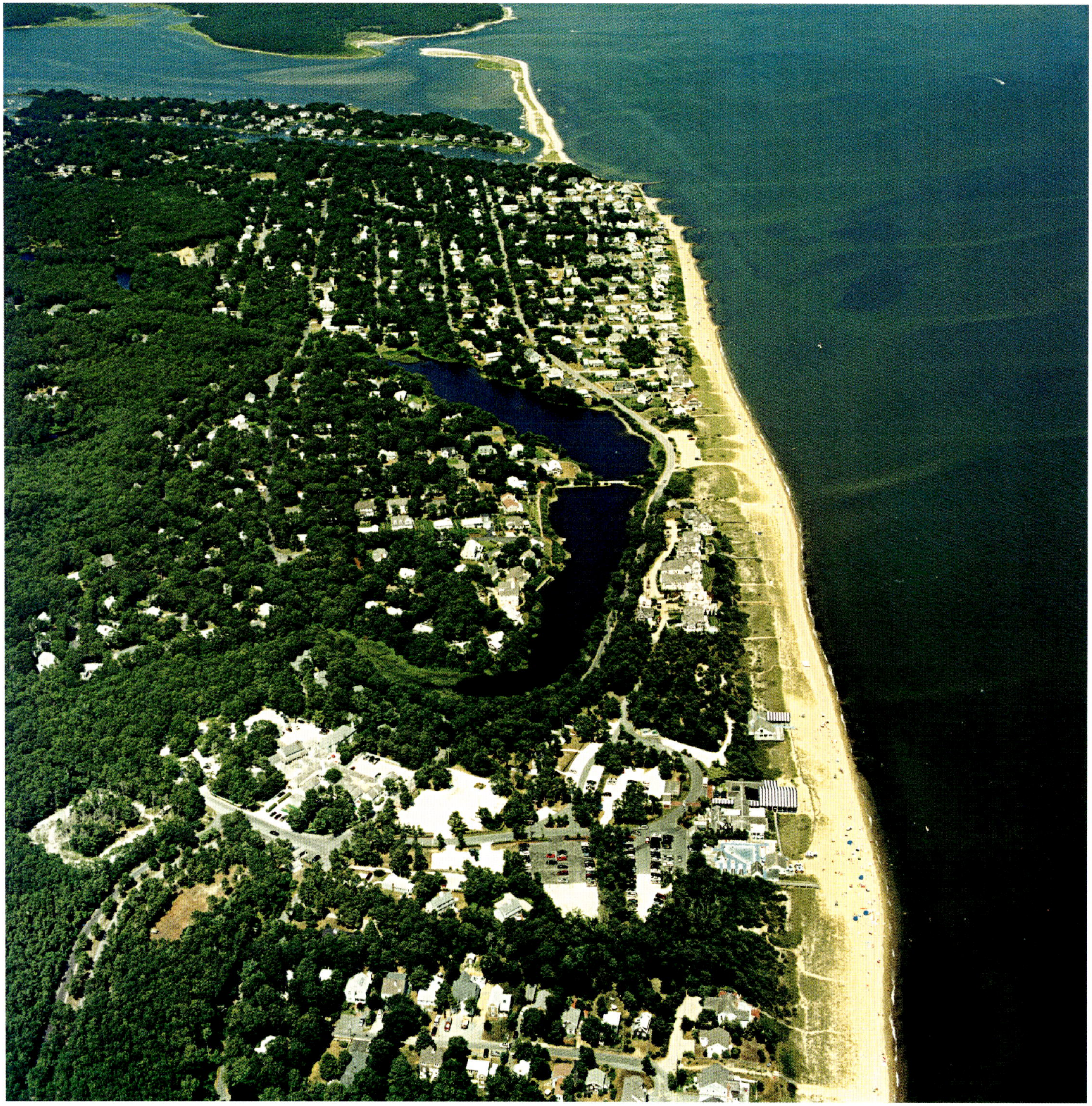

Mashpee looking north-east to Poponesset.

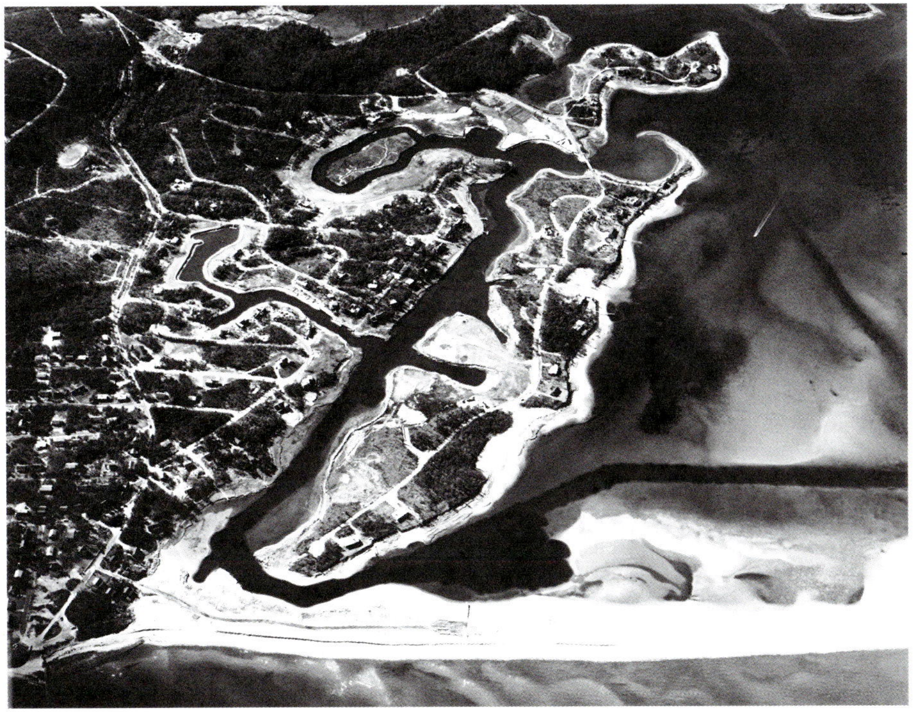

Poponesset in 1964 and 39 years later.

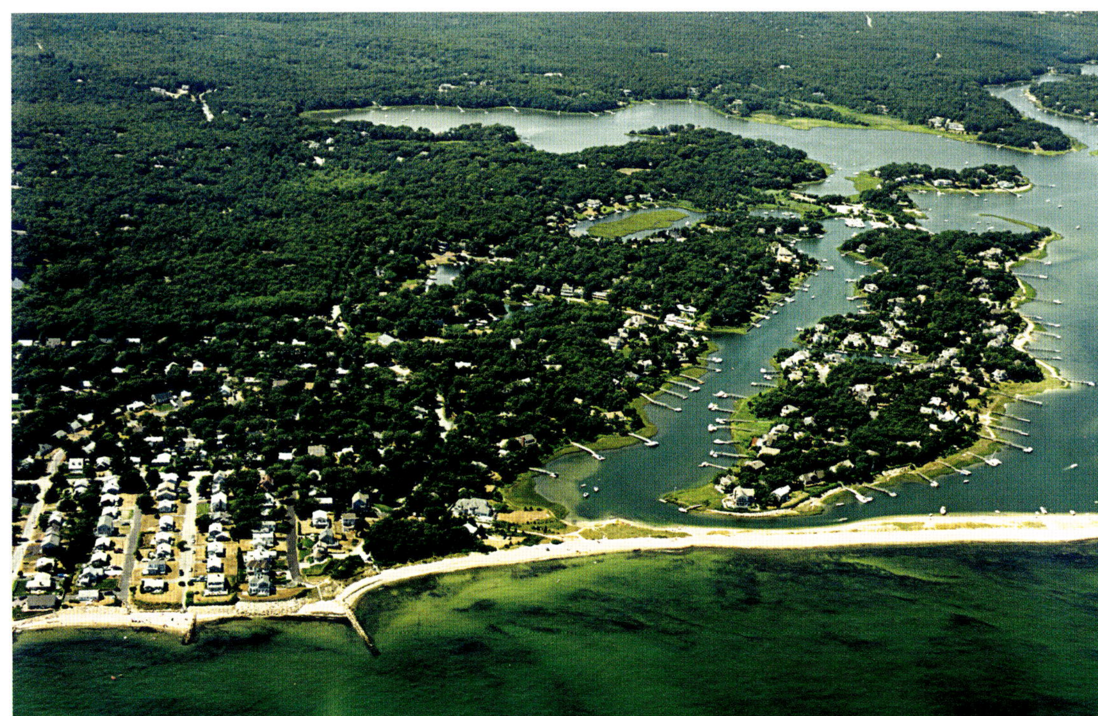

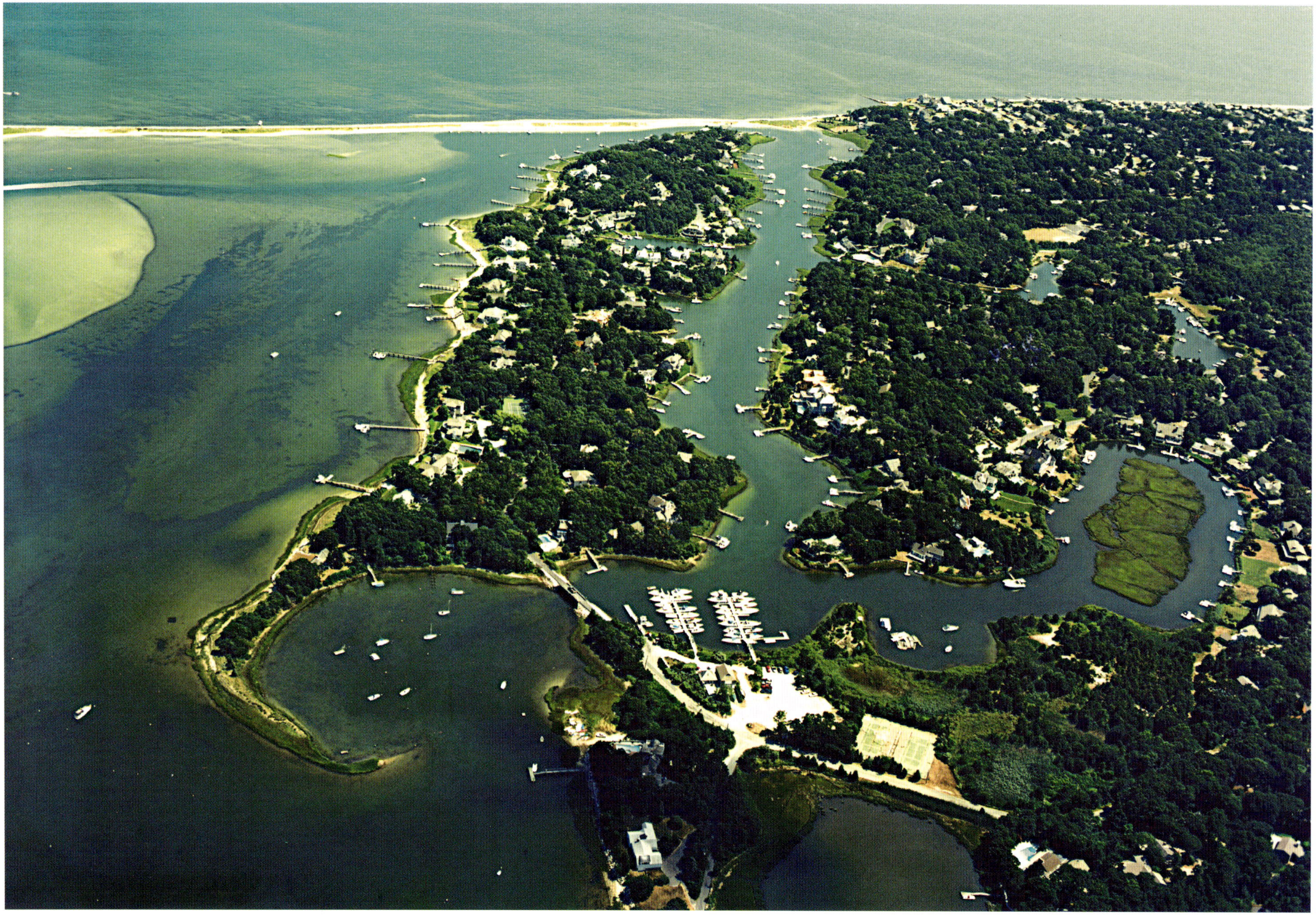

Poponesset Bay to Nantucket Sound.

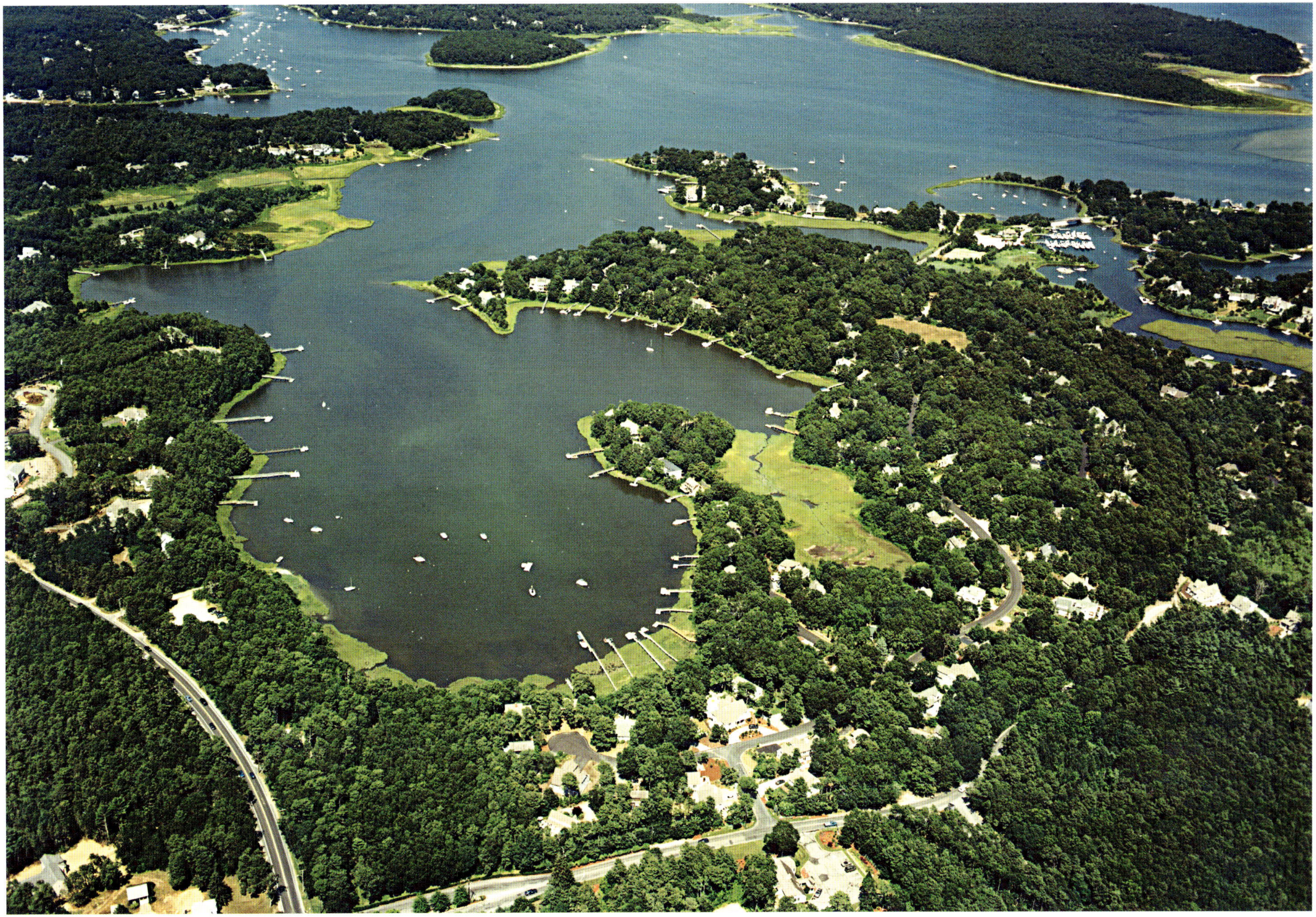

Ockway Bay to Barnstable.

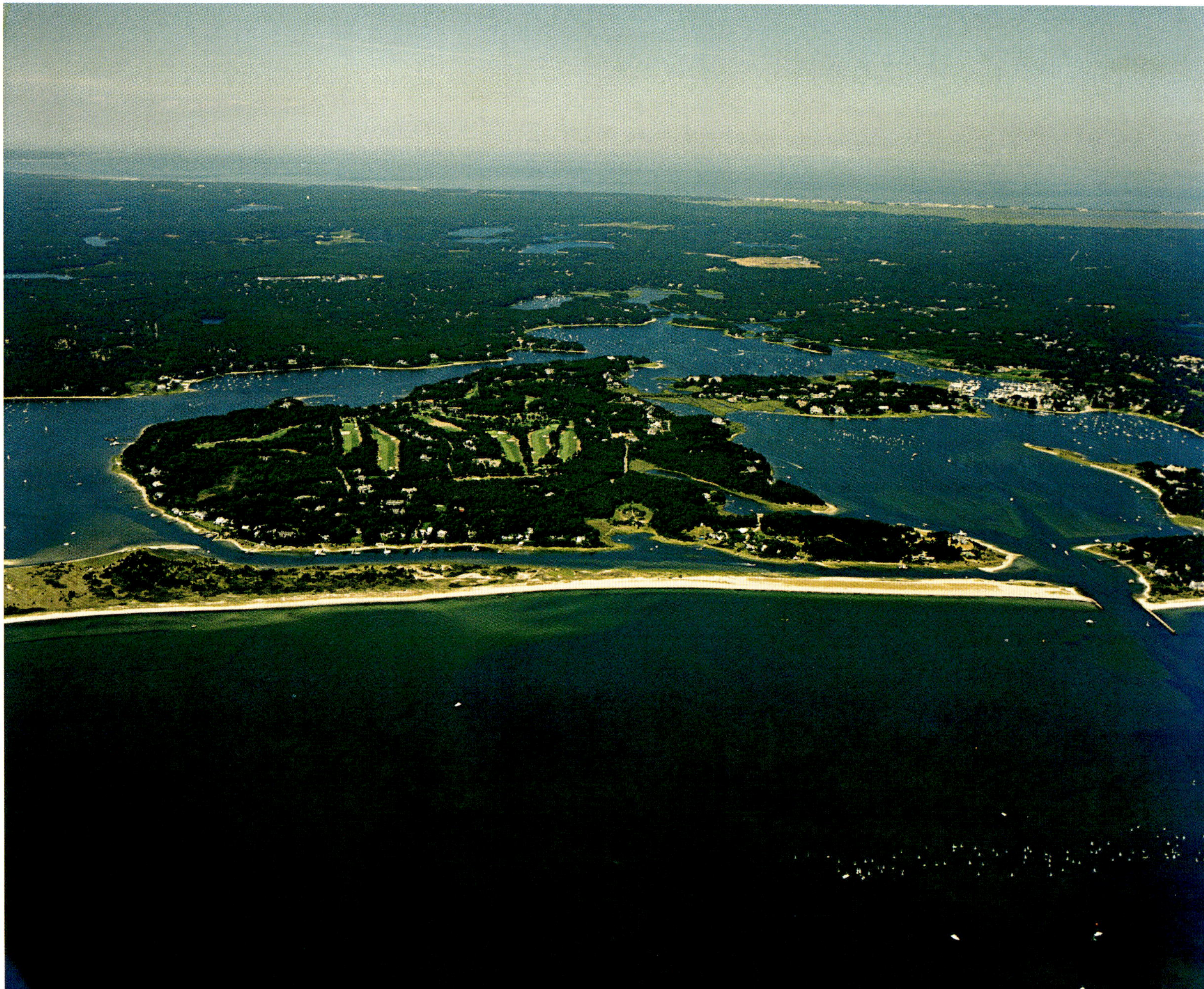

Oyster Harbors, Osterville.

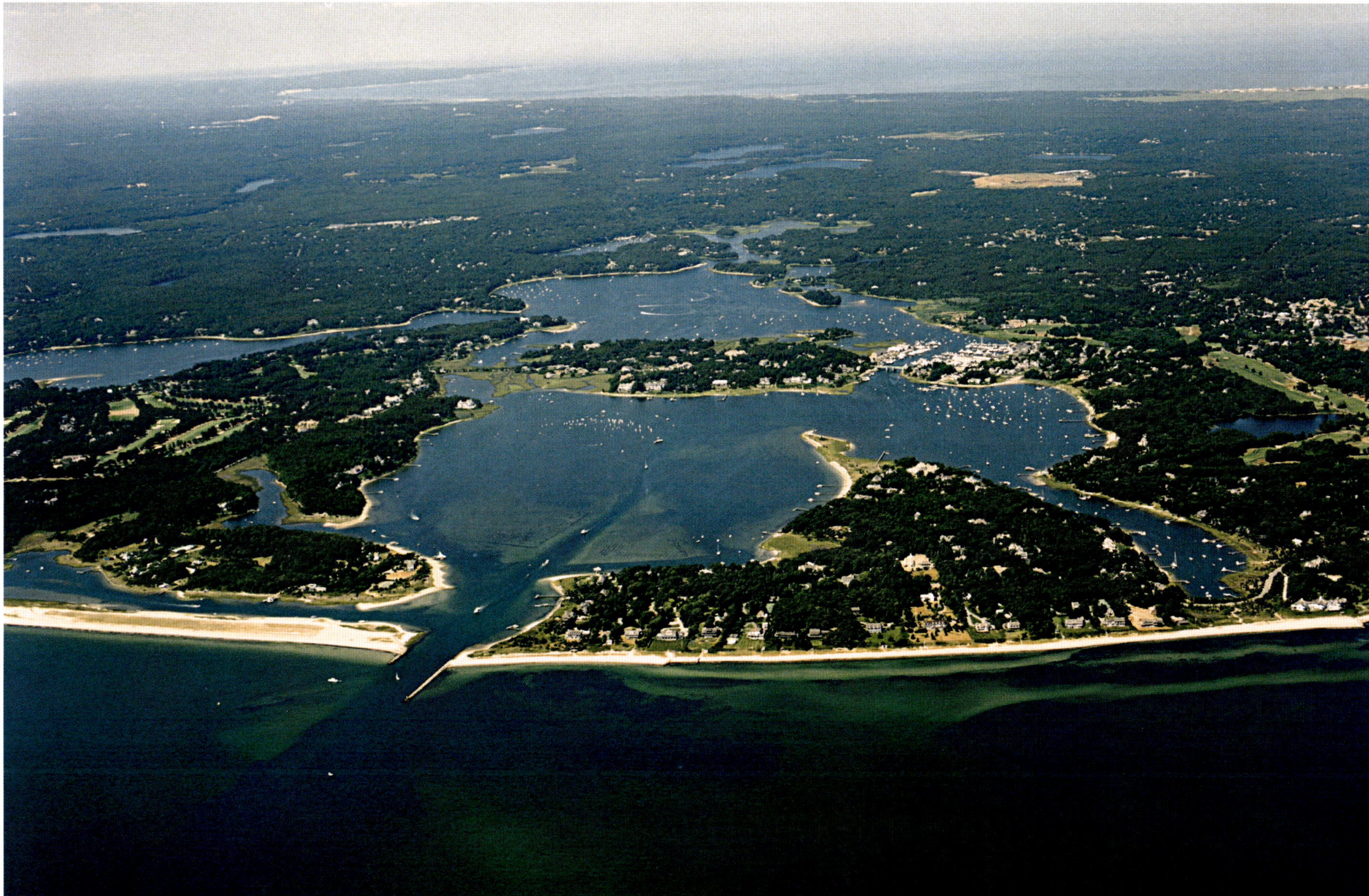

Three Bays, Osterville to Cape Cod Bay.

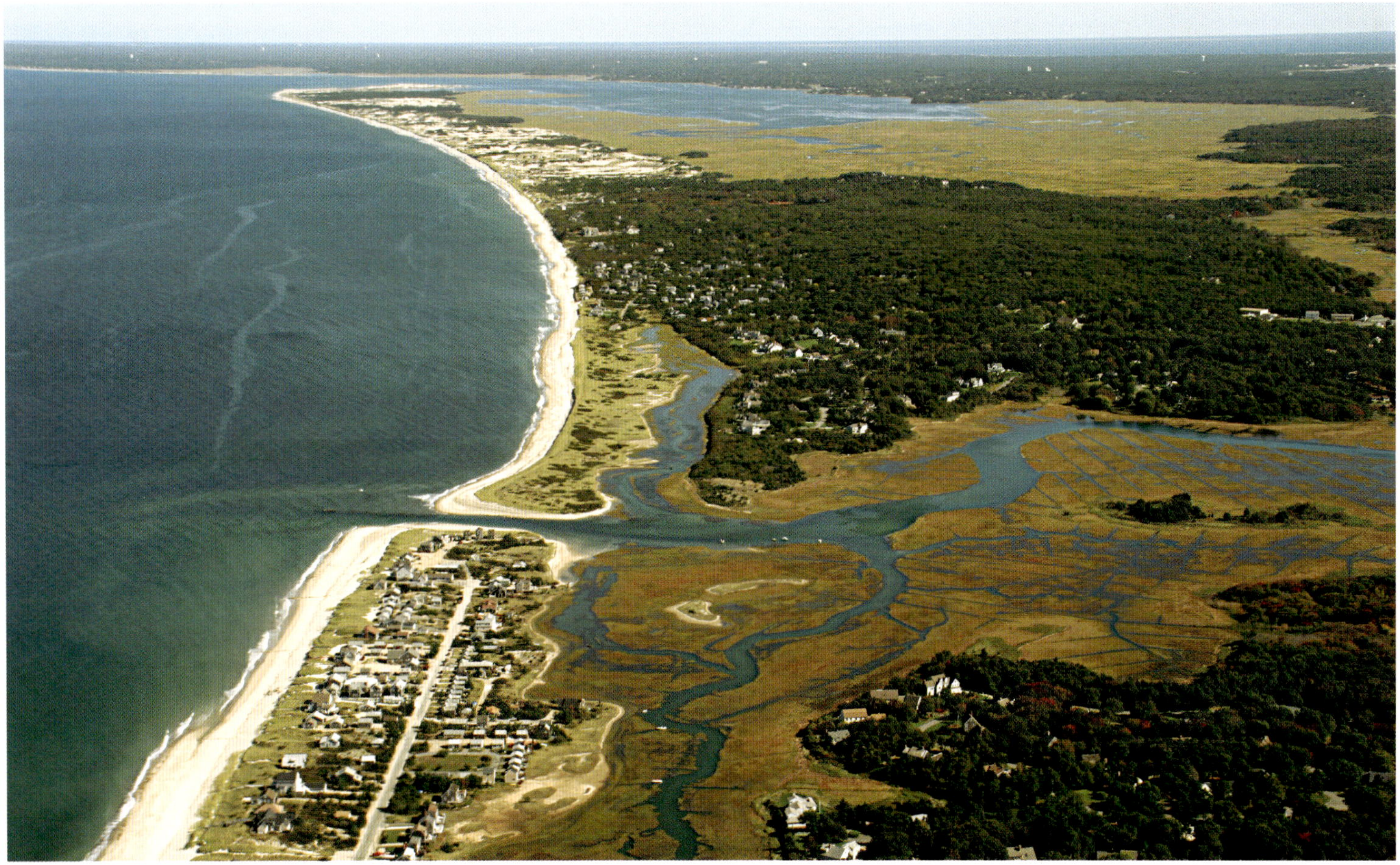

Scorton Creek, Sandwich, looking east to Sandy Neck.

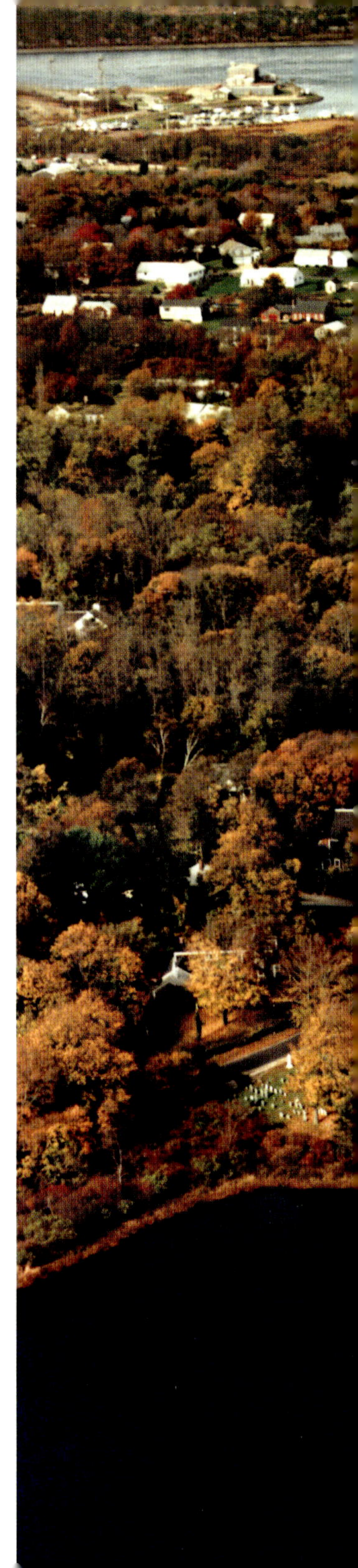

Lower Shawme Pond and Sandwich in fall foliage.

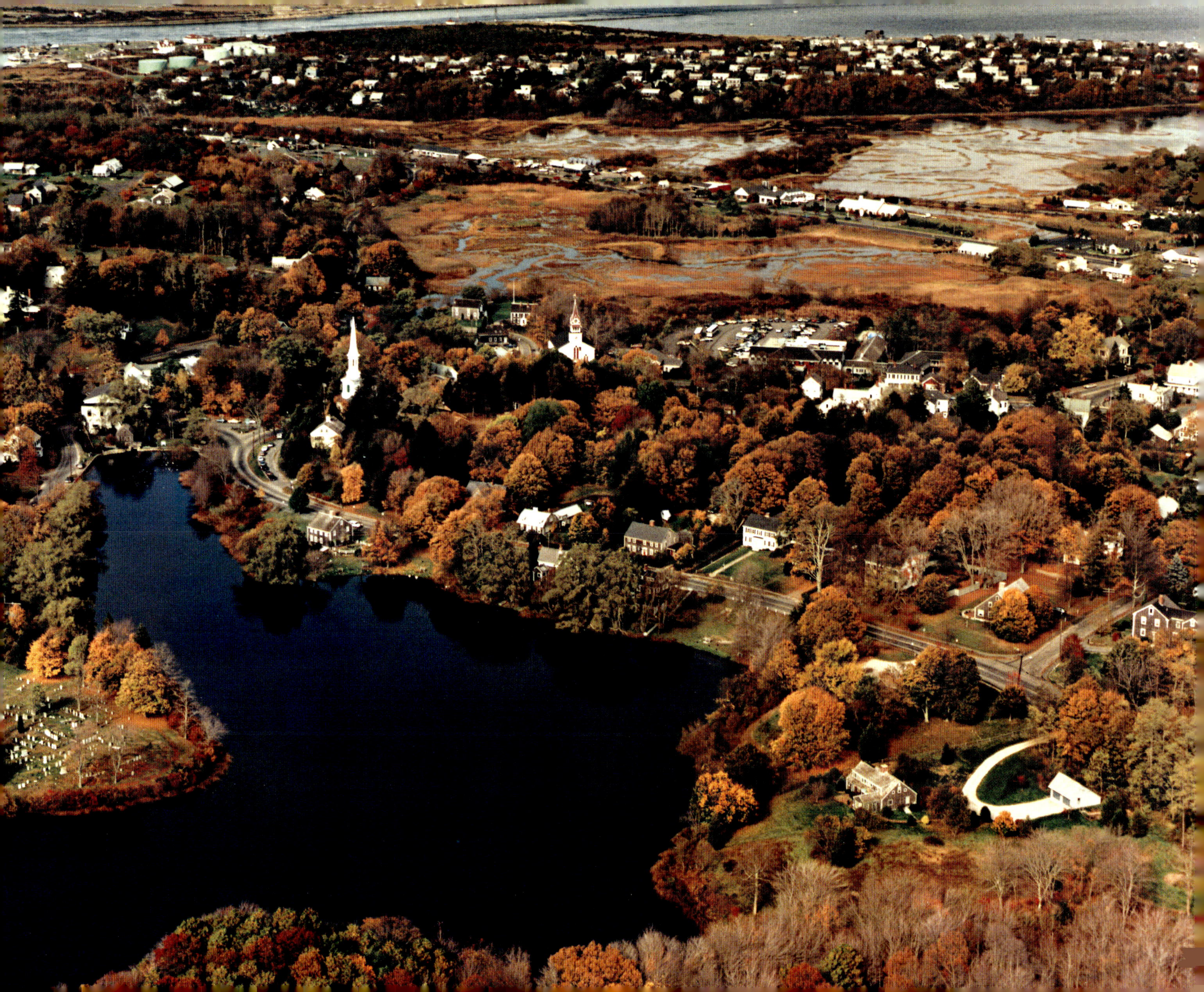

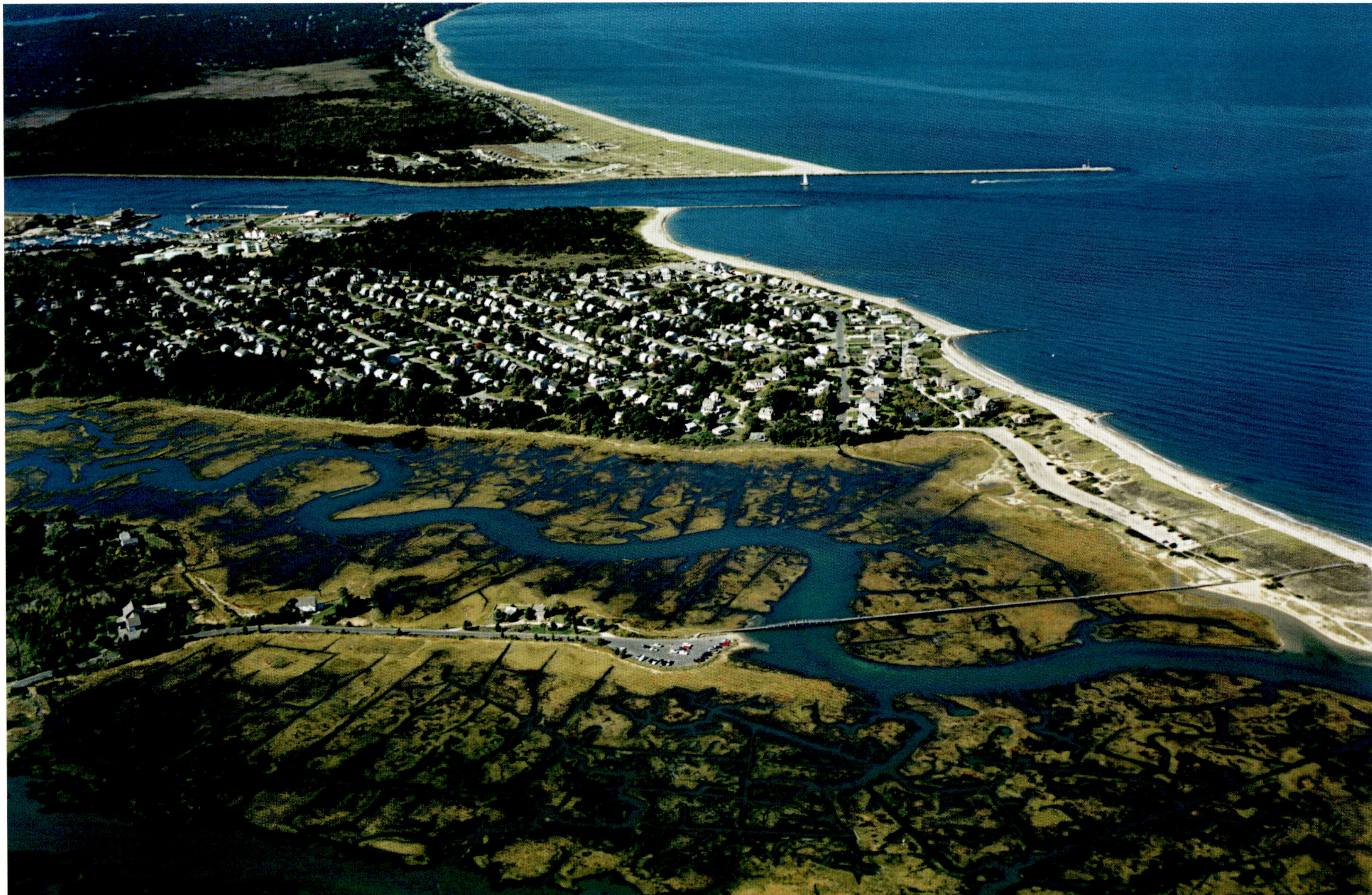

The Sandwich boardwalk to Cape Cod Canal.

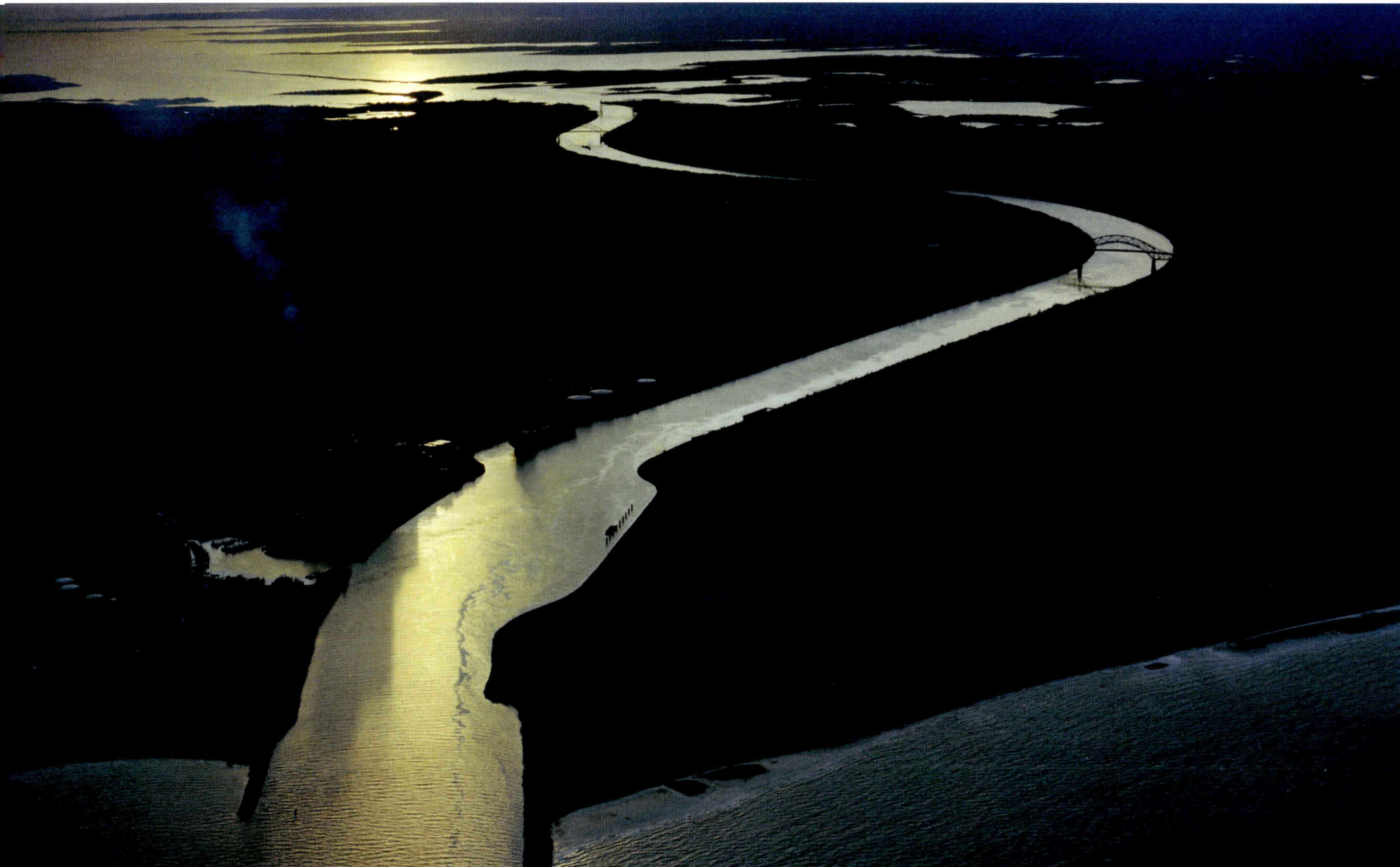

Cape Cod Canal at sunset.

Chapter 3
Barnstable, Hyannis, Yarmouth, & Dennis

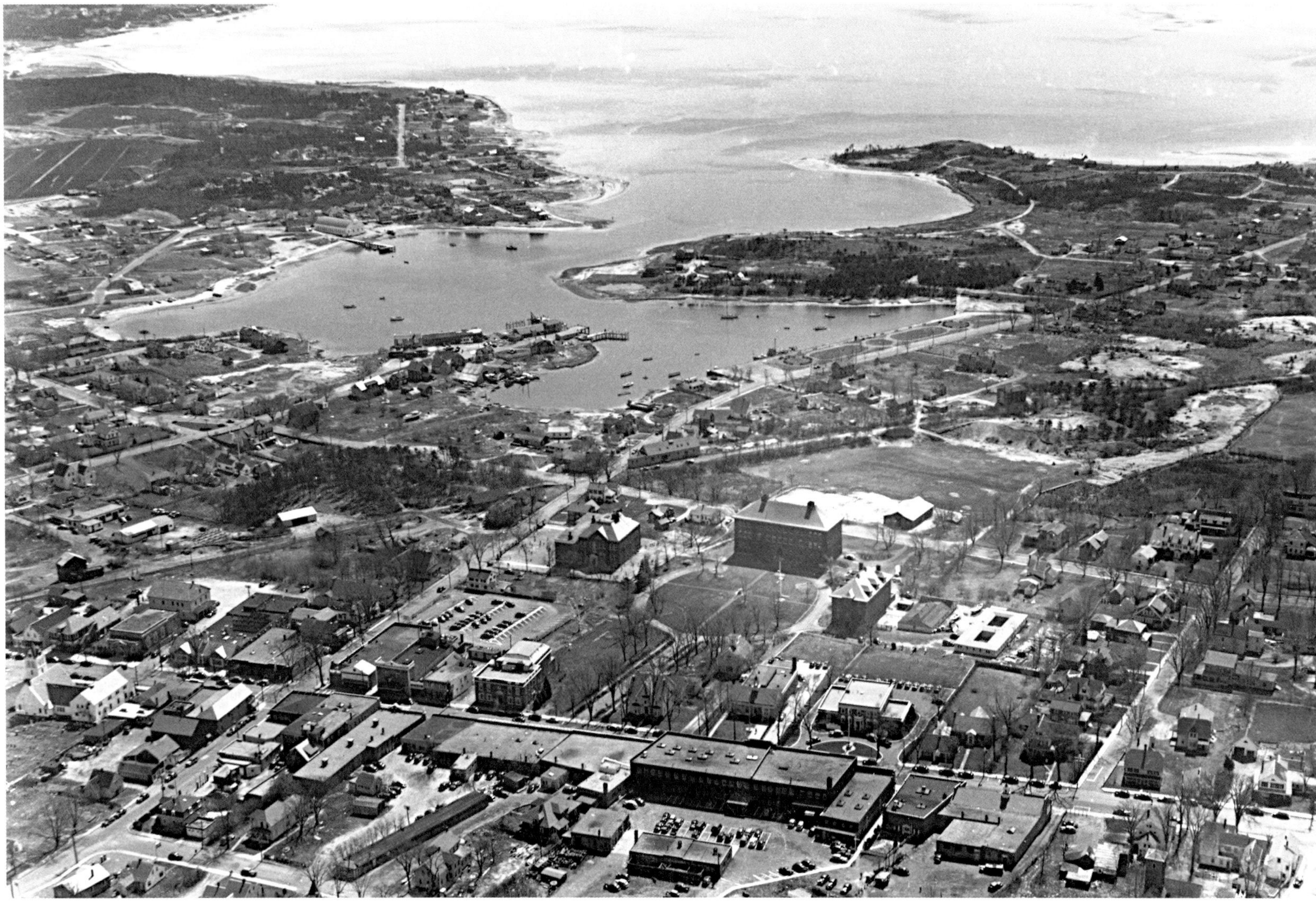

Downtown Hyannis looking towards Hyannis Harbor, this 1946 view is printed from one of our oldest negatives.

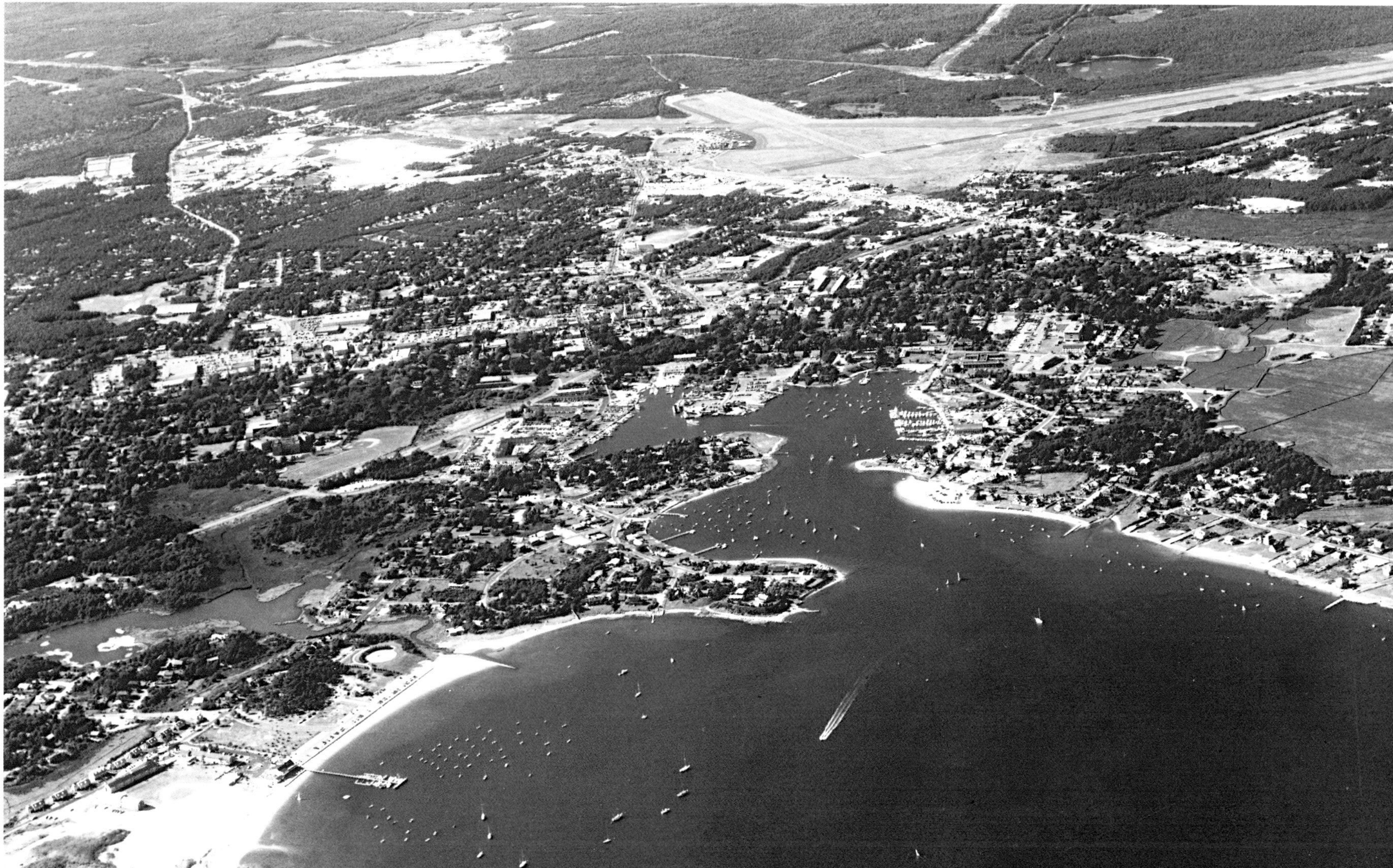

Looking in at Hyannis Harbor in 1969.

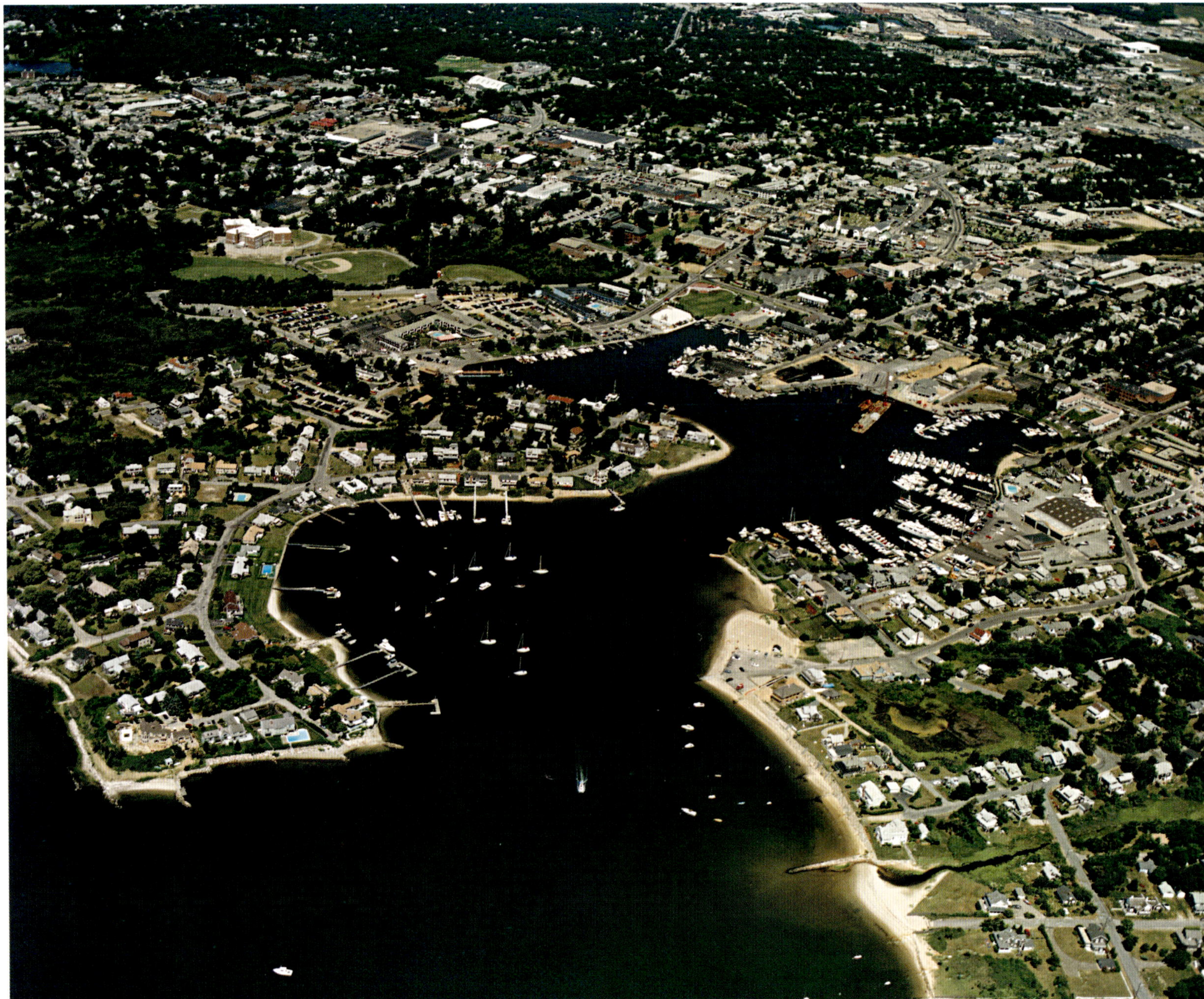

Hyannis Harbor.

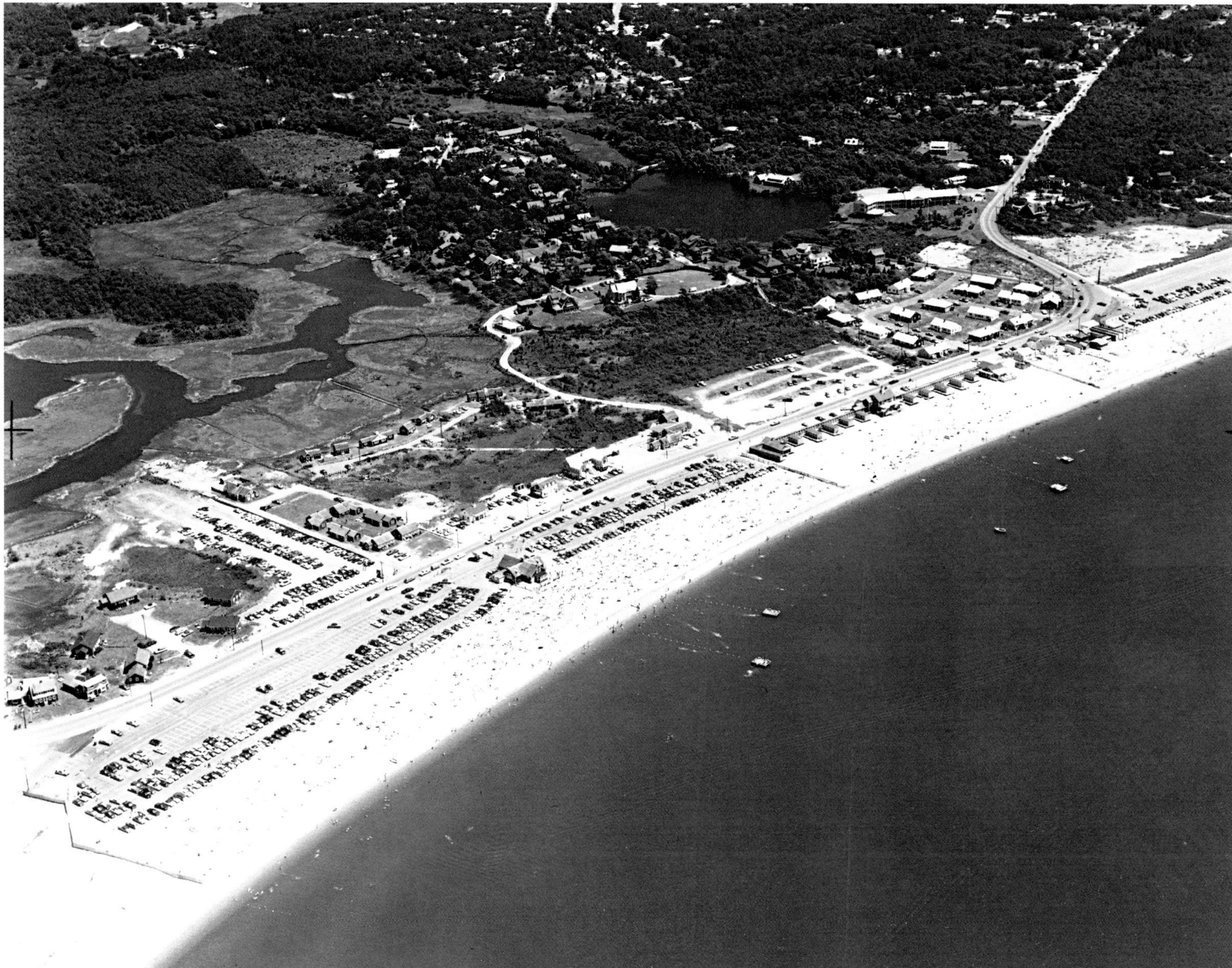

Craigville Beach in 1968.

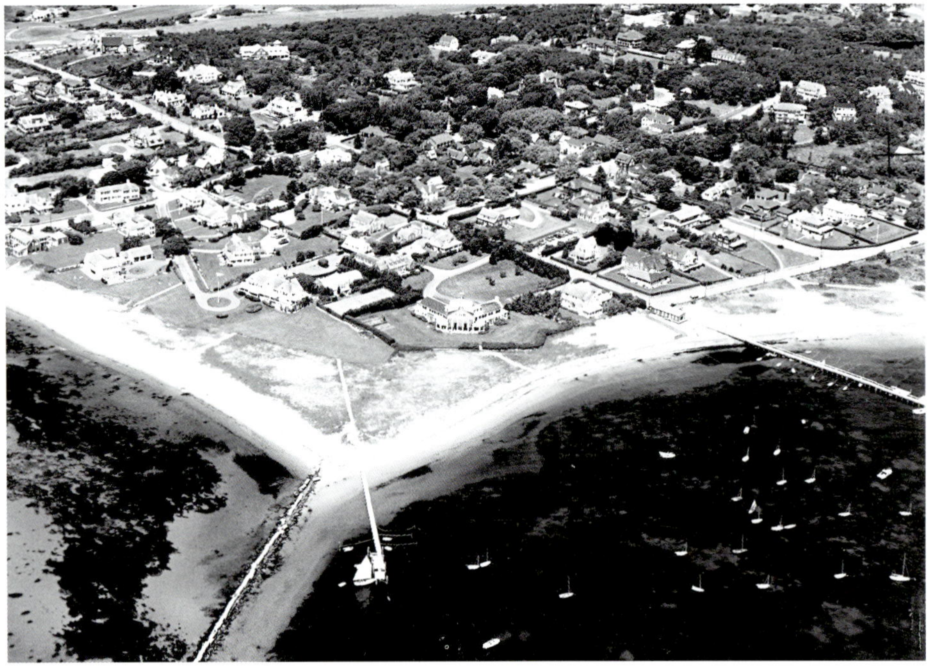

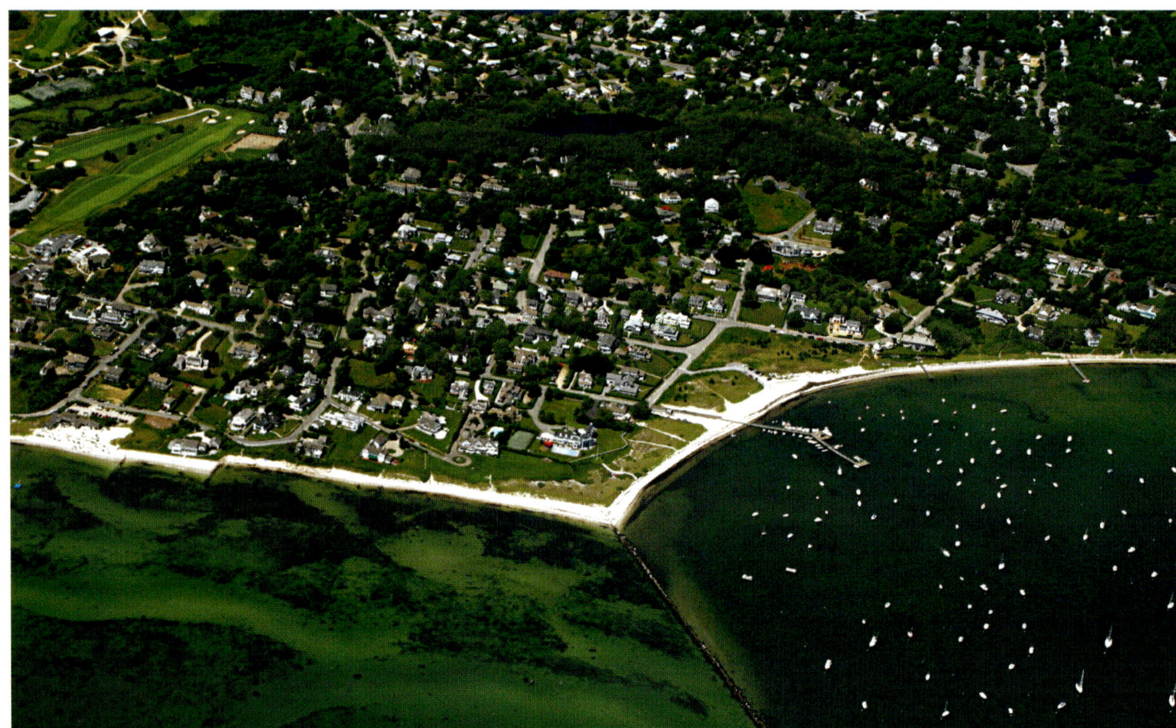

Hyannisport features the Kennedy compound, Hyannisport, in 1968 and 2006.

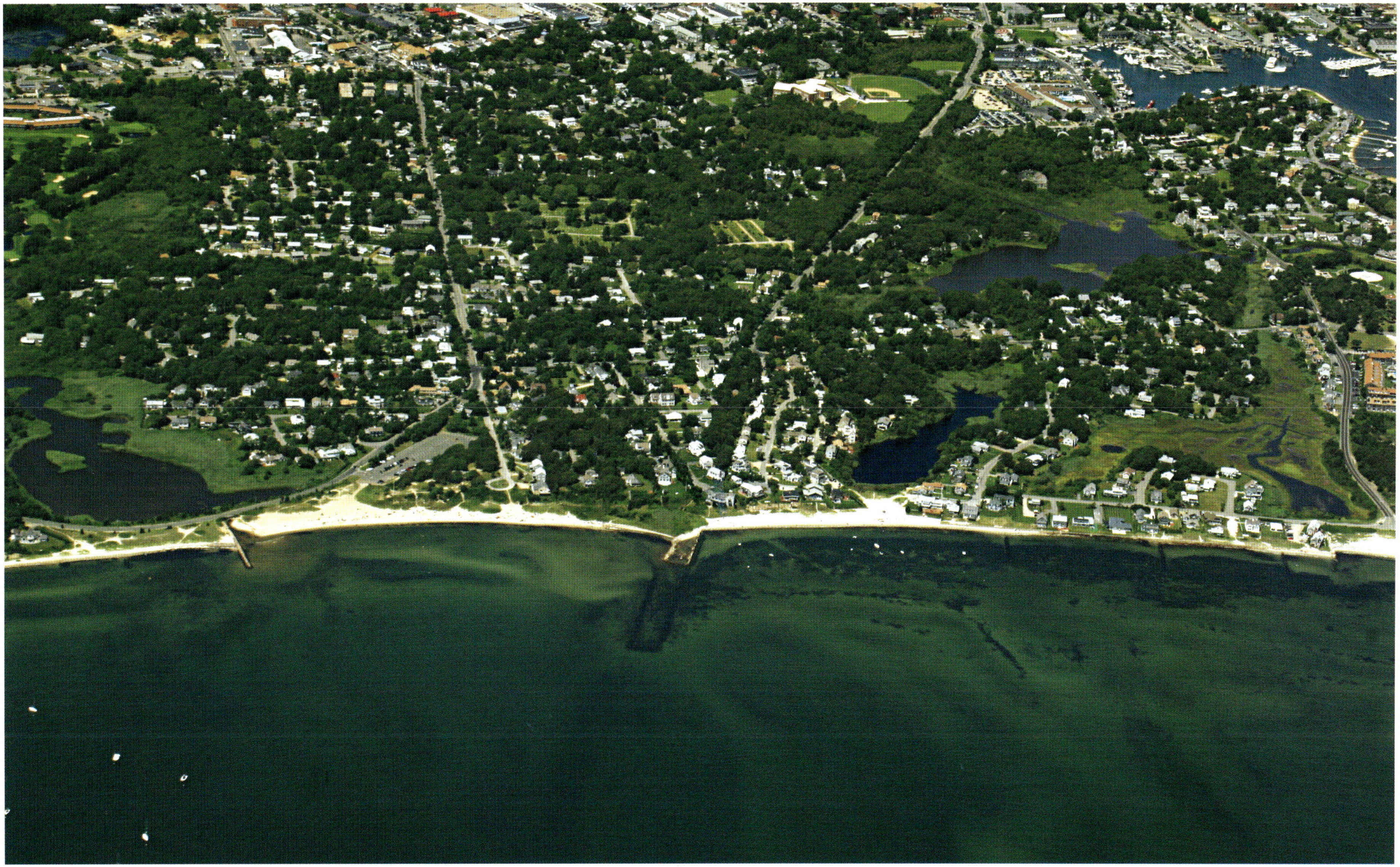

Hyannisport, Sea Street and Keyes Memorial Beach.

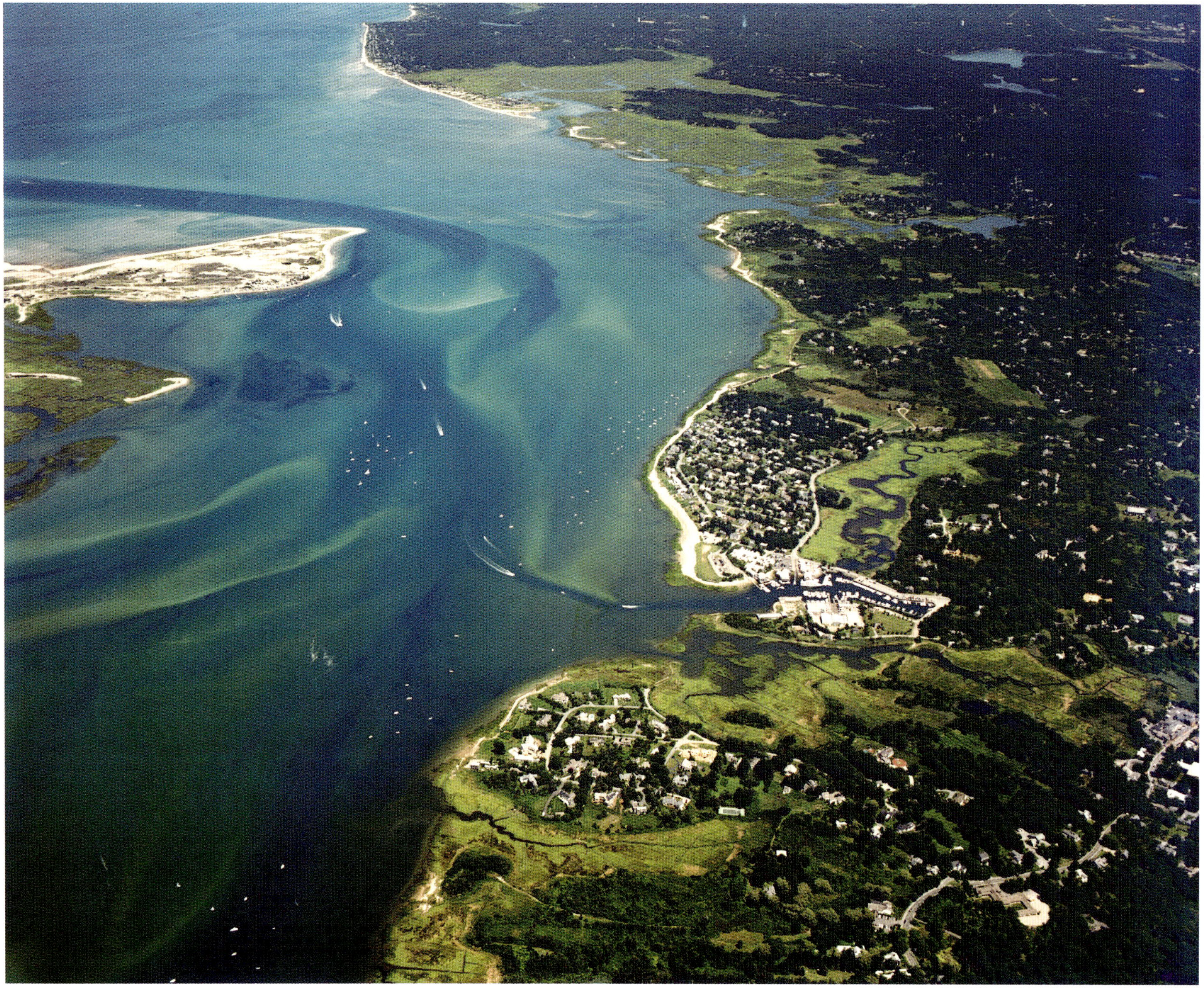

Barnstable Harbor and Sandy Neck looking east.

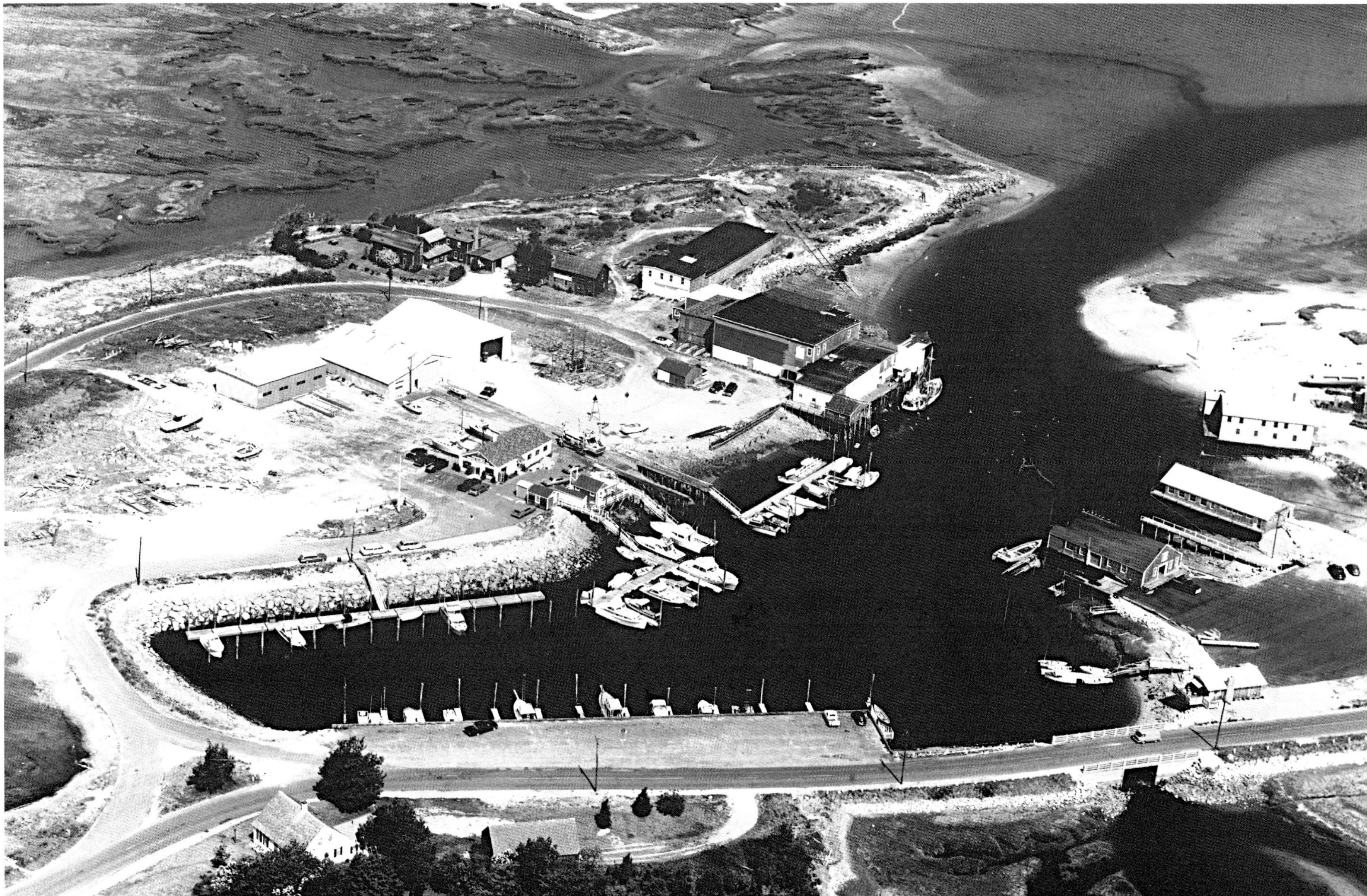

Barnstable Harbor Marina in 1964.

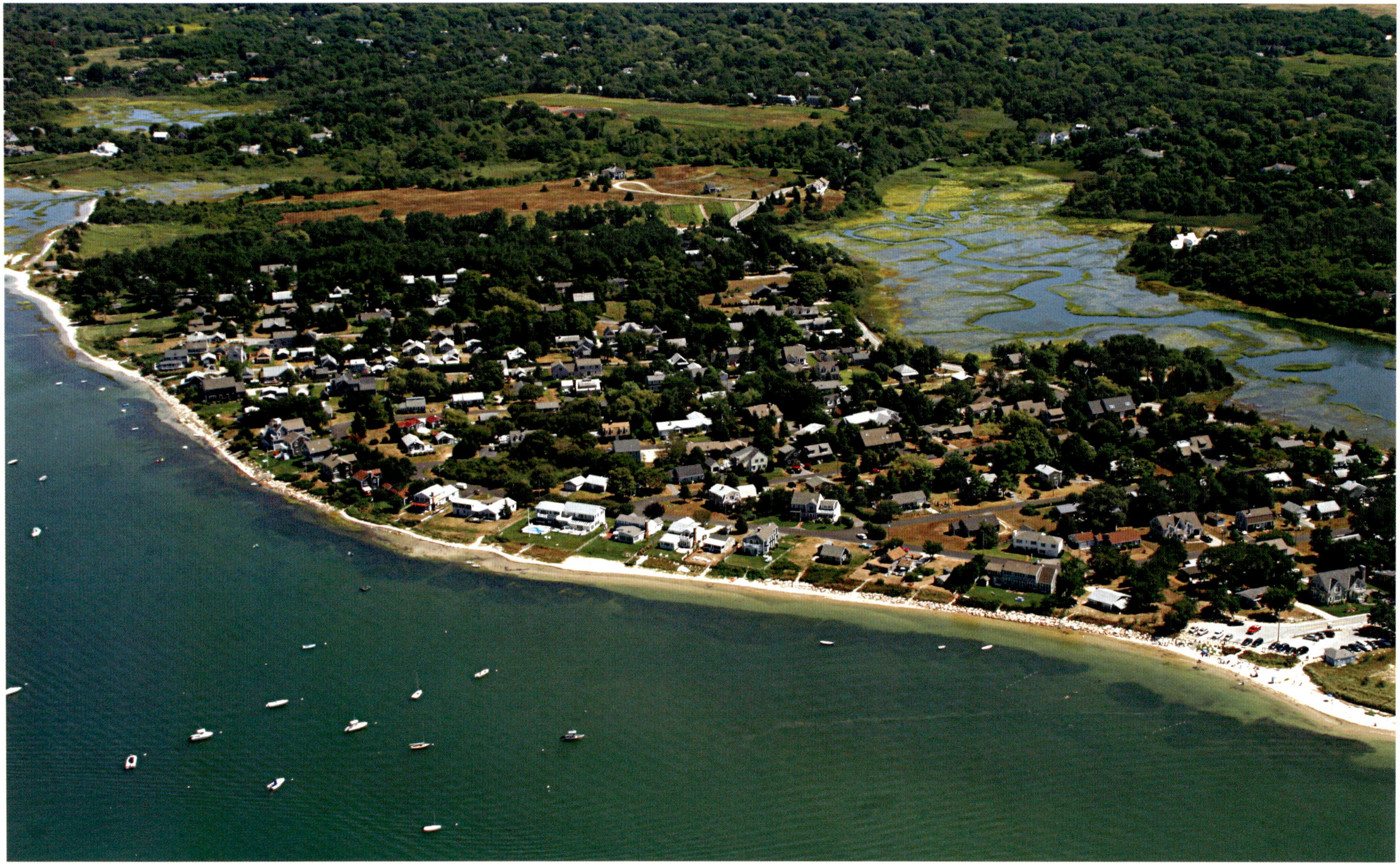

Village colony at Millway Beach, Barnstable.

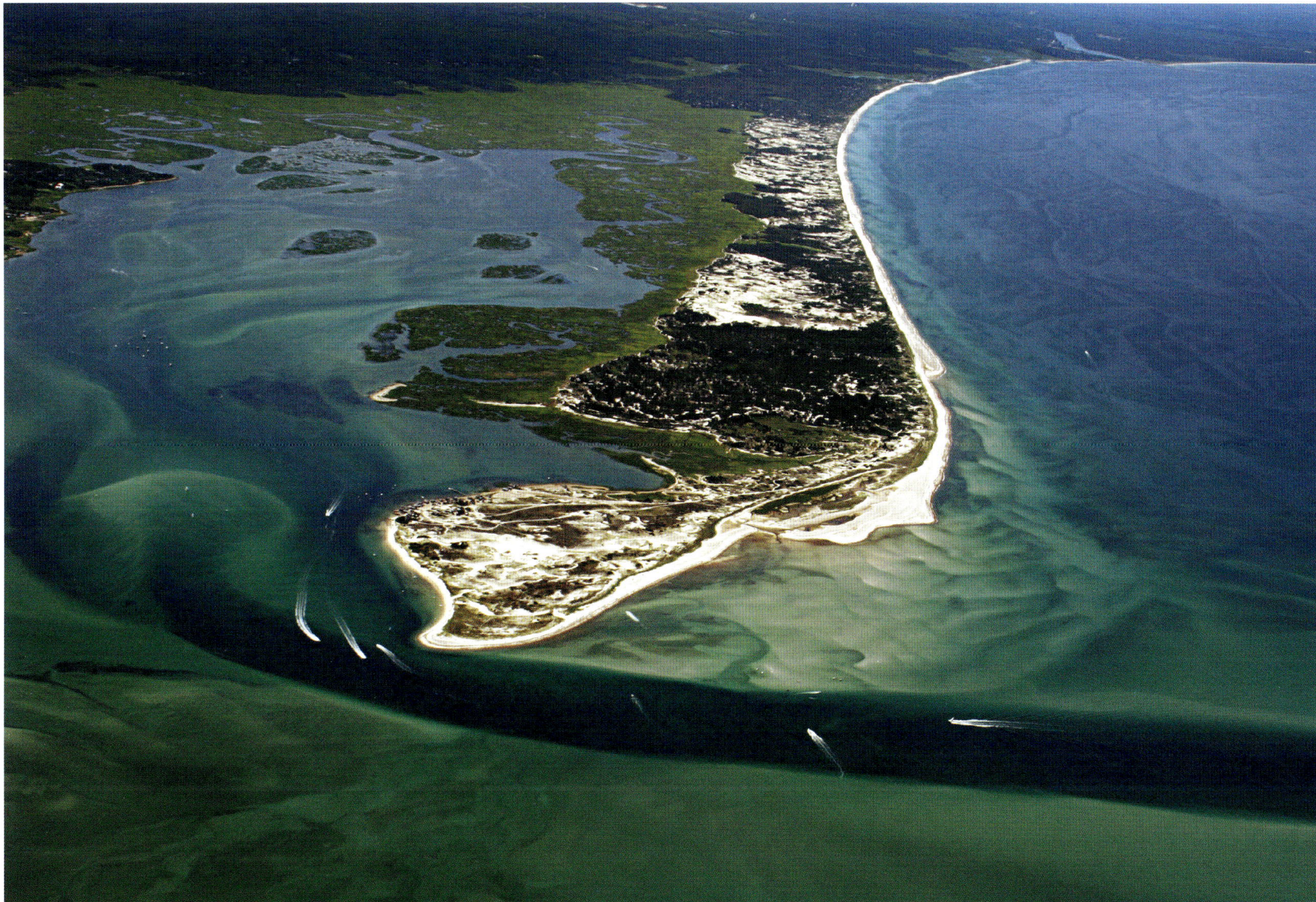

Sandy Neck looking west.

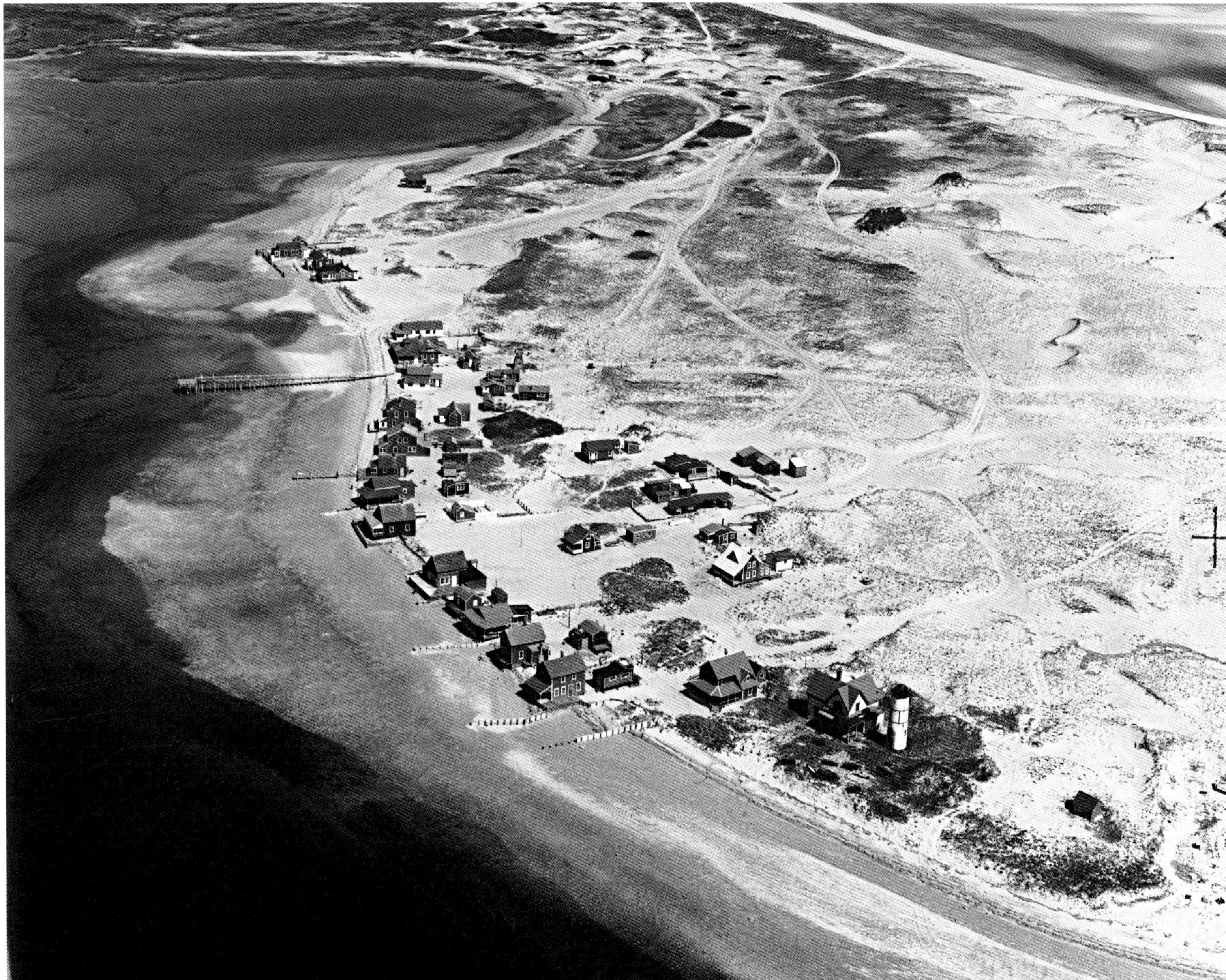

Sandy Neck Lighthouse and village in 1964.

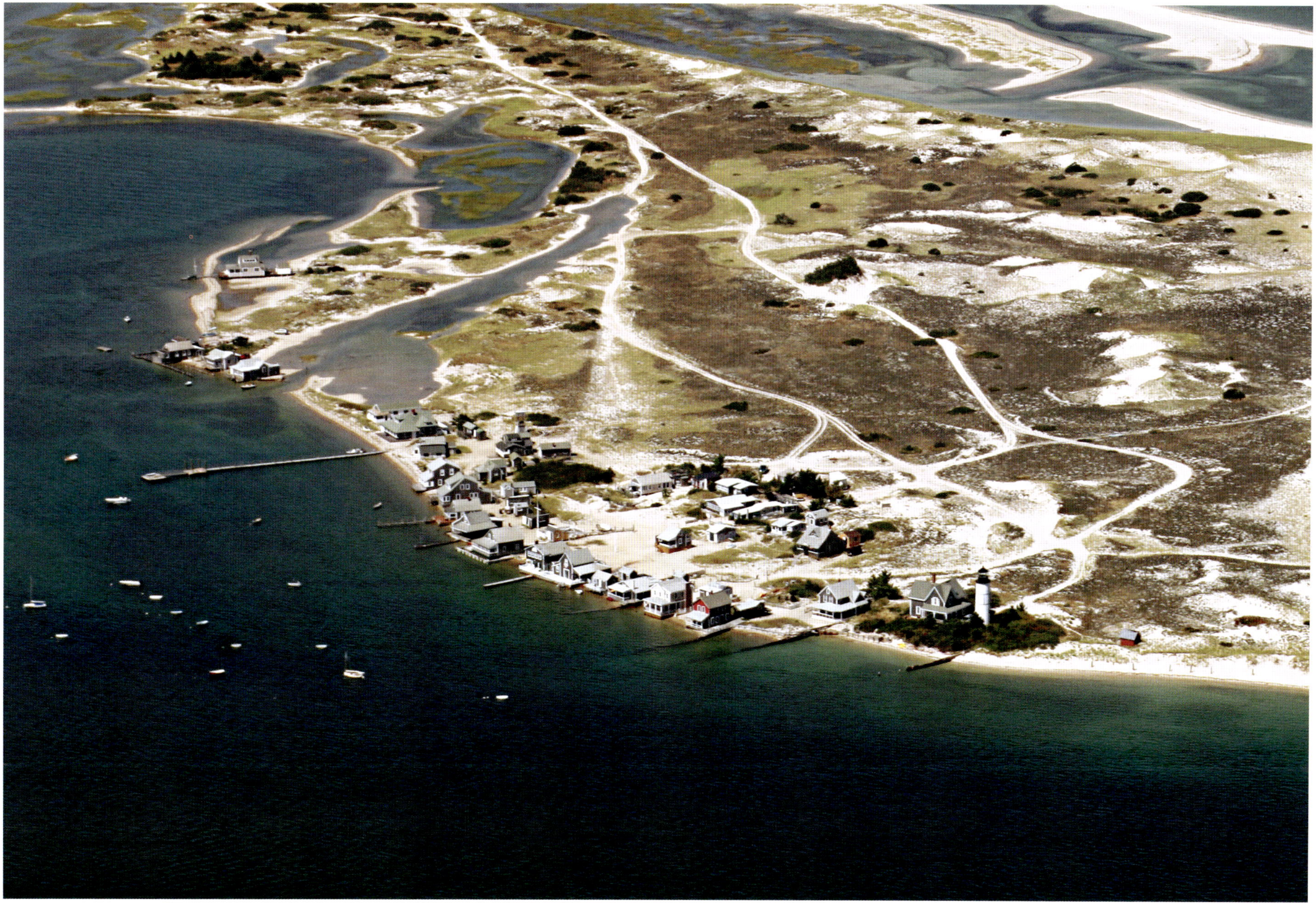

Sandy Neck village 43 years later.

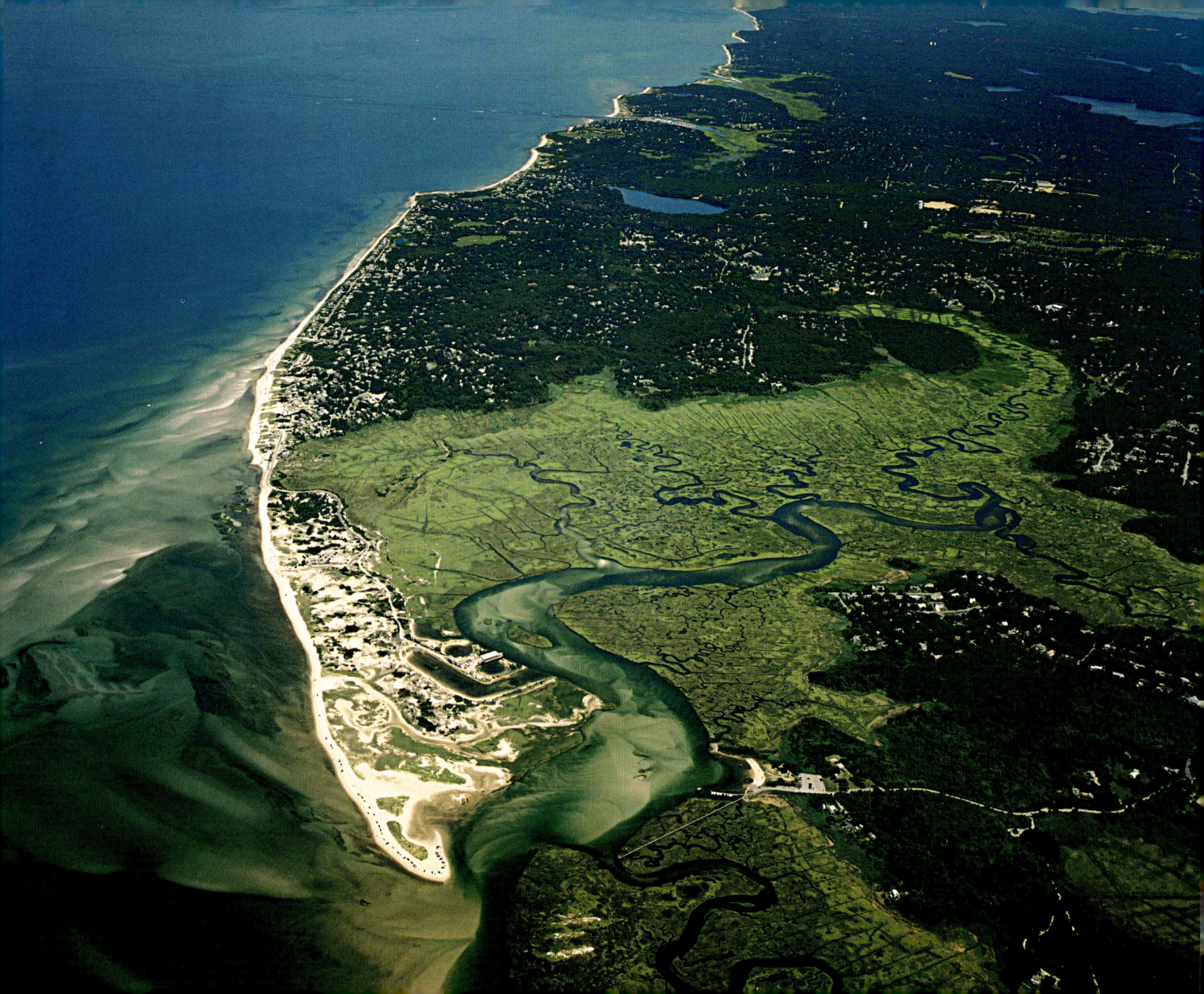

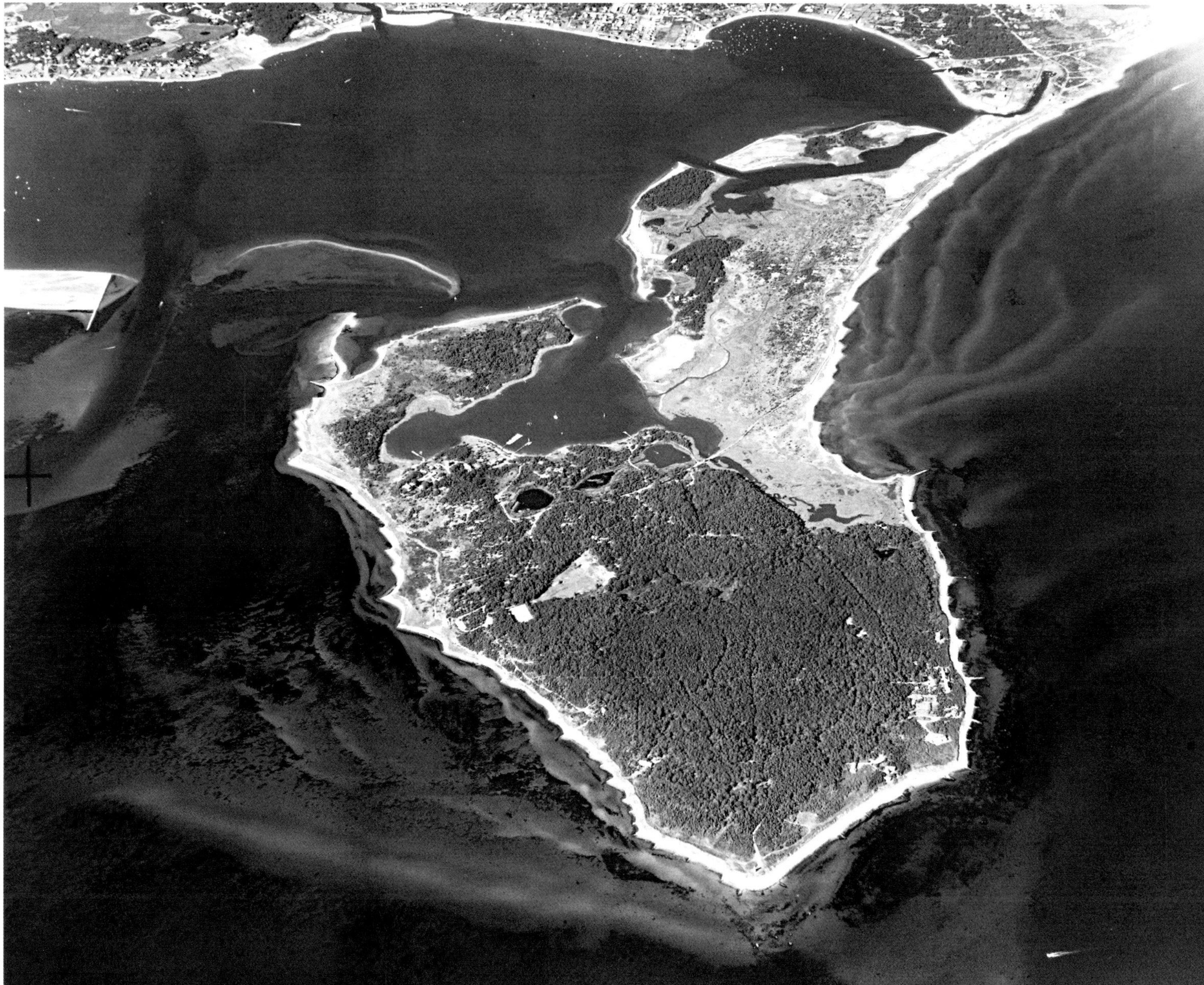

A steep oblique of Great Island with Lewis Bay on the left, taken in 1969.

Bass Hole, Yarmouth, looking east.

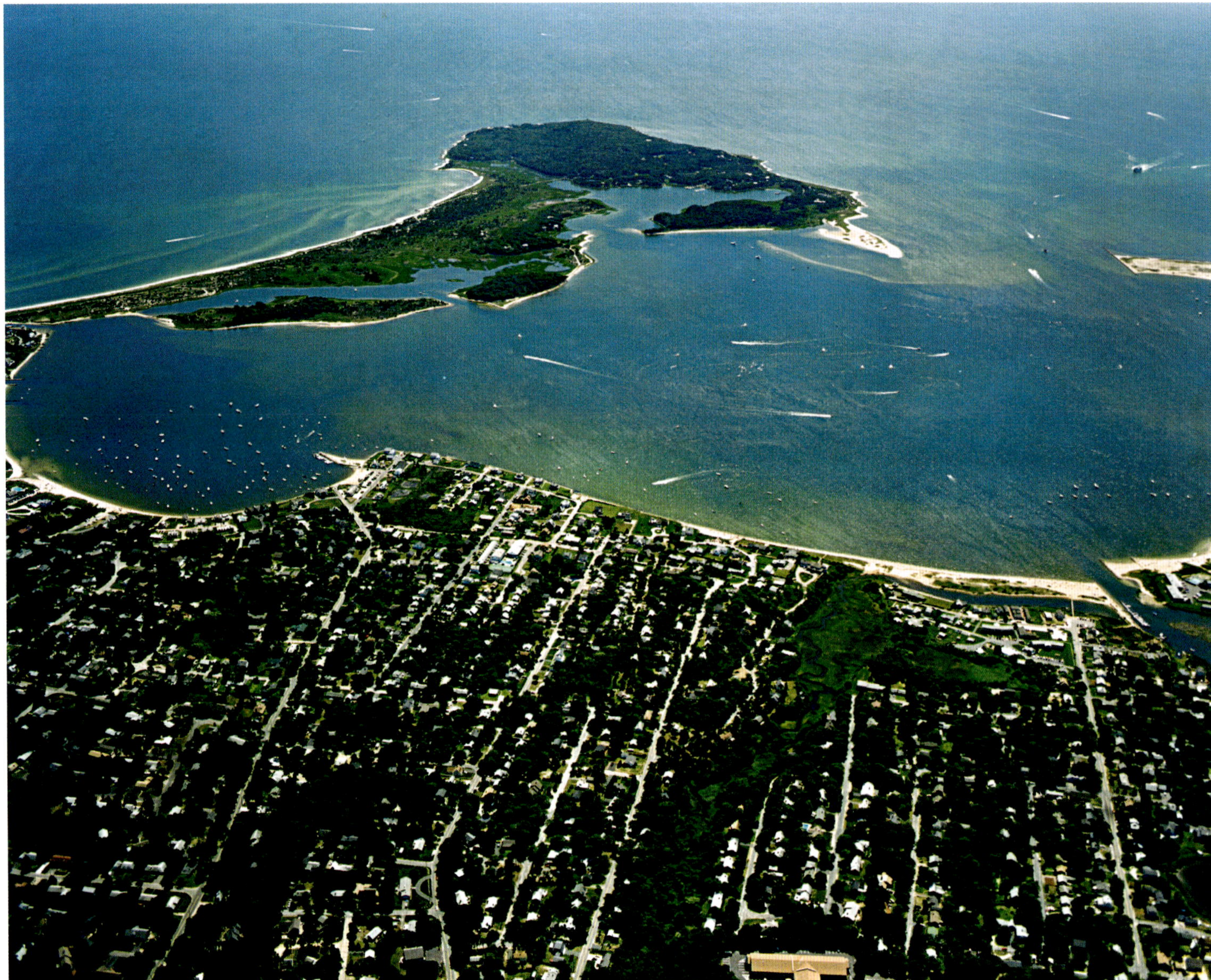

Lewis Bay and Great Island, Yarmouth.

Parker River, Lewis Pond and Seagull Beach.{opposite}

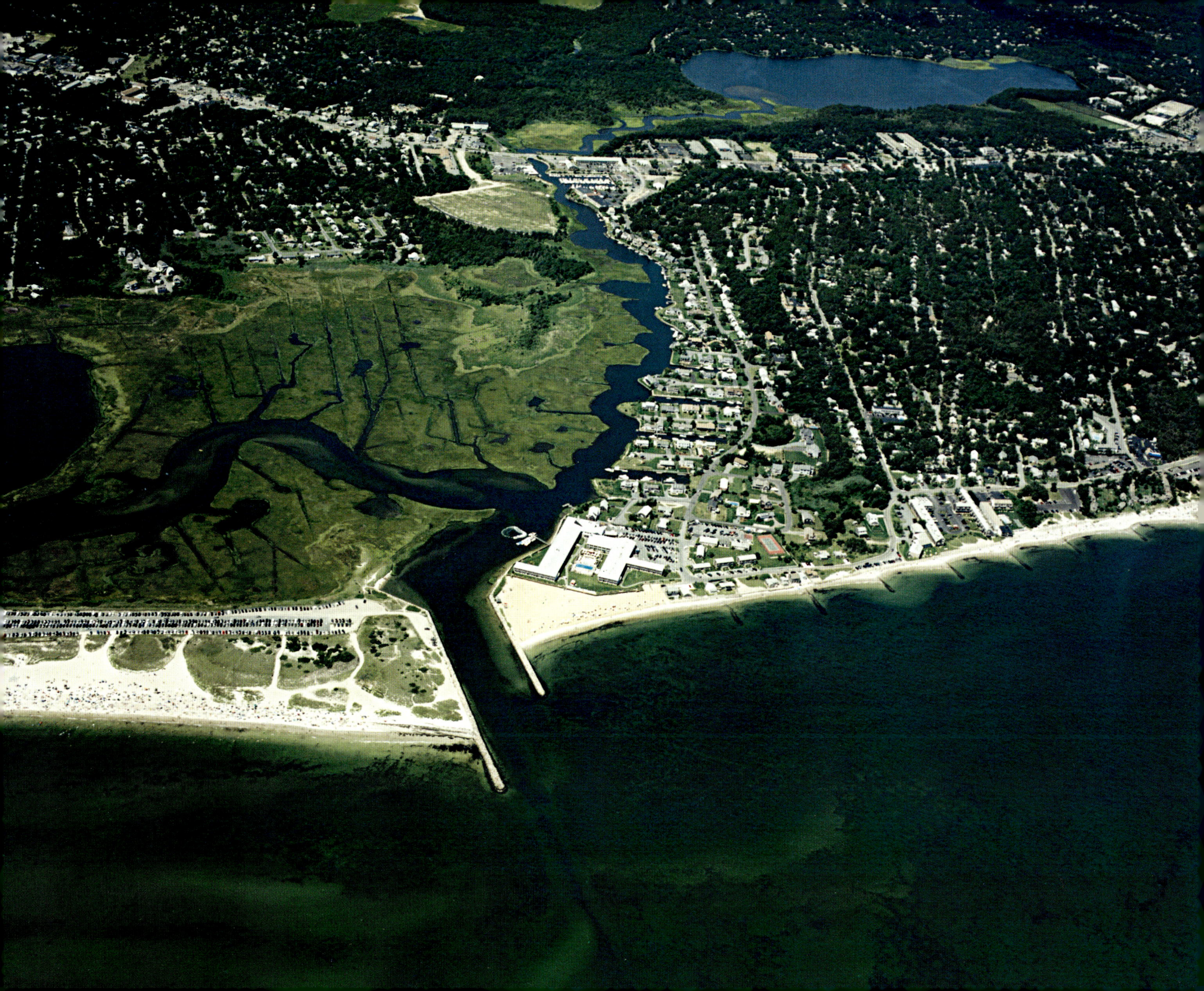

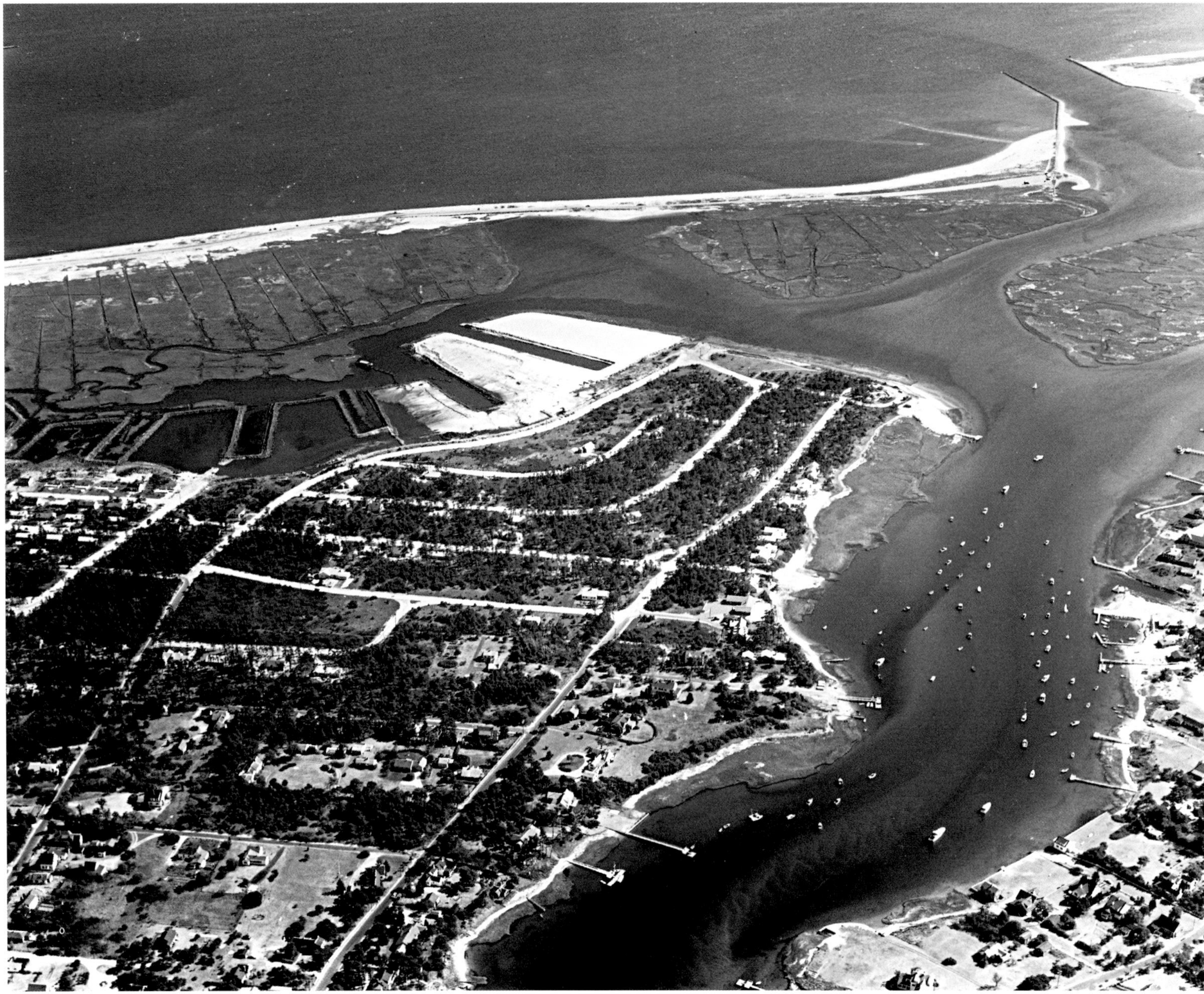

The Dennis "Fingers" being built on Wrinkle Point near the mouth of Bass River. in 1957.

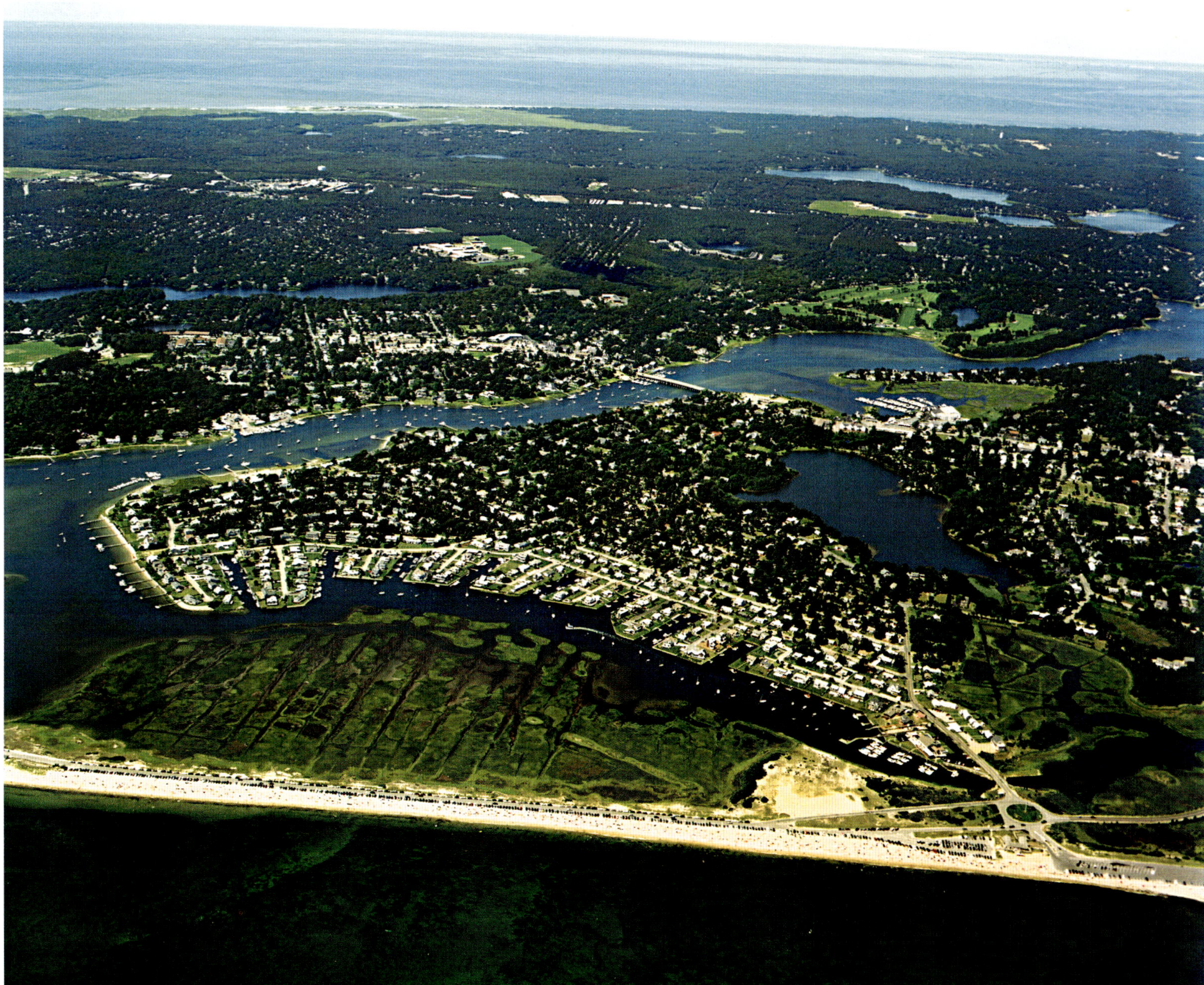

West Dennis Beach looking north up Bass River to Cape Cod Bay. The Dennis Fingers are in the foreground.

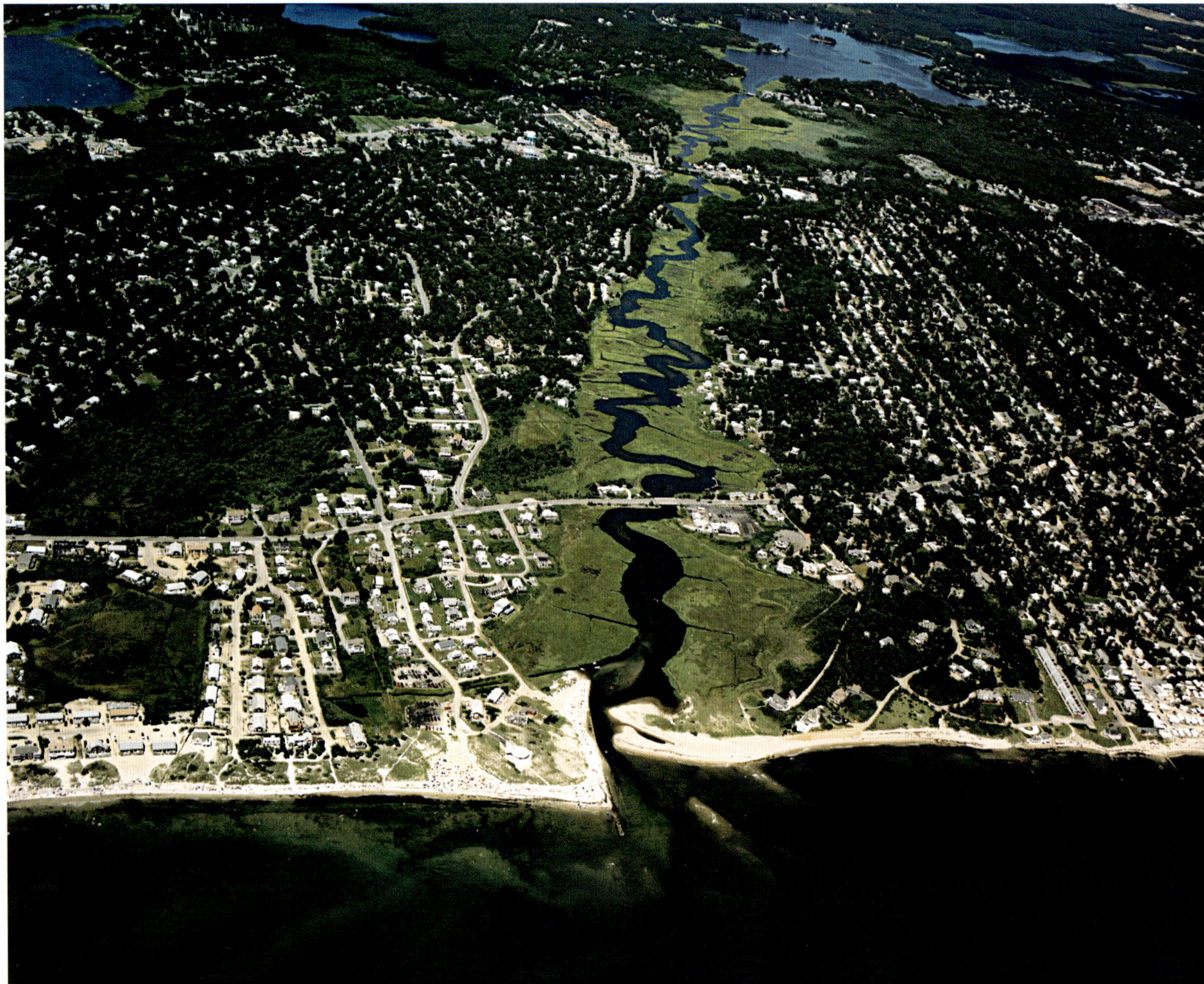

The serpentine Swan River and Swan Pond seen from above Nantucket Sound.

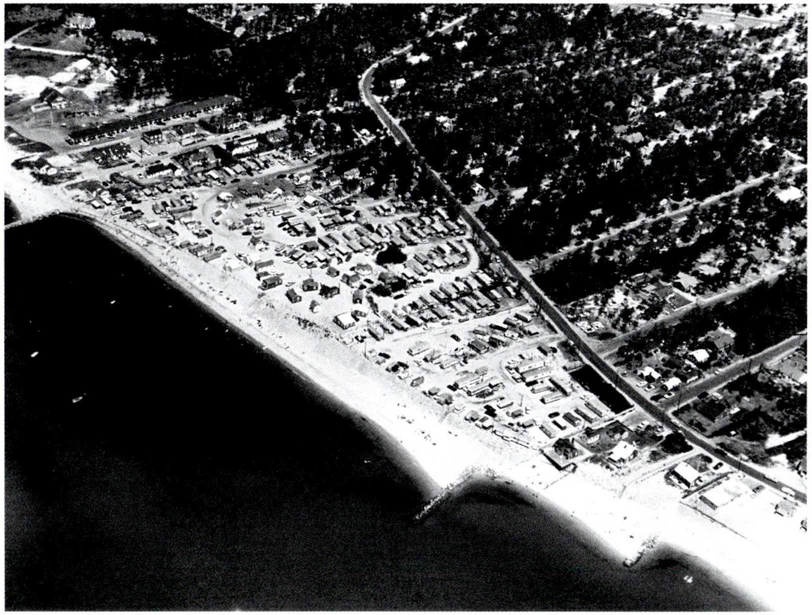

The Trailer Park on Nantucket Sound in Dennis-port, in 1963 and again 43 years later.

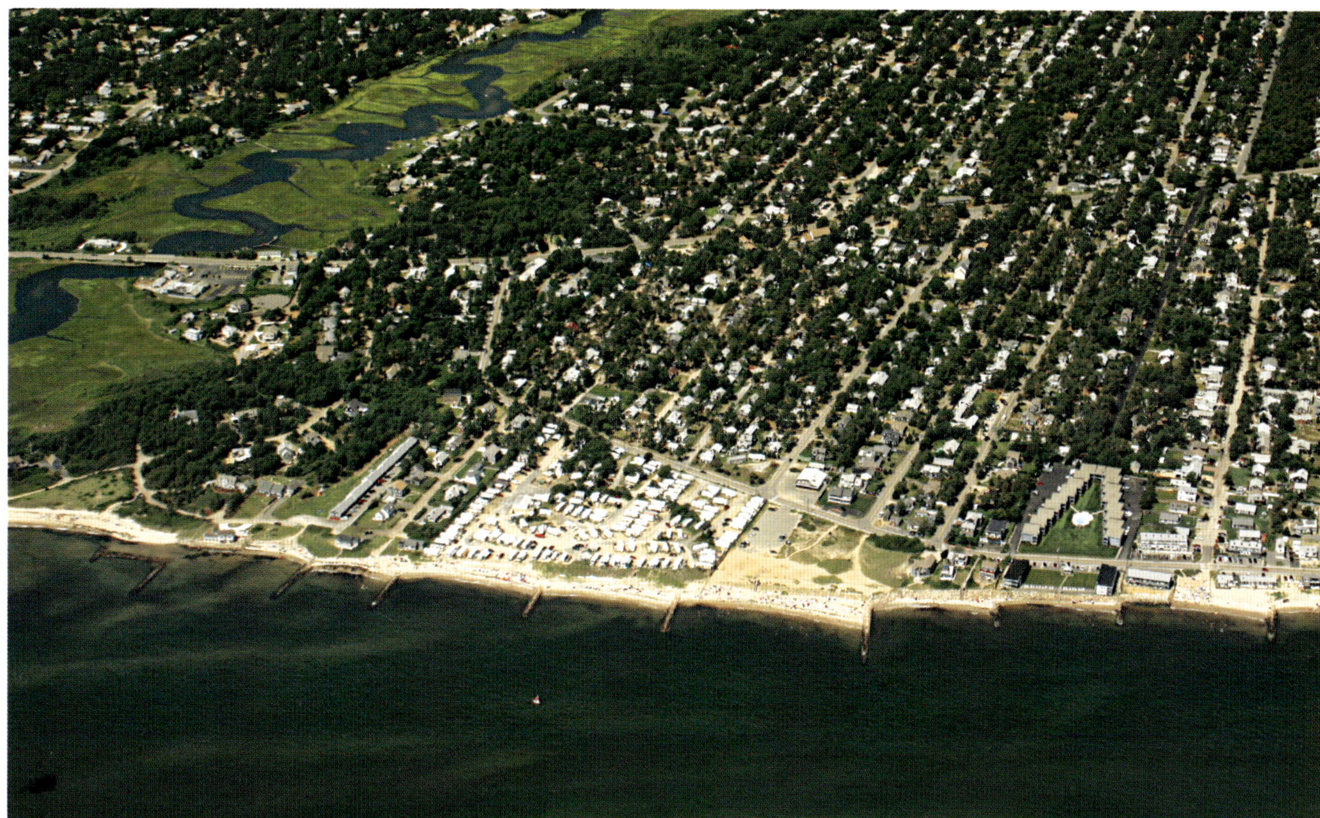

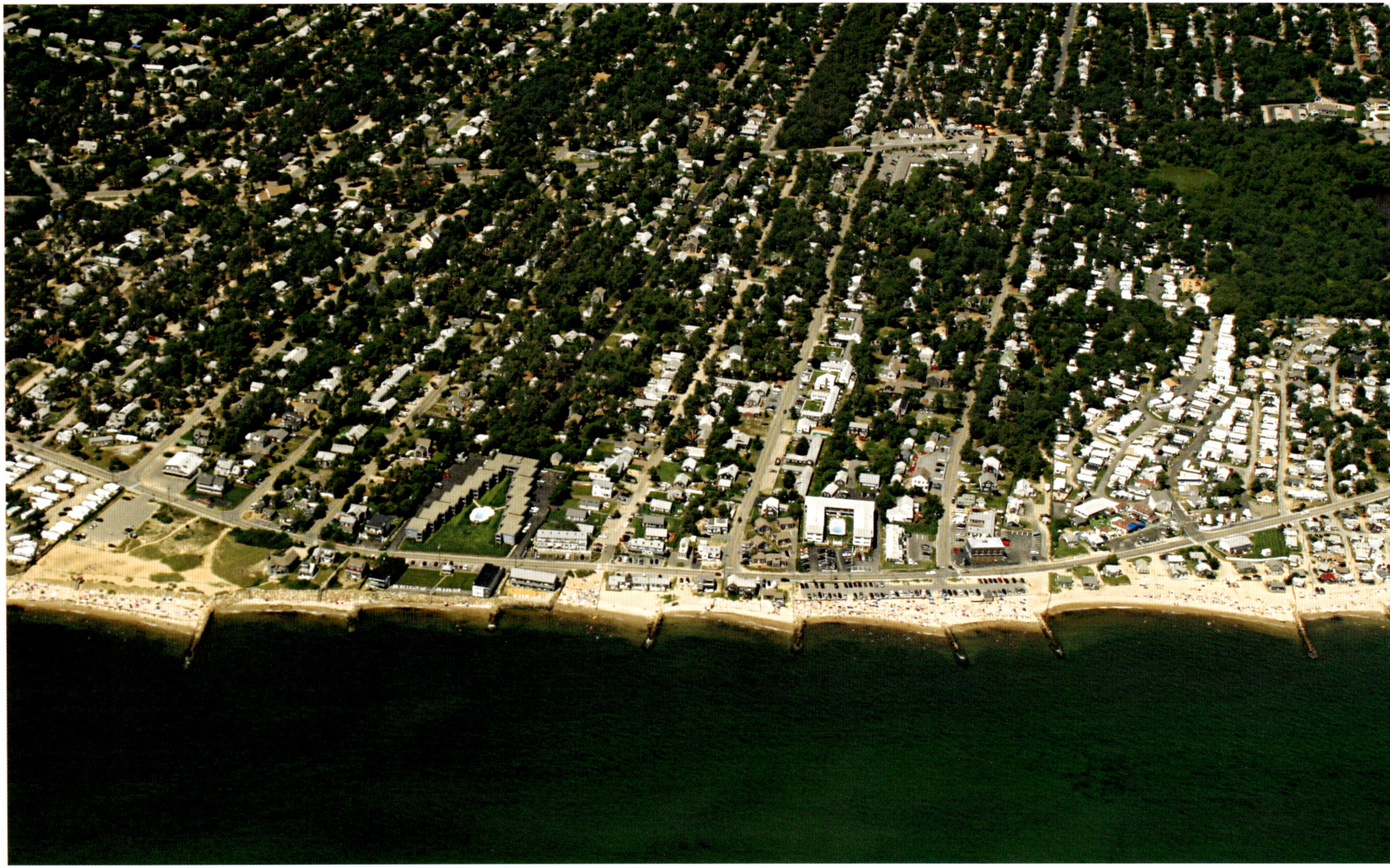

The Dennisport coastline, viewed while flying east along Nantucket Sound, shown on pages 68 to 74.

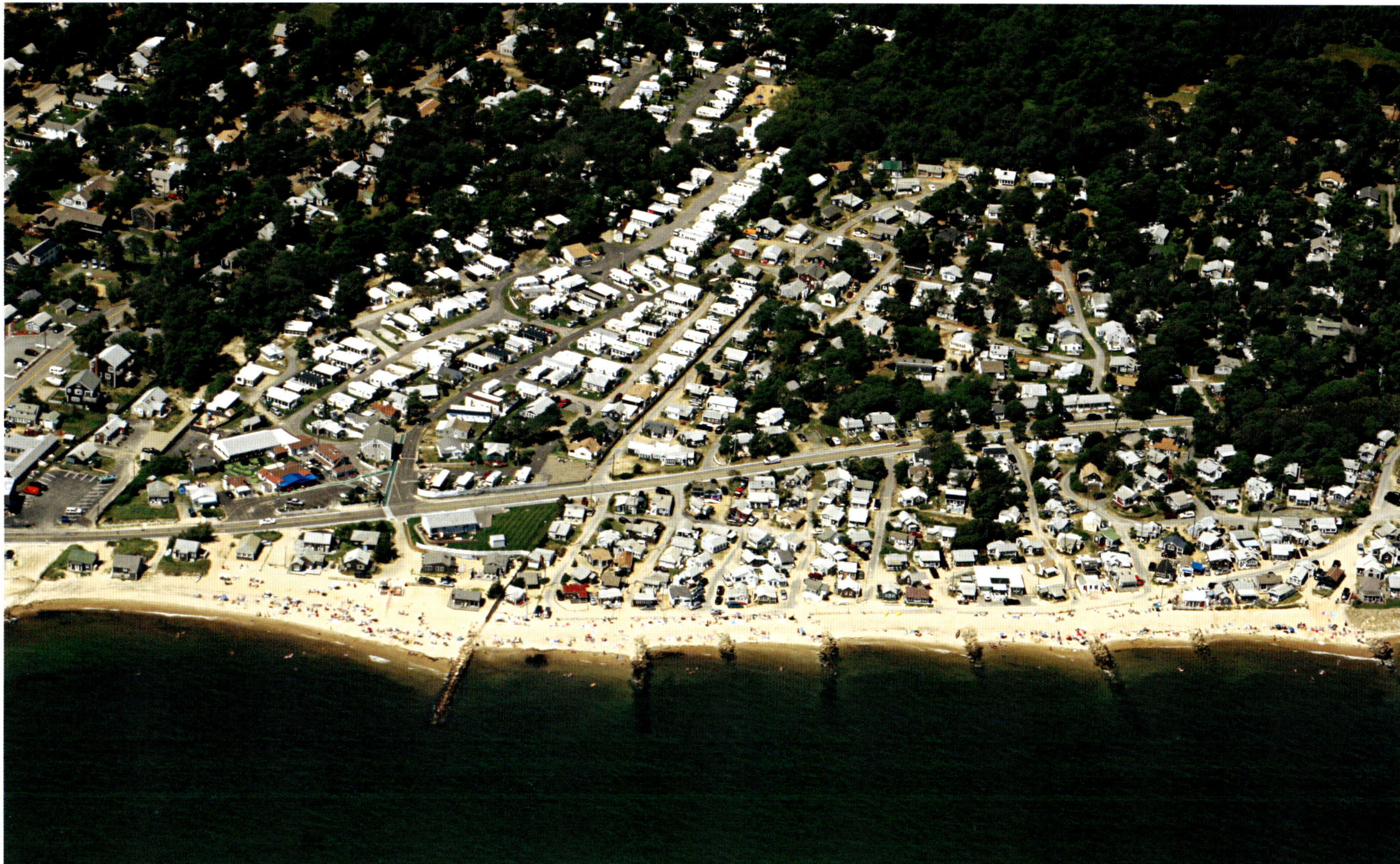

Continuing along the Dennisport coastline, viewed while flying east along Nantucket Sound.

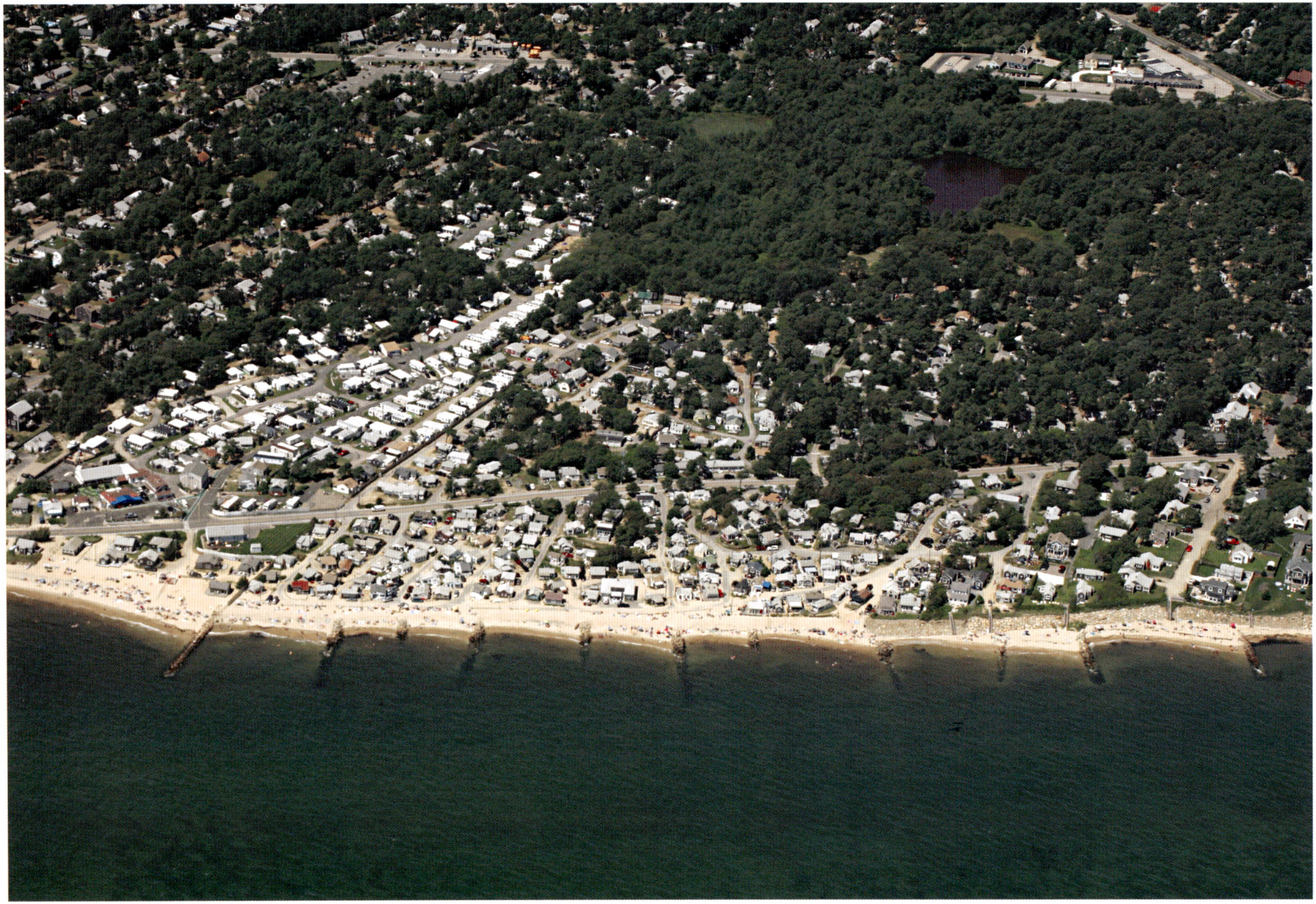

Farther on the Dennisport coastline, viewed while flying east along Nantucket Sound.

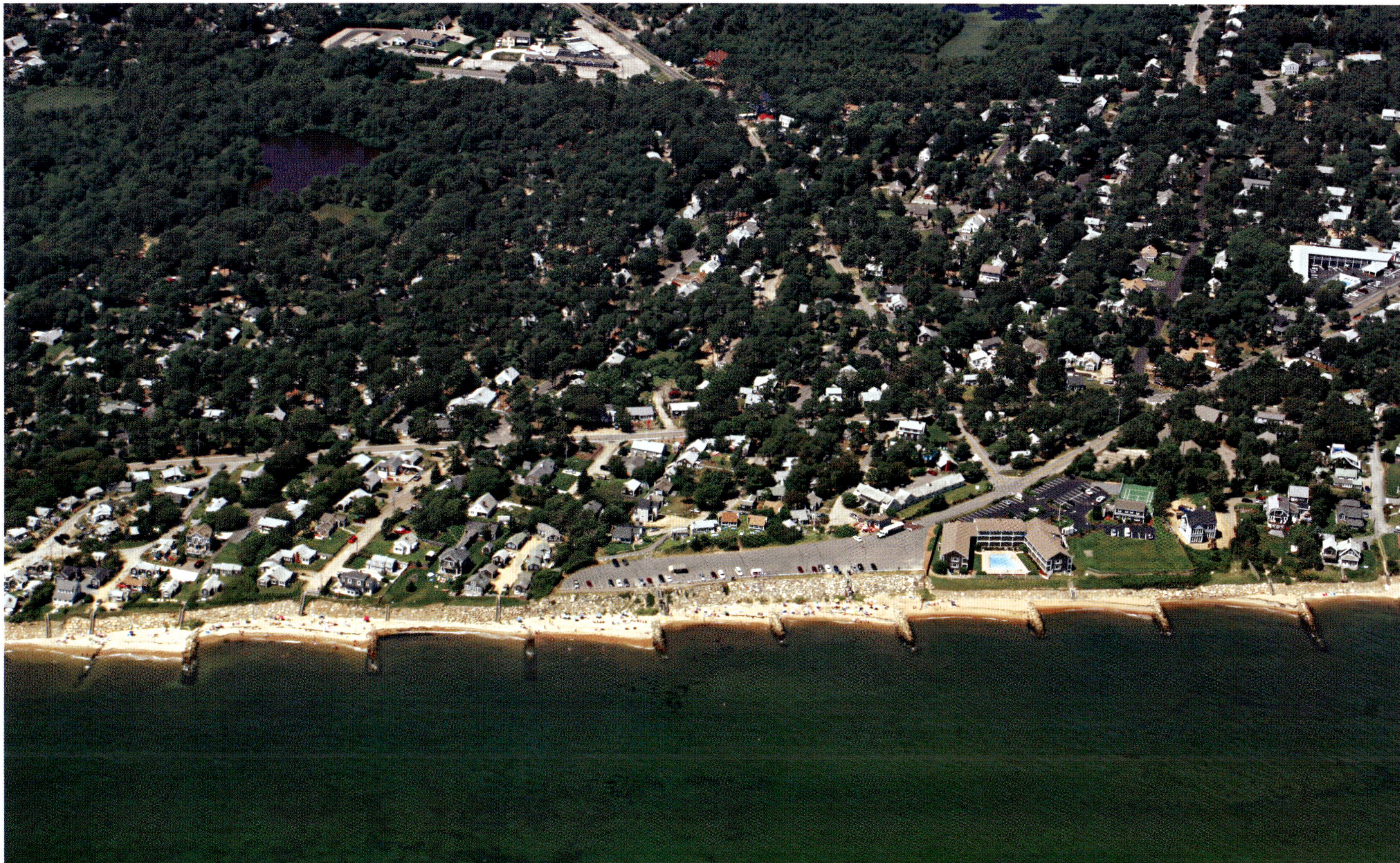

More of the Dennisport coastline, viewed while flying east along Nantucket Sound.

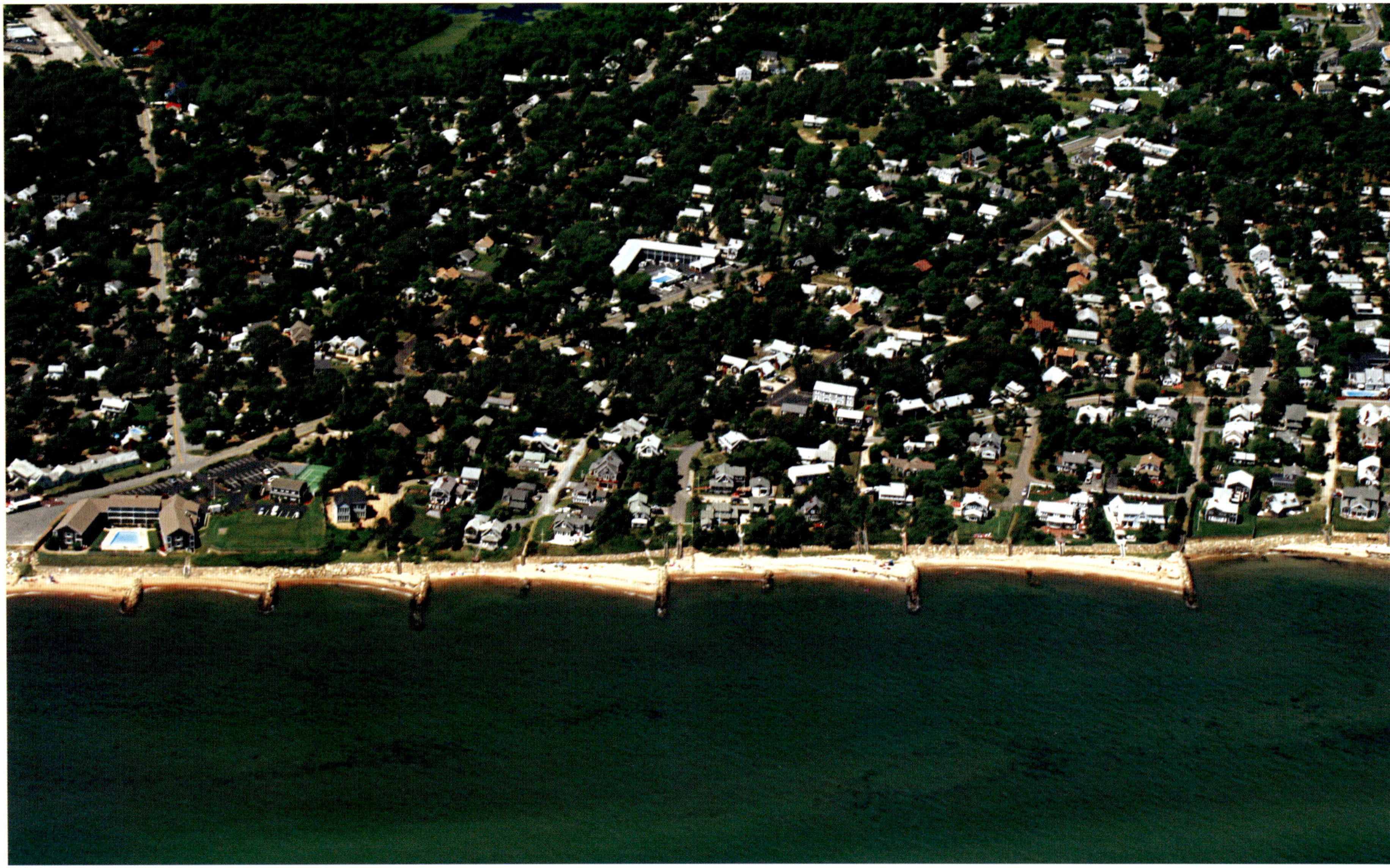

Another view of the Dennisport coastline, viewed while flying east along Nantucket Sound.

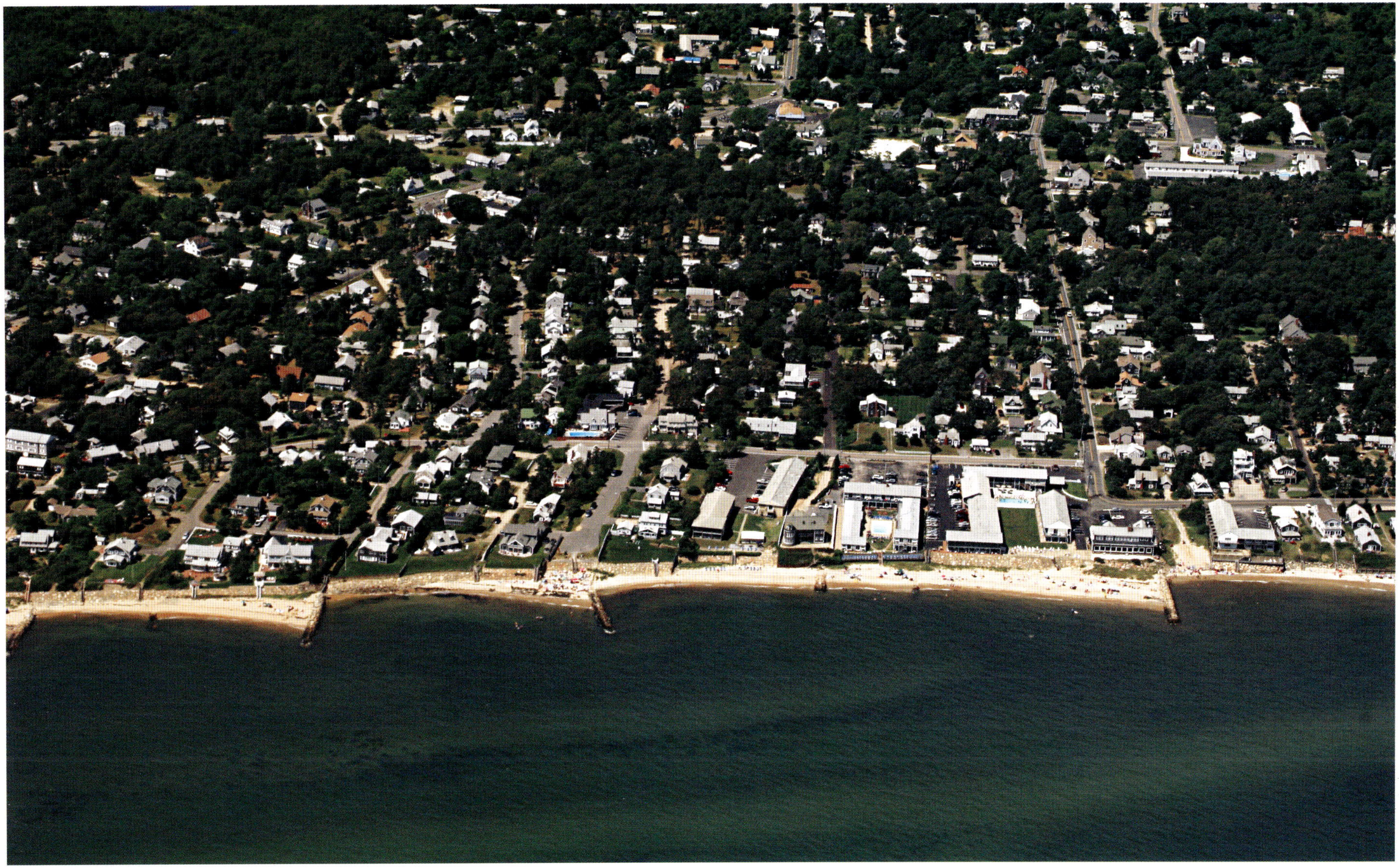

And more of the Dennisport coastline viewed, while flying east along Nantucket Sound.

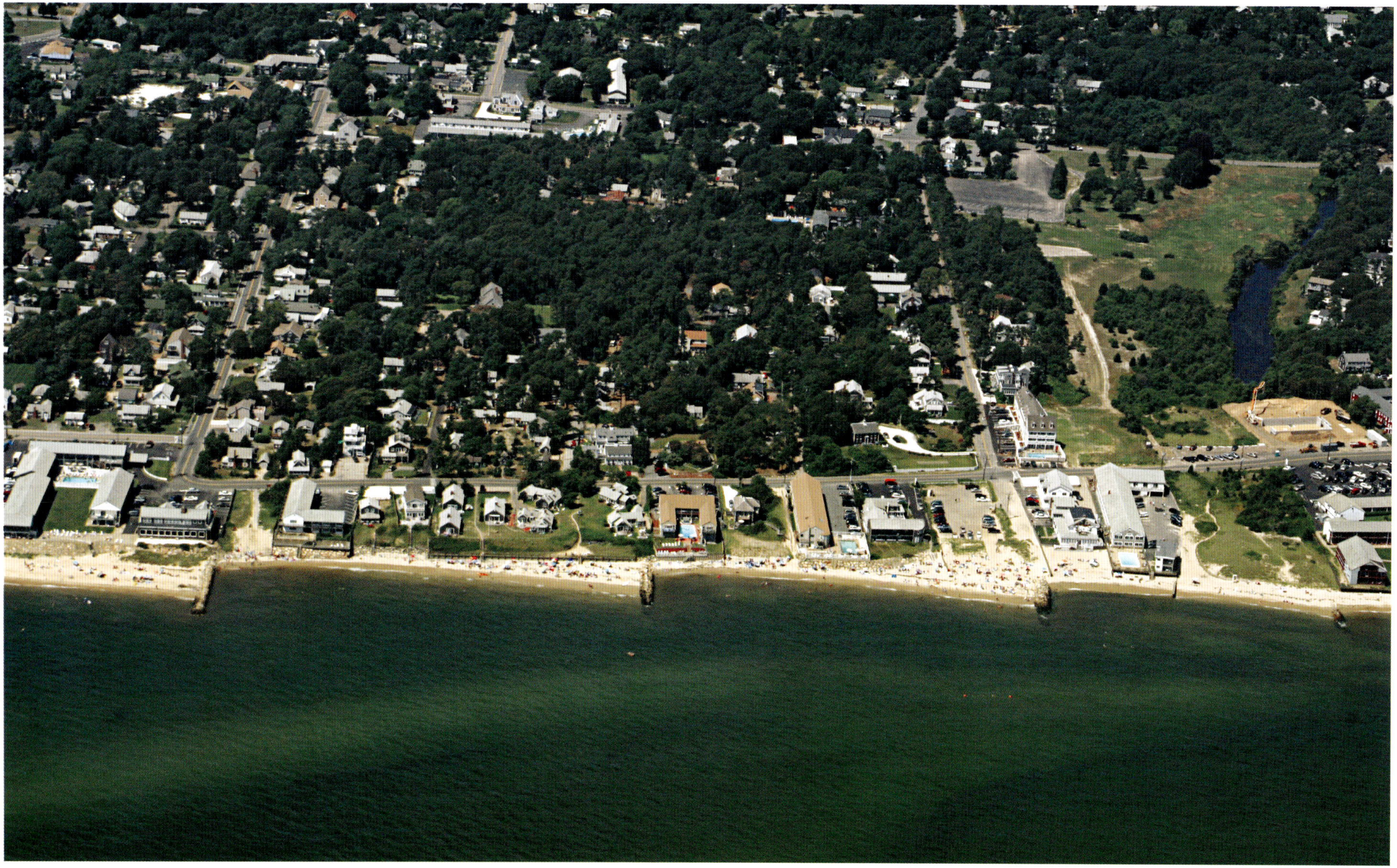

The end of the Dennisport coastline, viewed while flying east along Nantucket Sound.

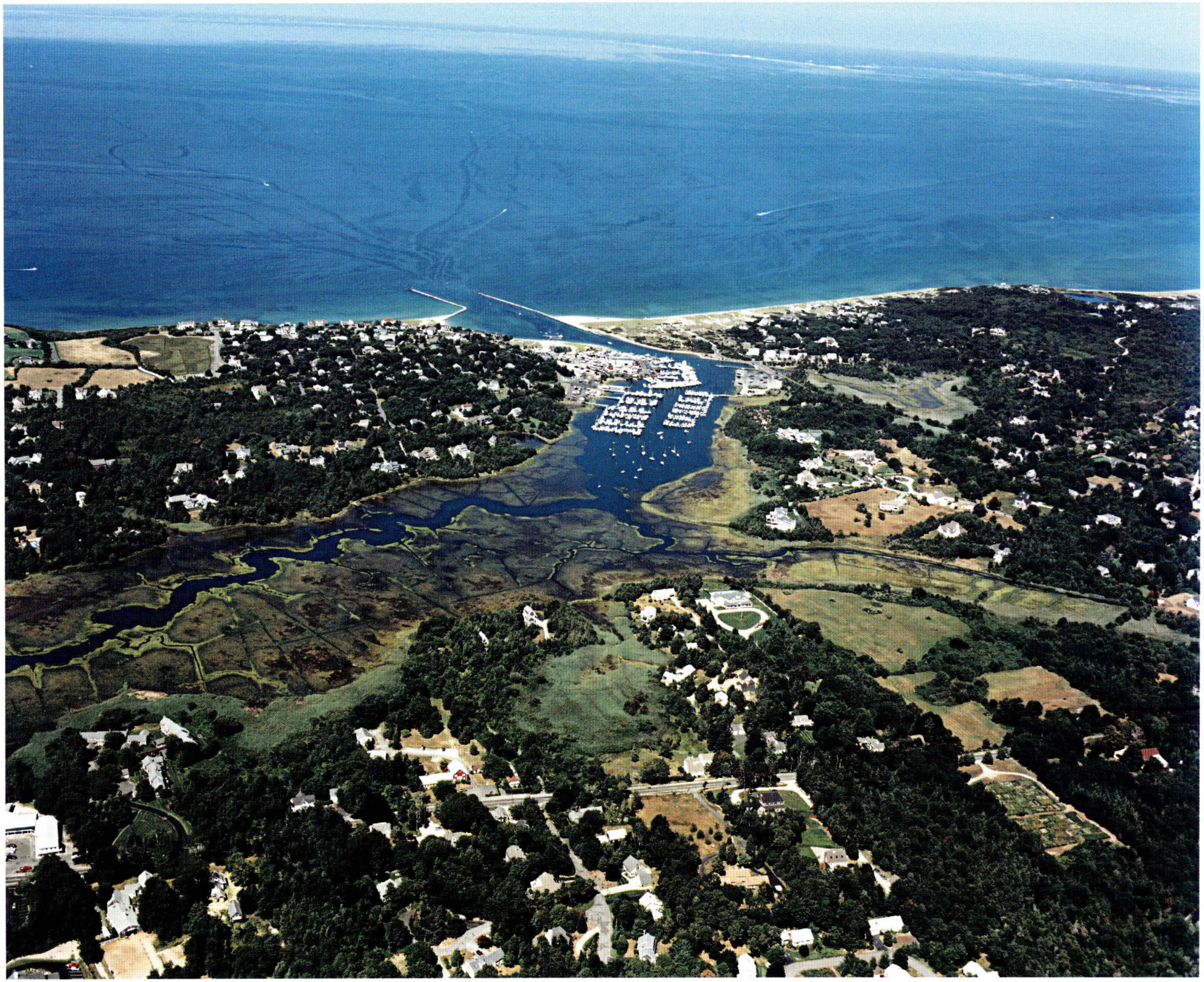

Sesuit Harbor in Dennis leads into Cape Cod Bay.

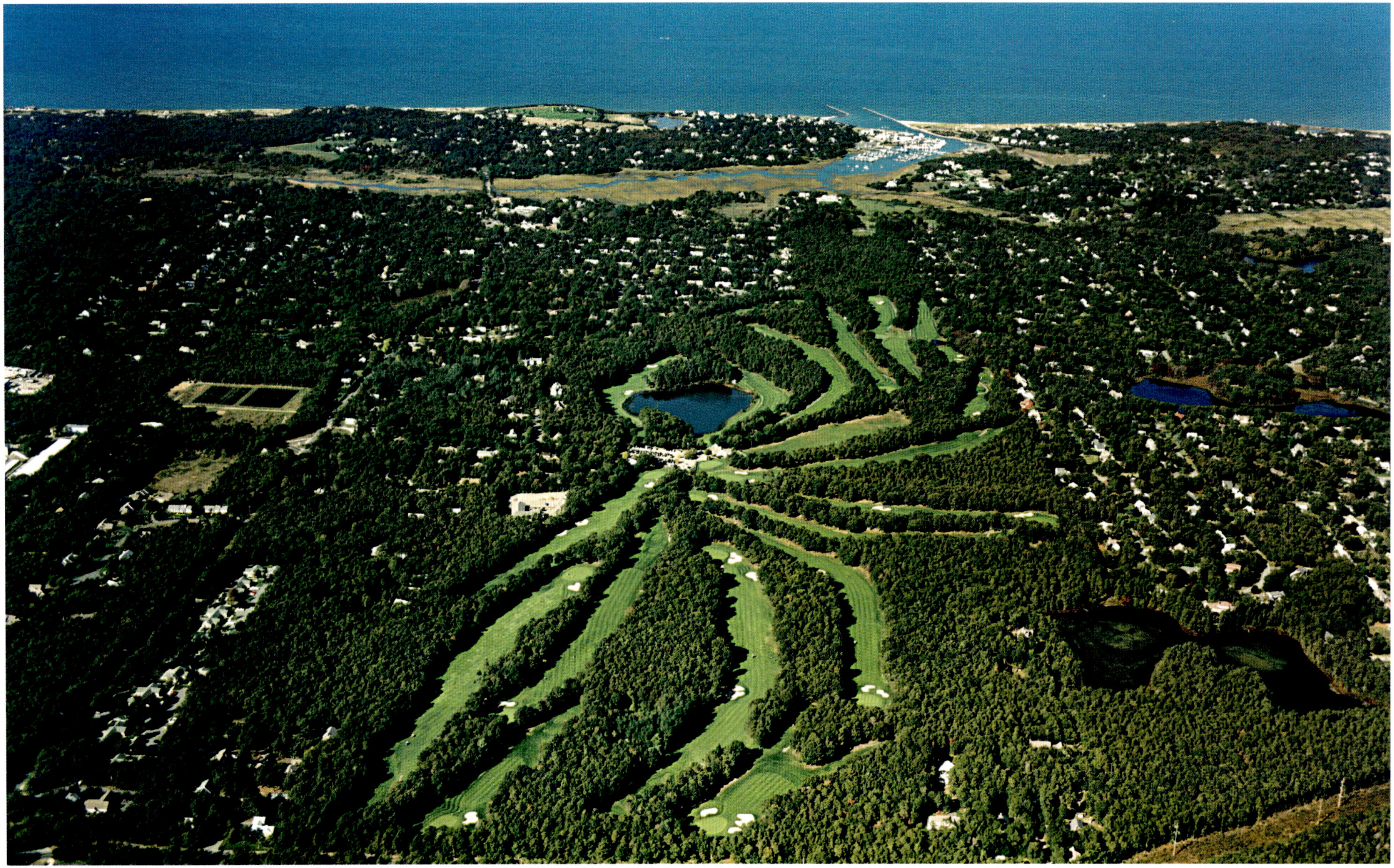

The Dennis Pines golf course looking north to Cape Cod Bay.

Chapter 4

Harwich, Brewster, & Chatham

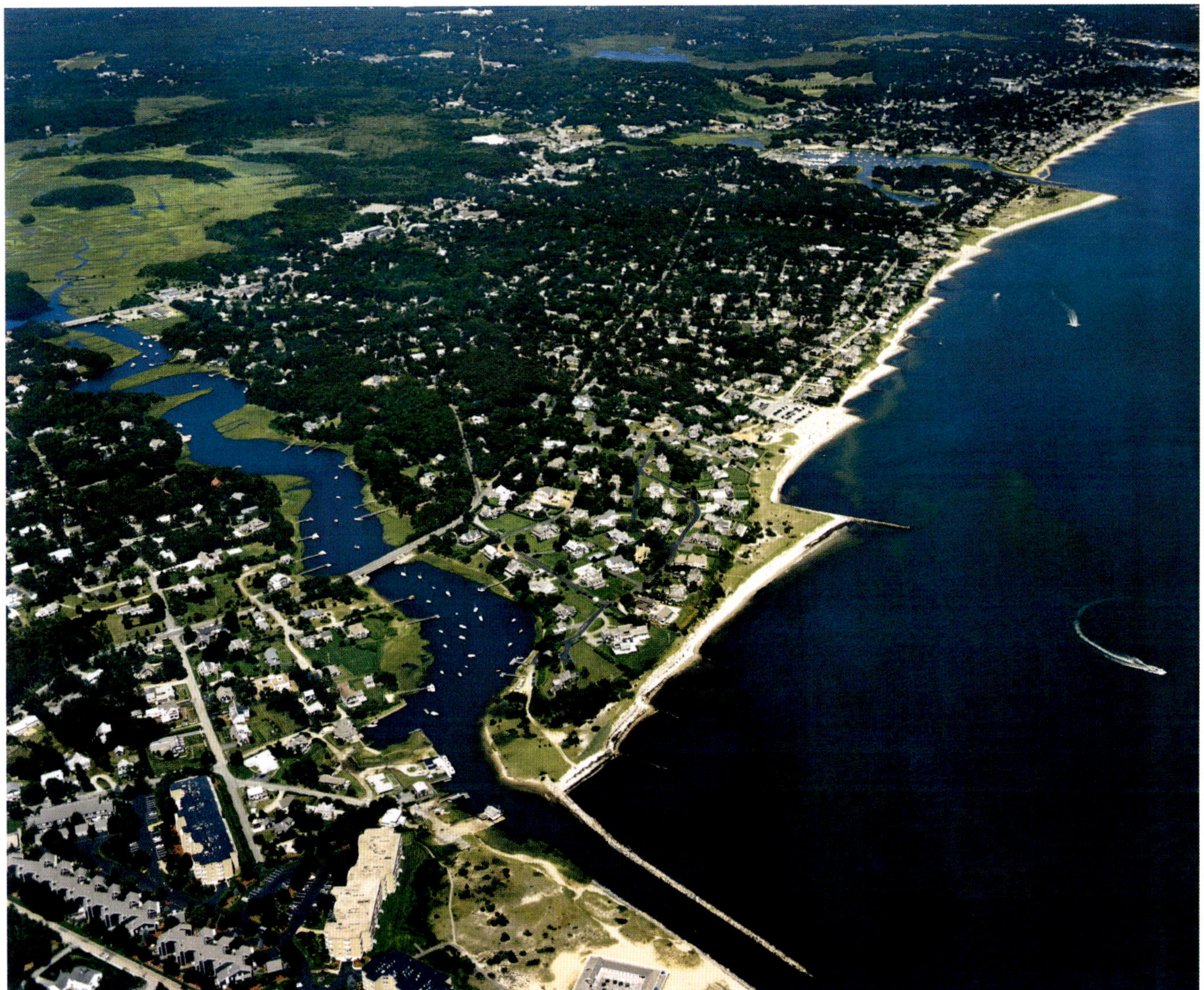

Looking east across Harwich, the Belmont, Herring River and Old Mill Point are in the foreground.

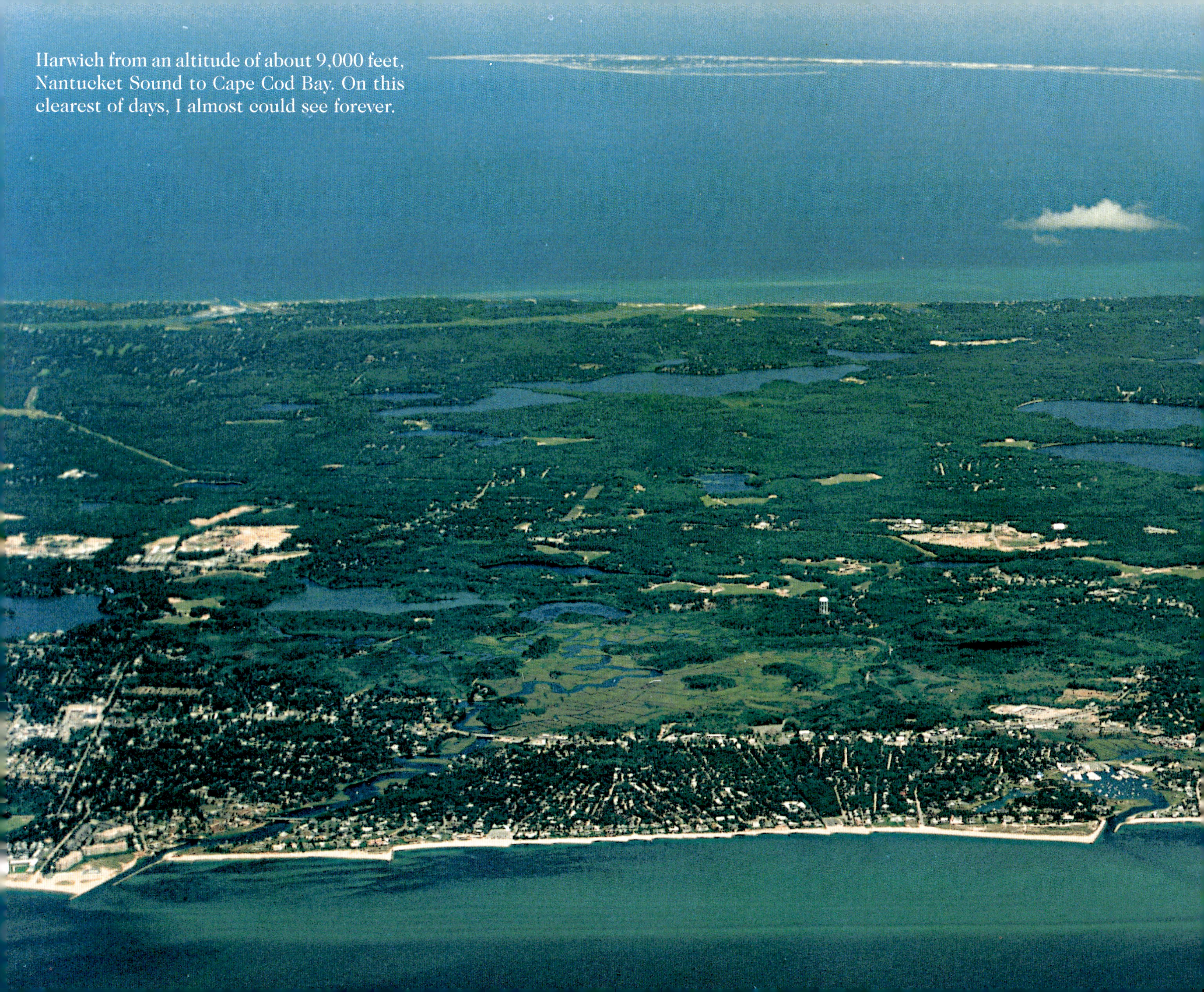

Harwich from an altitude of about 9,000 feet, Nantucket Sound to Cape Cod Bay. On this clearest of days, I almost could see forever.

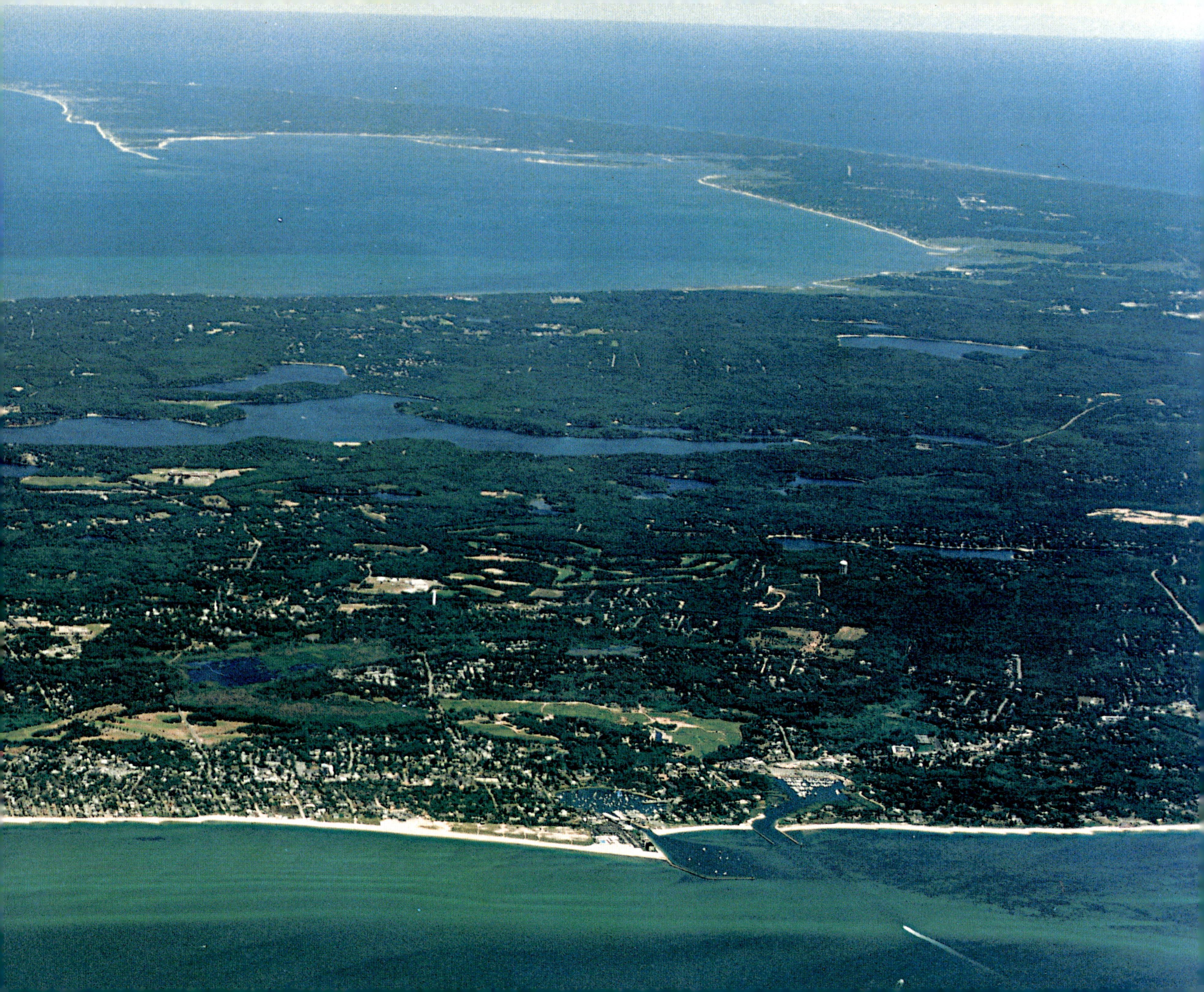

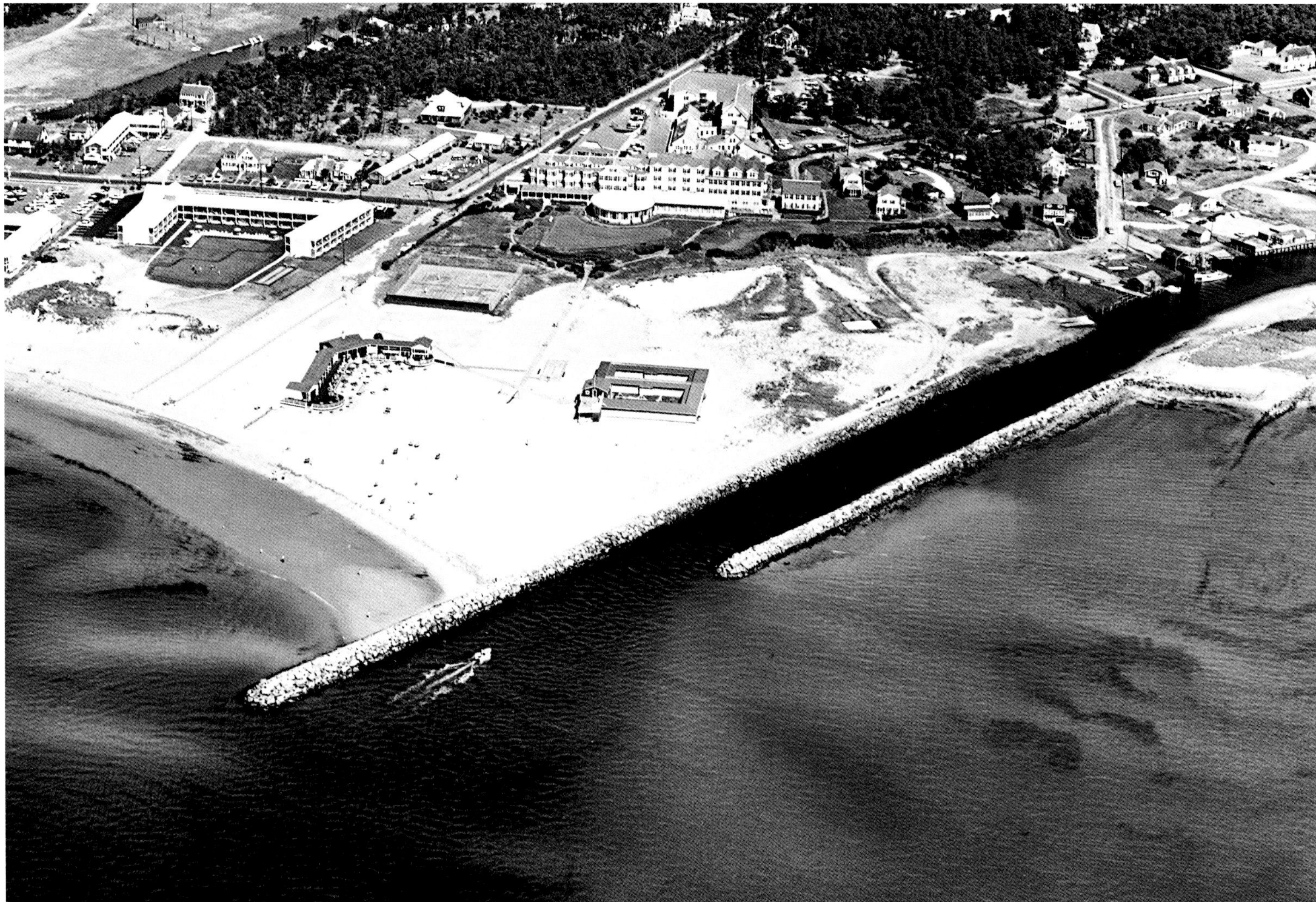

The Belmont Inn in 1963.

Looking south over Allen's Harbor.

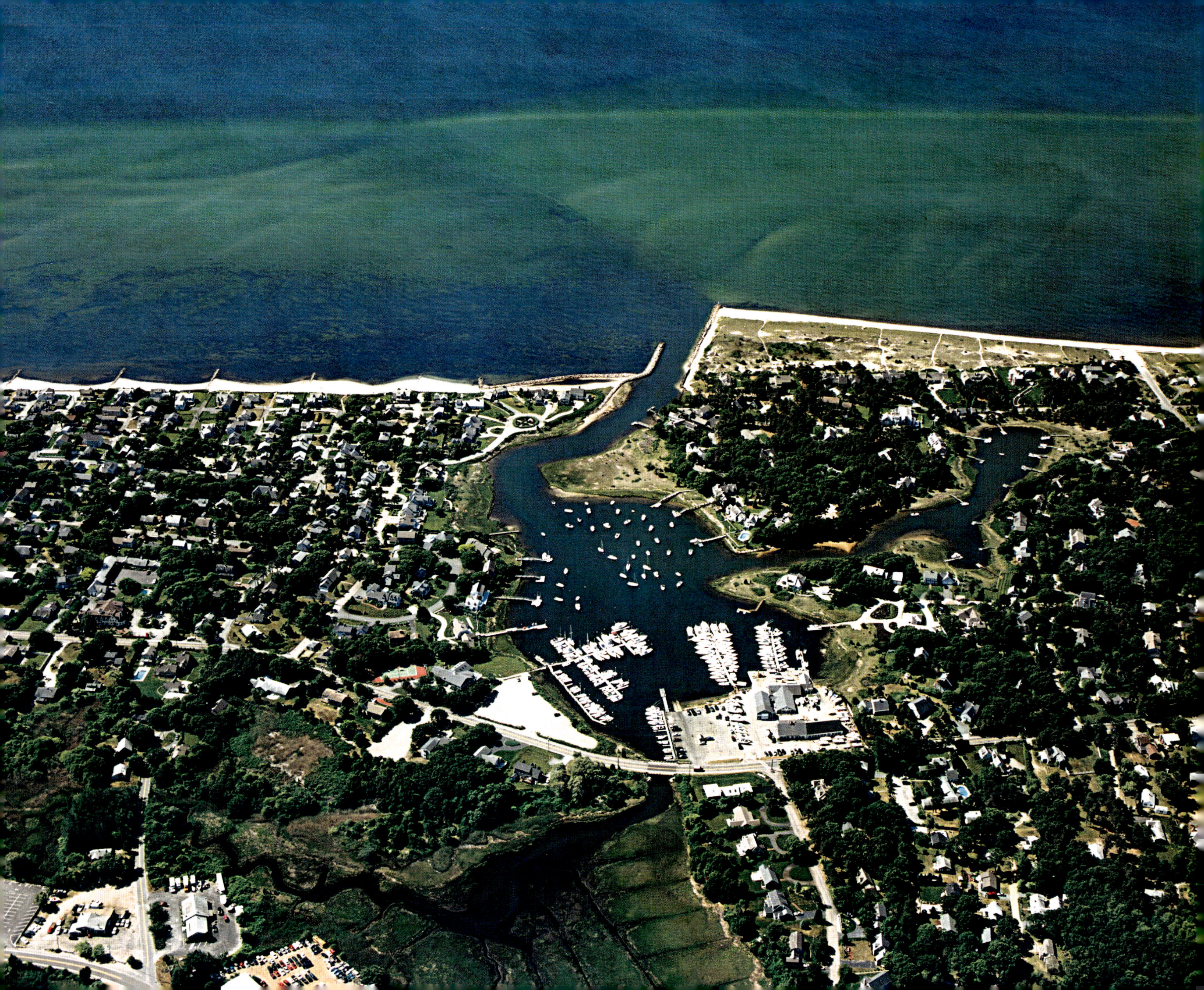

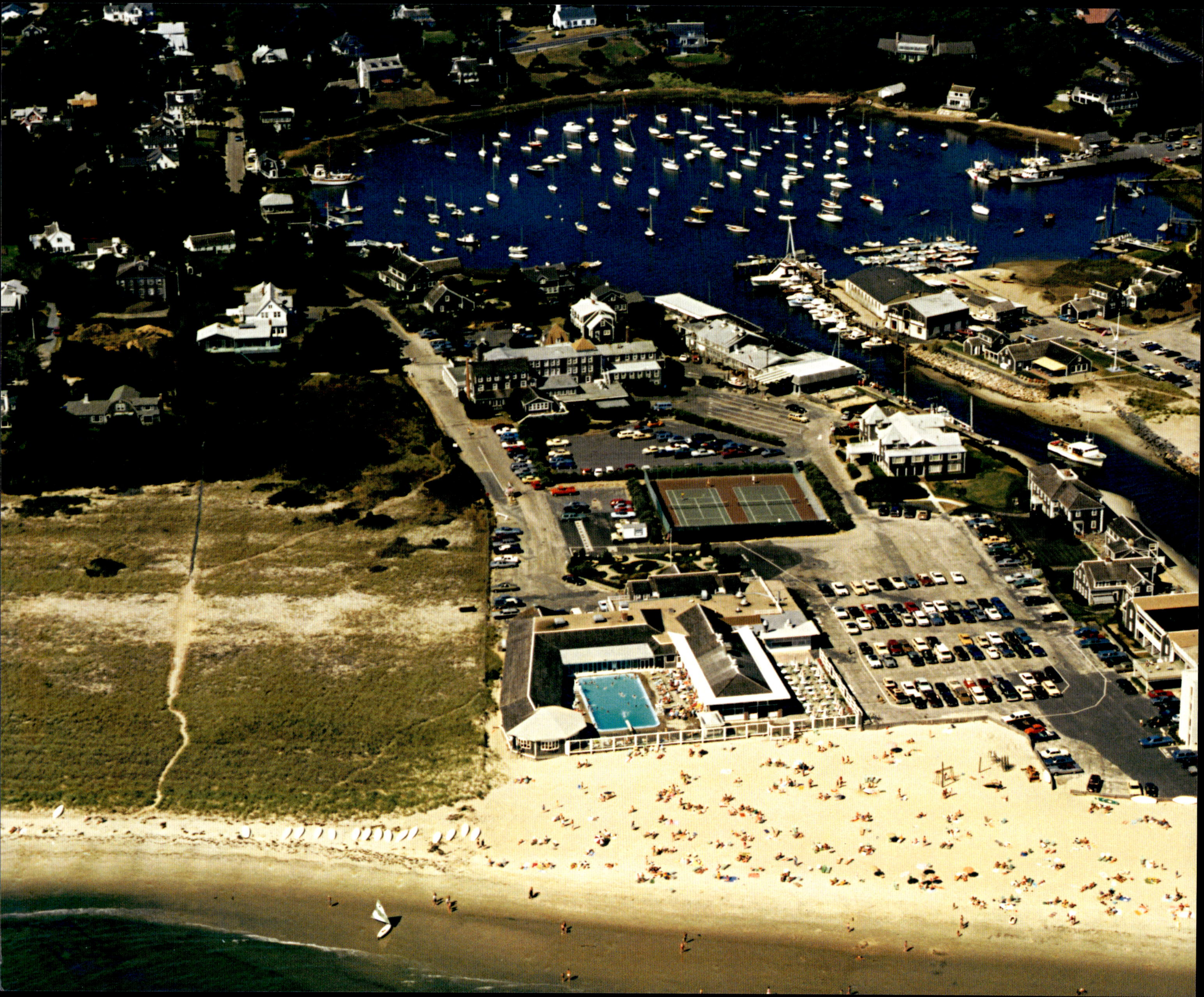

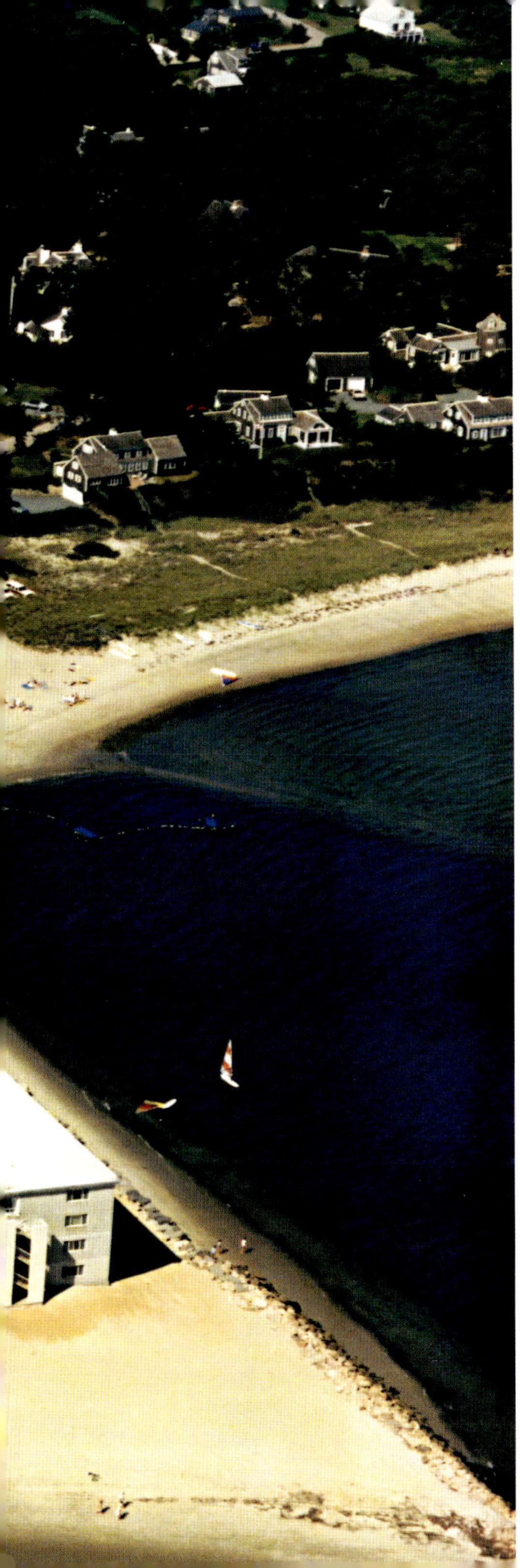

Wychmere Harbor, Stonehorse Yacht Club, the Harbor Club, and Thompson's Clam Bar. "Hey! Where you going…?" in 1981 and 26 years later.

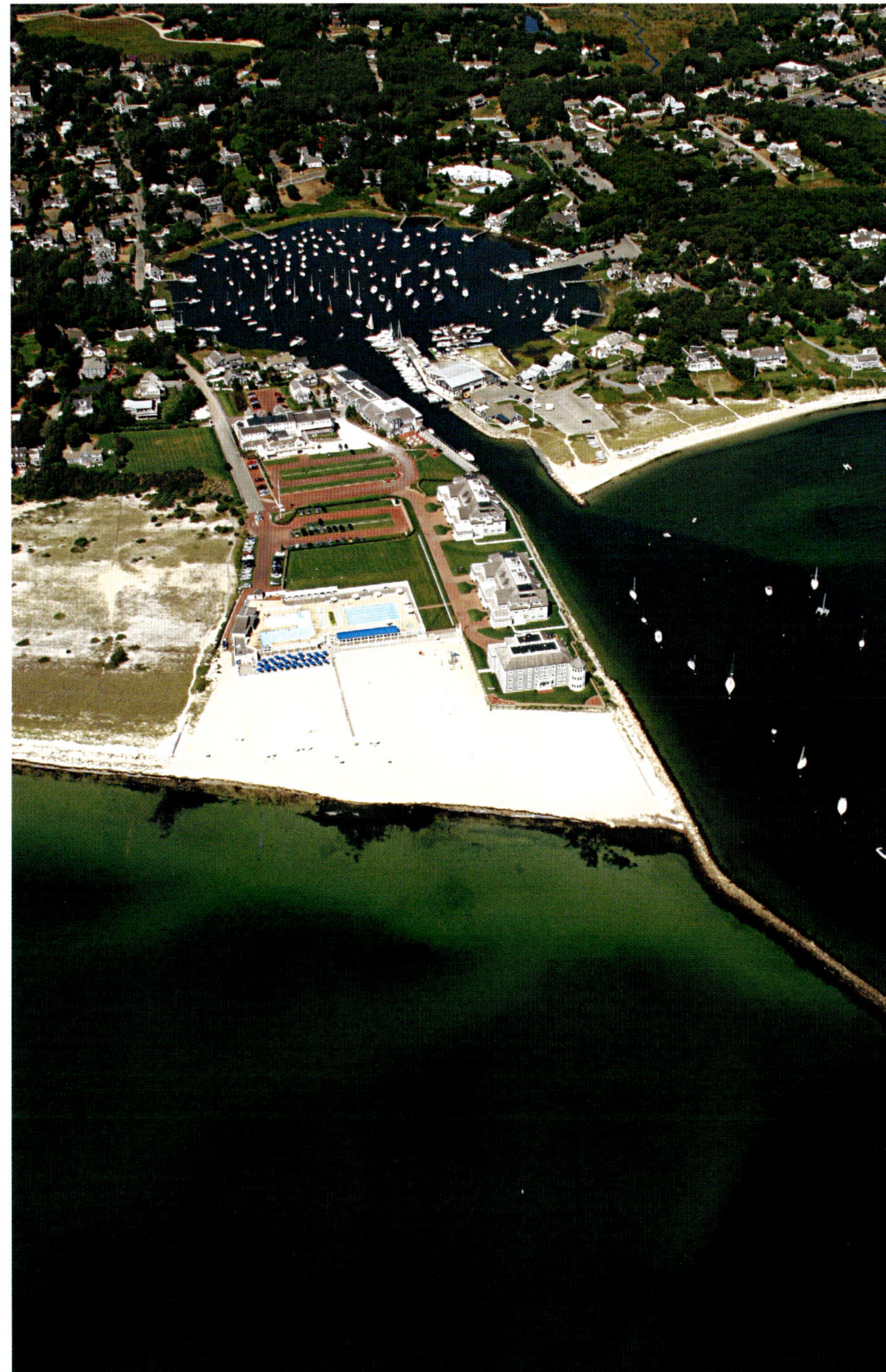

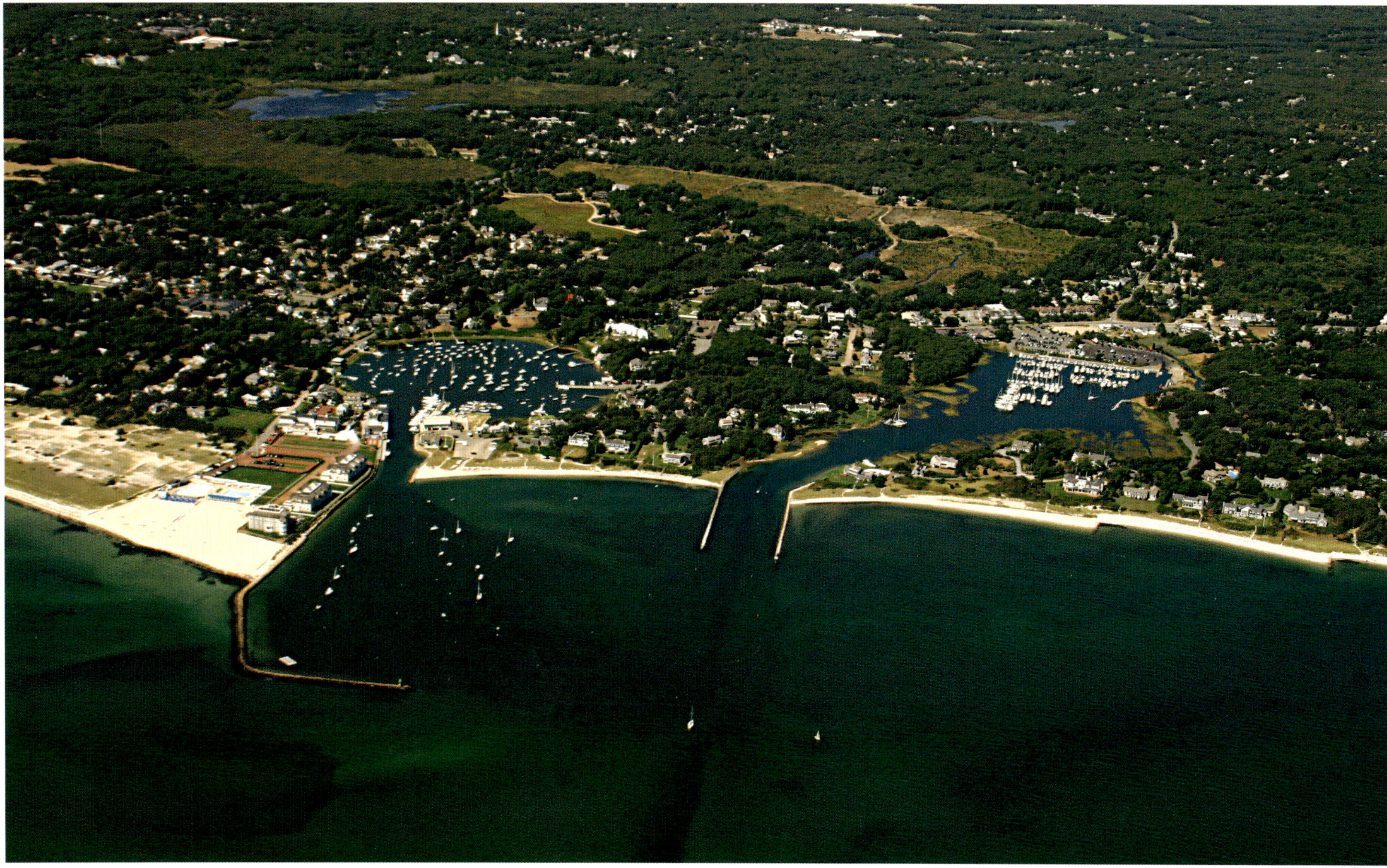

Looking in on Wychmere and Saquatucket Harbors.

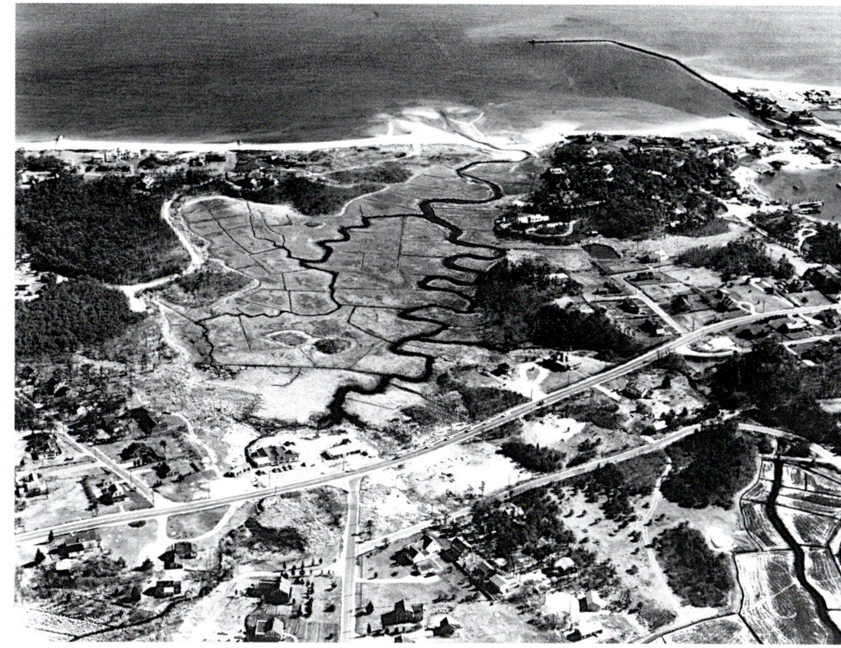

Andrews River in 1964. Later to become Saquatucket Harbor.

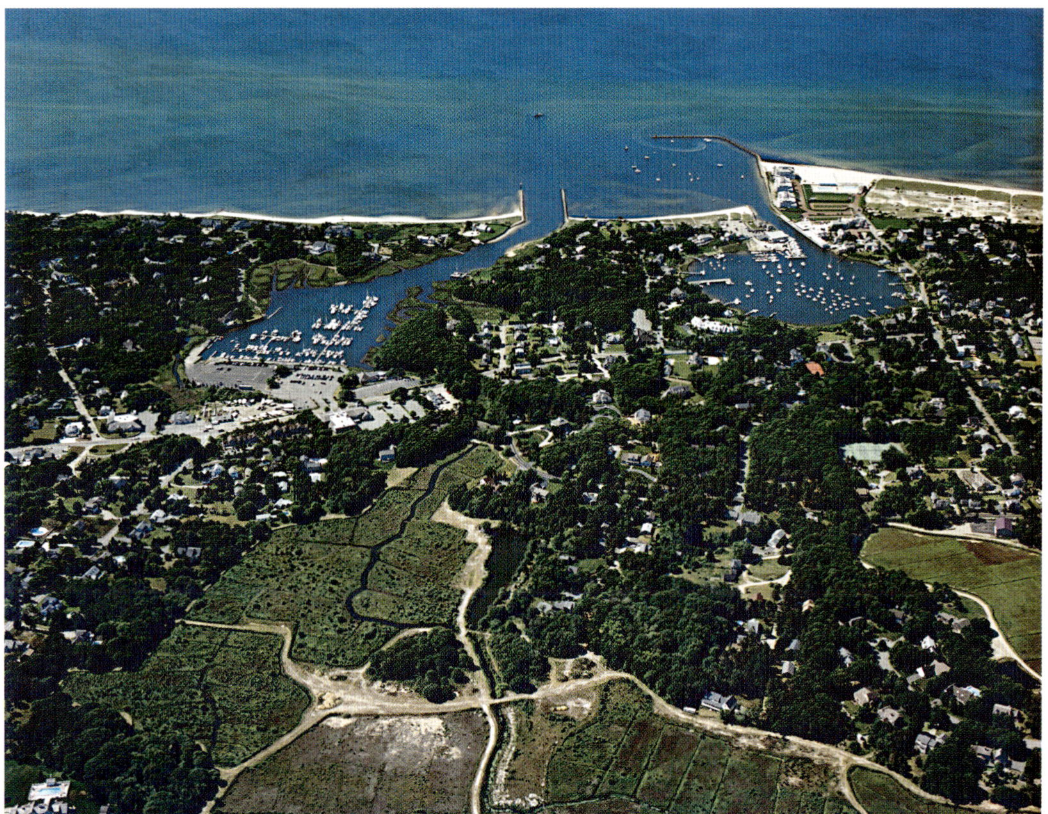

Looking south across Saquatucket and Wychmere Harbors. The green swaths in the foreground are cranberry bogs.

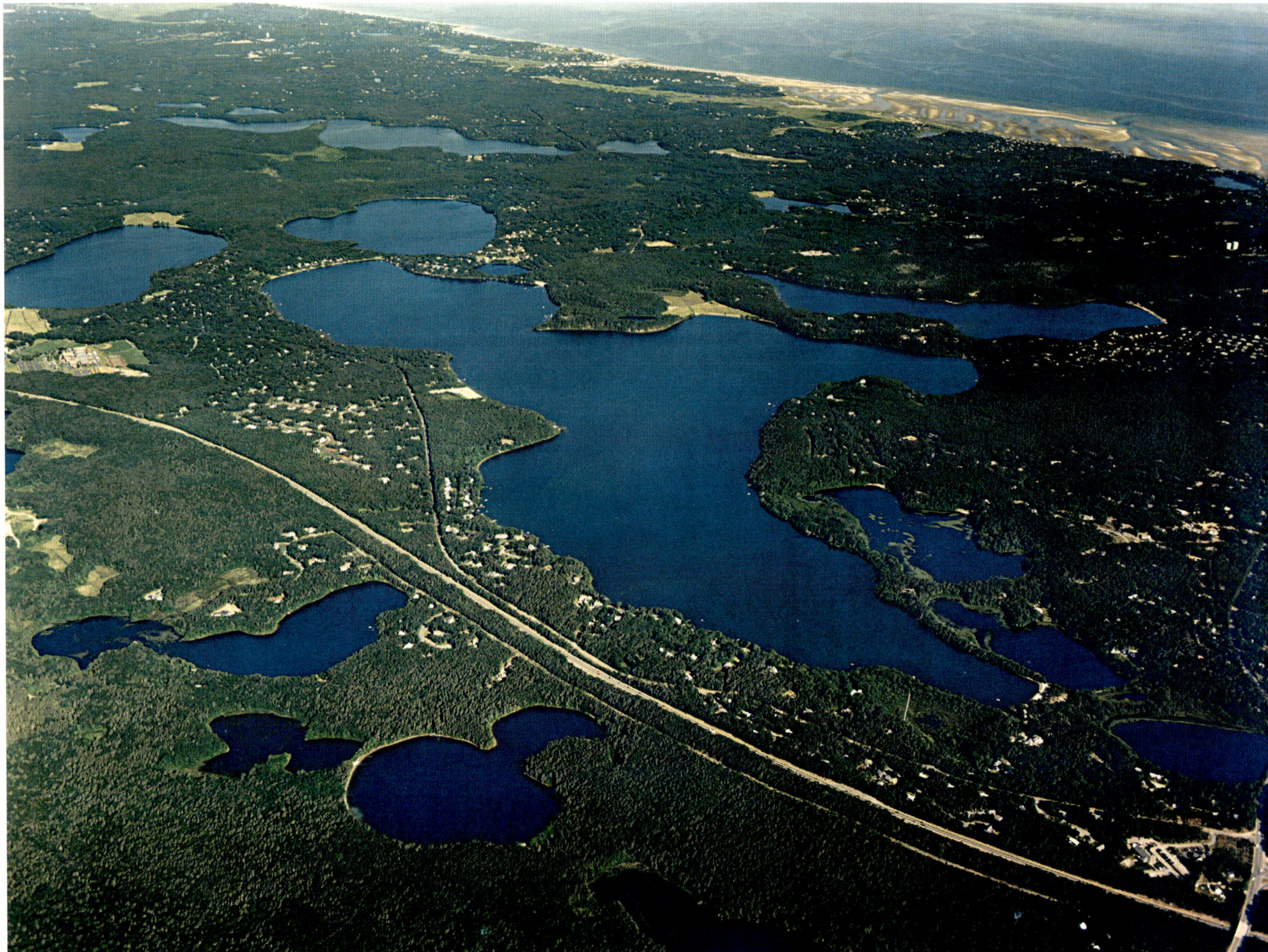

Looking northwest across Harwich and Brewster towards Cape Cod Bay. The largest pond is Long Pond.

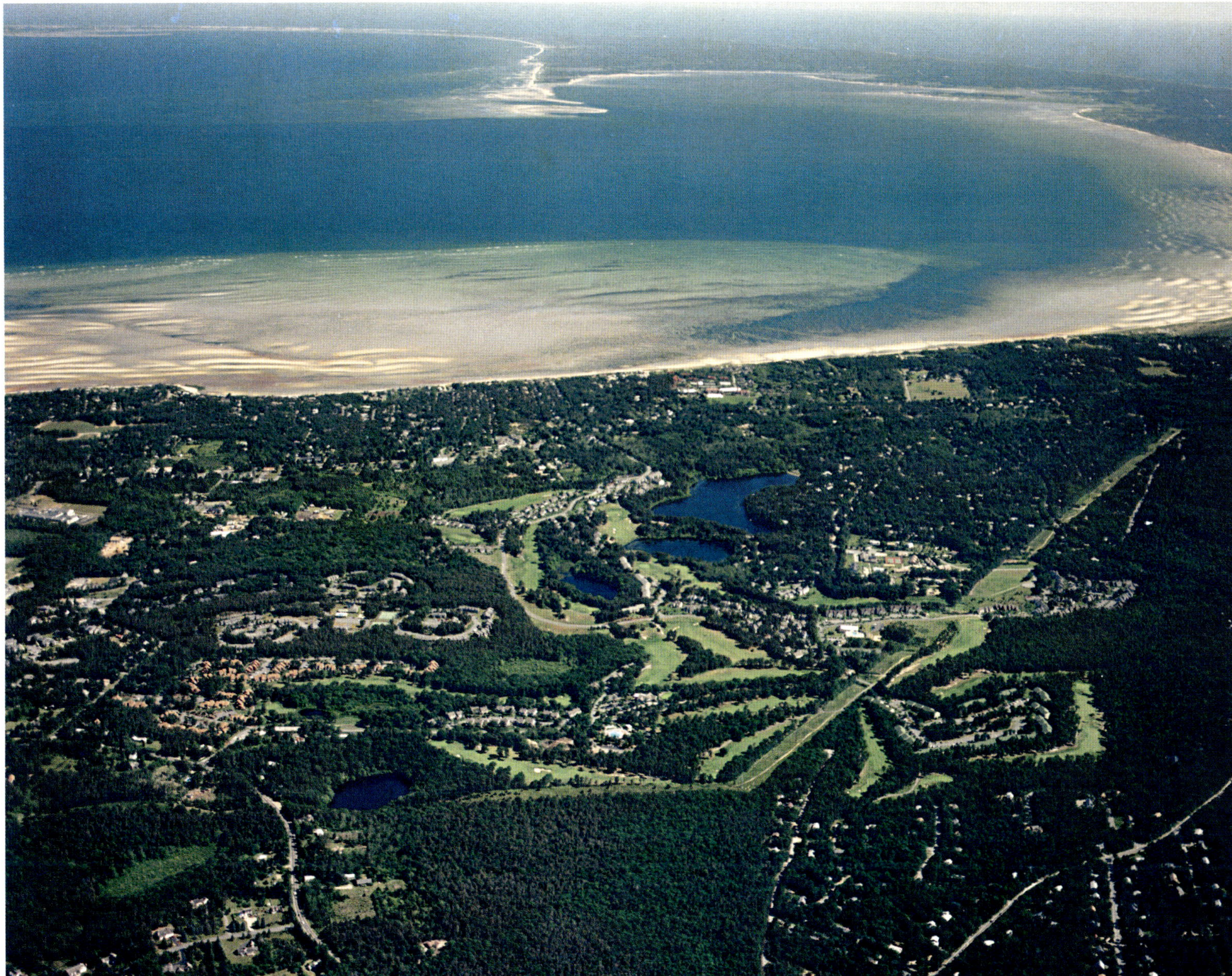

The Ocean Edge golf course to Cape Cod bay.

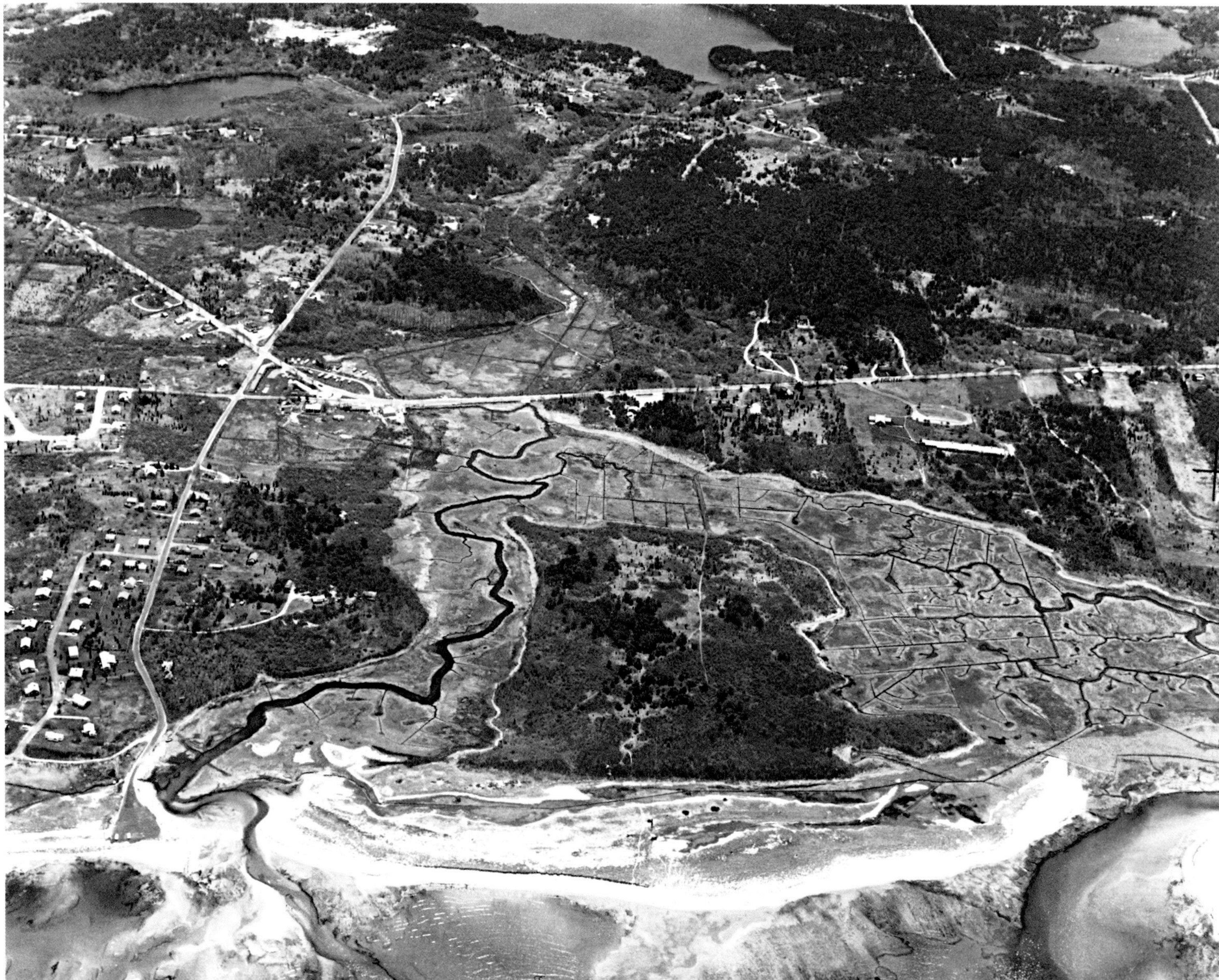

From the bayside looking south, Wing's Island and Stony Brook in 1967.
This area is home to the Cape Cod Museum of Natural History.

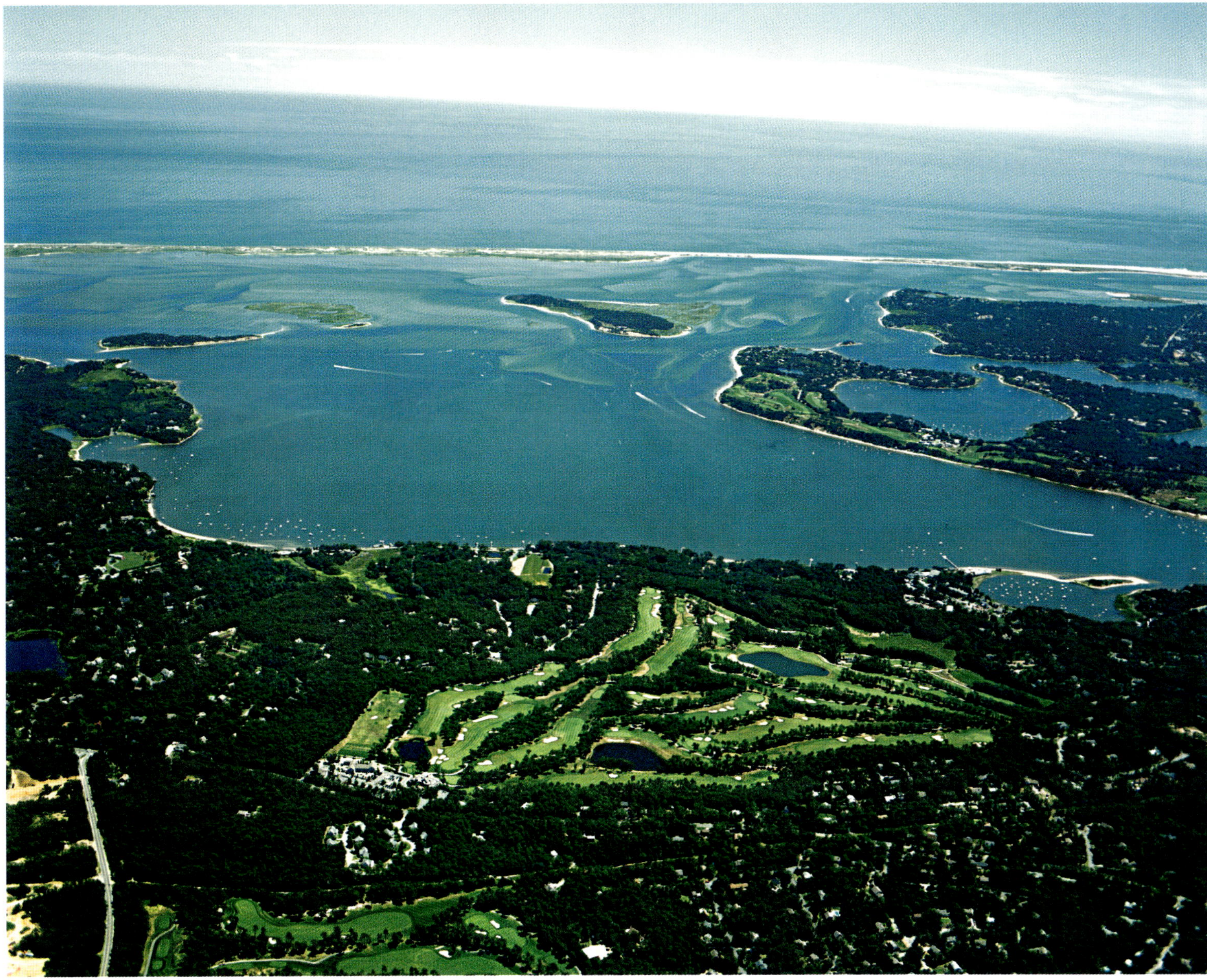

The Cape Cod National Golf Course looks east towards Pleasant Bay and North Beach.

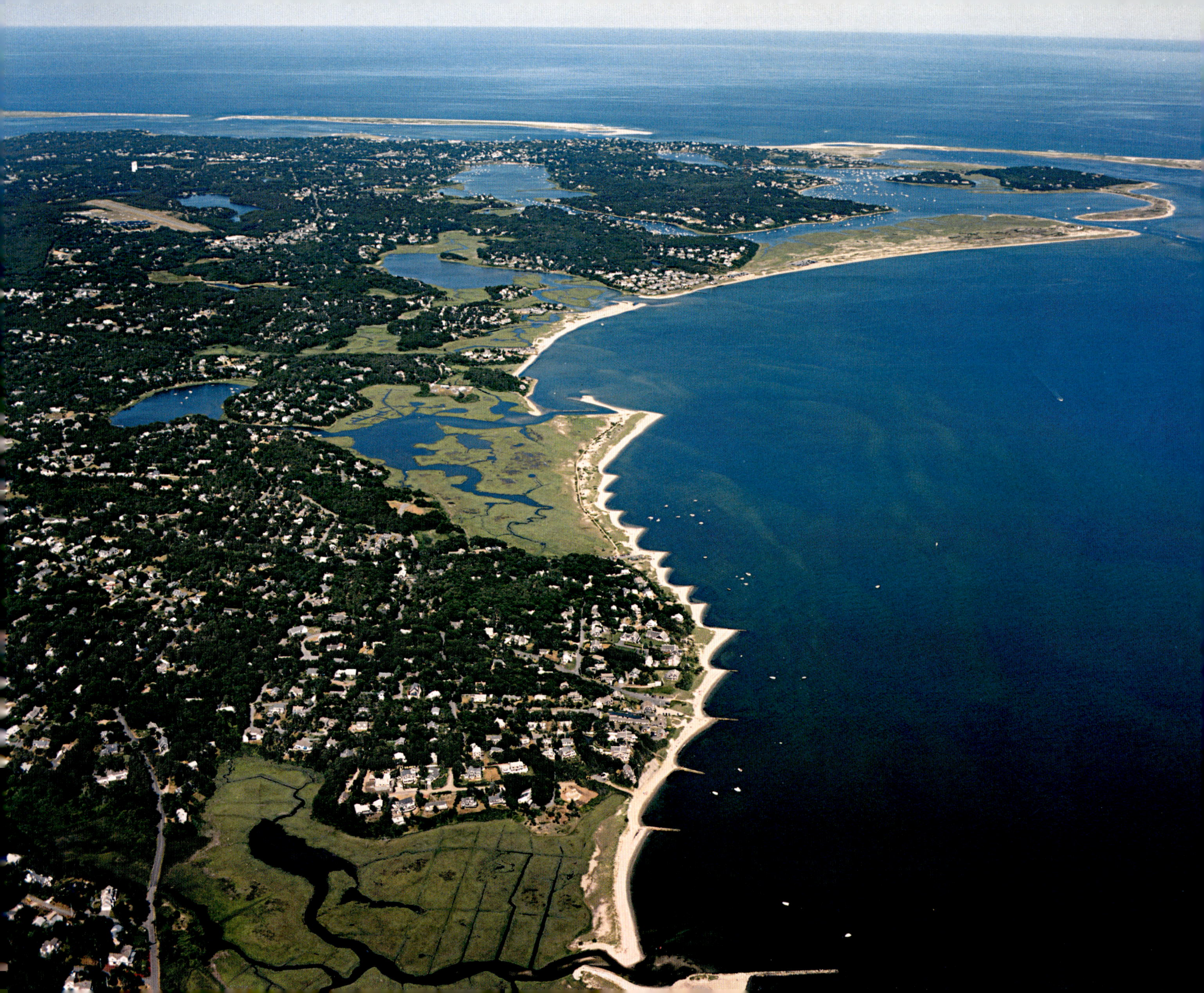

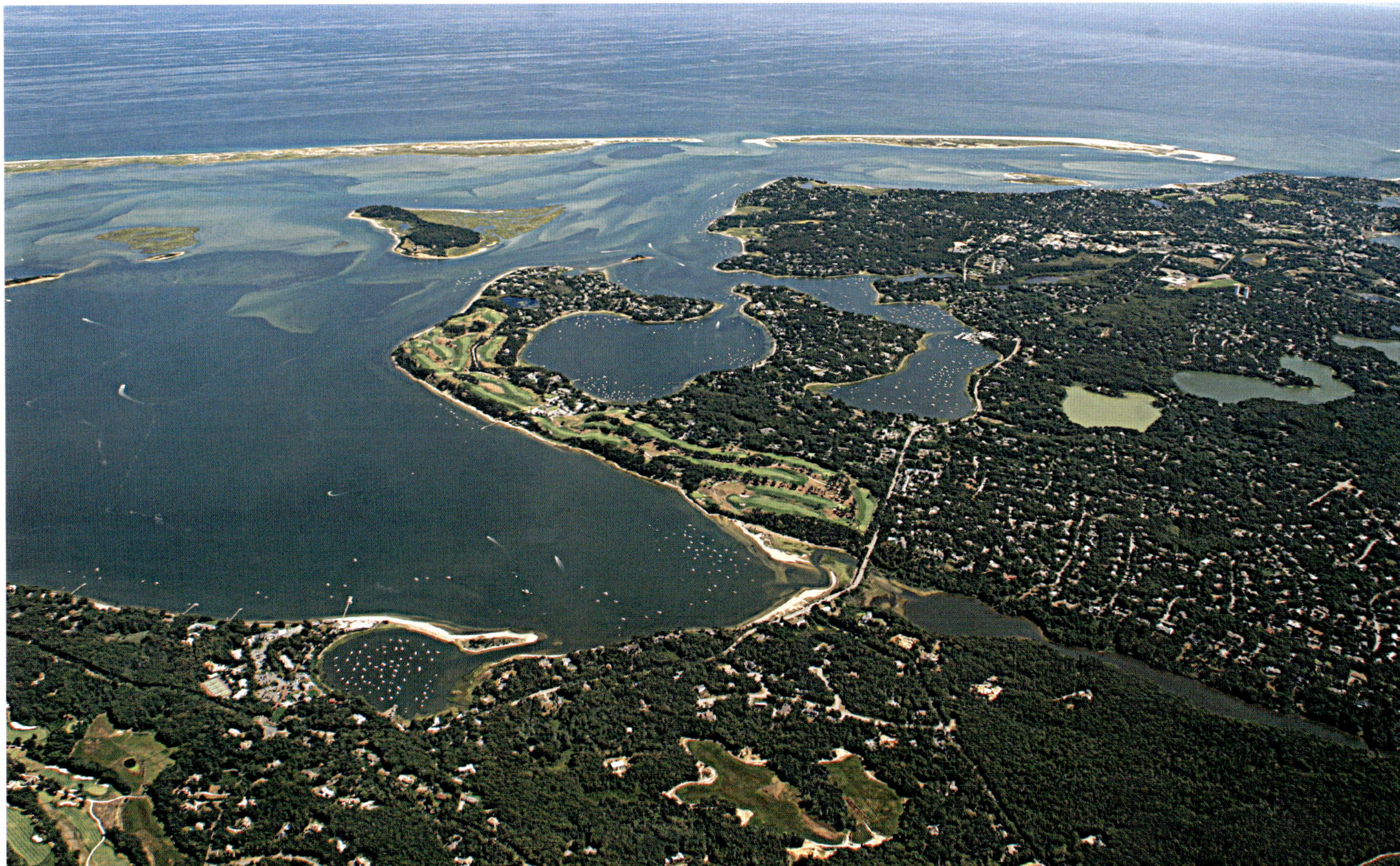

Round Cove and the Wequassett Inn looking east across Eastward Ho! Country Club.

Looking east across South Chatham to Chatham.

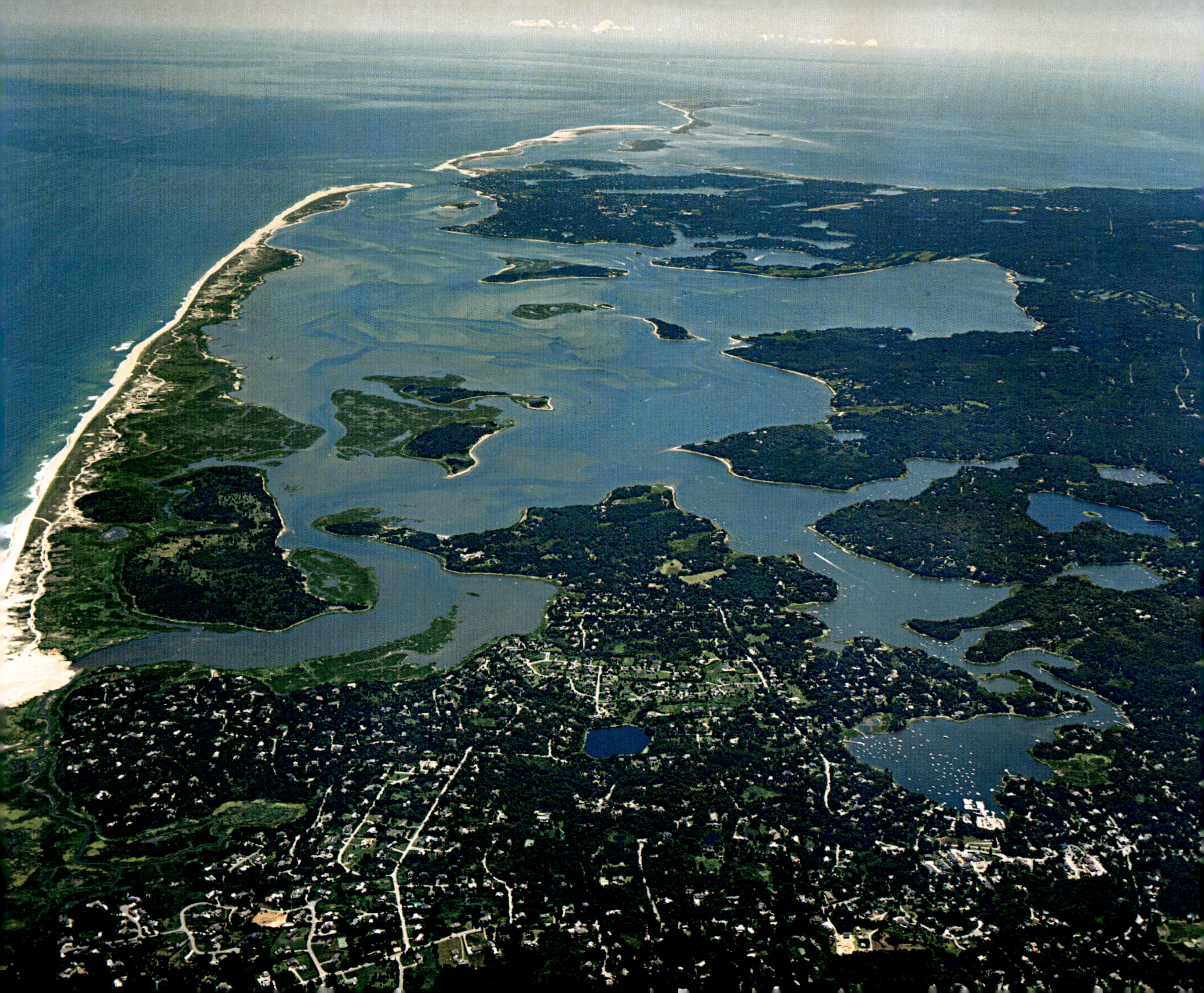

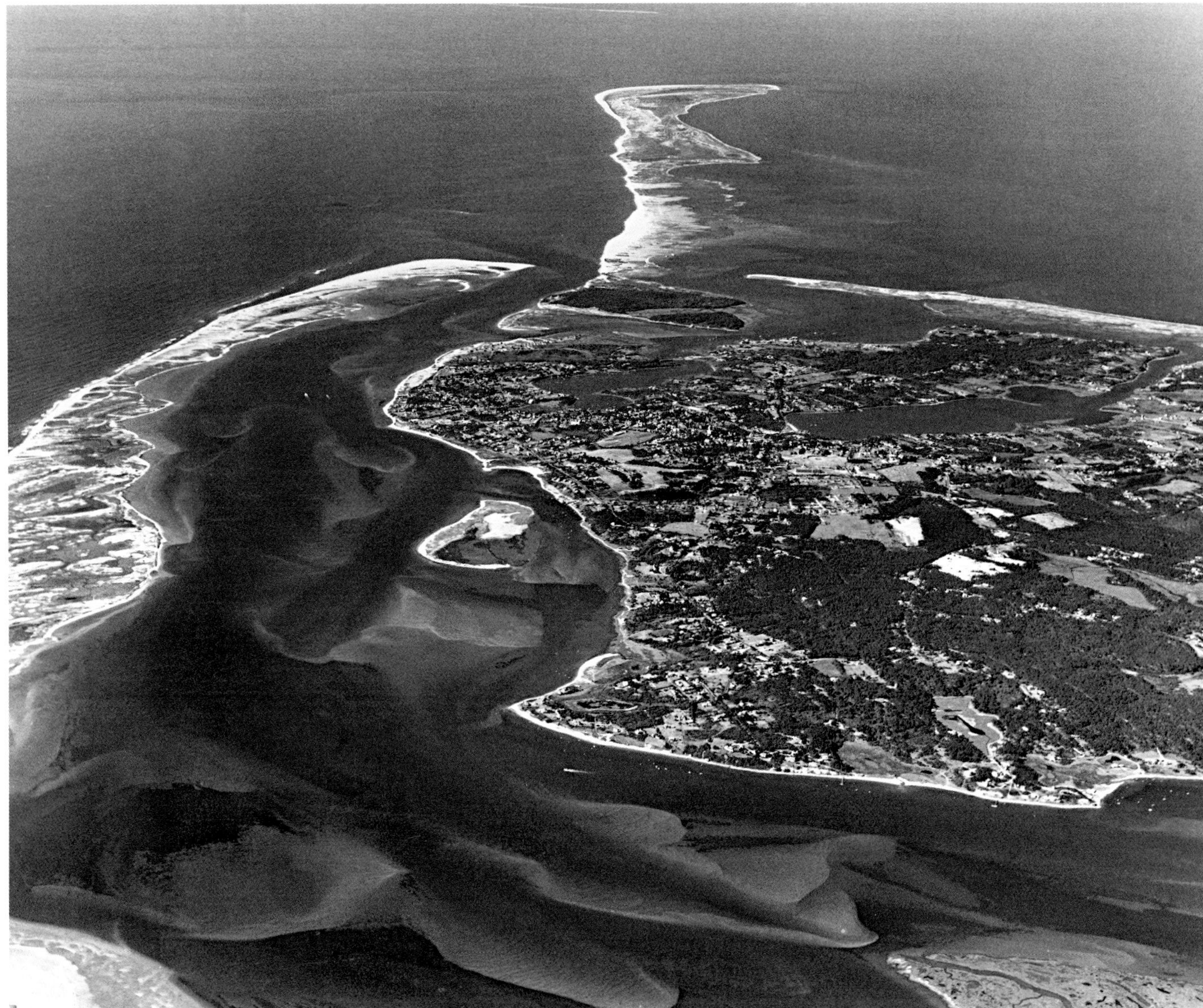

This series of three looks south across Chatham in 1957.

Orleans south to Chatham. Meetinghouse Pond and all of Pleasant Bay.{opposite}

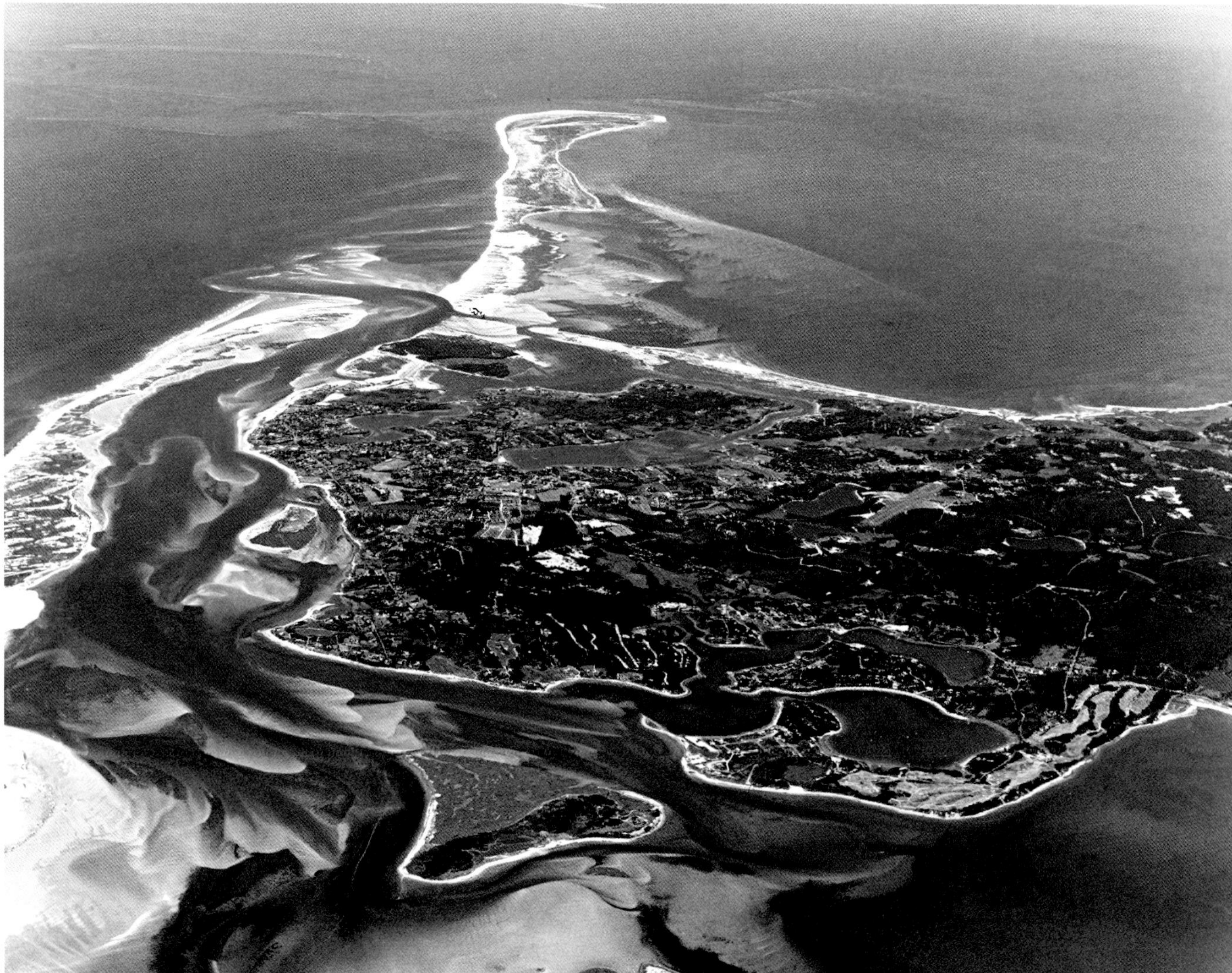

Look closely at the changes around Monomoy Island, Morris and Stage Islands and the barrier beach in 1961.

There have been many natural and man-made changes over 50 years, 2007.{opposite}

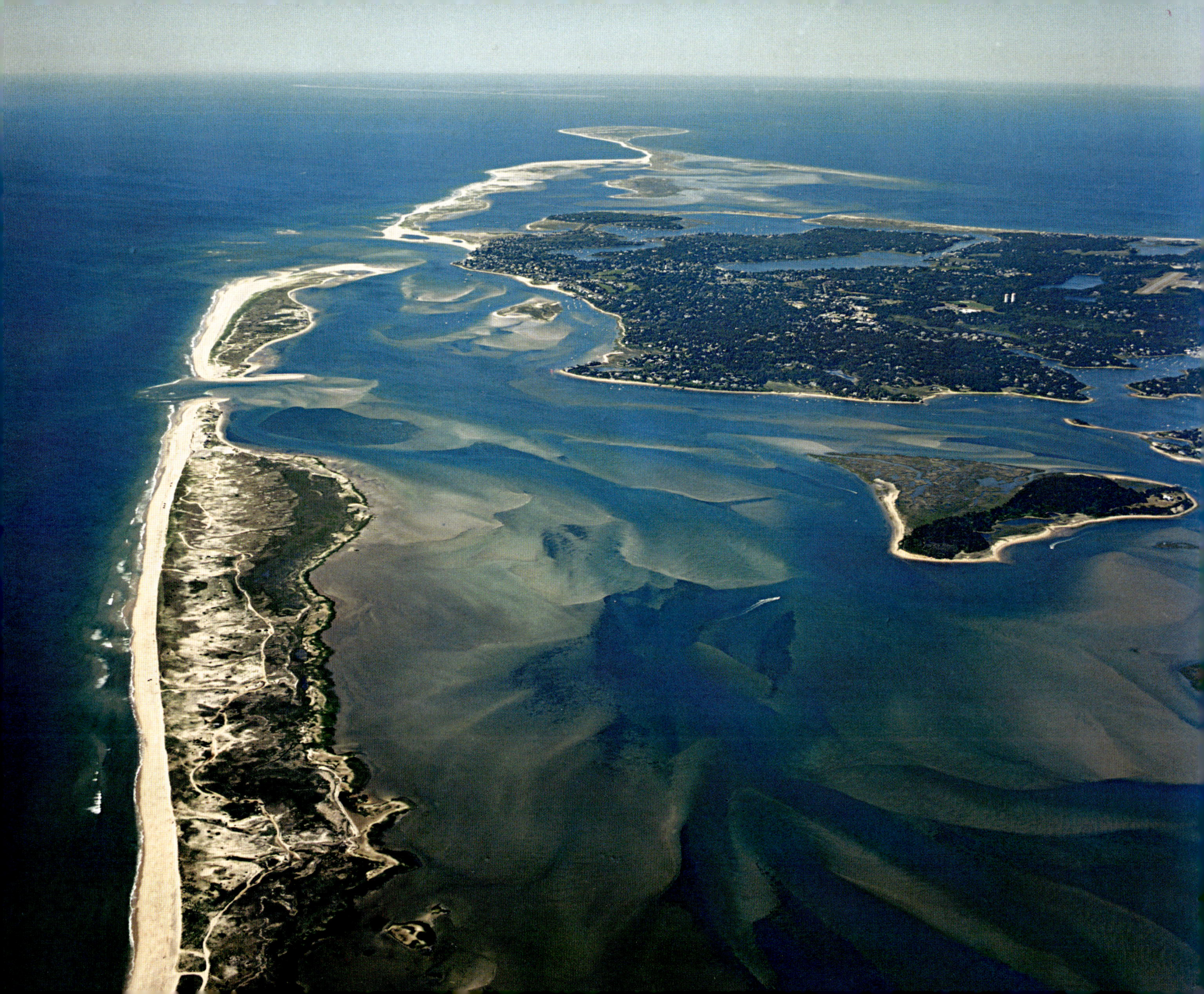

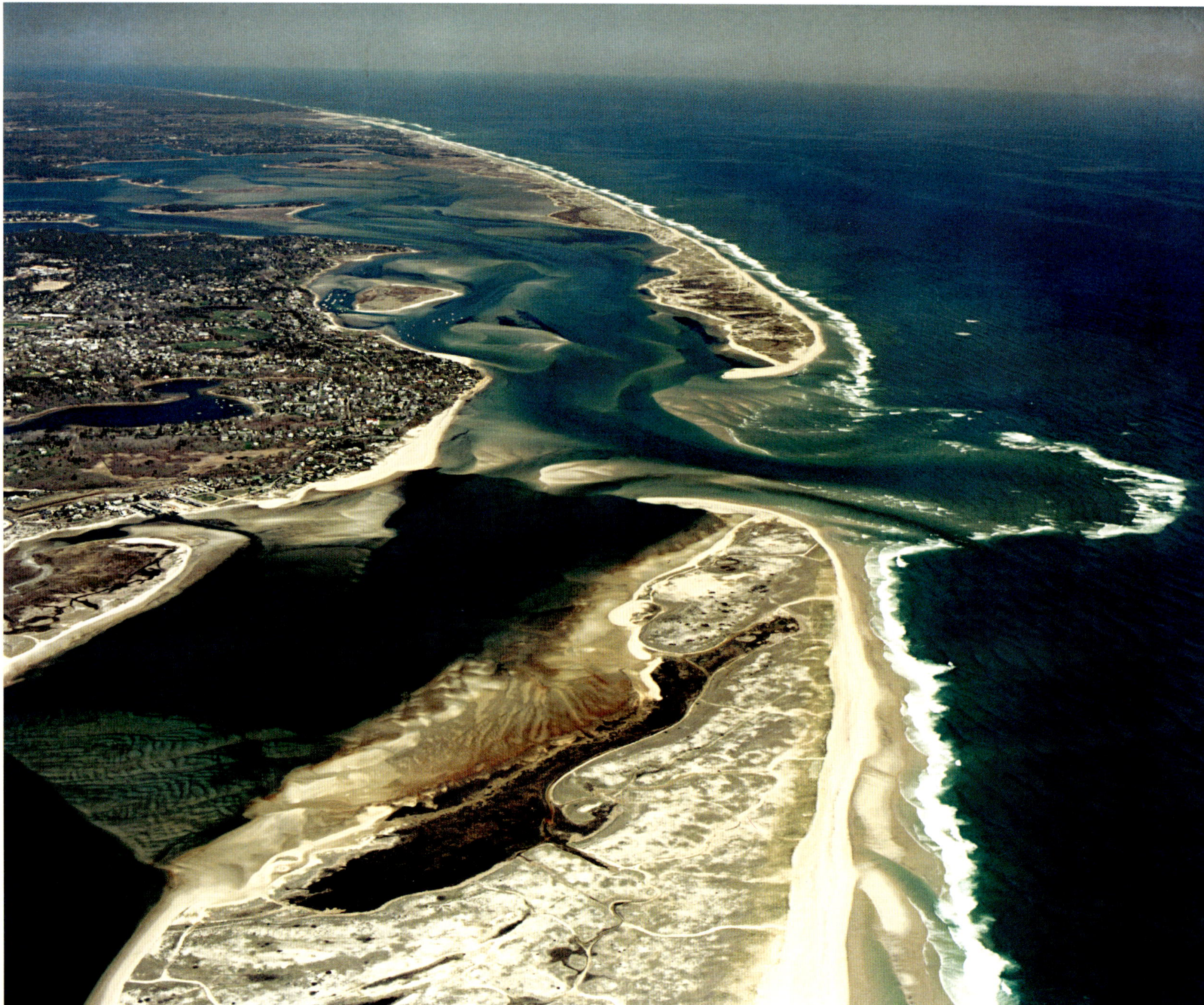

The Chatham Break in 1988 looking north, about a year and a half after a Noreaster caused a breech in the barrier beach.

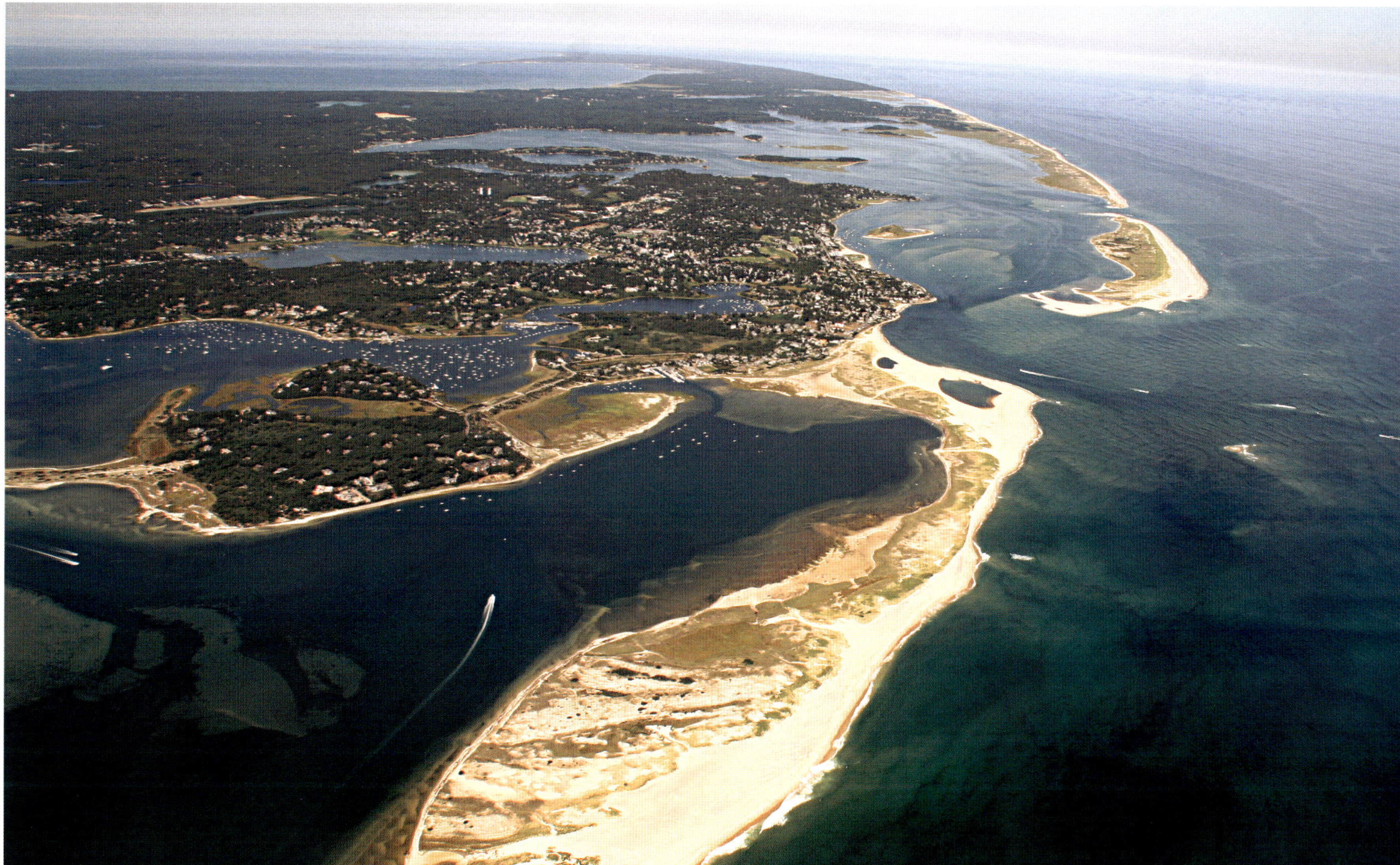

Looking north 19 years later, 2007.

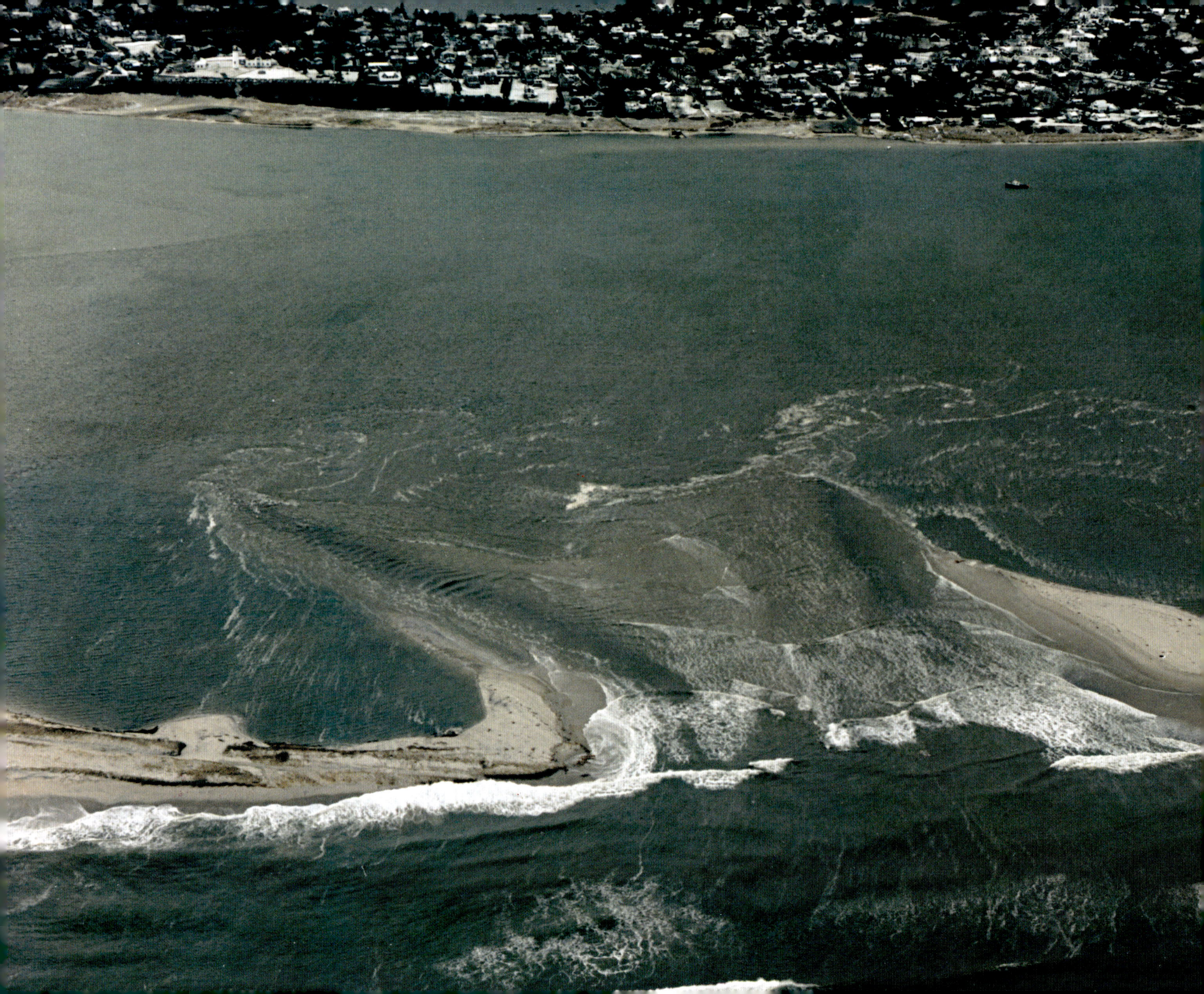

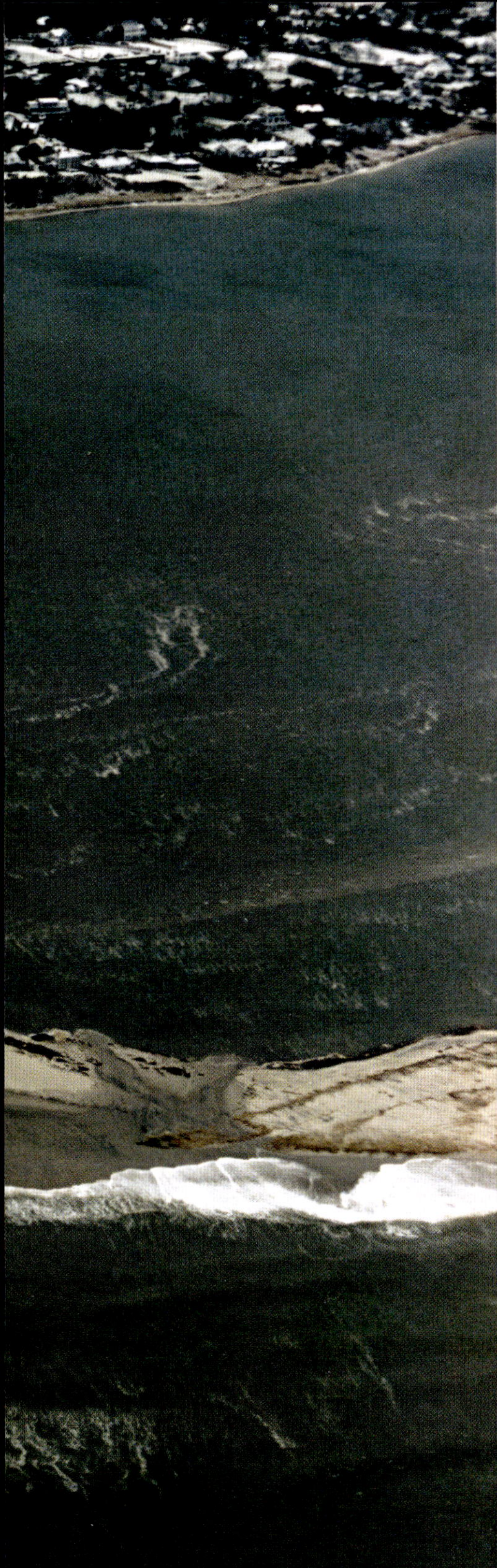

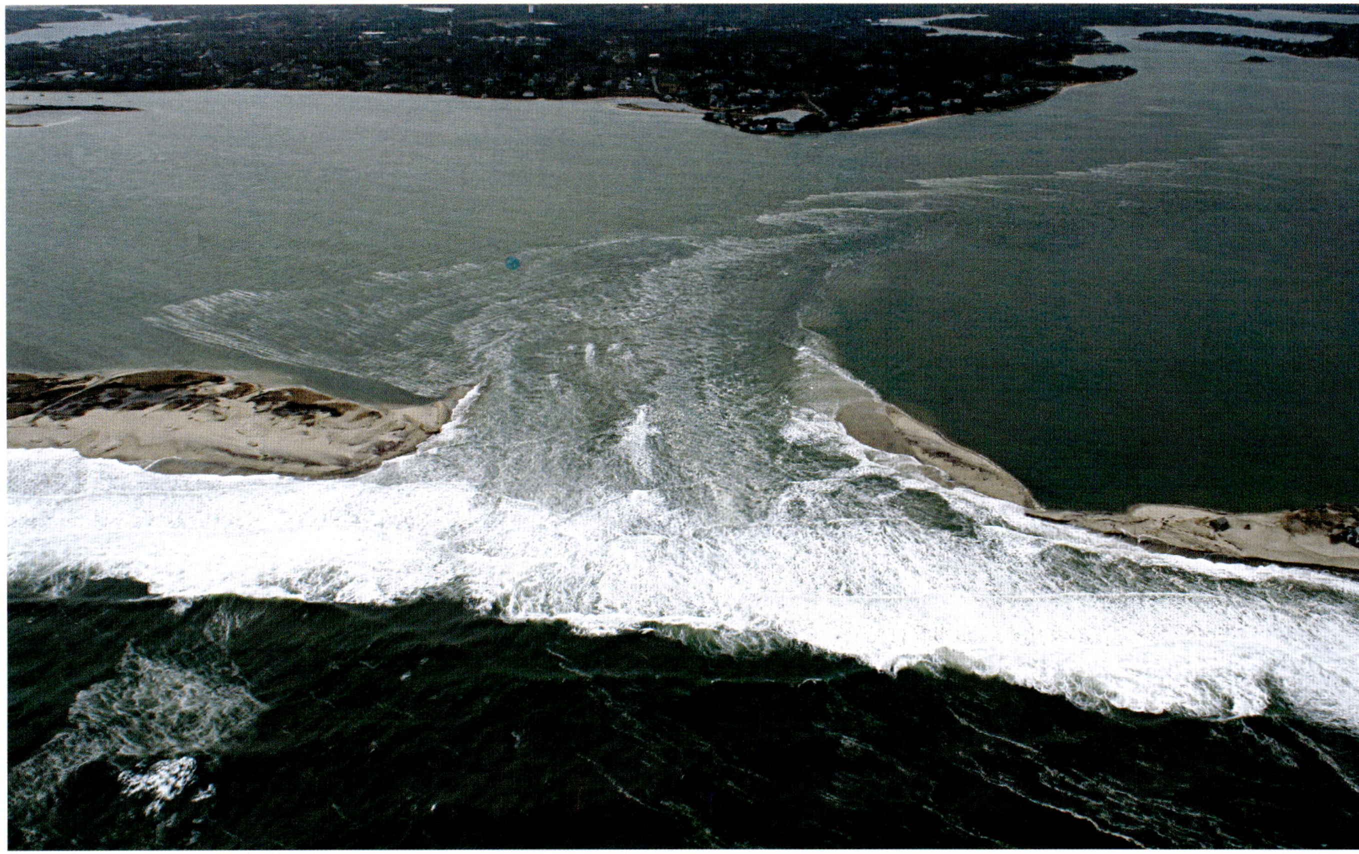

Two different breeches on the same beach, 1987 and 2007. About 20 years and one-and-a-half miles apart.

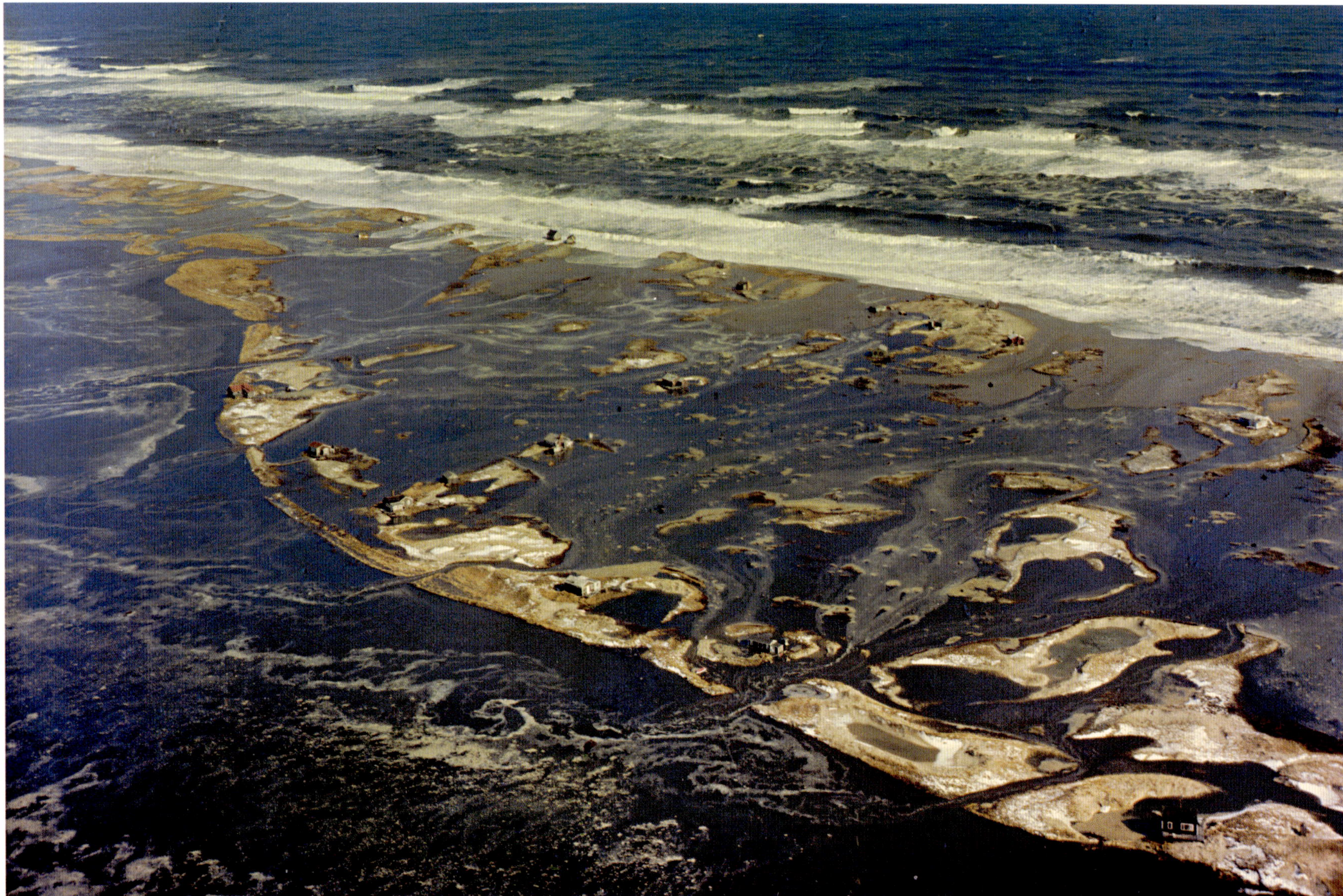

North Beach during the Blizzard of 1978.

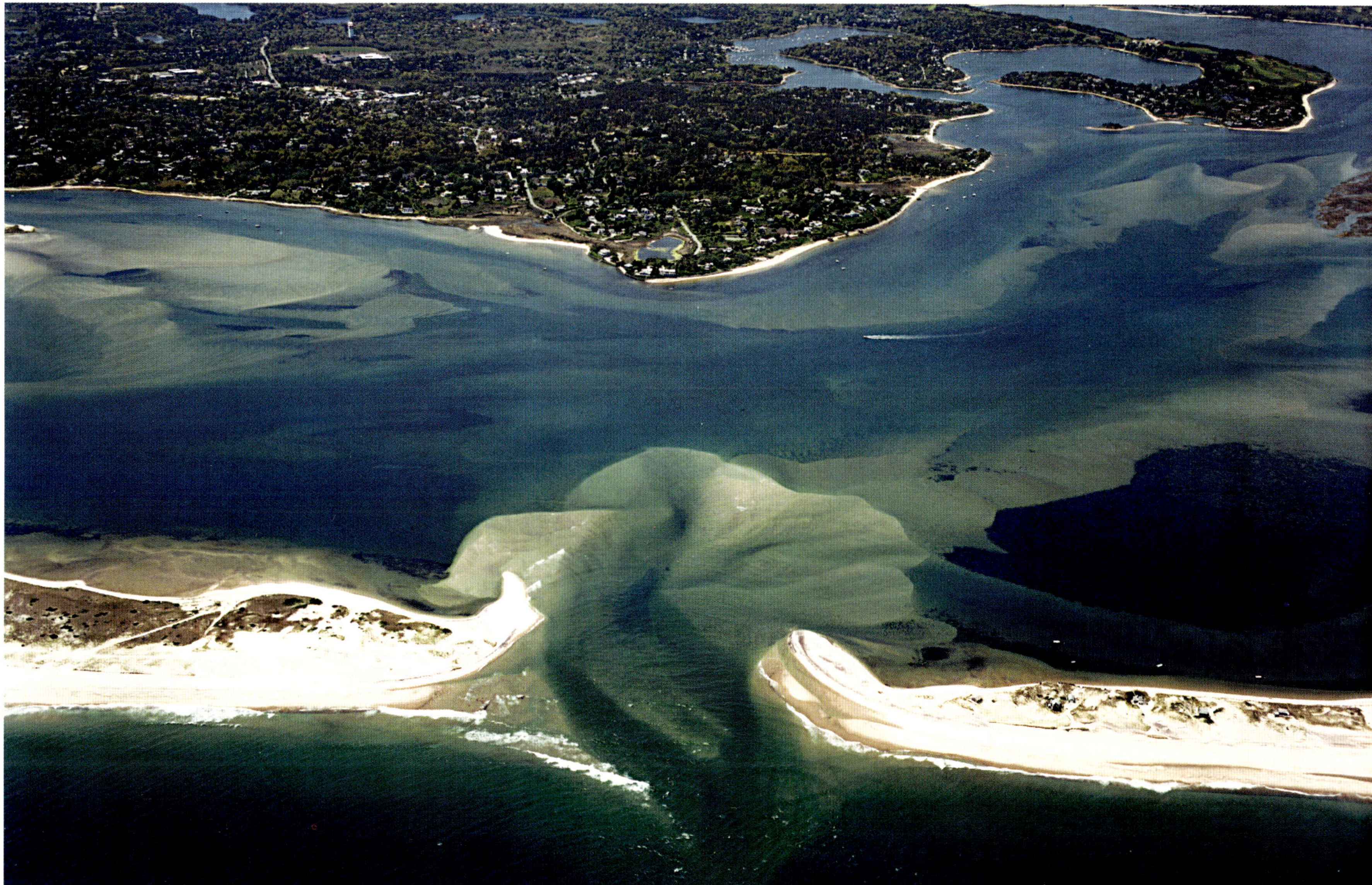

New Break caused by the Patriots Day Nor'easter of 2007.

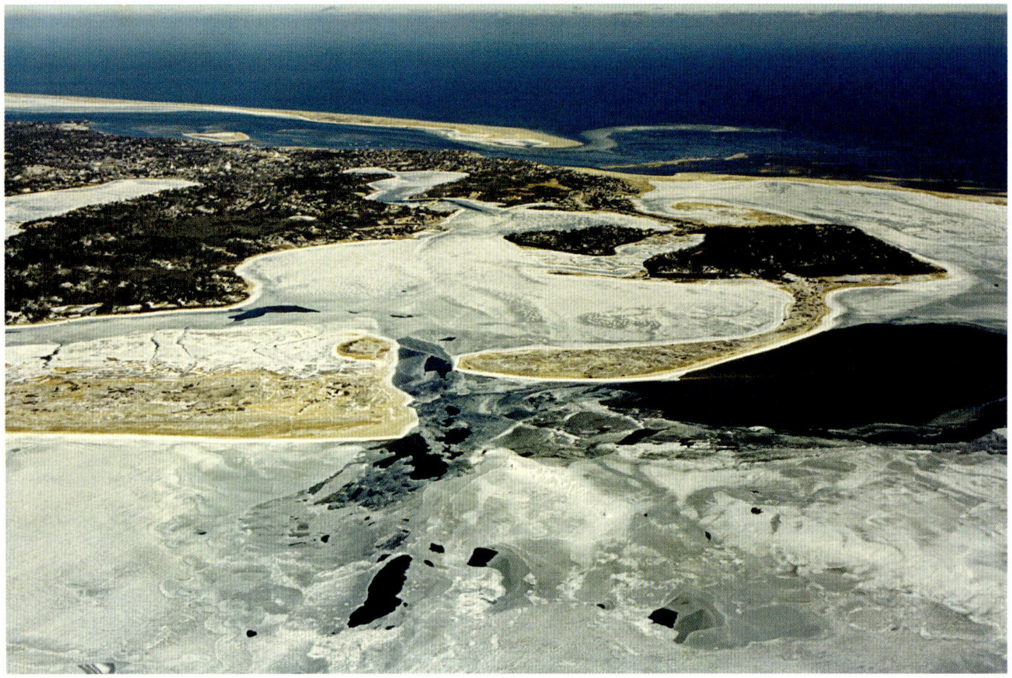

Stage Harbor during a winter freeze.

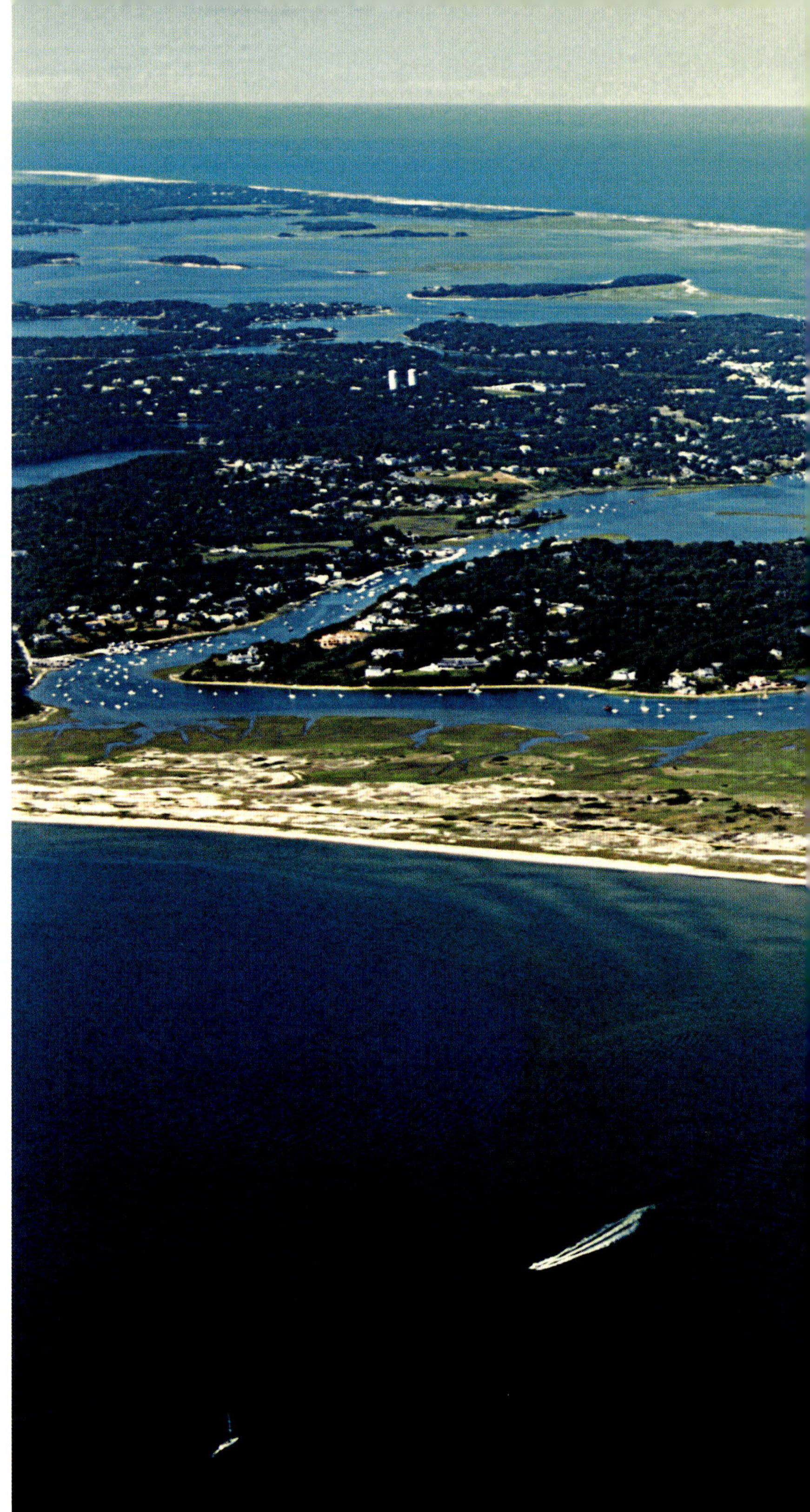

Looking into Stage Harbor during the summer.

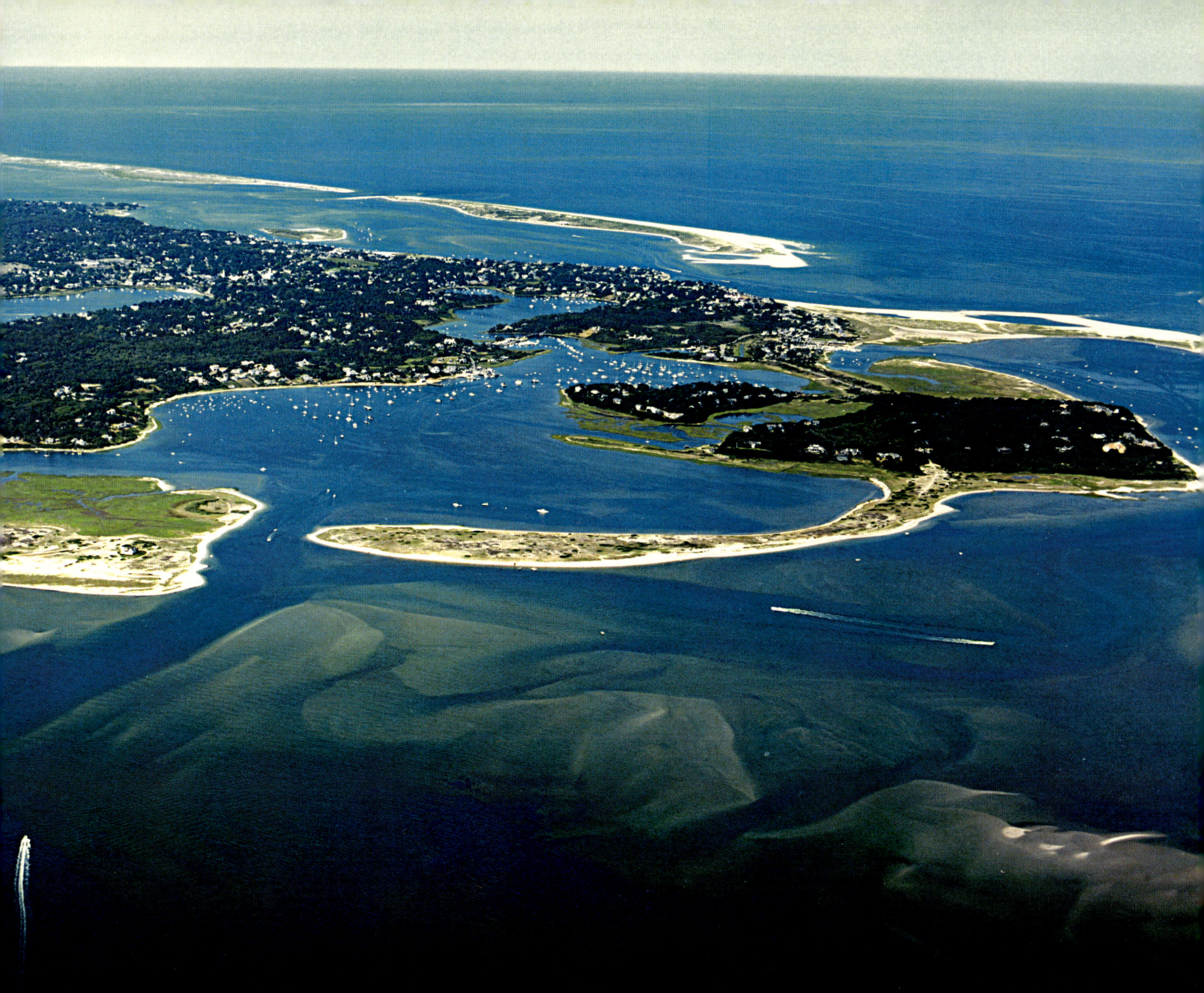

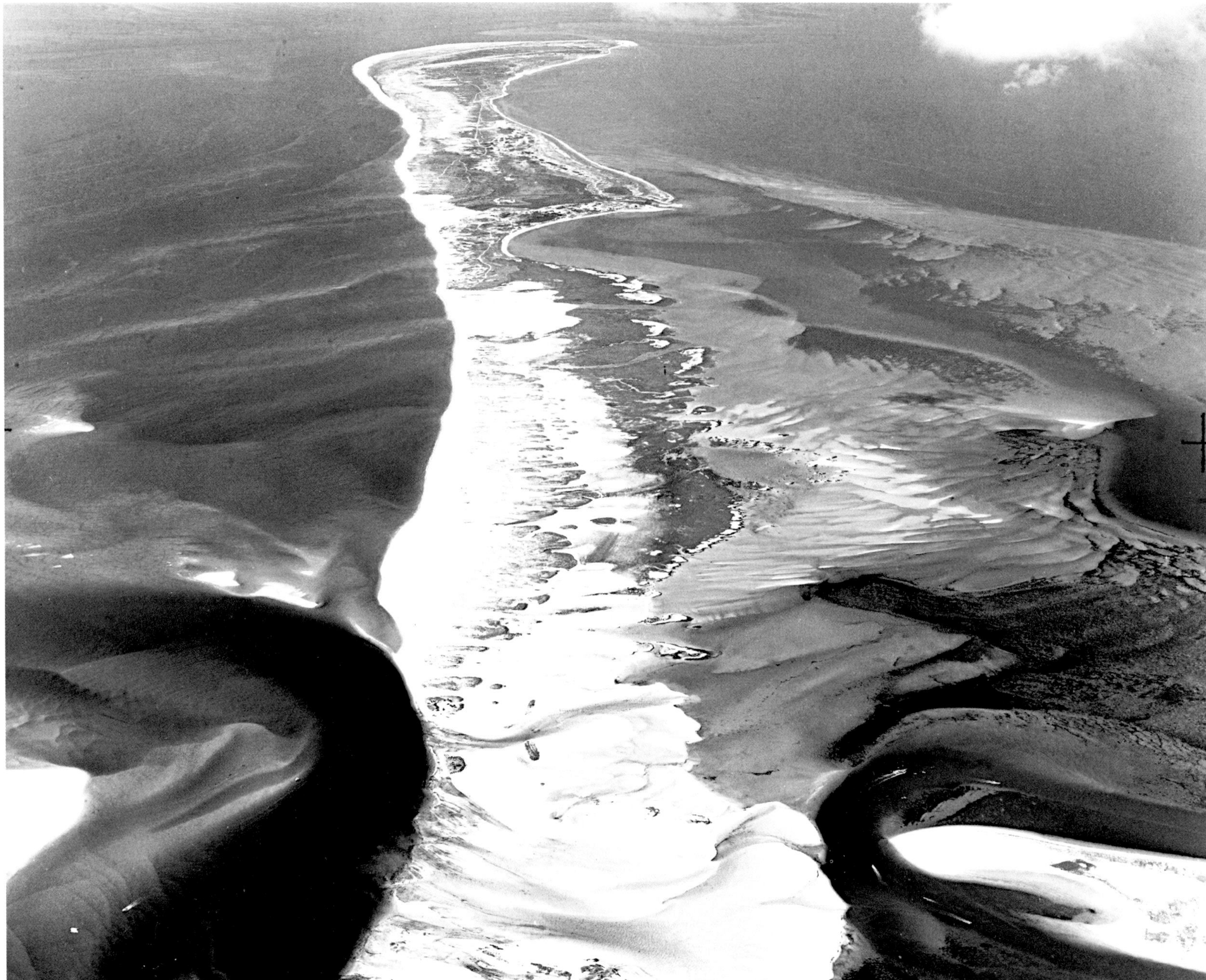

Monomoy Island in 1960. The bigger black spot on the left is the Pendleton shipwreck.

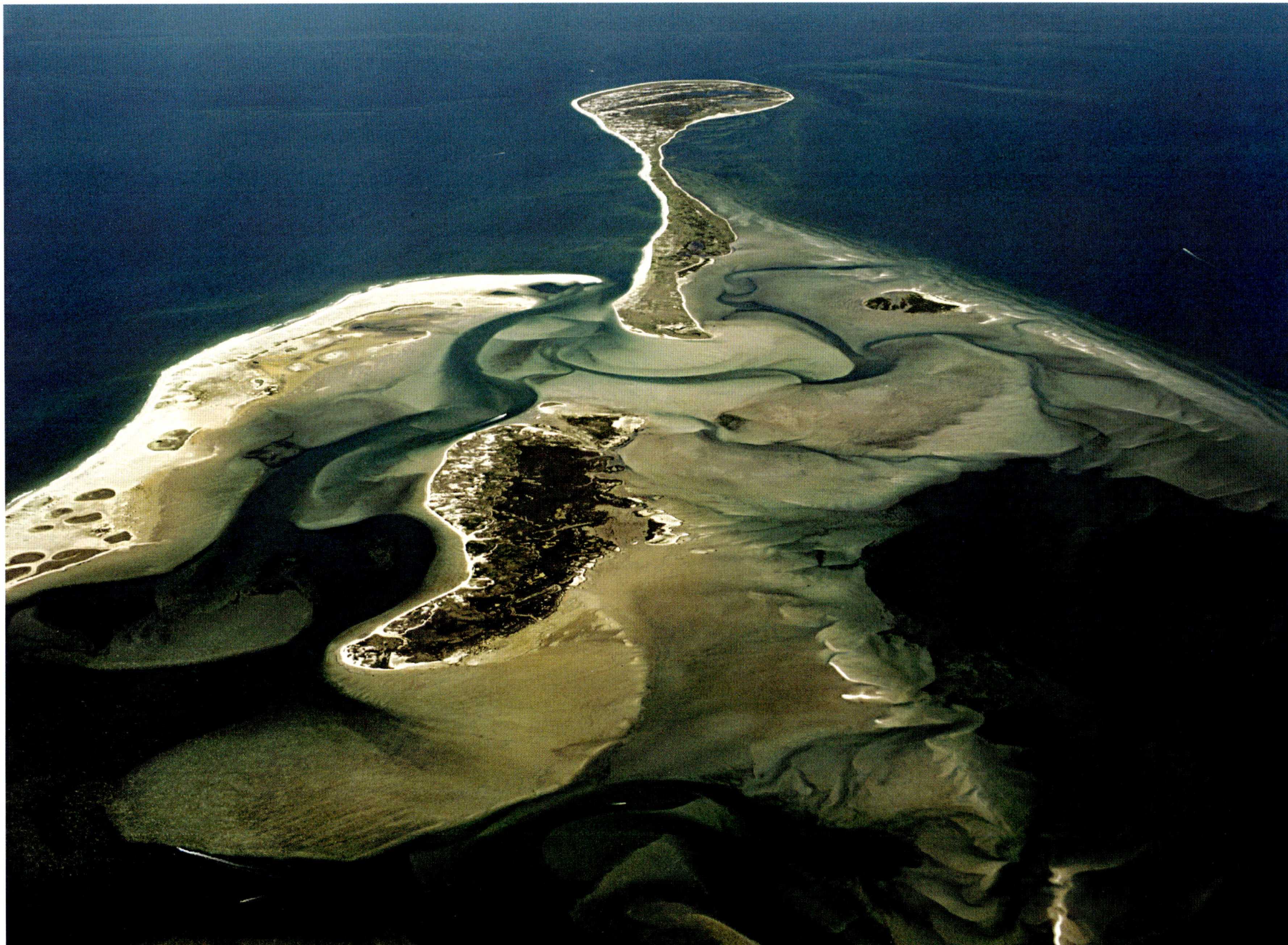

Monomoy 44 years later. Nature's storms are constantly changing the island's shape. Monomoy is the most consistently appearing landmark in our Airviews.

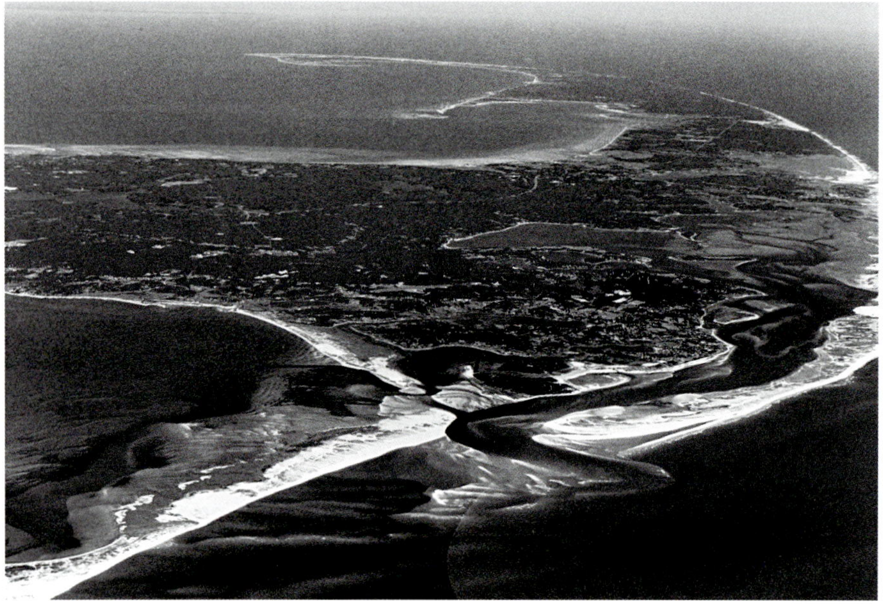

1961

The story of a barrier beach can be seen in this series of Airviews, showing Monomoy to Provincetown over a period of 46 years. Taken from altitudes between 6,000 and 10,000 feet, clear days are needed for this shot!

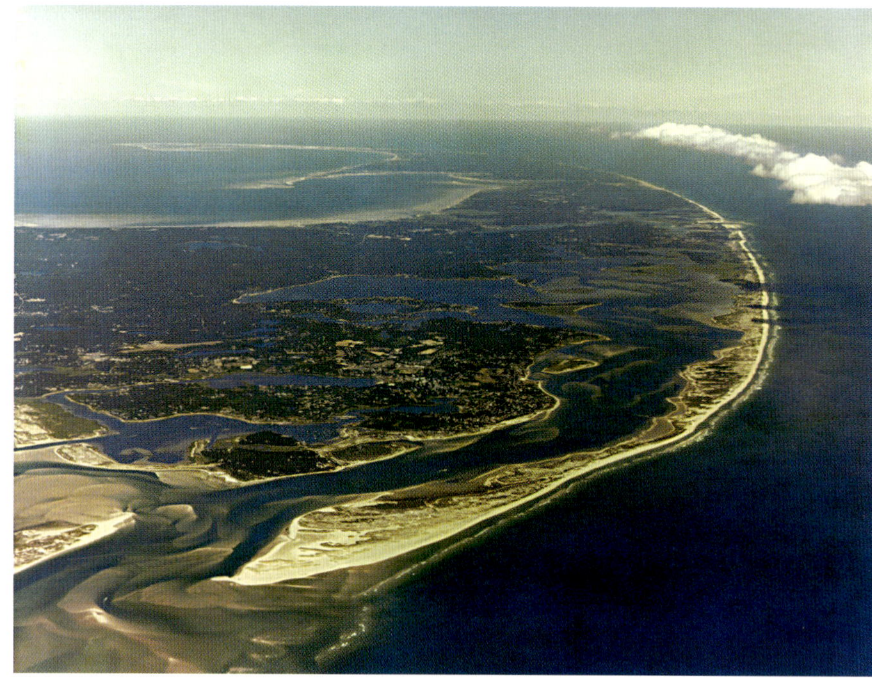

1977

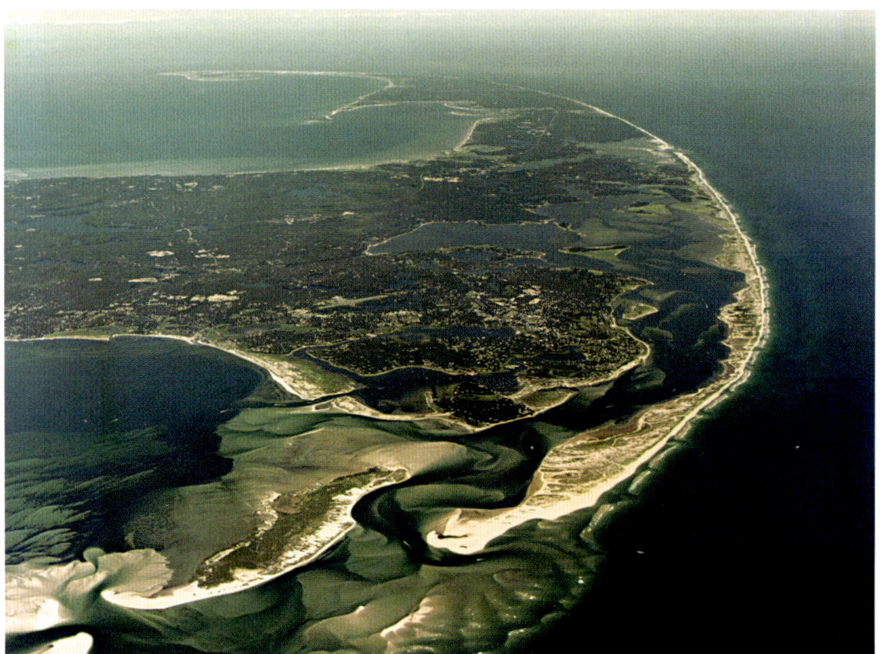

1984

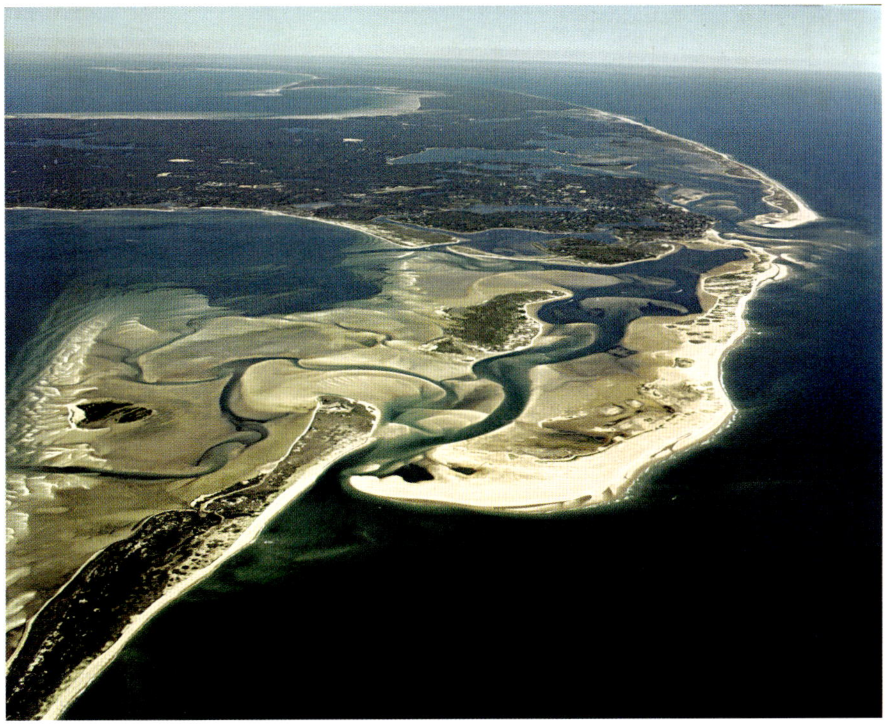

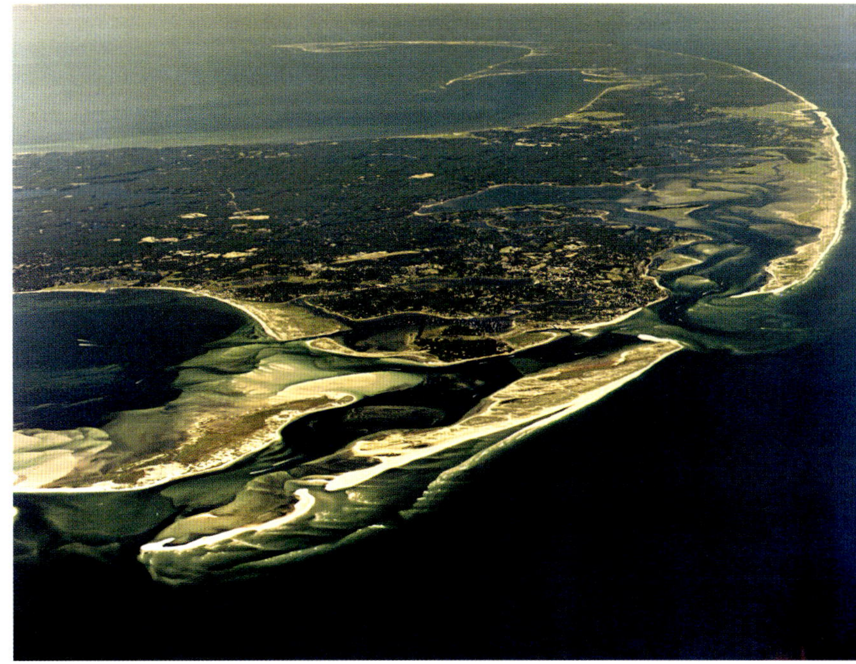

1989

2004

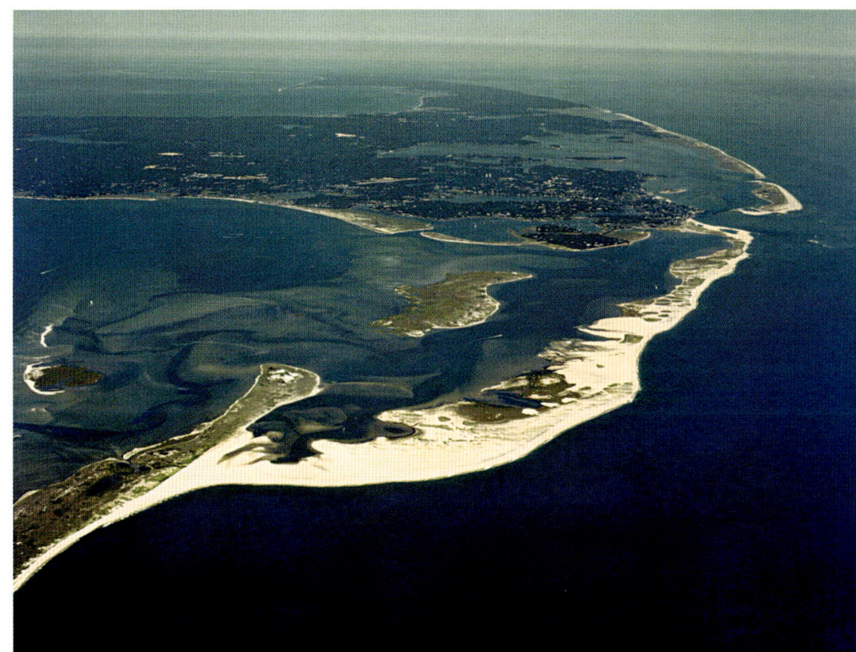

2007

Chapter 5

Orleans, Eastham, Wellfleet, Truro, & Provincetown

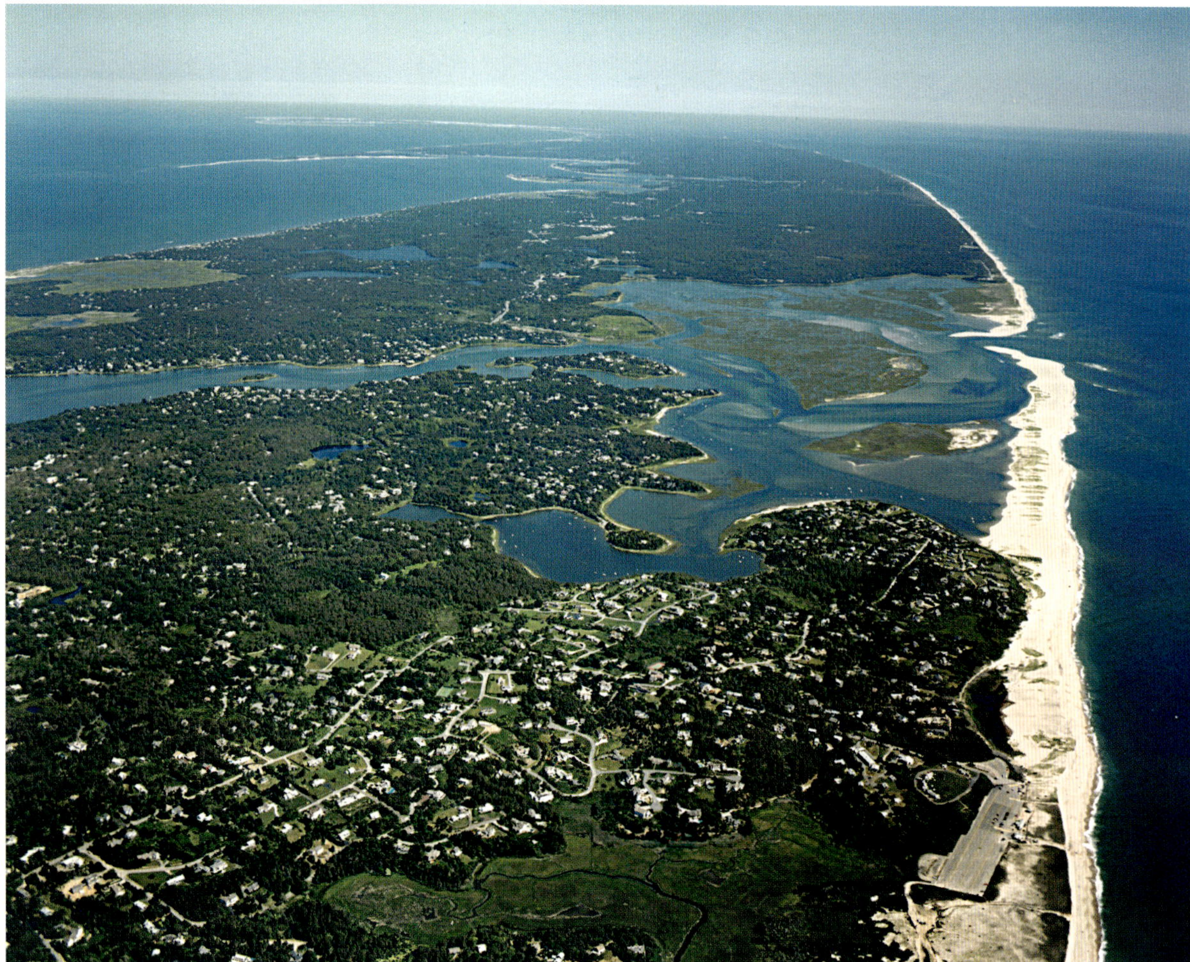

Nauset Beach parking lot looking north to Provincetown.

Coast Guard Beach looking south t
Chatham. Nauset Inlet and Town Cov
are the prominent waterways in th
middle of the picture.{opposite}

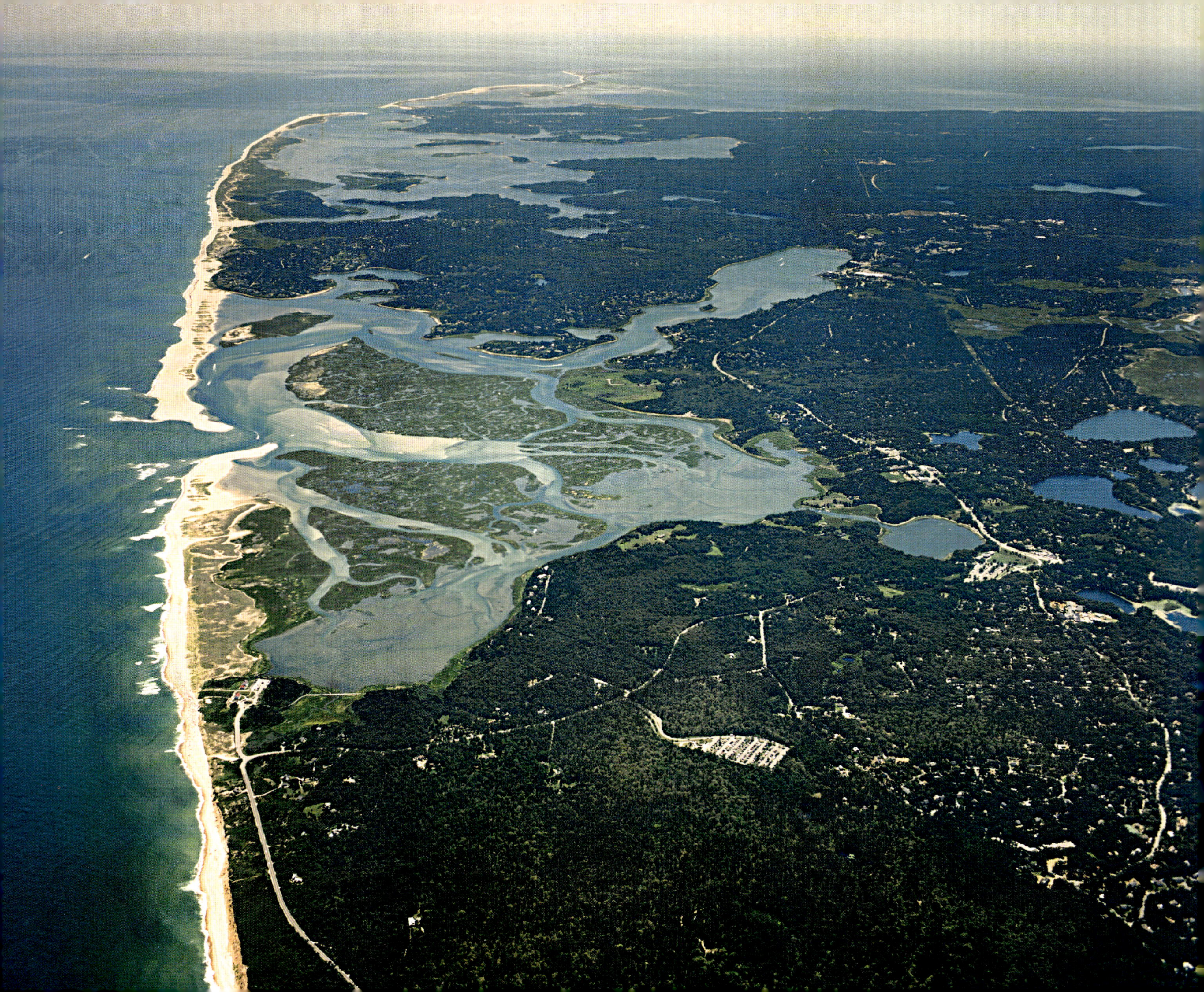

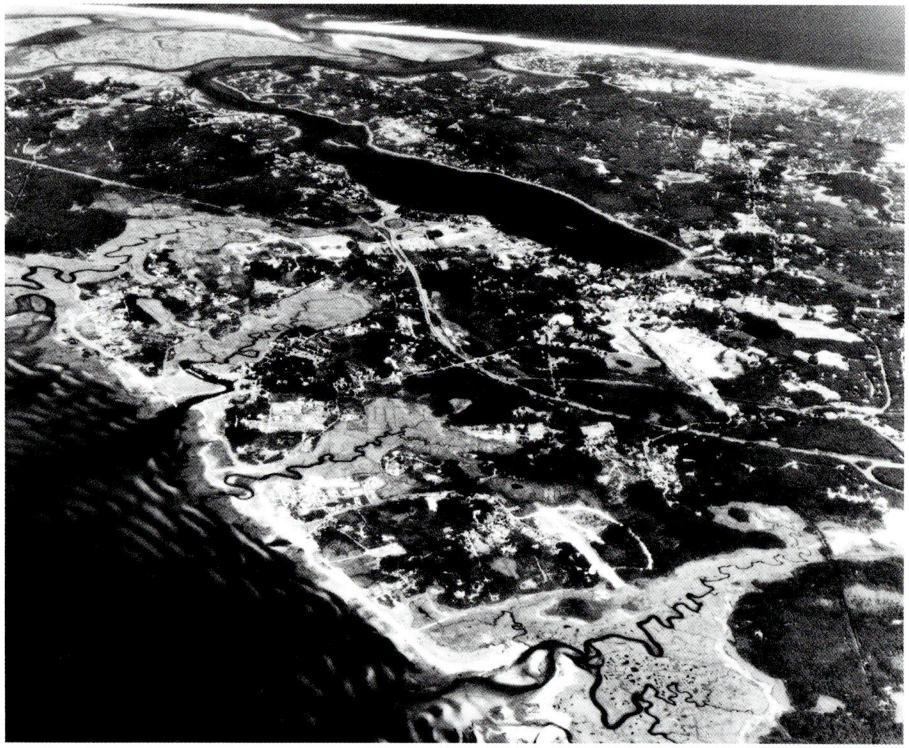

An older and recent view showing the bayside of Orleans, 1974 and 2007. From the bottom up: Namskaket Creek, Skaket Beach, and Rock Harbor. The white streak off Namskaket Creek was a grass airstrip called Sky Meadow.

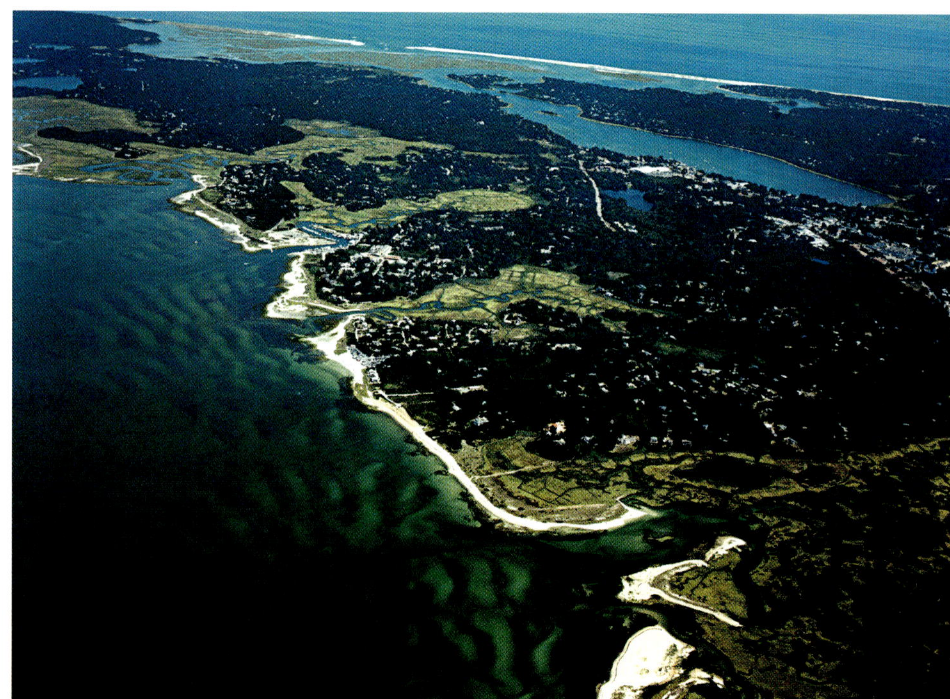

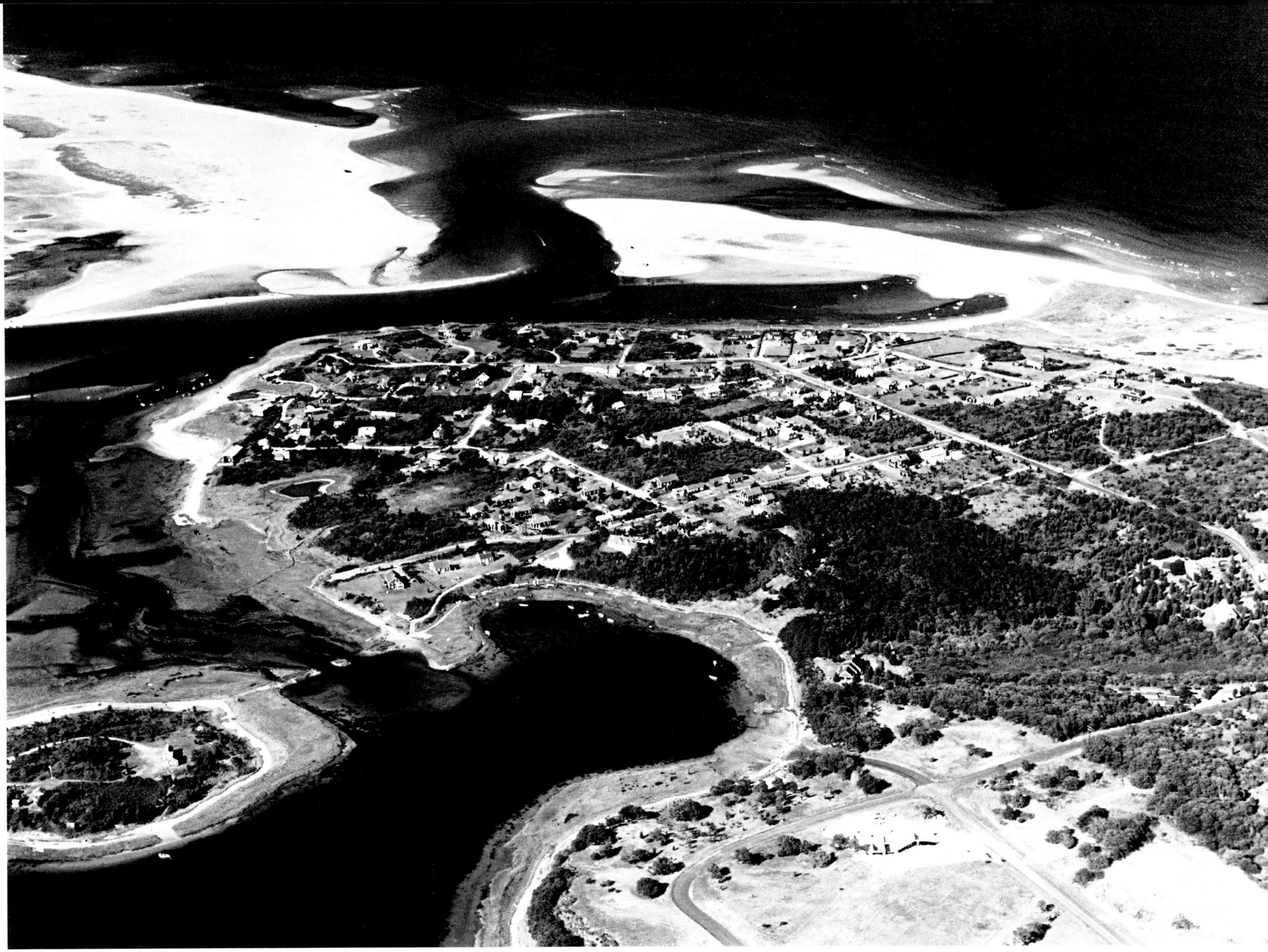

The opening of Nauset Inlet has changed location and shape numerous times. In the 1960s it was very close to Nauset Heights. Over the years the beach has grown moving the opening to the north, 1966.

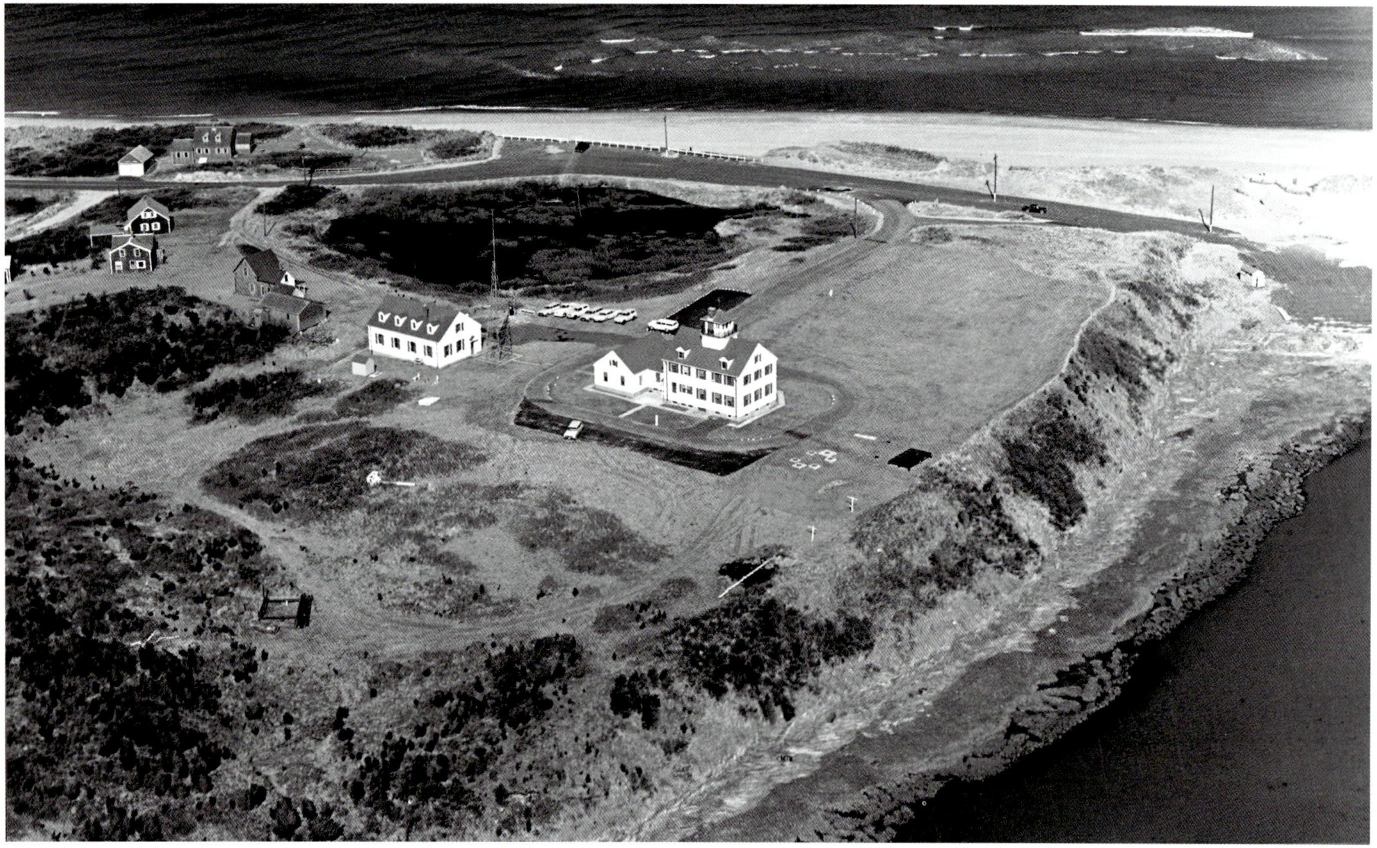

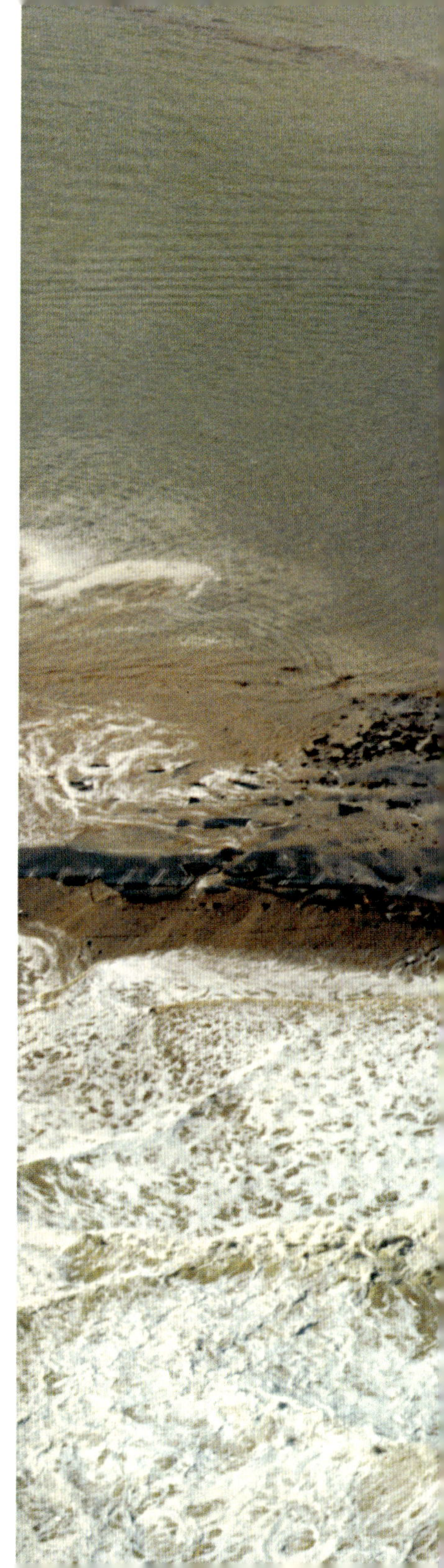

Two older views of the Nauset Coast Guard Station, 1967 and 1978. The blizzard of 1978 did a lot of damage to the Atlantic coastline, including the parking lot shown here.

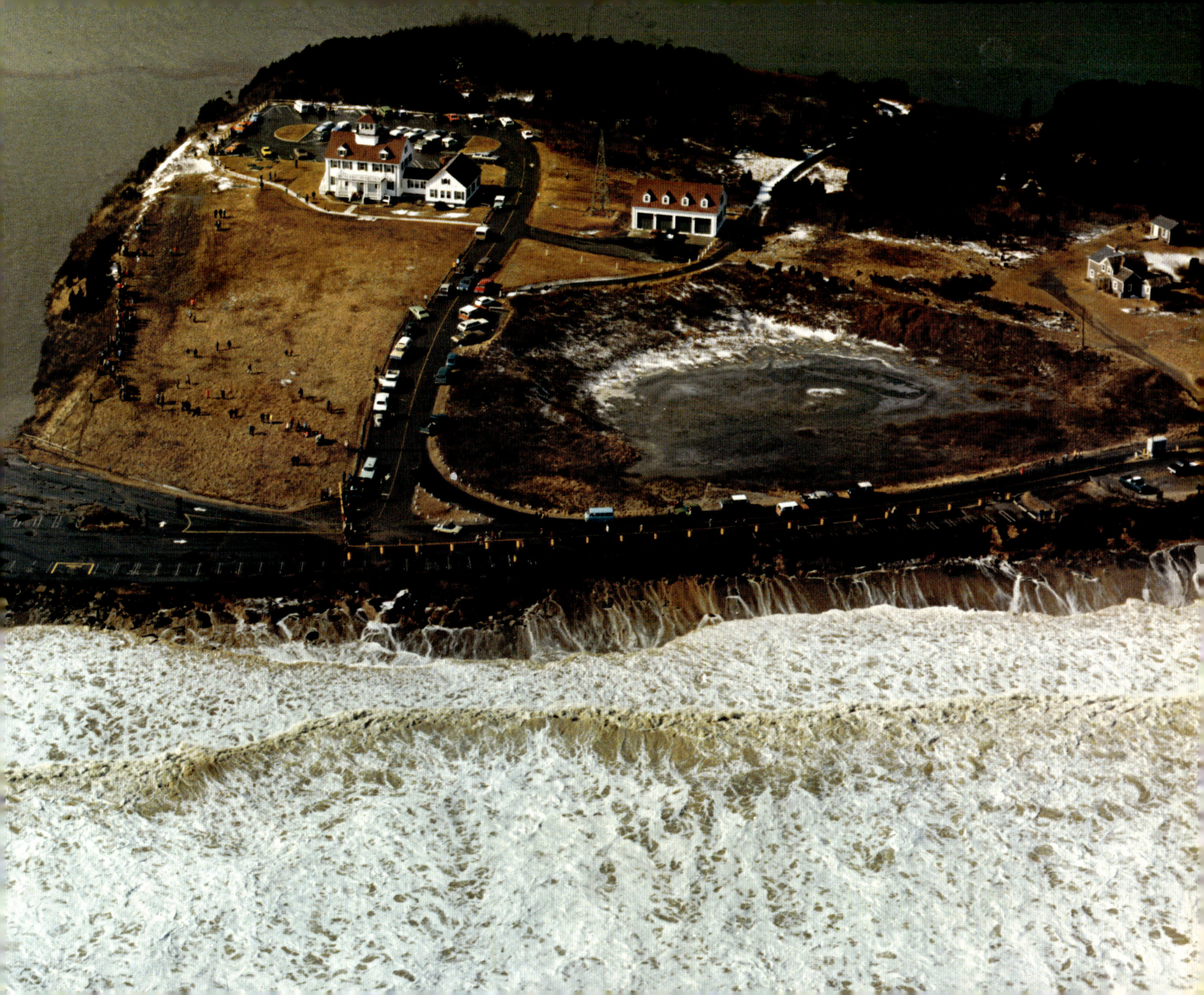

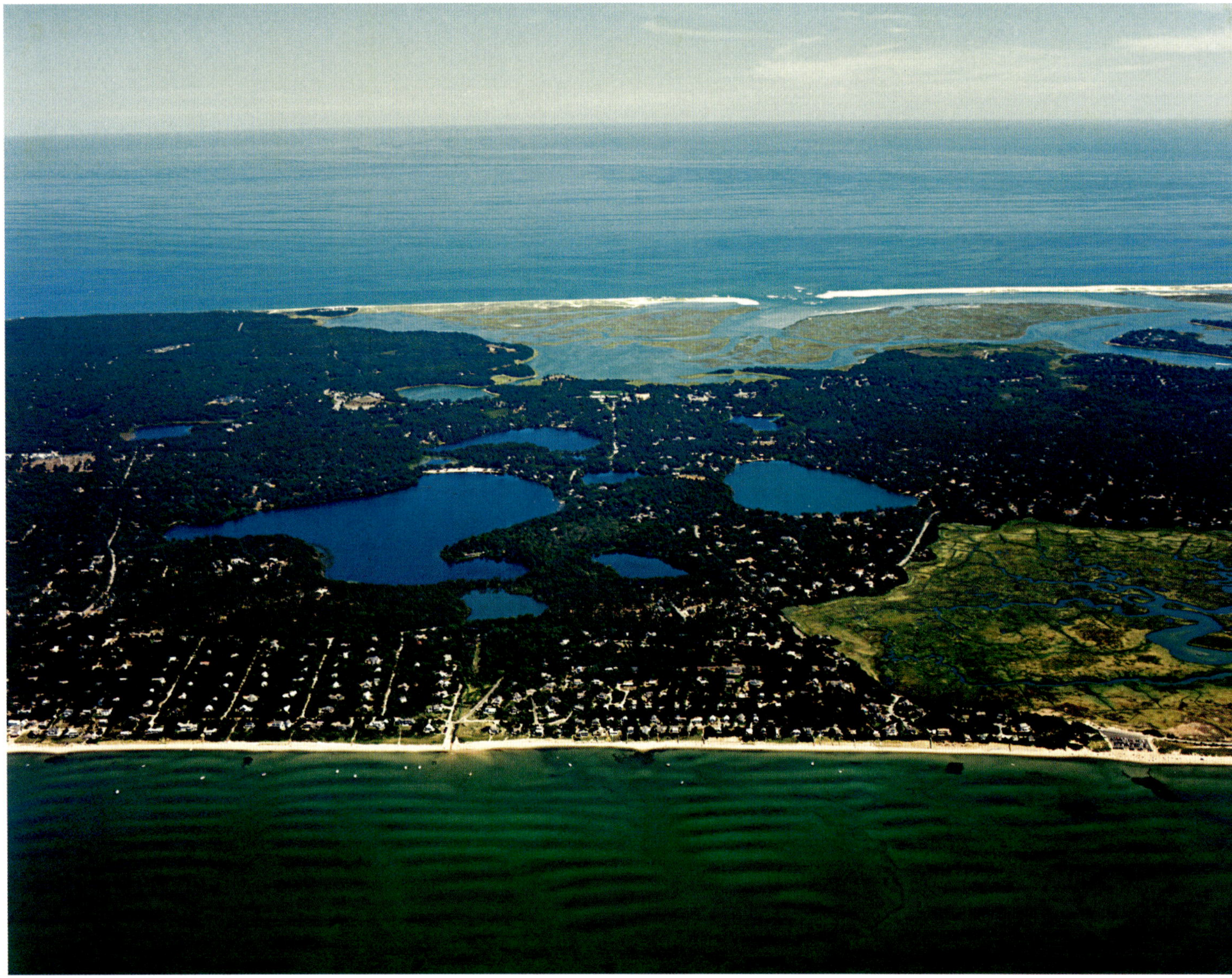

Bayside looking across Eastham to the Atlantic. Great Pond, Herring Pond and Long Pond are three largest ponds seen in the middle of the picture.

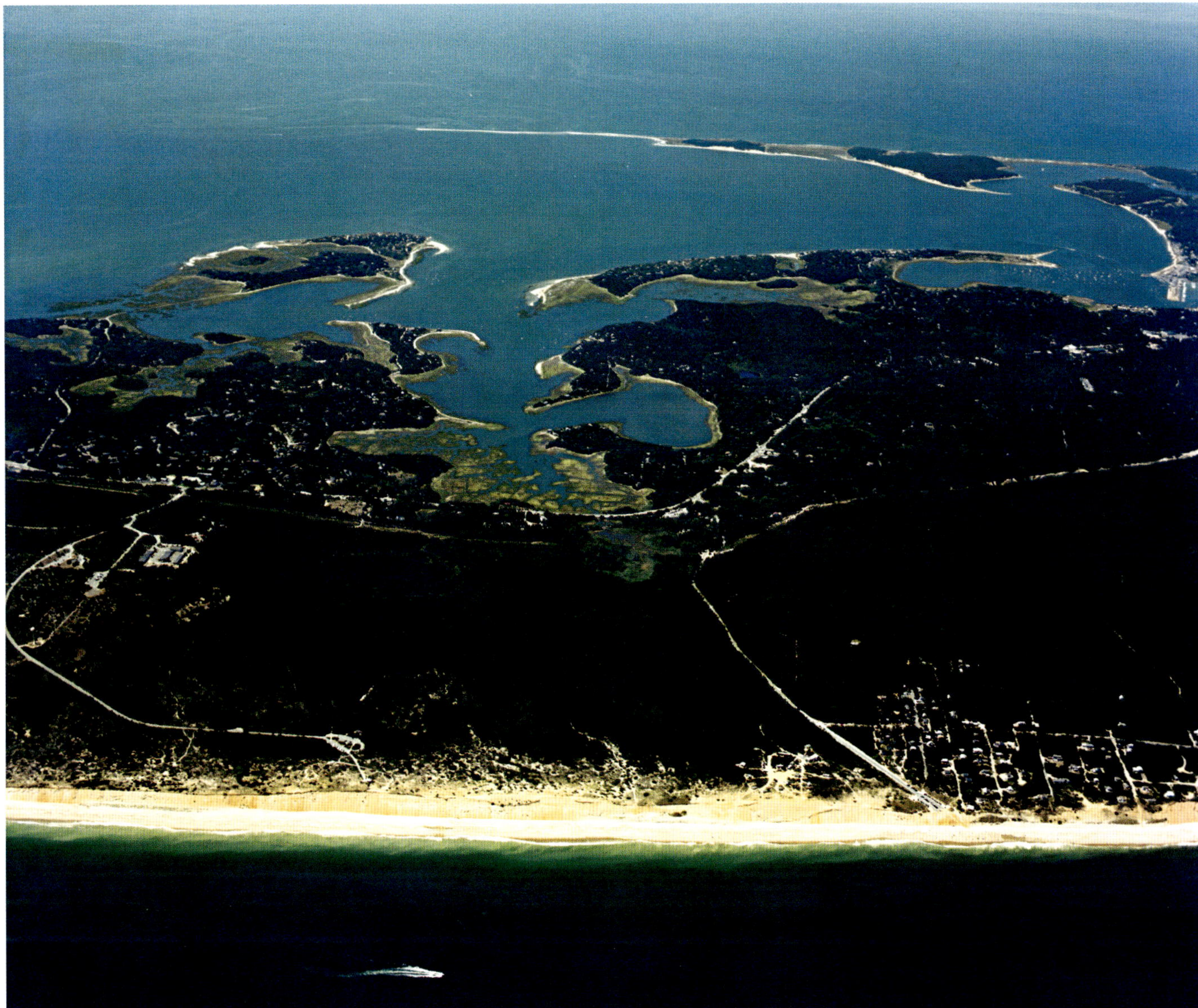

From the Atlantic looking across Wellfleet to Great Island and Cape Cod Bay. The road visible in the lower left leads to the Marconi Wireless Station, part of the Cape Cod National Seashore. In the upper middle Lieutenant Island (left) and Indian Neck are separated by Drummer Cove and Blackfish Creek.

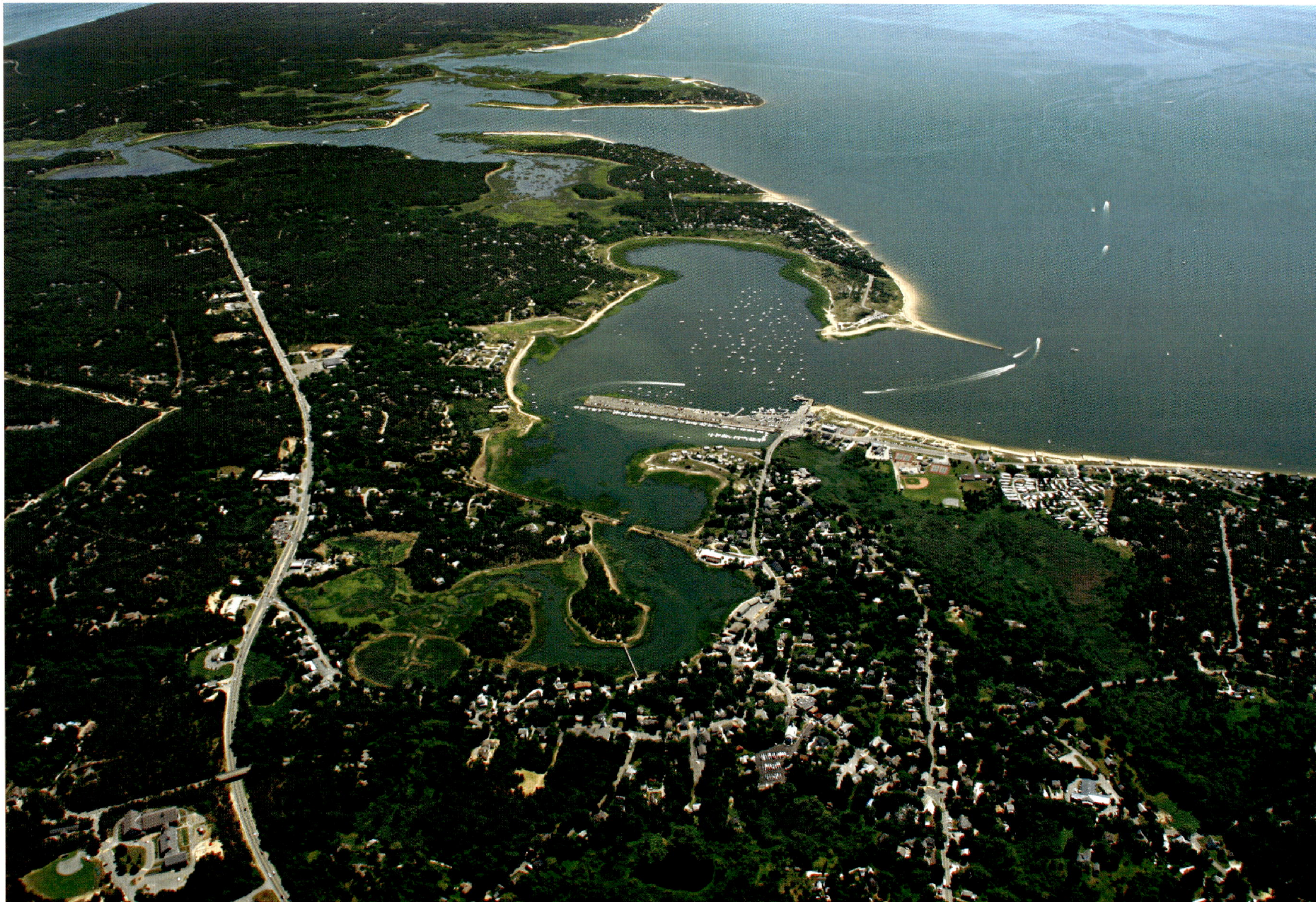

Wellfleet harbor looking towards Indian Neck.

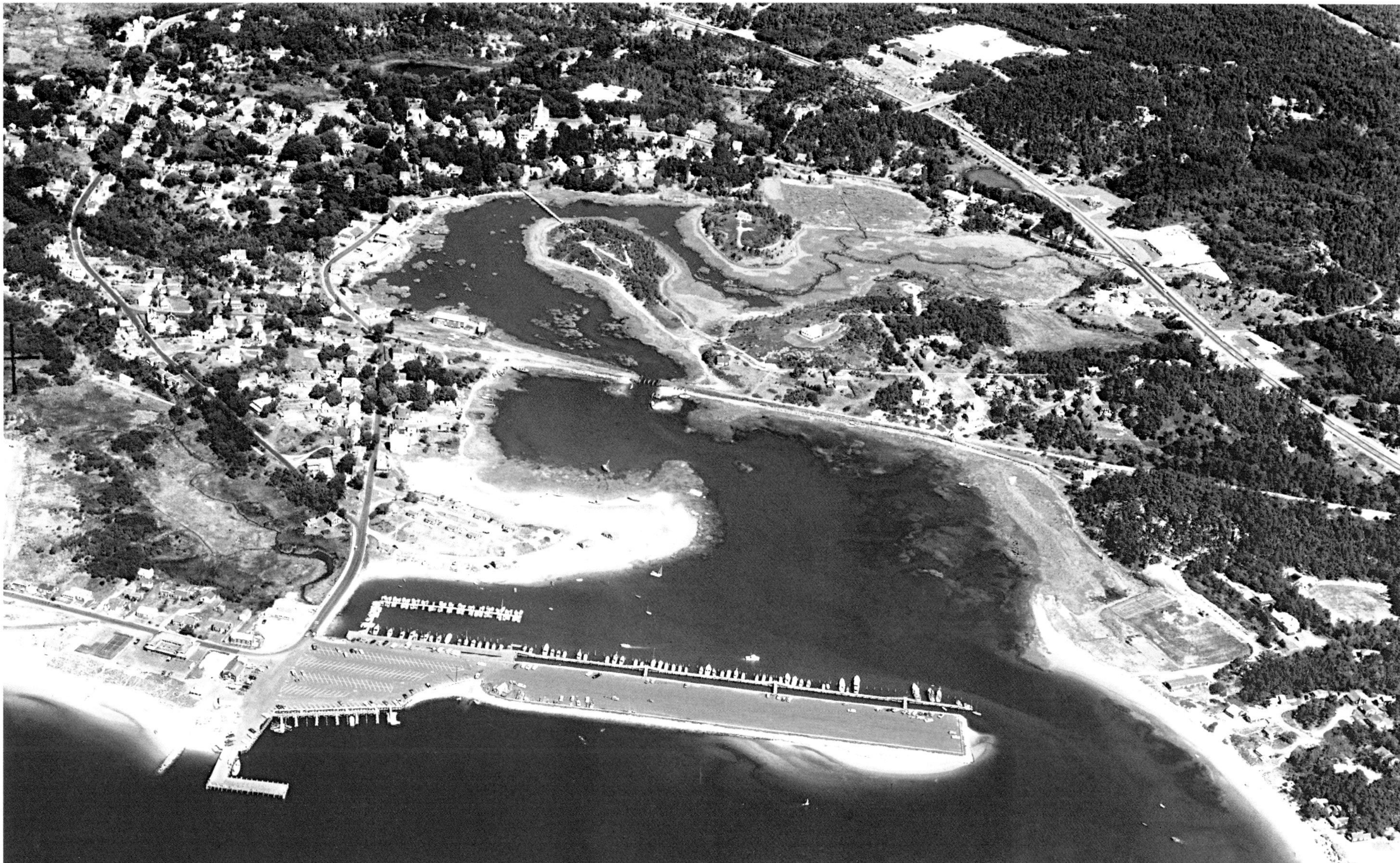

Wellfleet Harbor photographed in 1964.

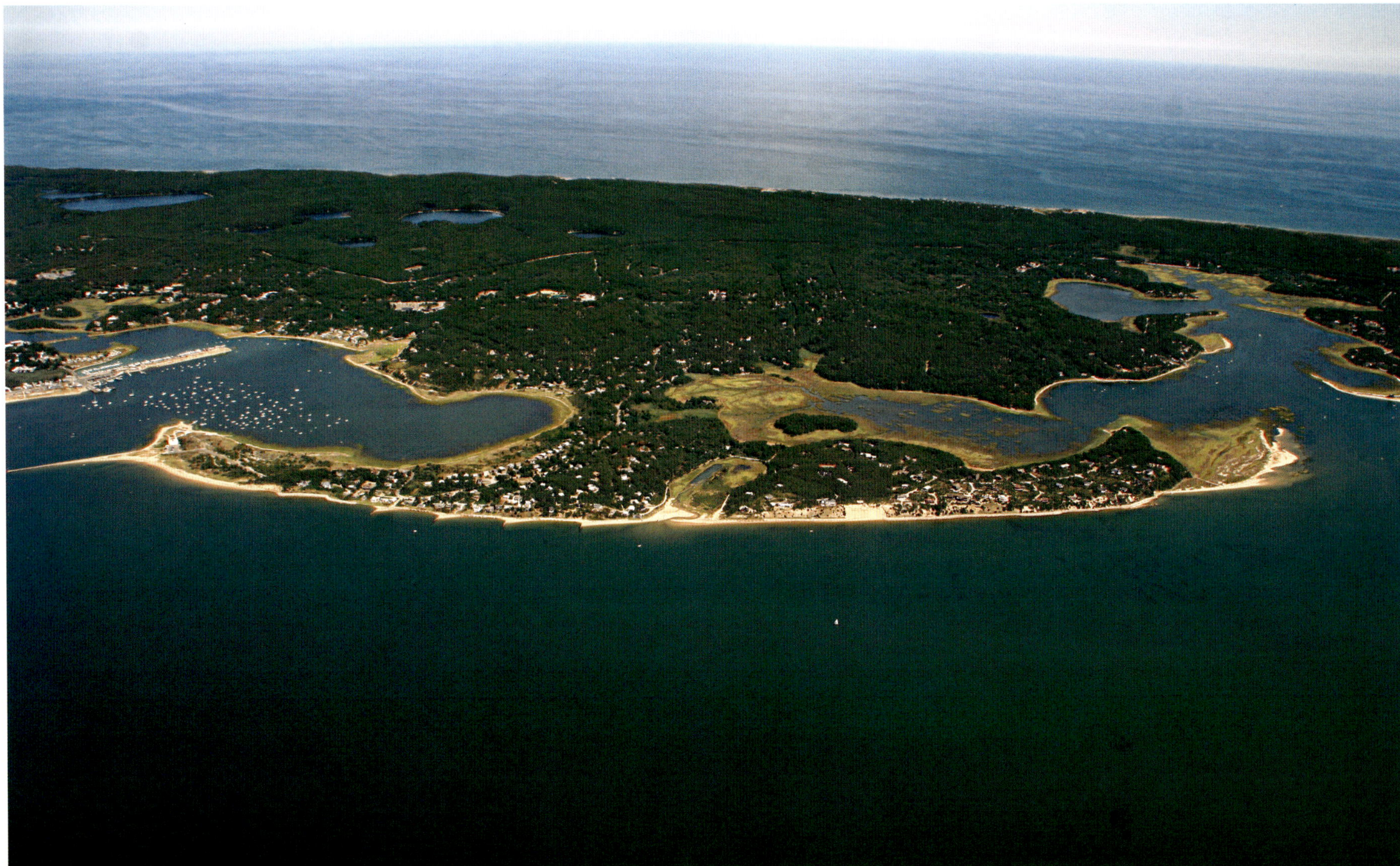

Indian Neck.

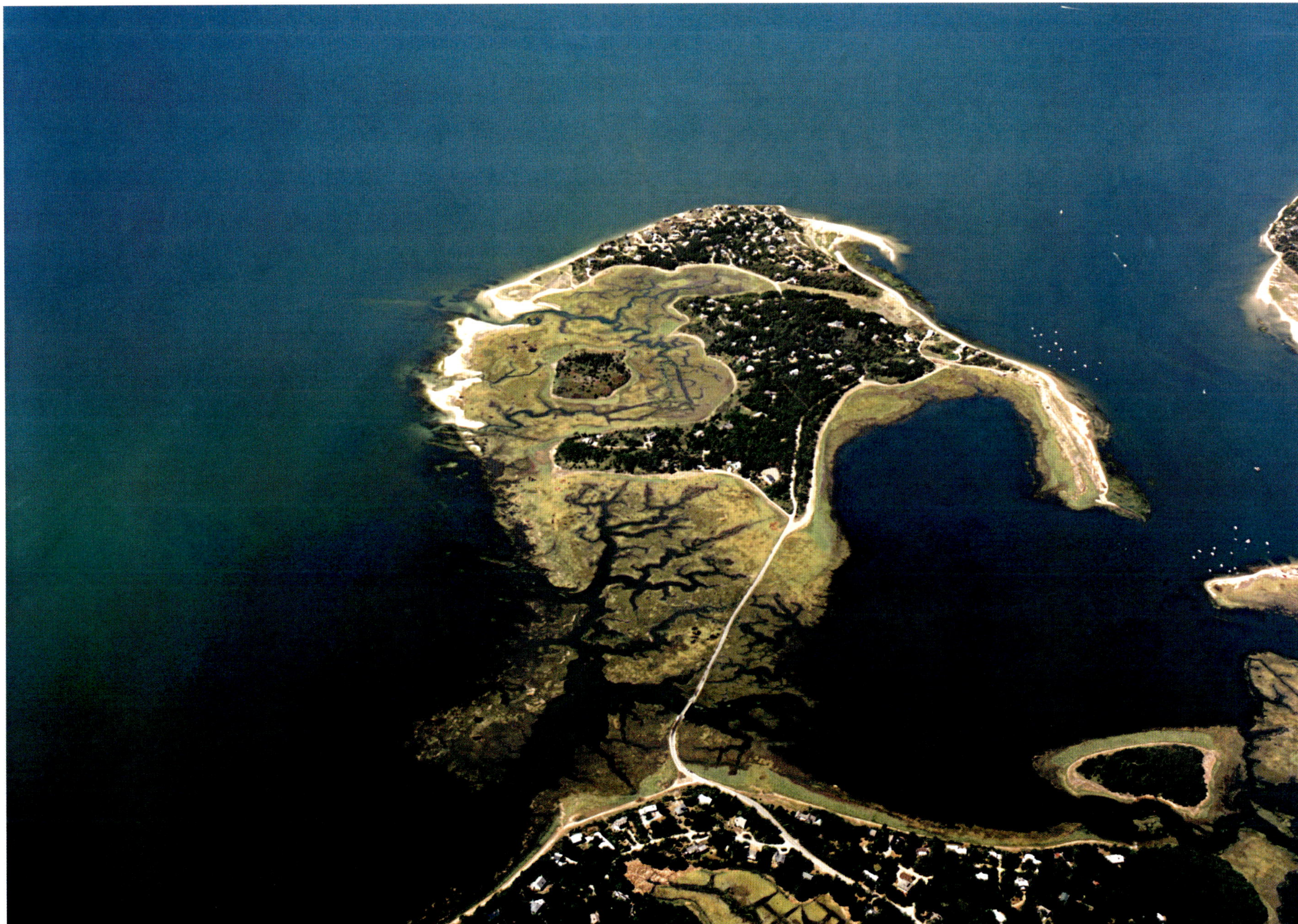

Lieutenant Island.

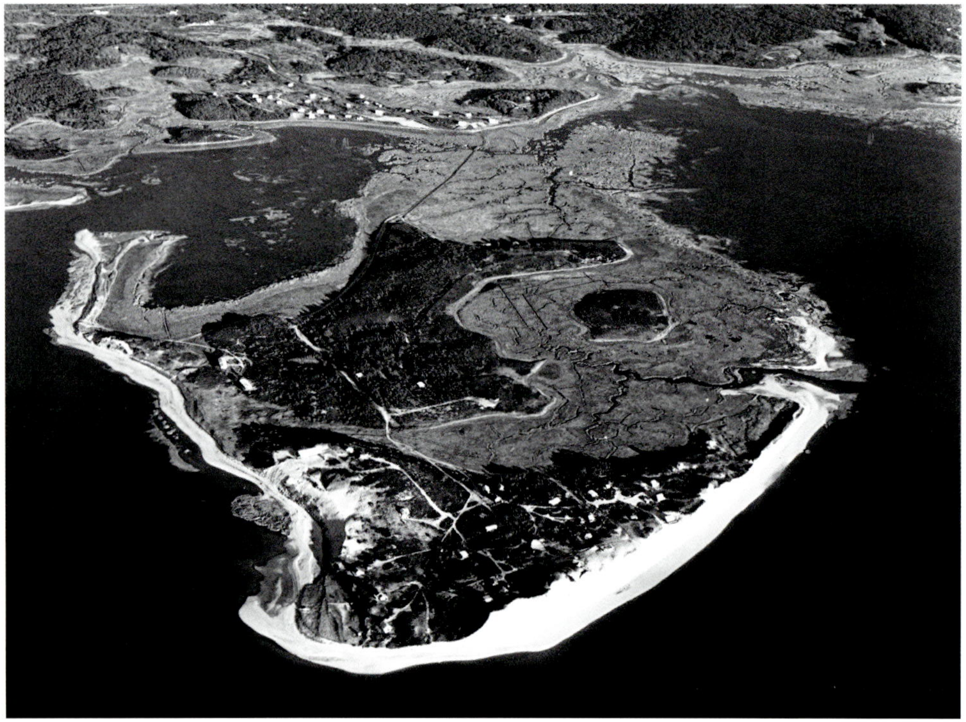

Lieutenant Island, natural, 1966, and
Lieutenant Island iced-in, 1981.

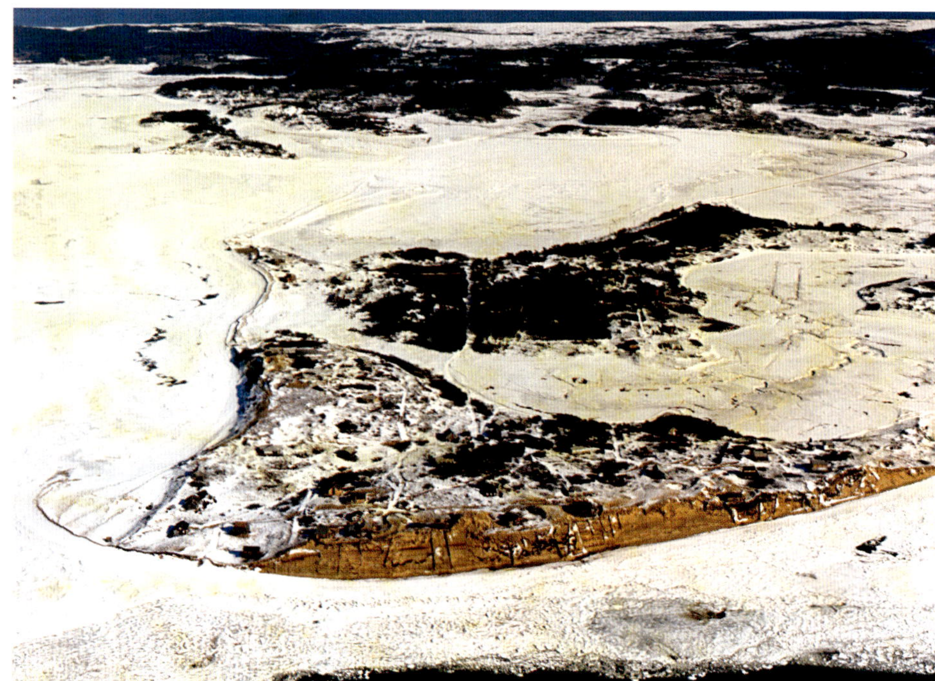

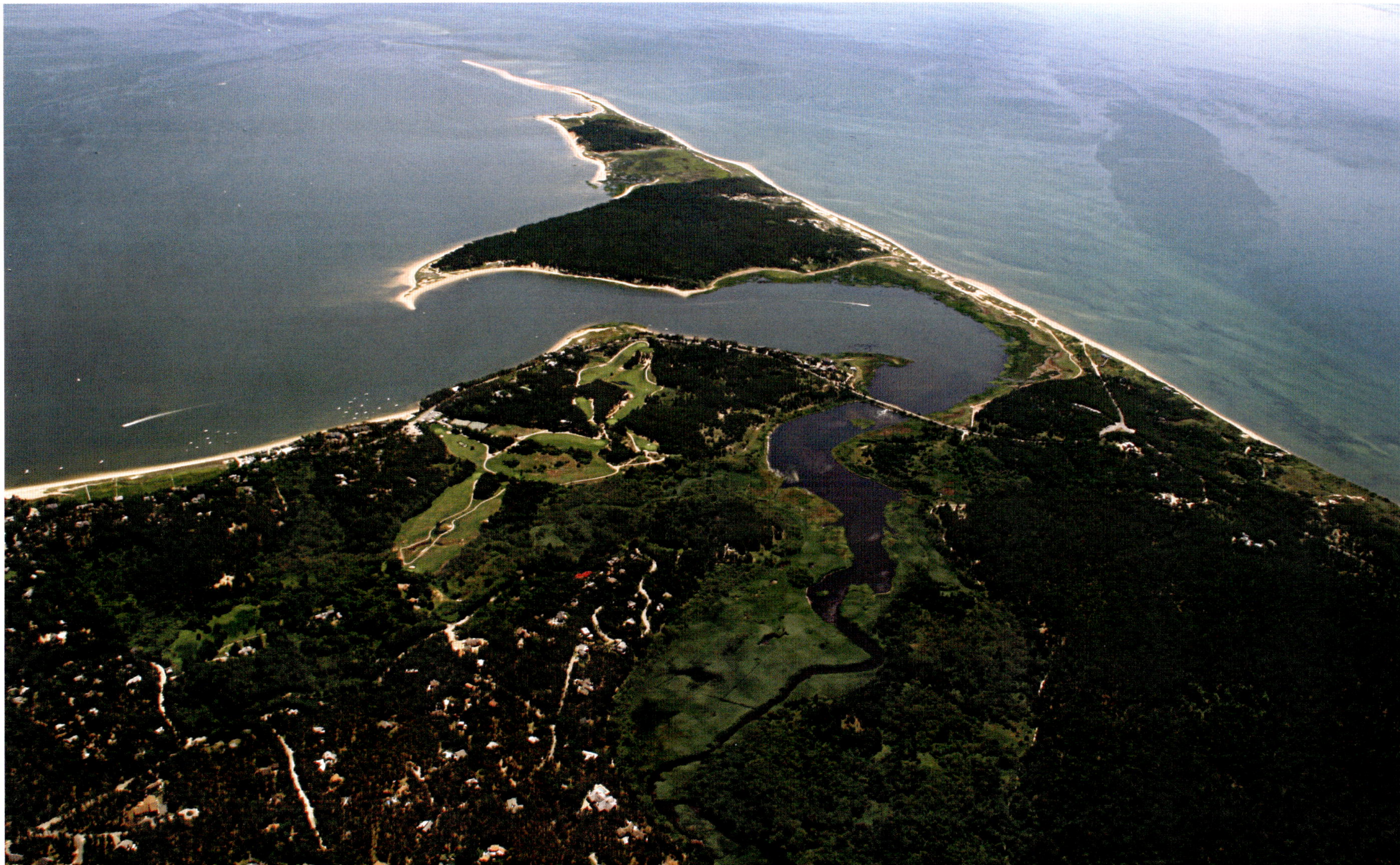

The Herring River marshes, Chequessett golf course and Great Island.

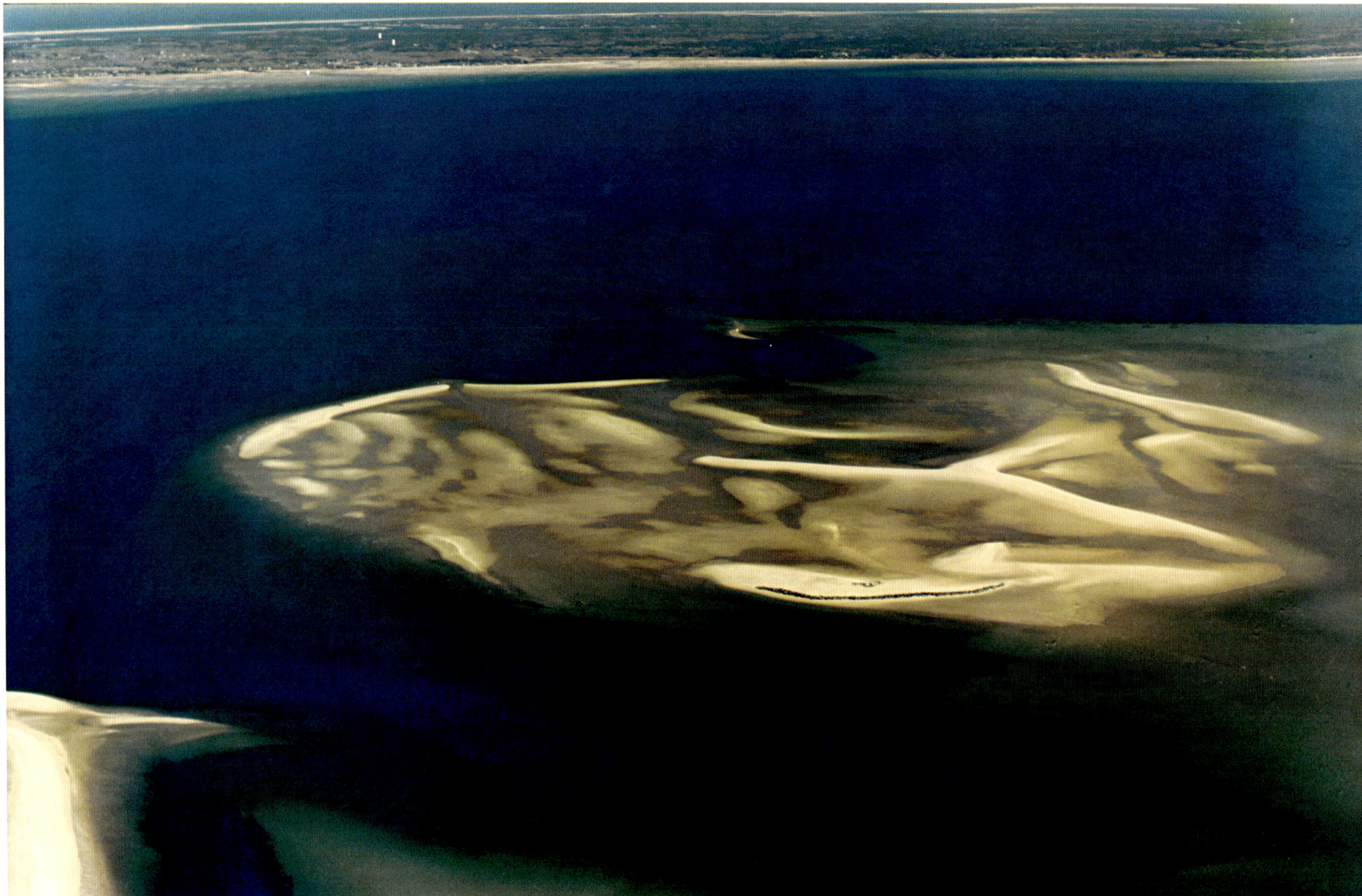

The tidal patterns of Billingsgate Shoal lies off of Great Island.

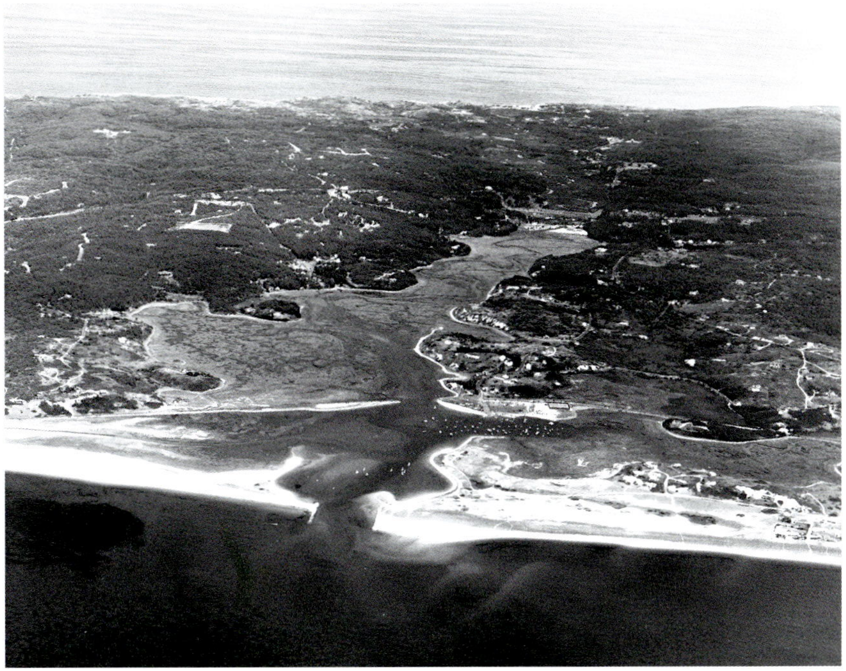

An older and recent view of Pamet harbor shown from Cape Cod Bay, 1970 and 2007. Pamet river runs across to Ballston Beach.

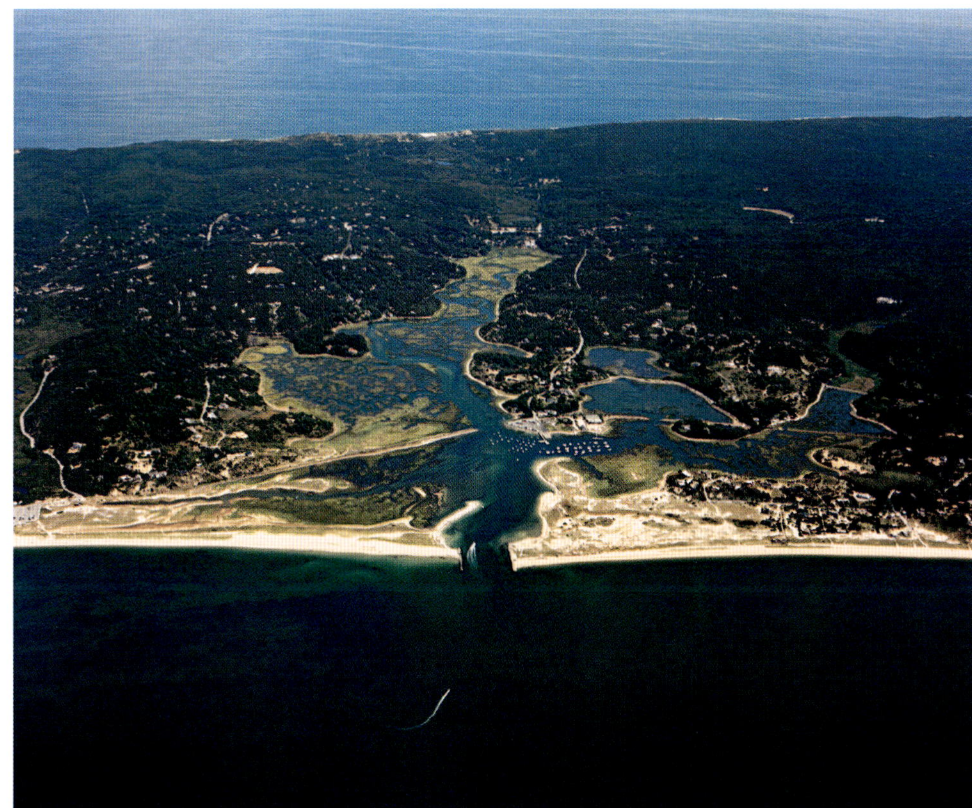

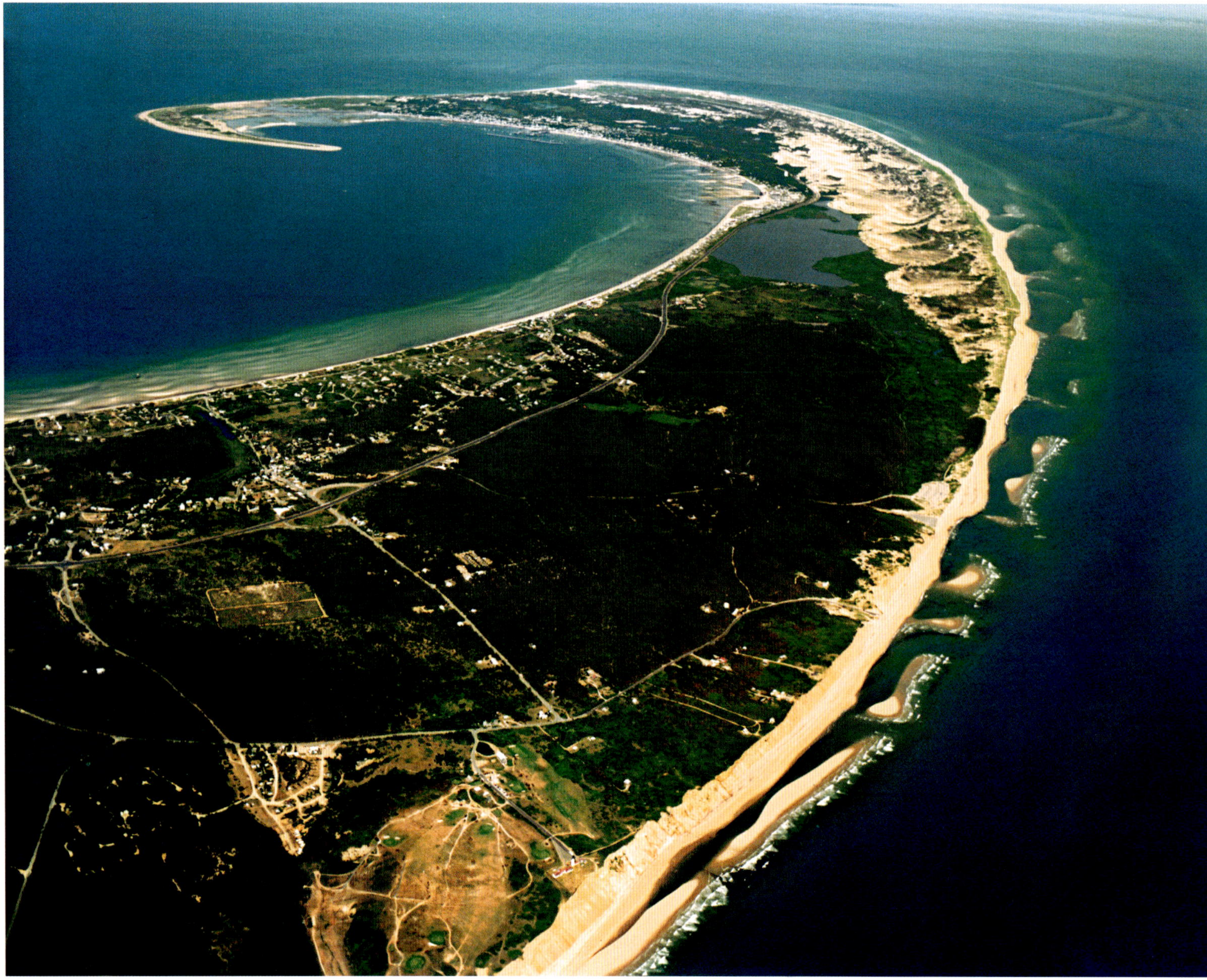

The outer arm of Cape Cod includes the Highland Lighthouse and golf course.

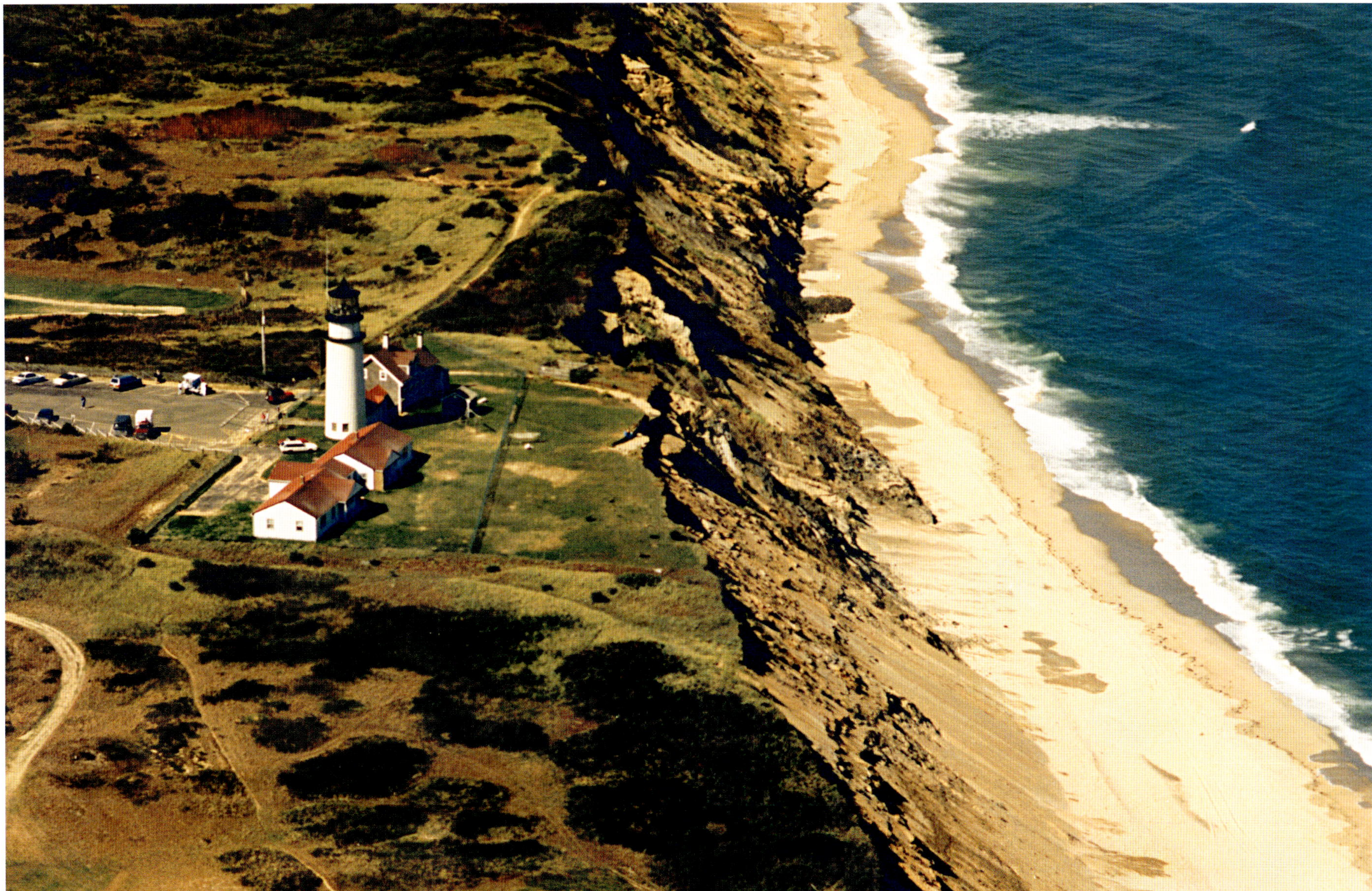

Erosion, as shown in this 1993 photo, is the main reason the lighthouse was moved back almost 500 feet in 1996.

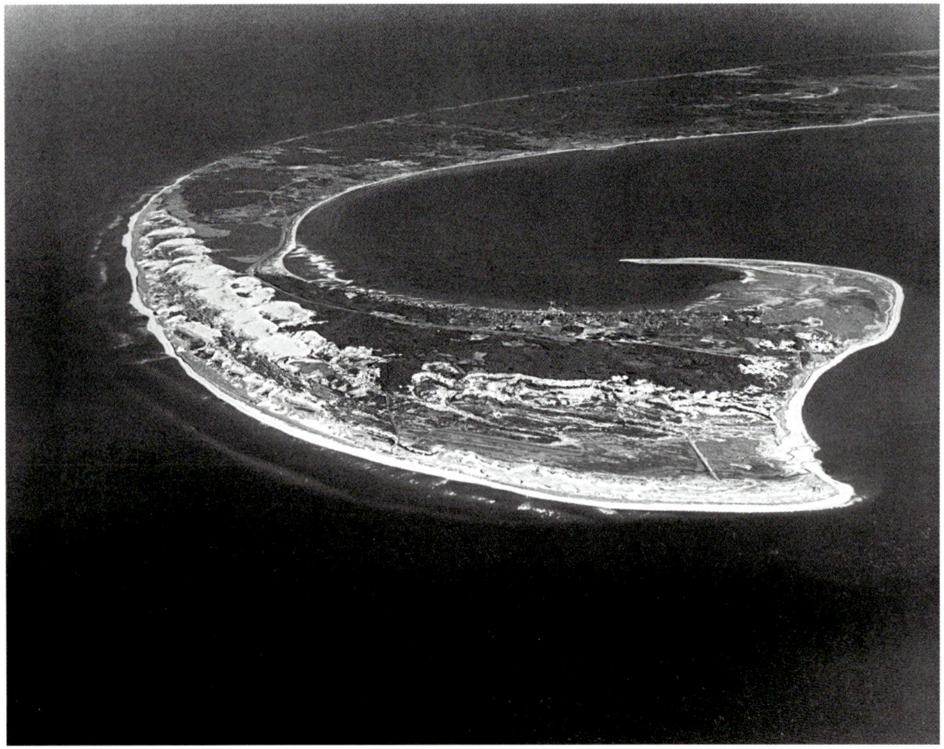

These two high-altitude Airviews of Provincetown show the outermost curve of Cape Cod, 1950 and 2007.

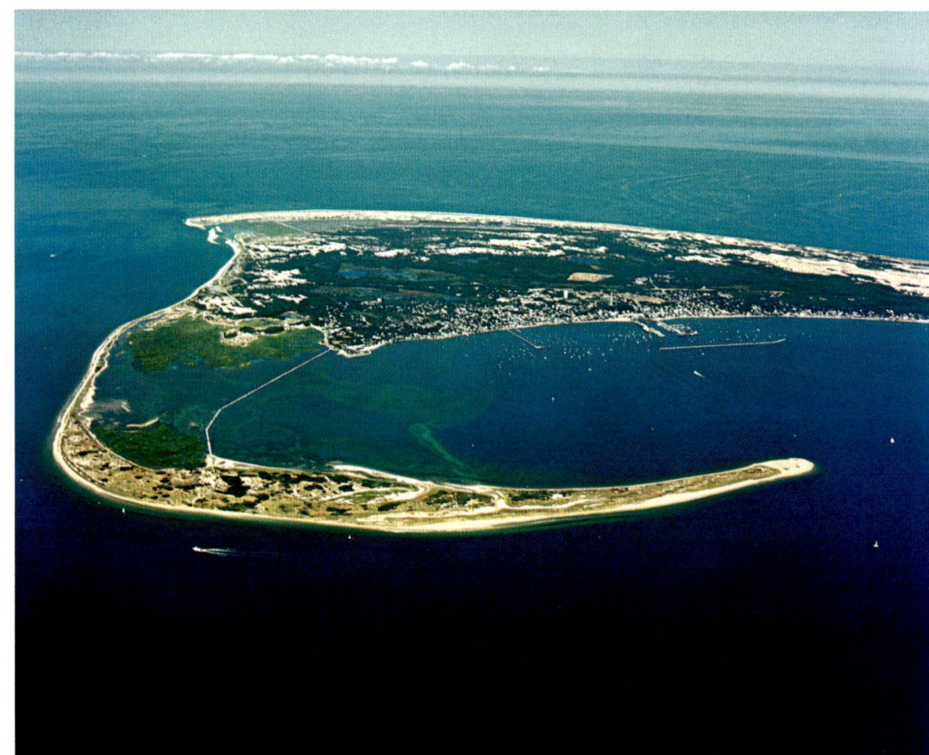

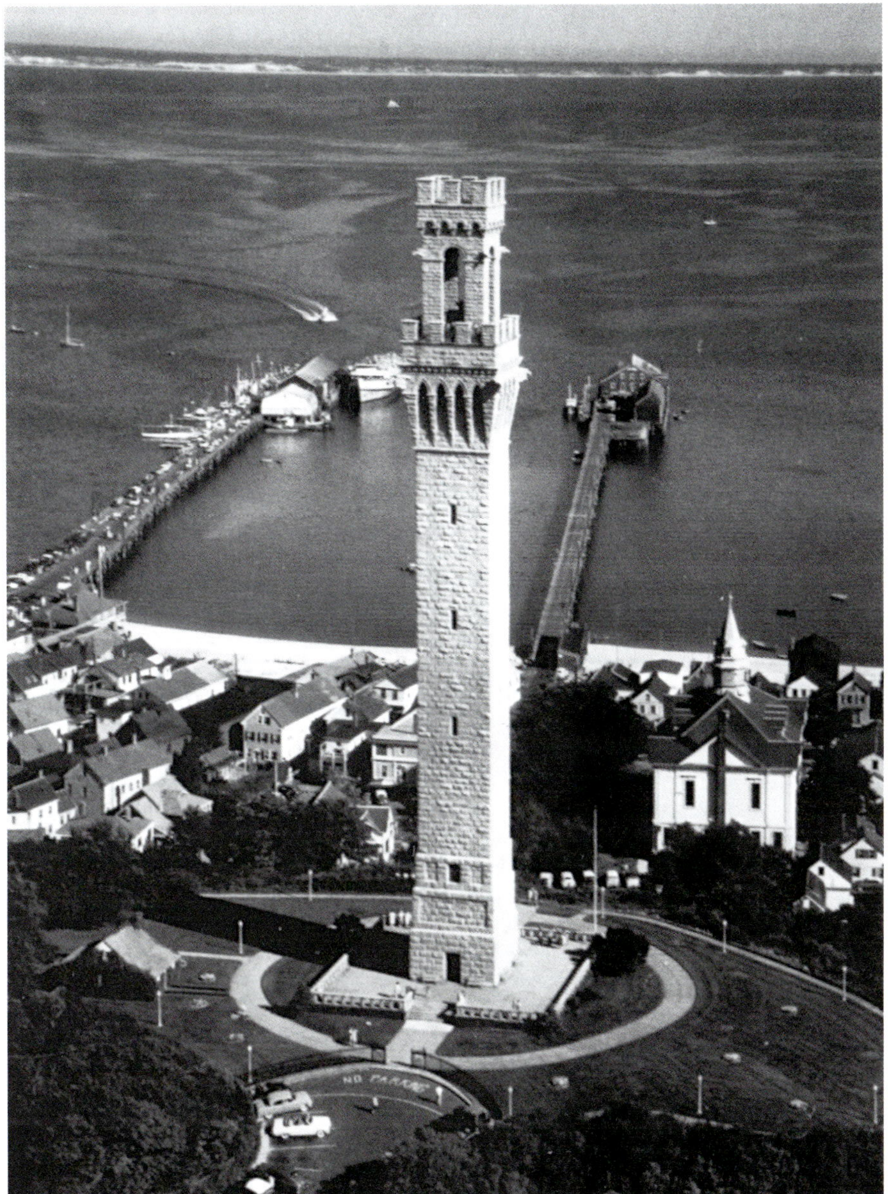

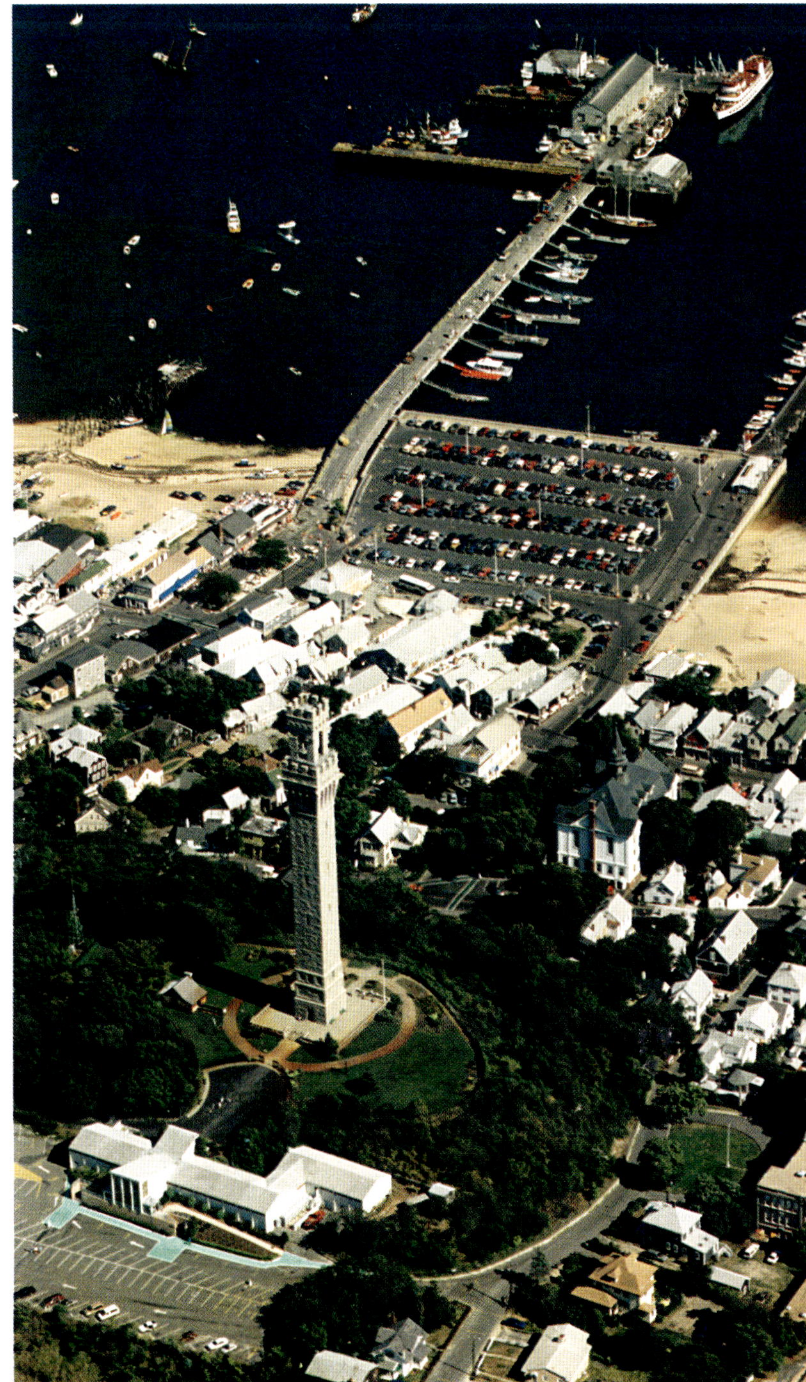

Provincetown's Pilgrim Monument, taken around 1955 and agin in 1987.

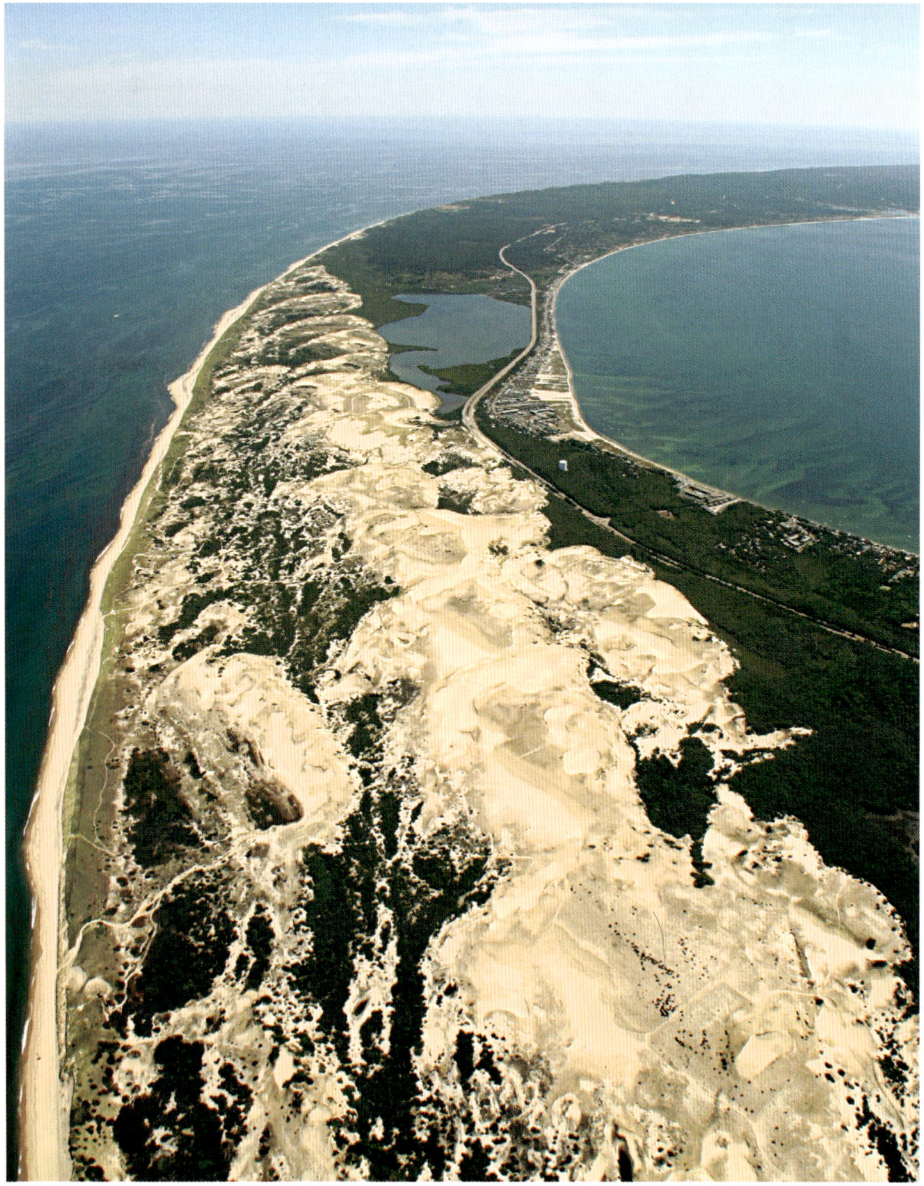

The sand dunes display a parabolic shape.

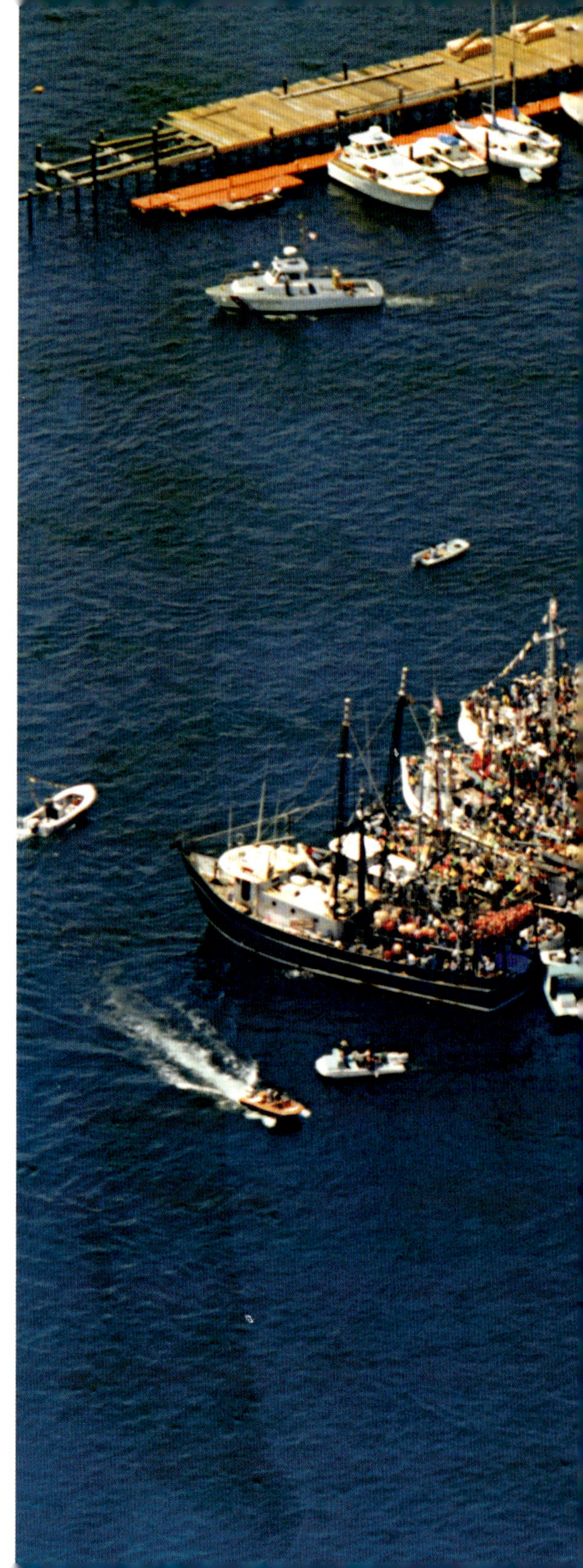

The Blessing of the Fleet is an annual celebration.

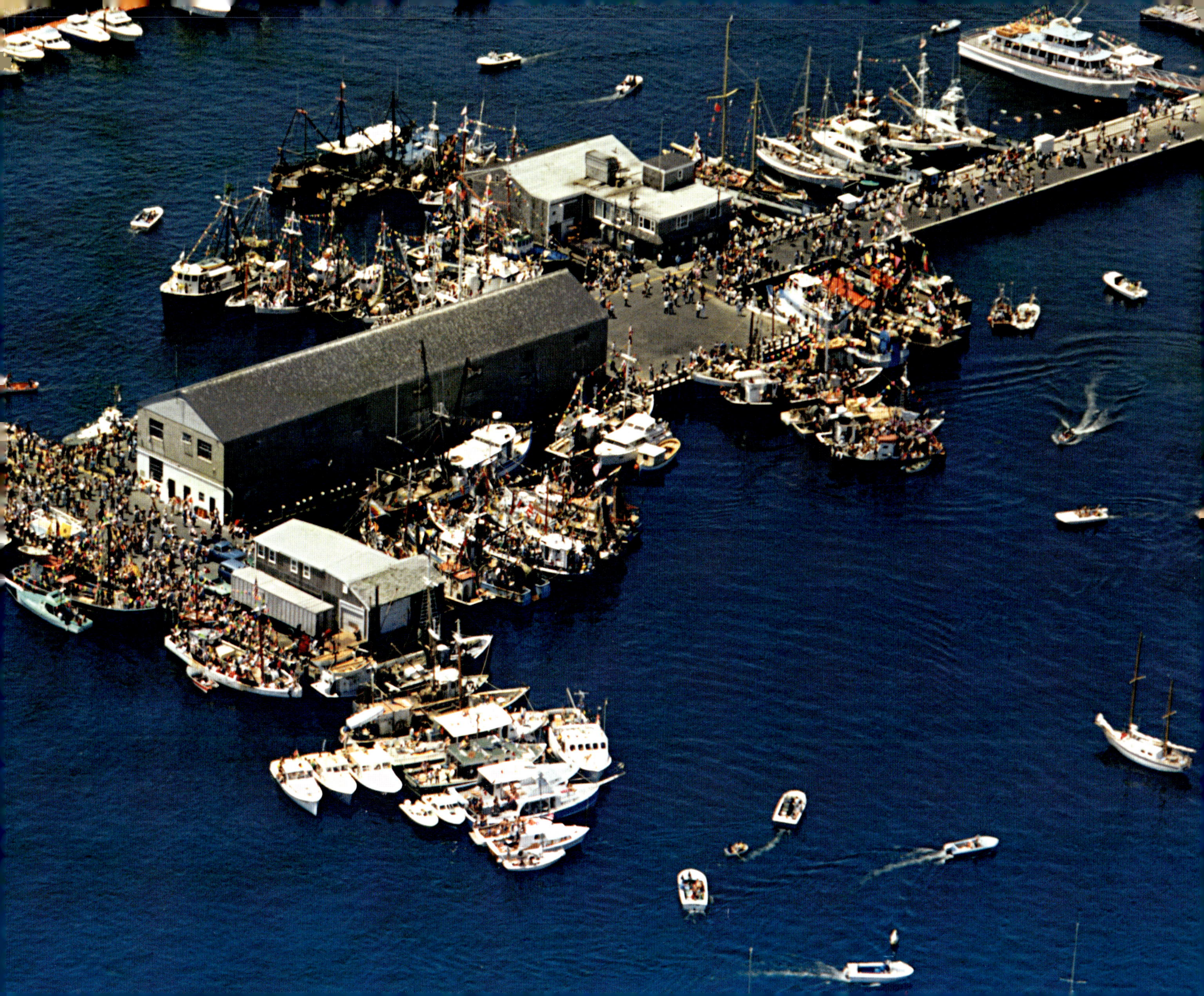

Chapter 6
Abstracts

Natural wonders are evident everywhere. While flying over sand and water I will many times see an artist's canvas in motion. Every angle will produce a different image of astounding color and form, some very tranquil others quite bizarre. In some cases the natural abstracts have fractal symmetry to them, the patterns of Mother Nature repeat themselves. The following images are some of our favorites.

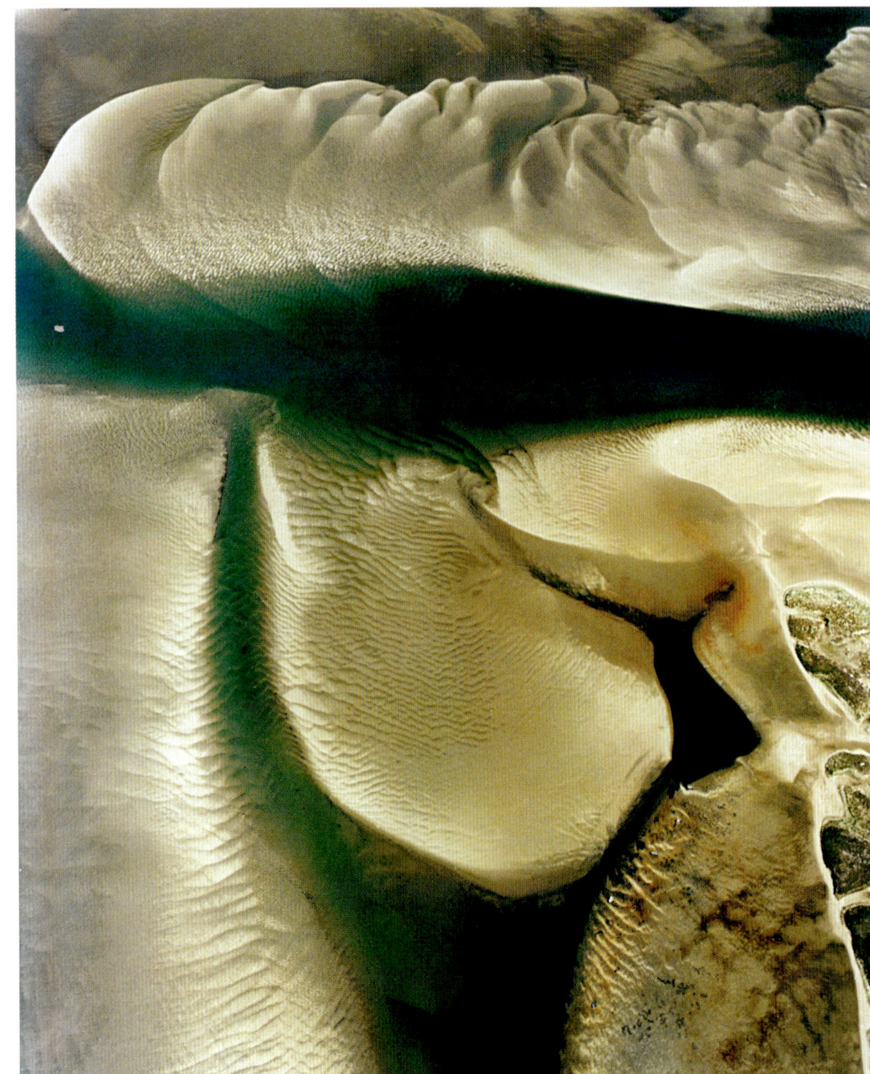

The Hand.

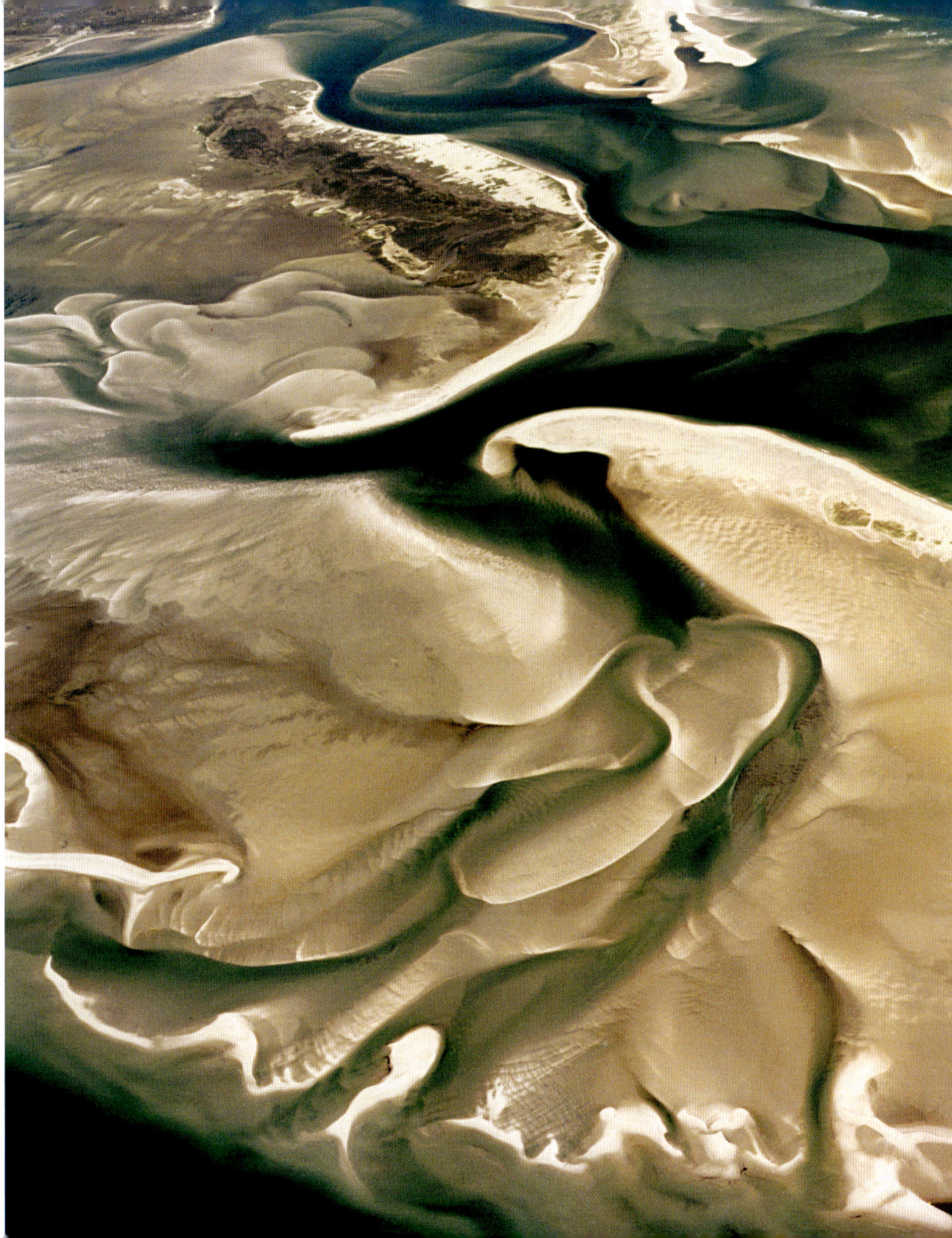

Sand Collar.

Angel Wings.
{next 2-pages}

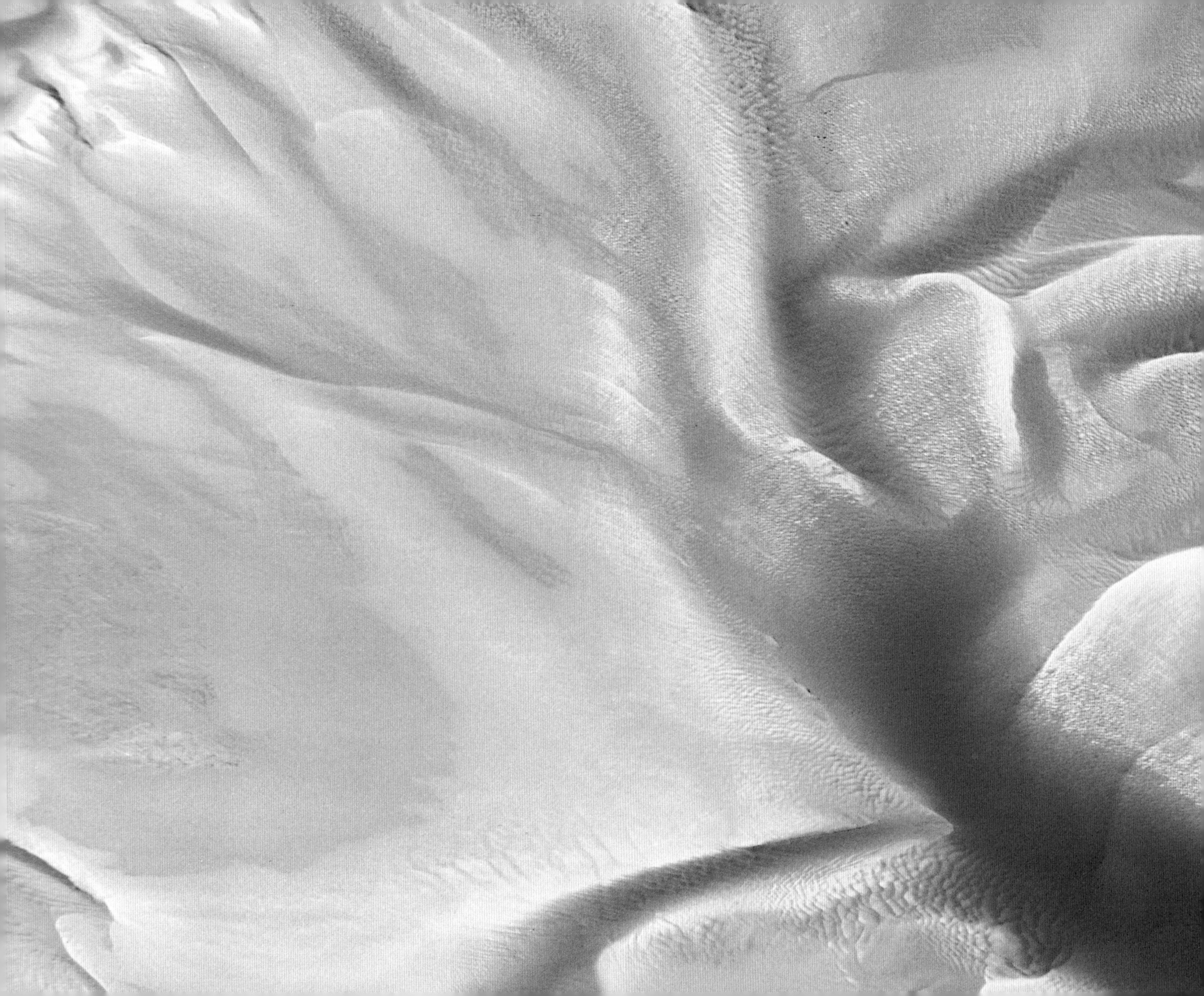

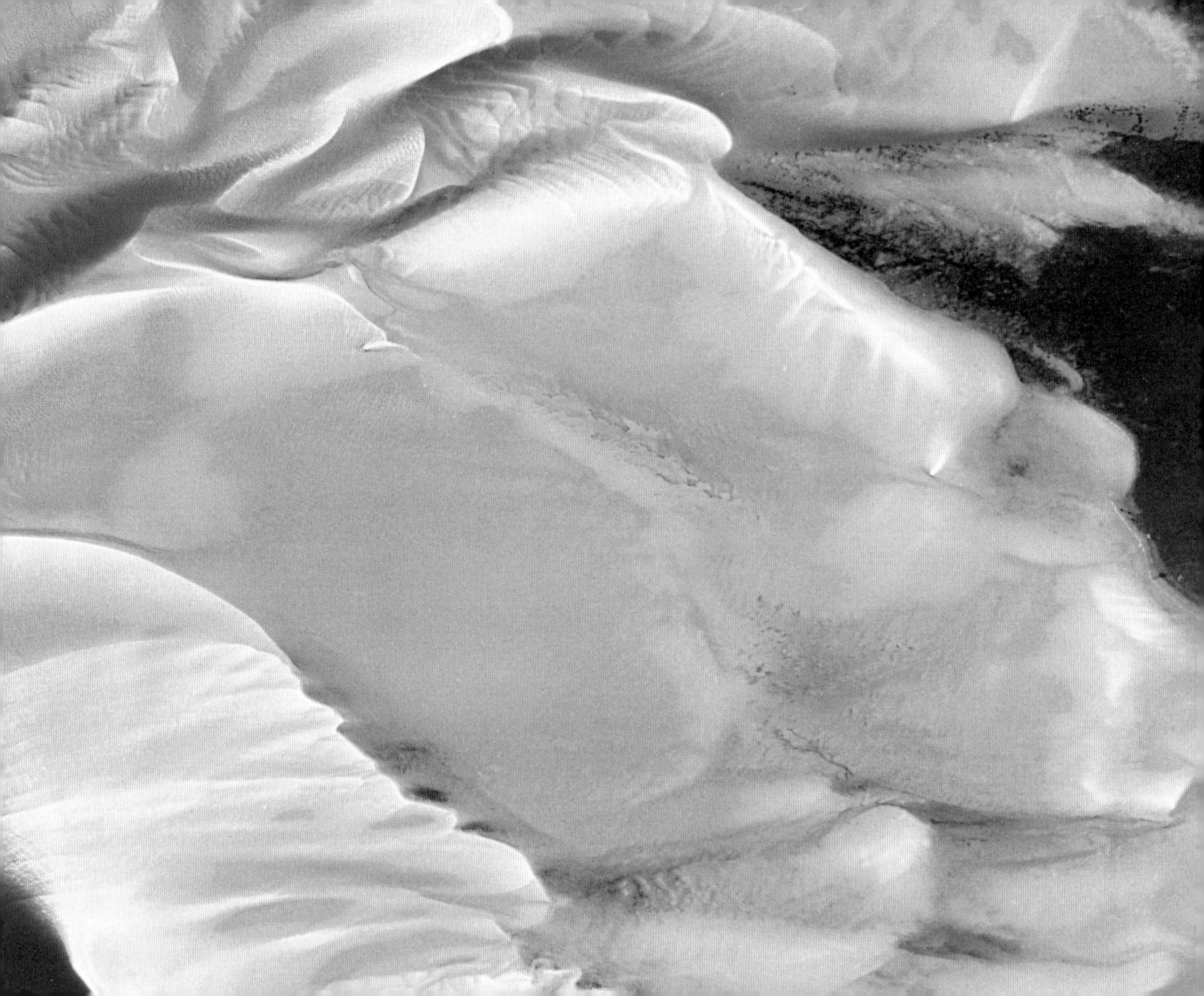

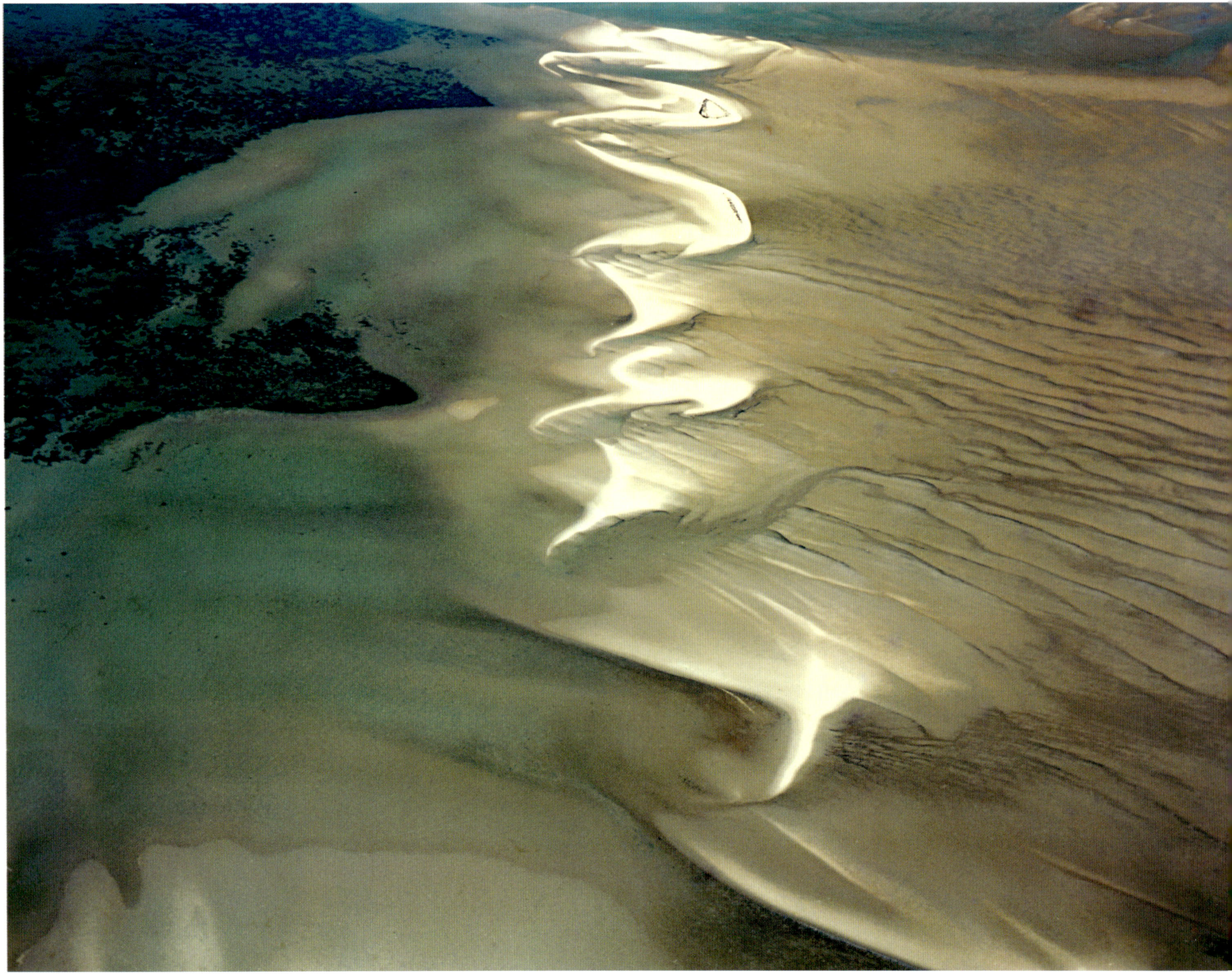

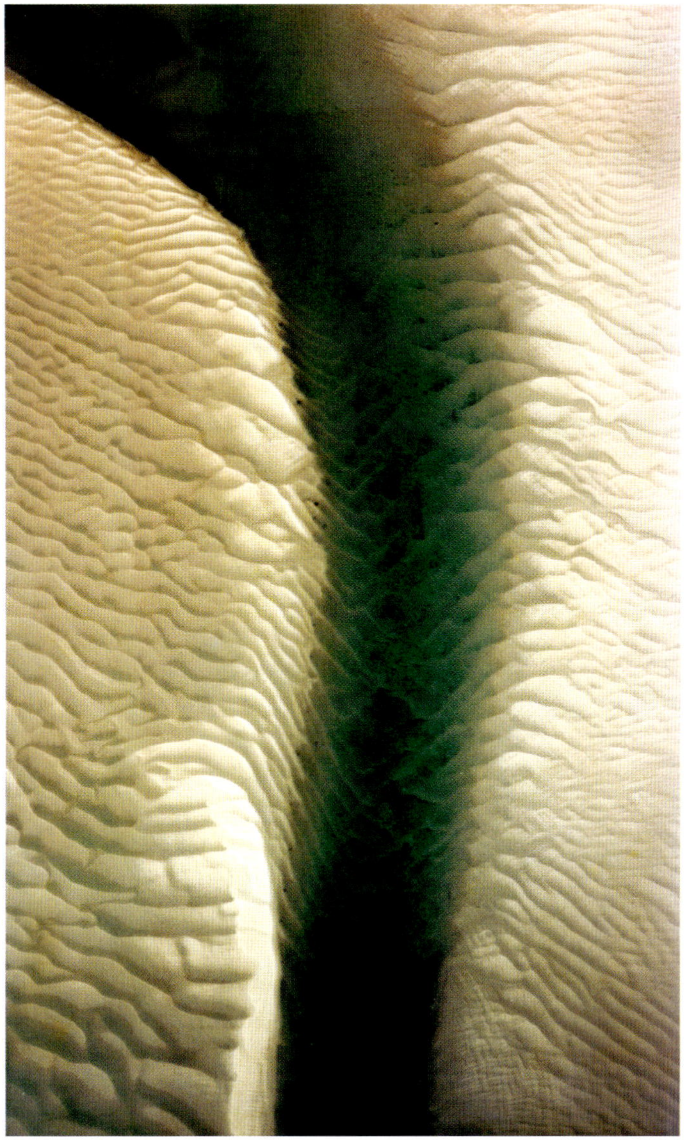

Worm Hole.

Neptune.

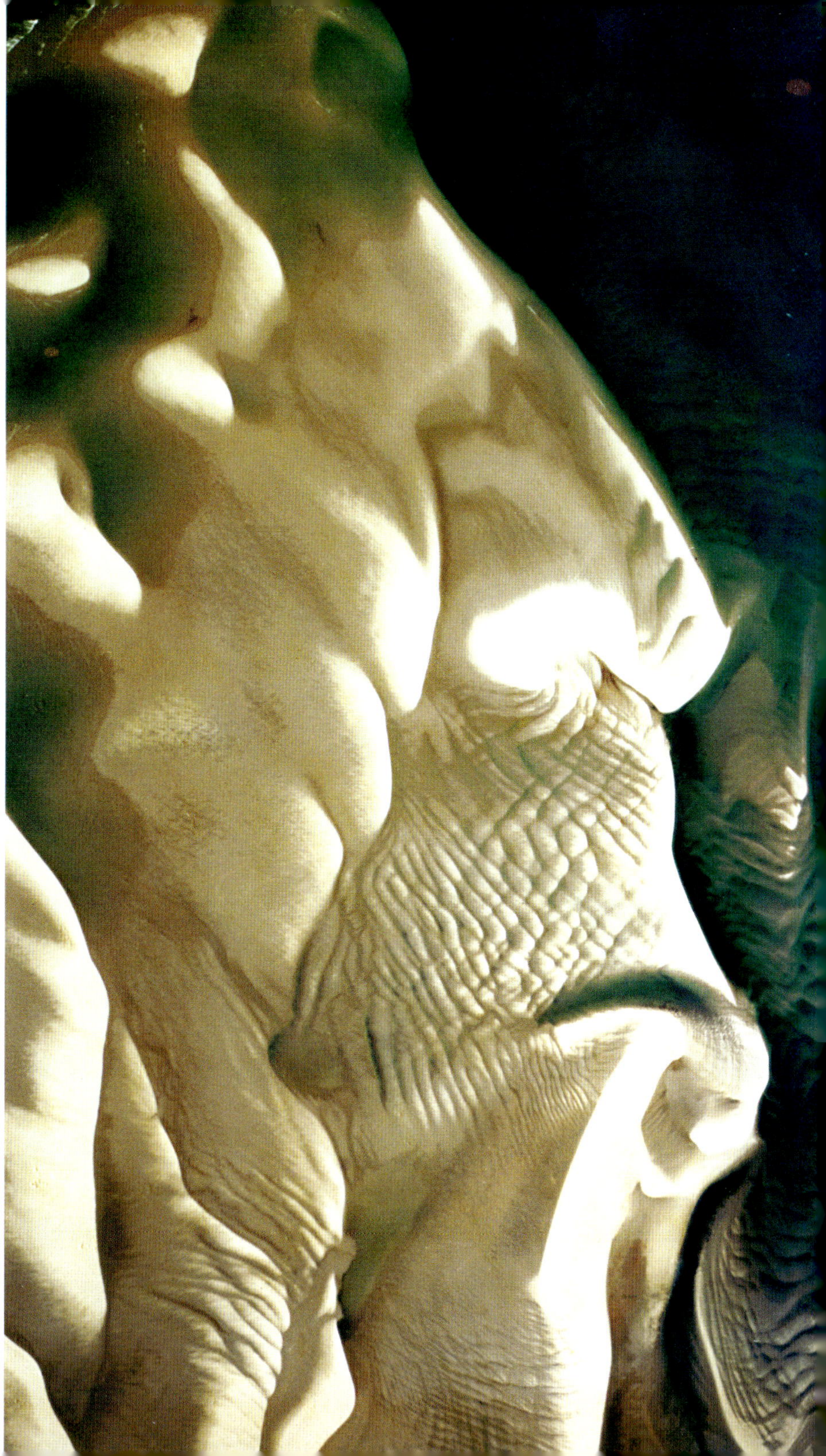

Sand Slalom.{opposite}

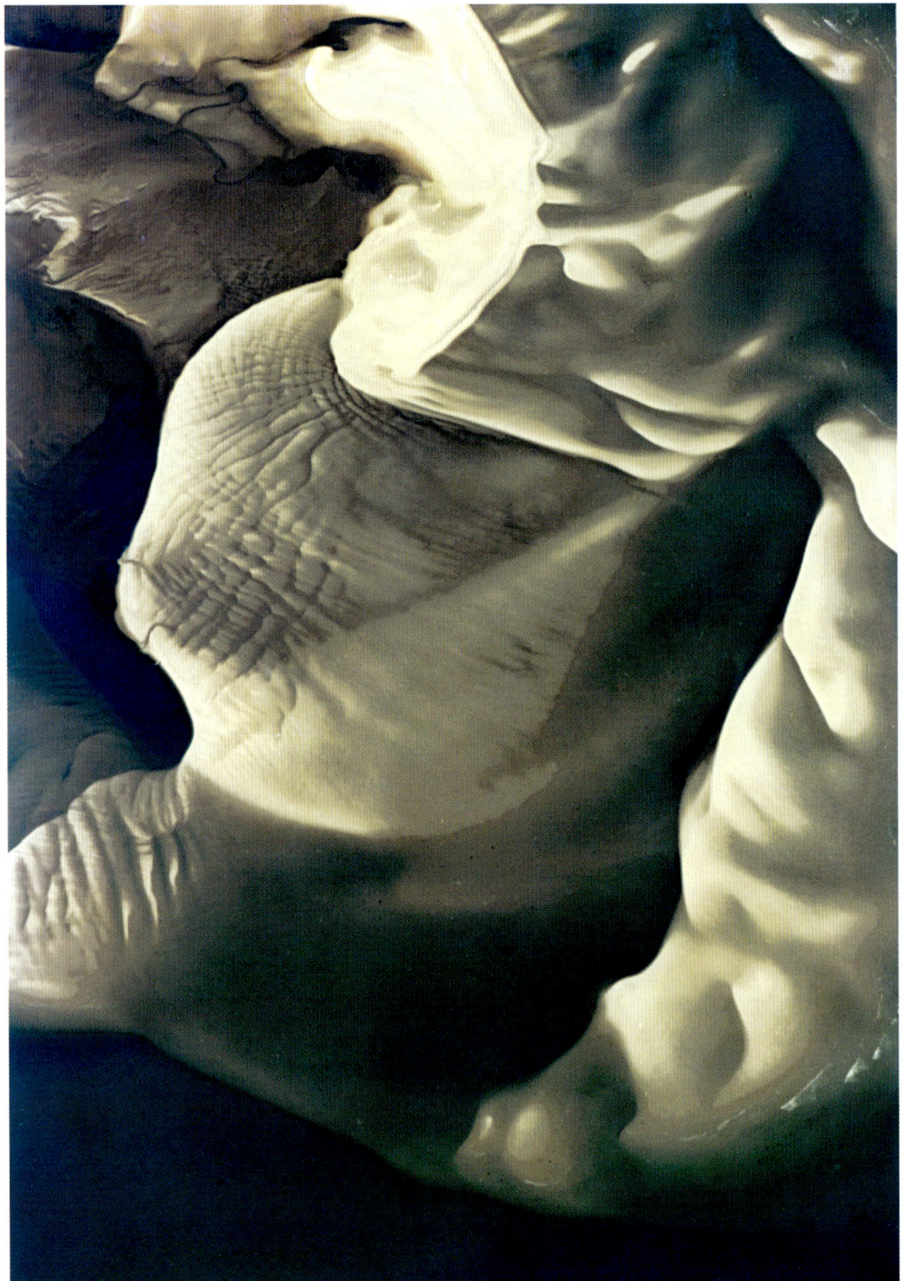

Untitled #1.

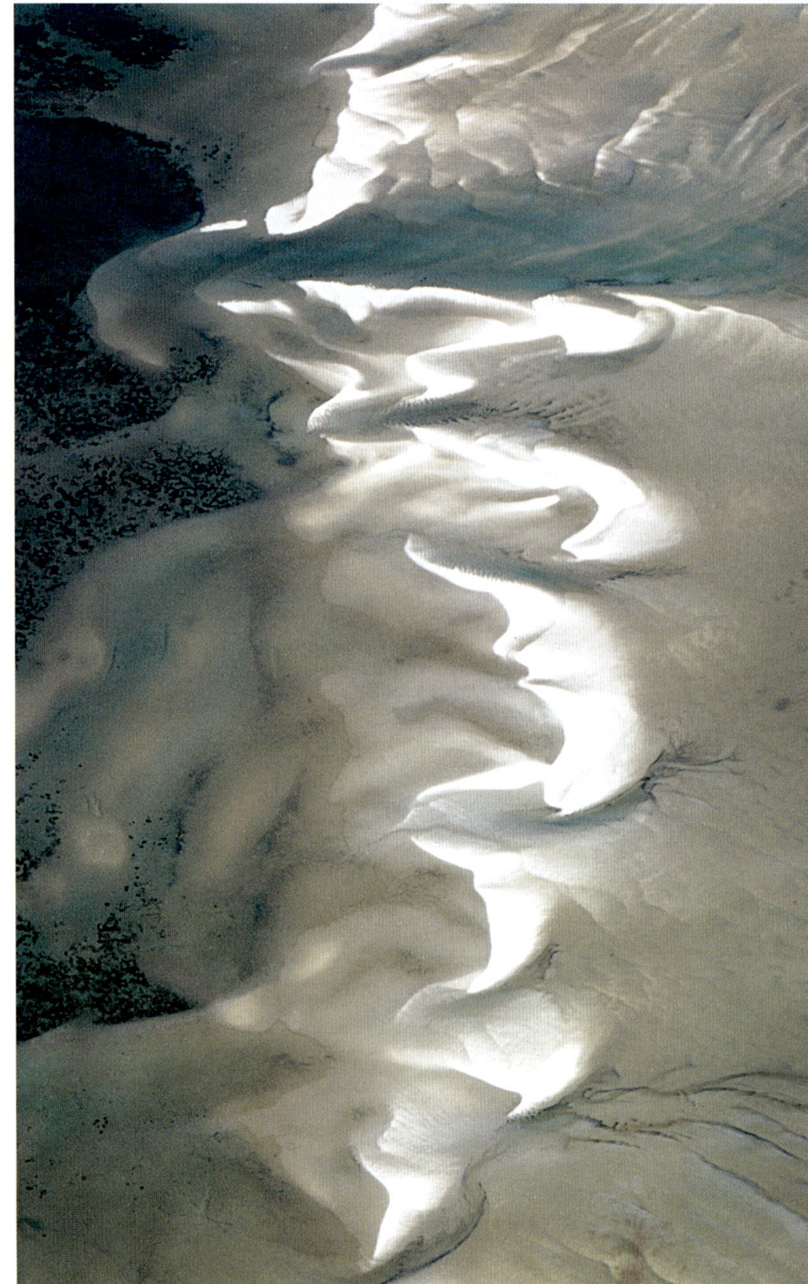

Whale Tail.

Funnel Cloud.{opposite}

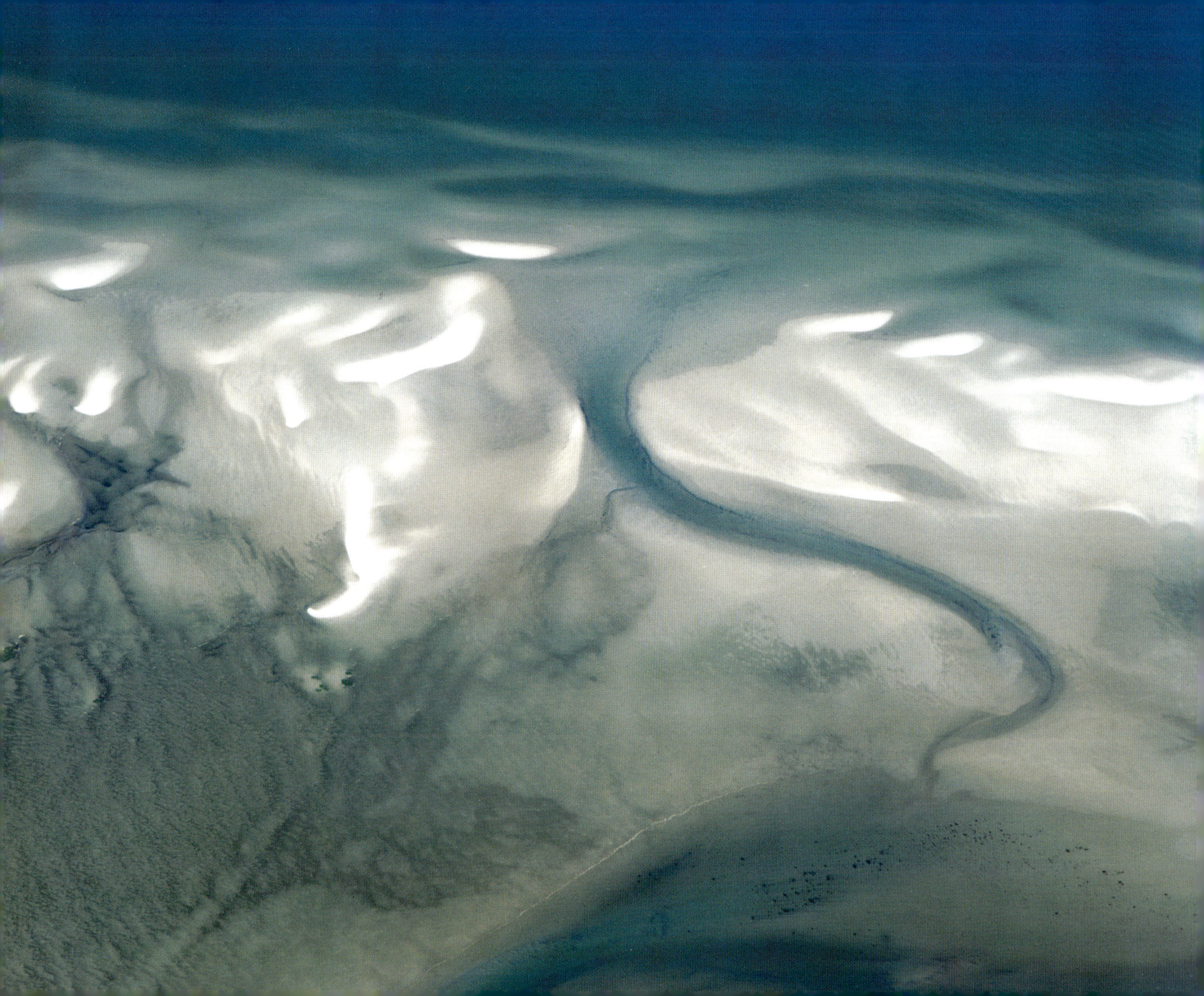

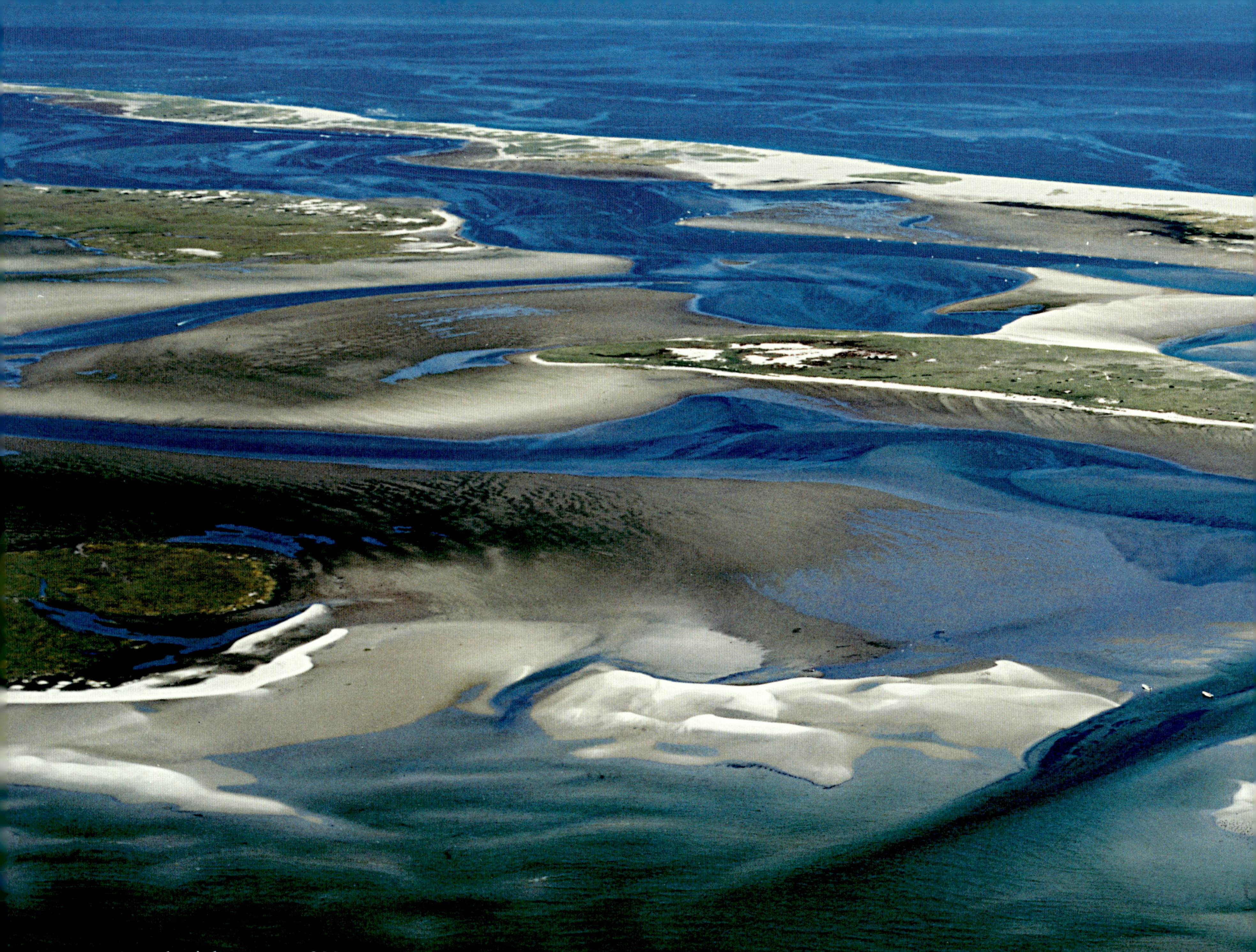

Spencer's pick of the season, 2006

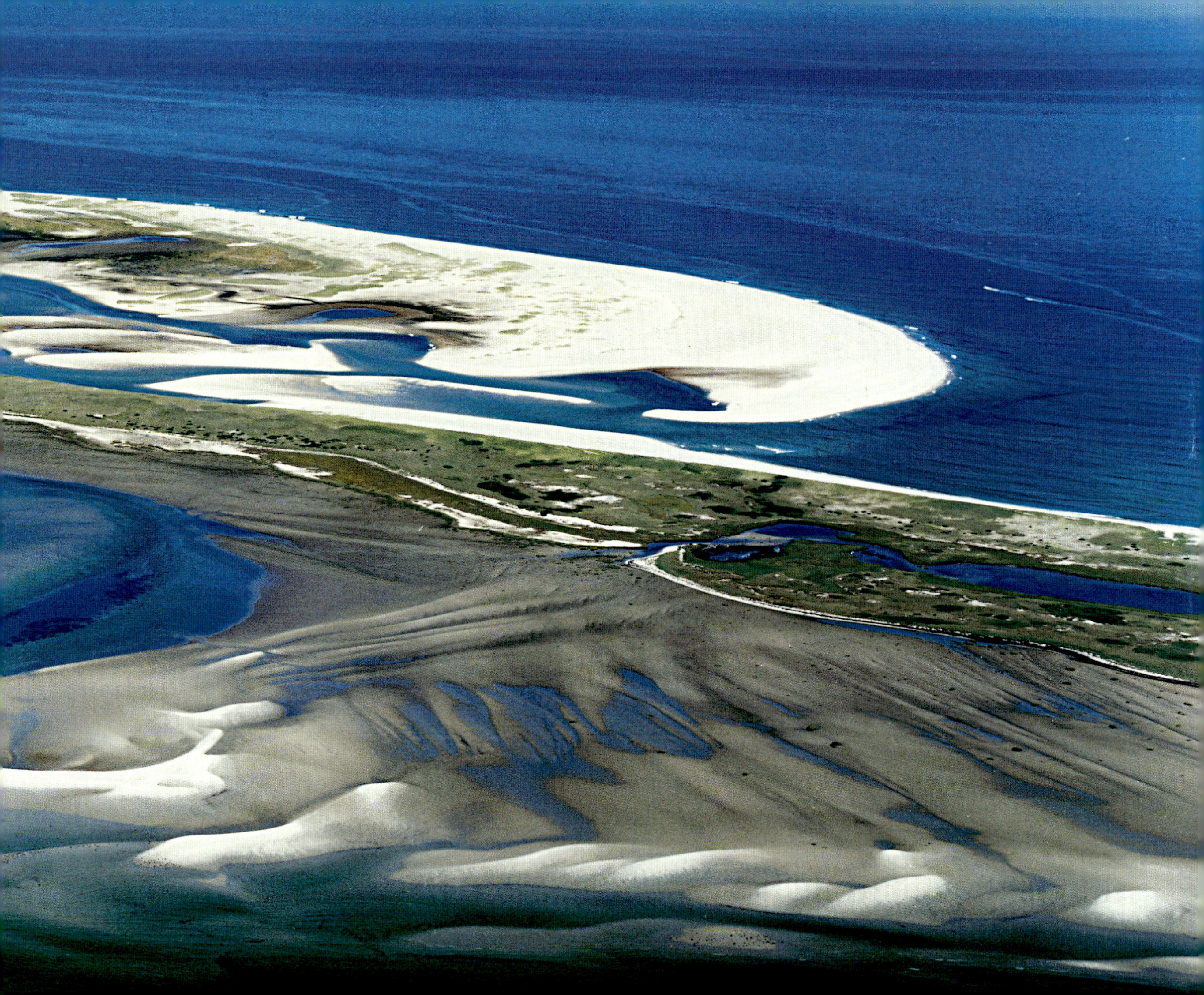

Chapter 7
Things You See While Flying

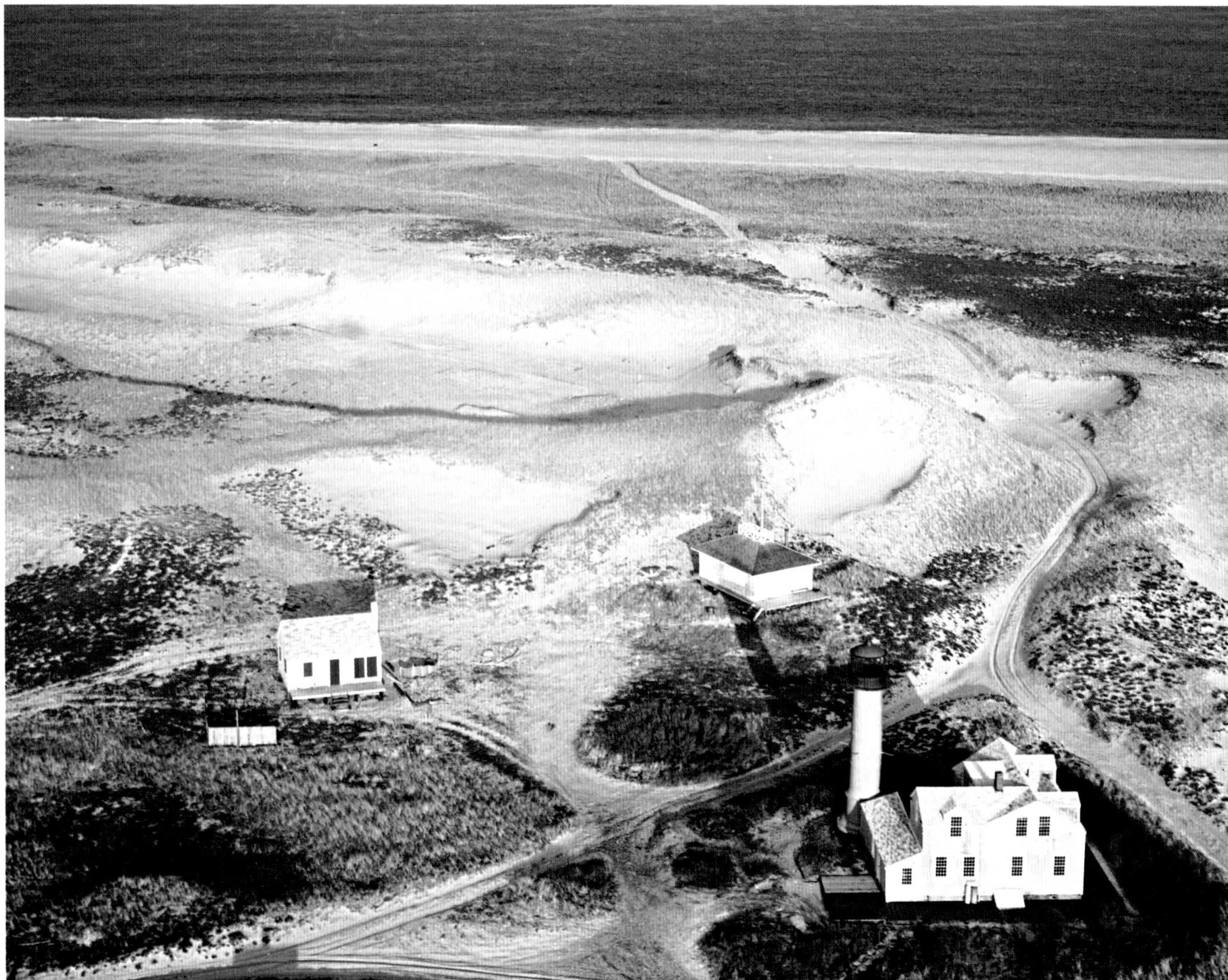

Monomoy Lighthouse, 1966.

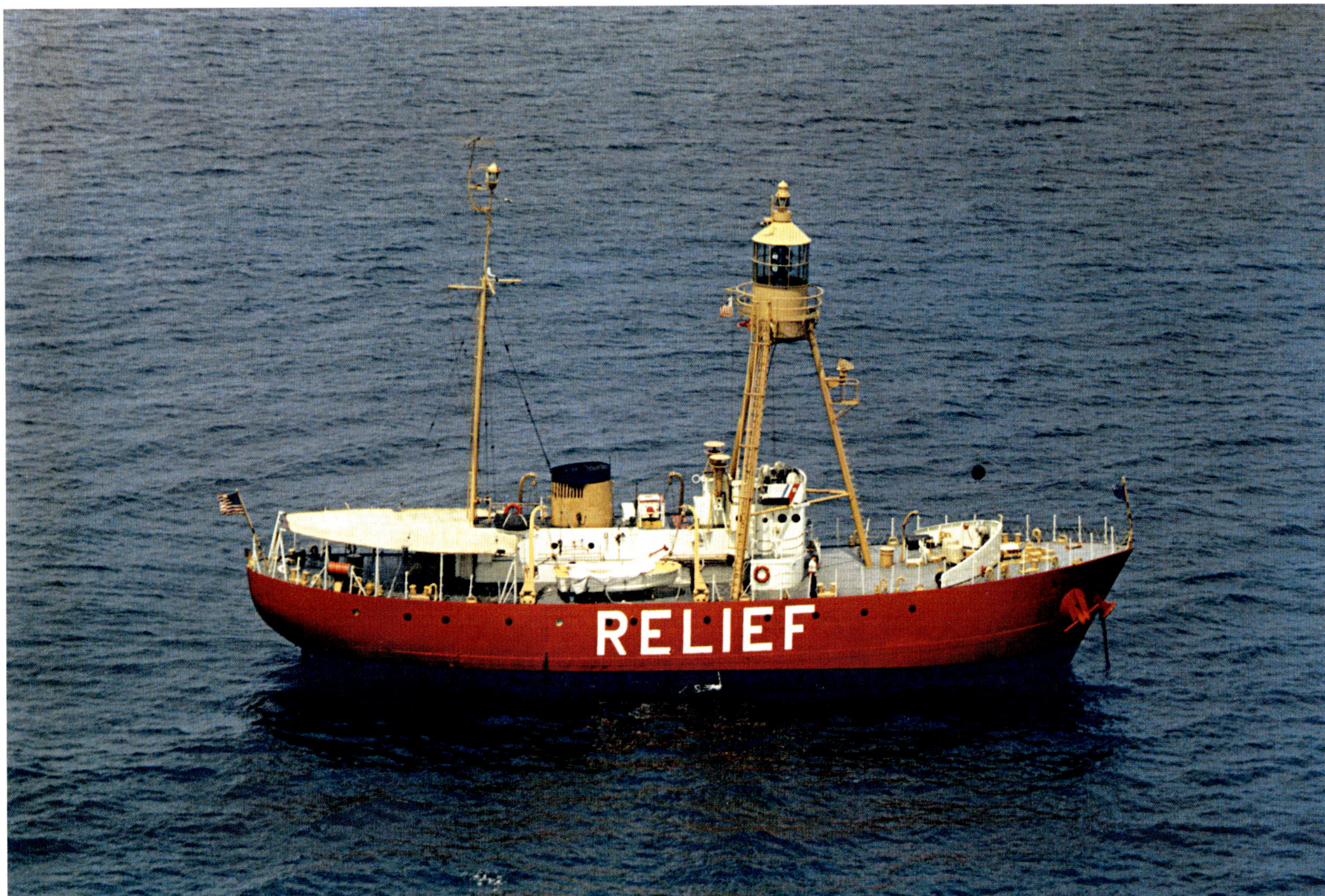

The lightship *Relief.* This is a big seller and adorns many bathroom doors.

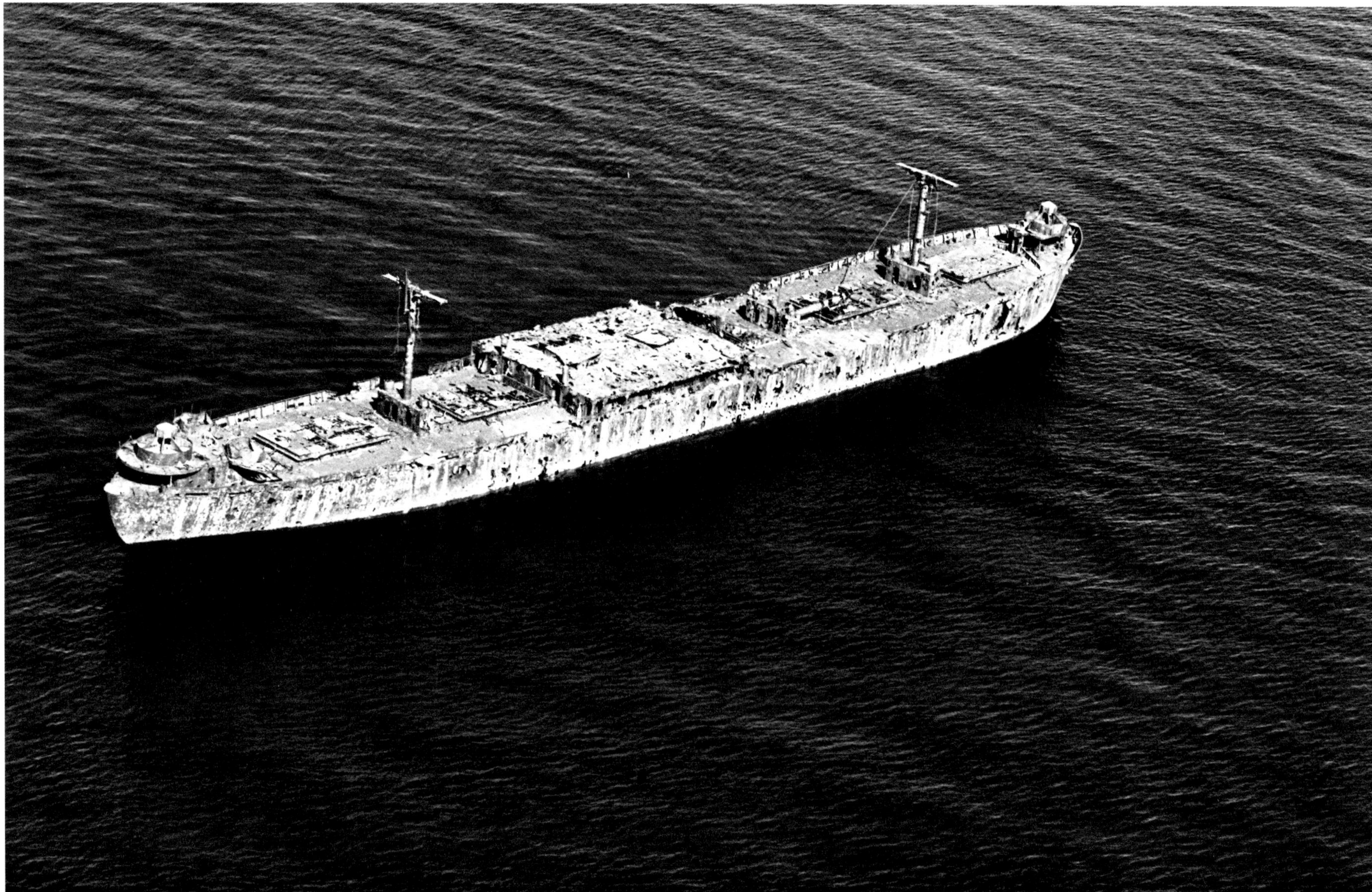

The James Longstreet, aka "The Target Ship," settled in Cape Cod Bay.

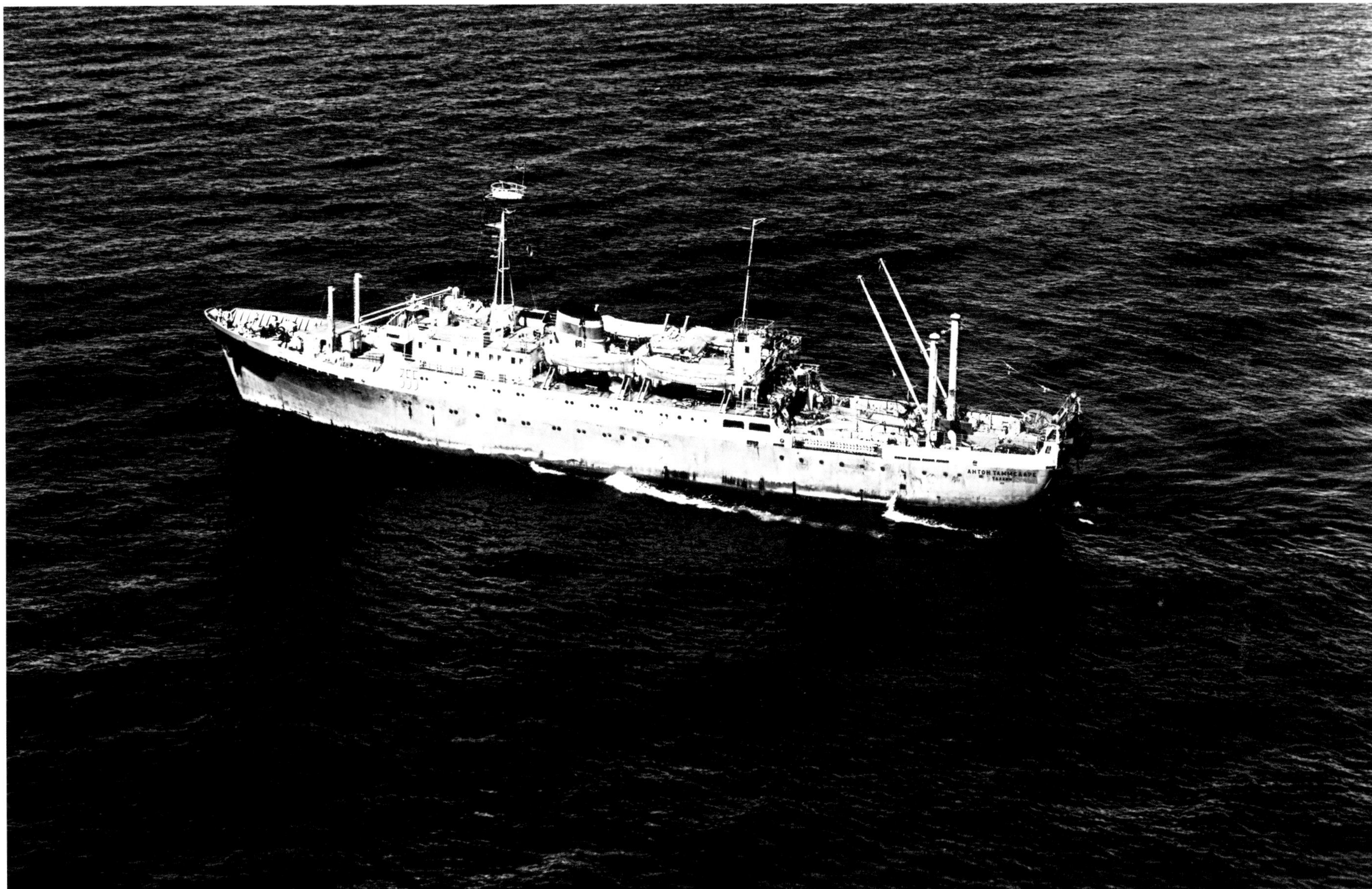

A Russian trawler that Dick Kelsey spotted off Chatham. These photos caused quite the sensation back then.

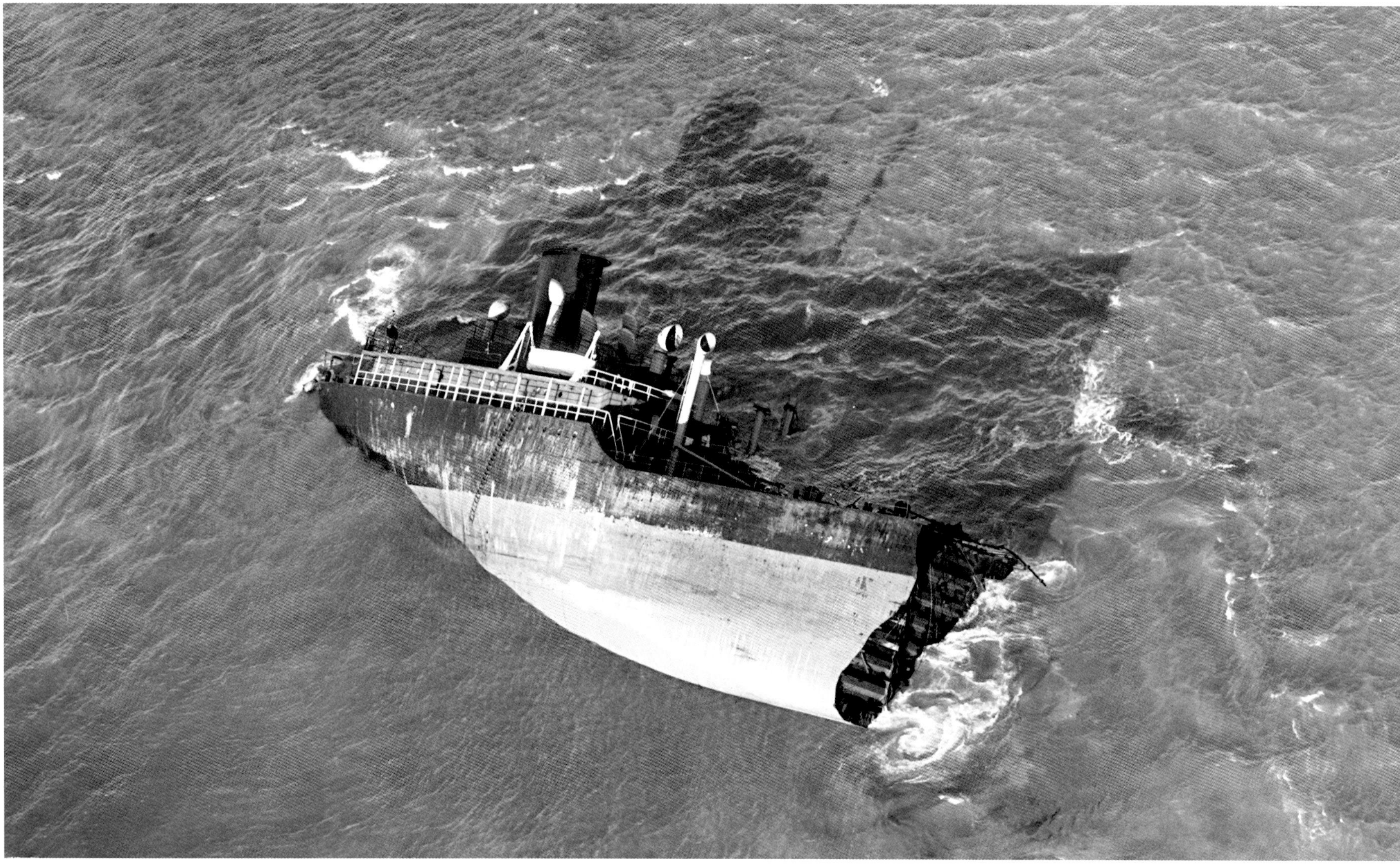

The Pendelton shipwreck.

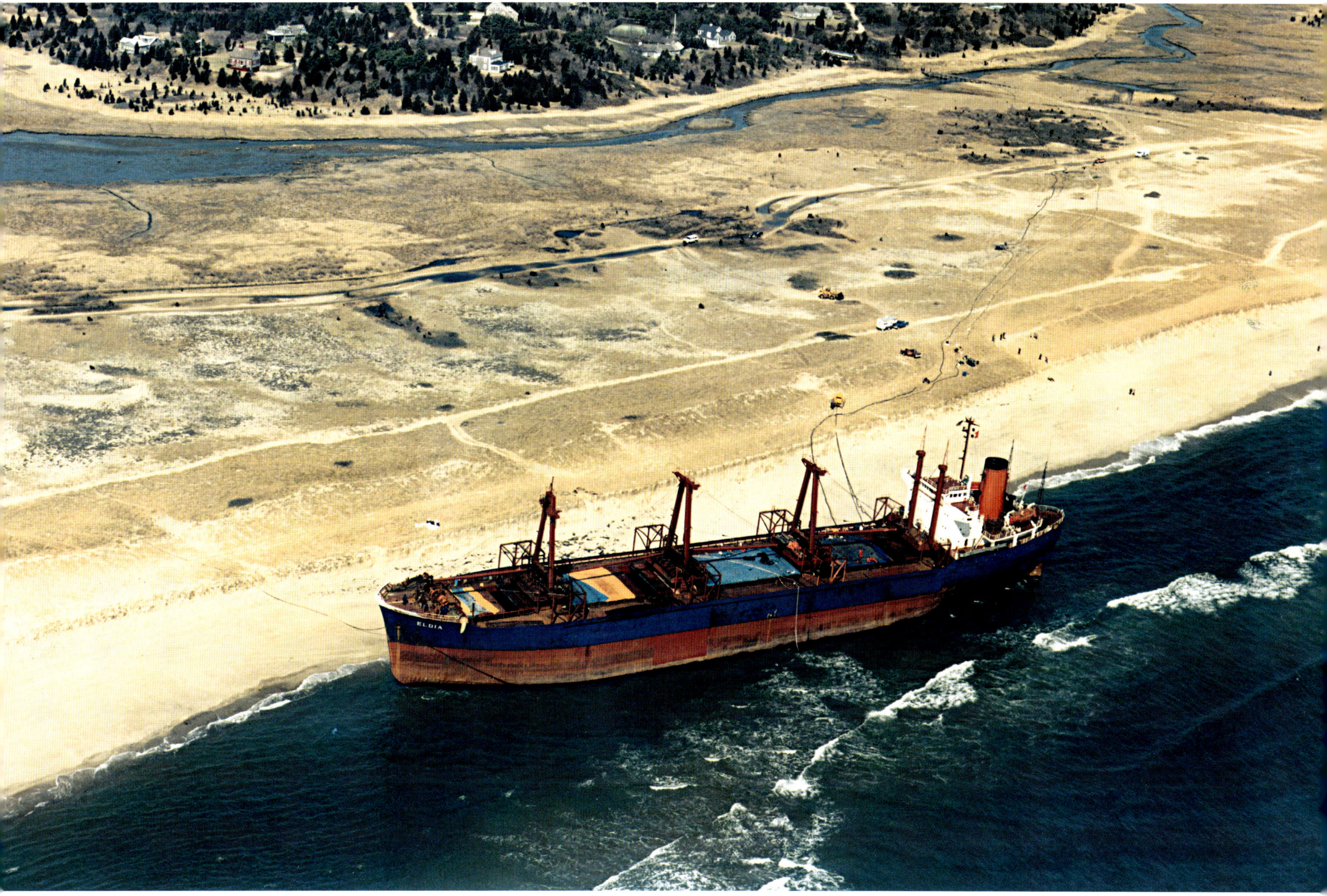

The Eldia blew ashore on Nauset Beach in 1984.

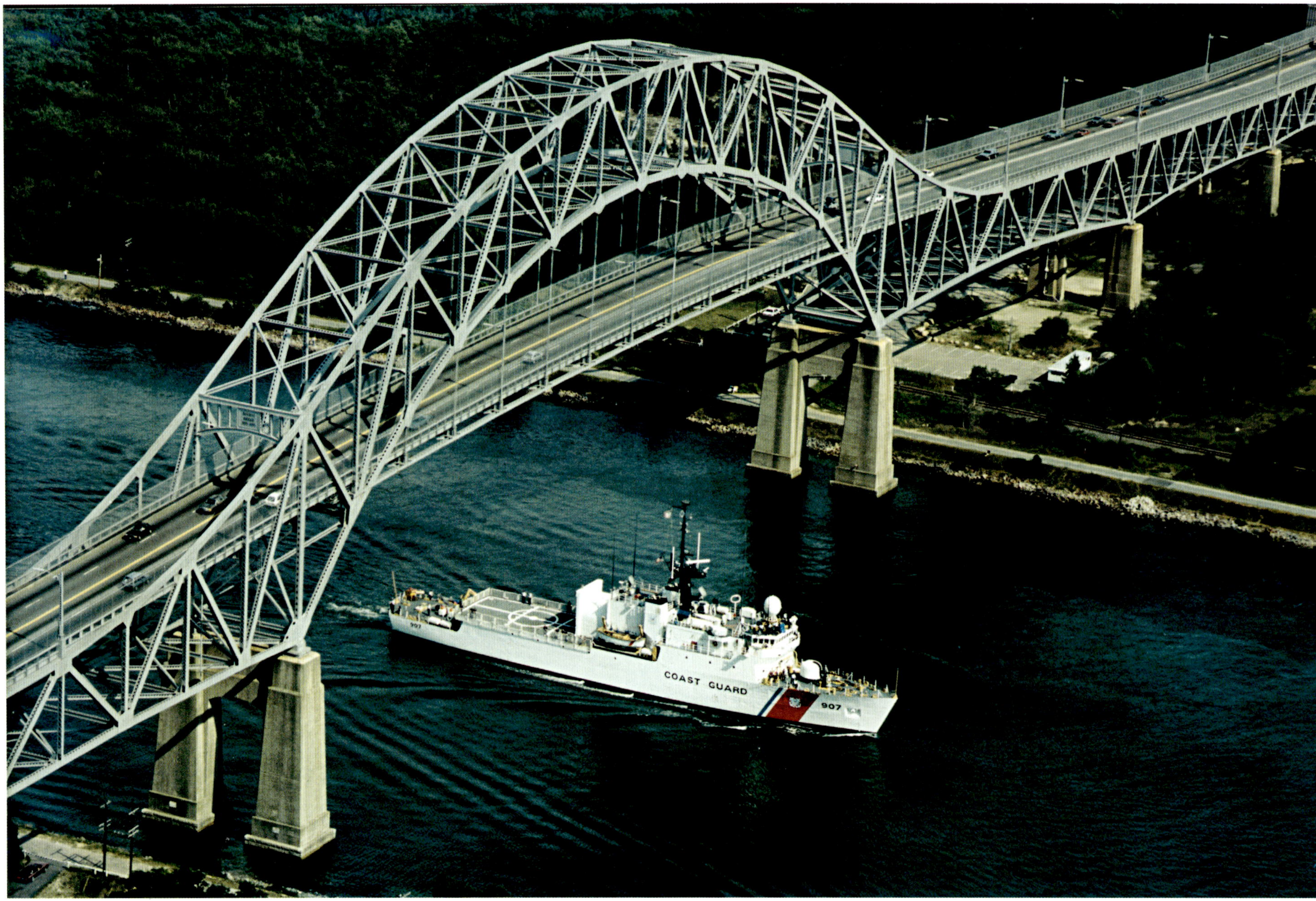

USCGC Escanaba in the Cape Cod Canal.

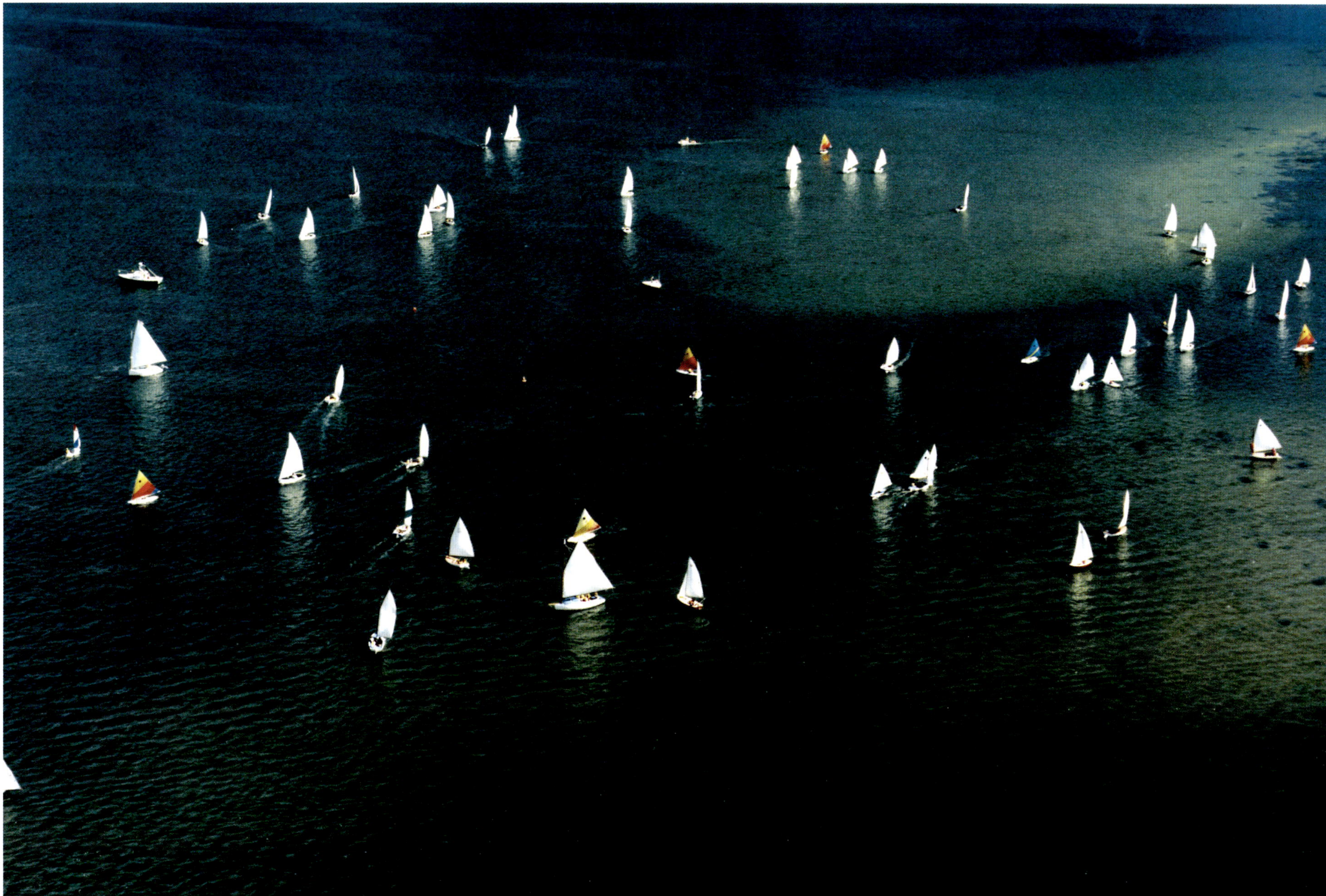

Richard Cooper Kelsey's last regatta, taken in August of 1987.

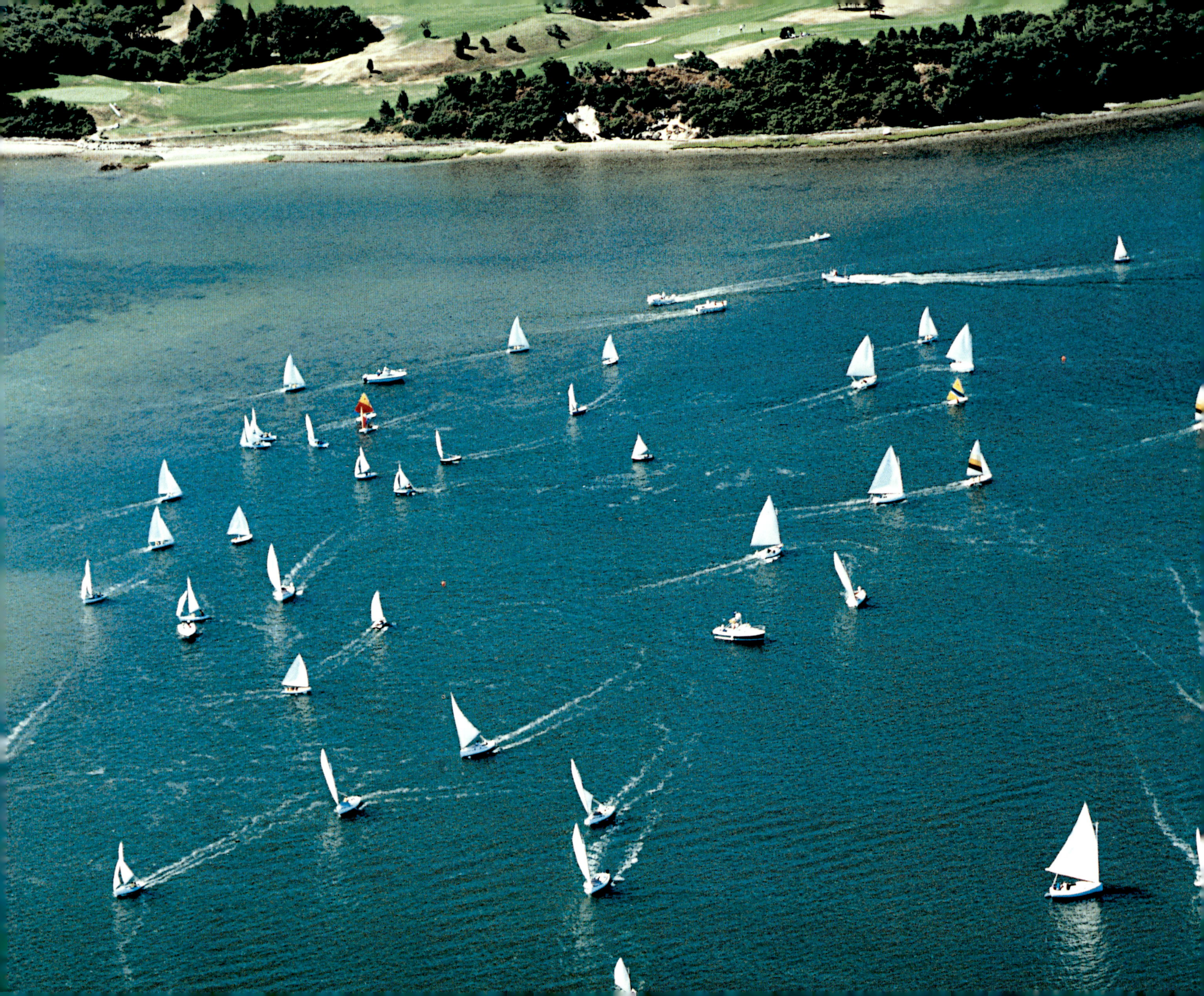

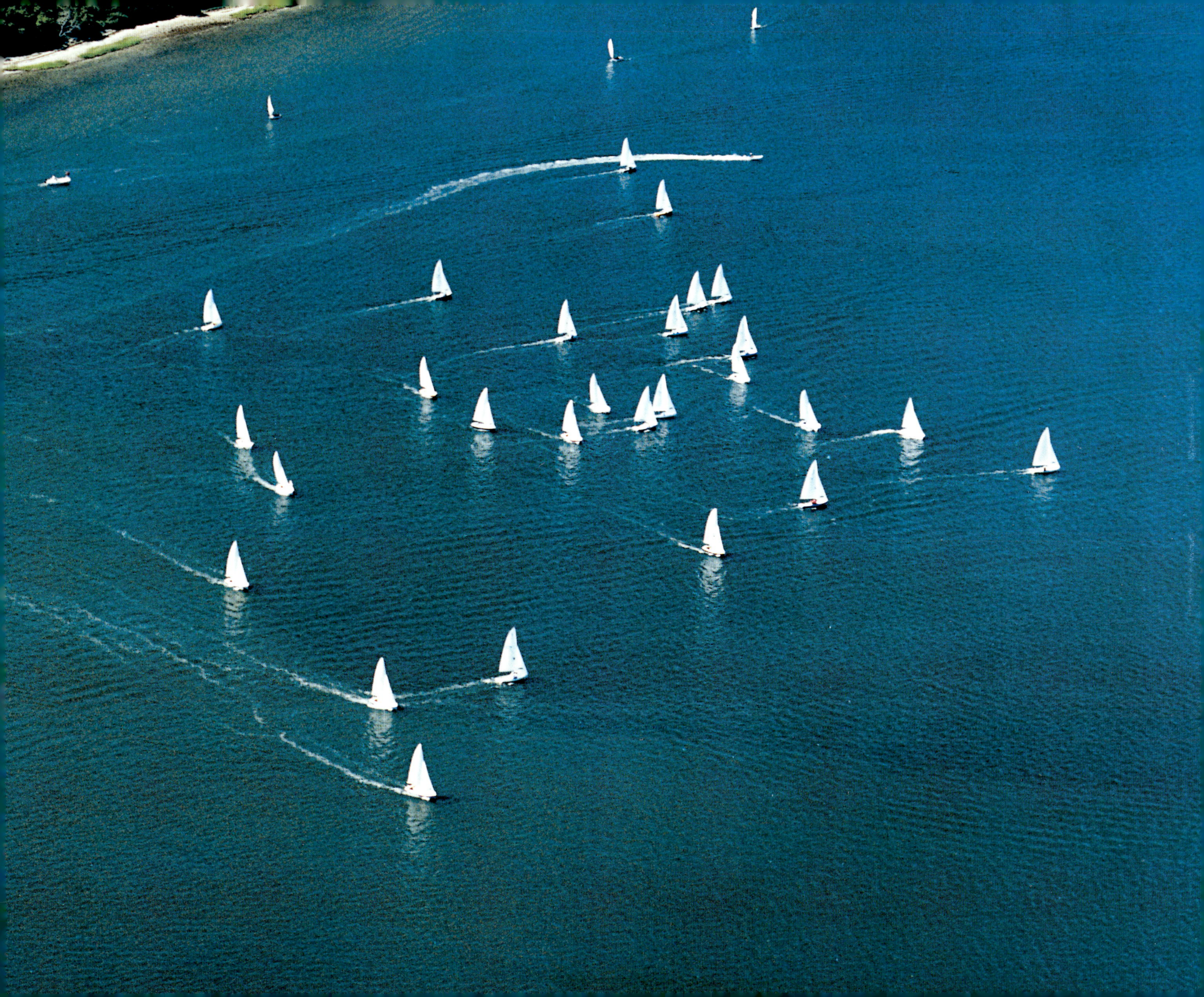

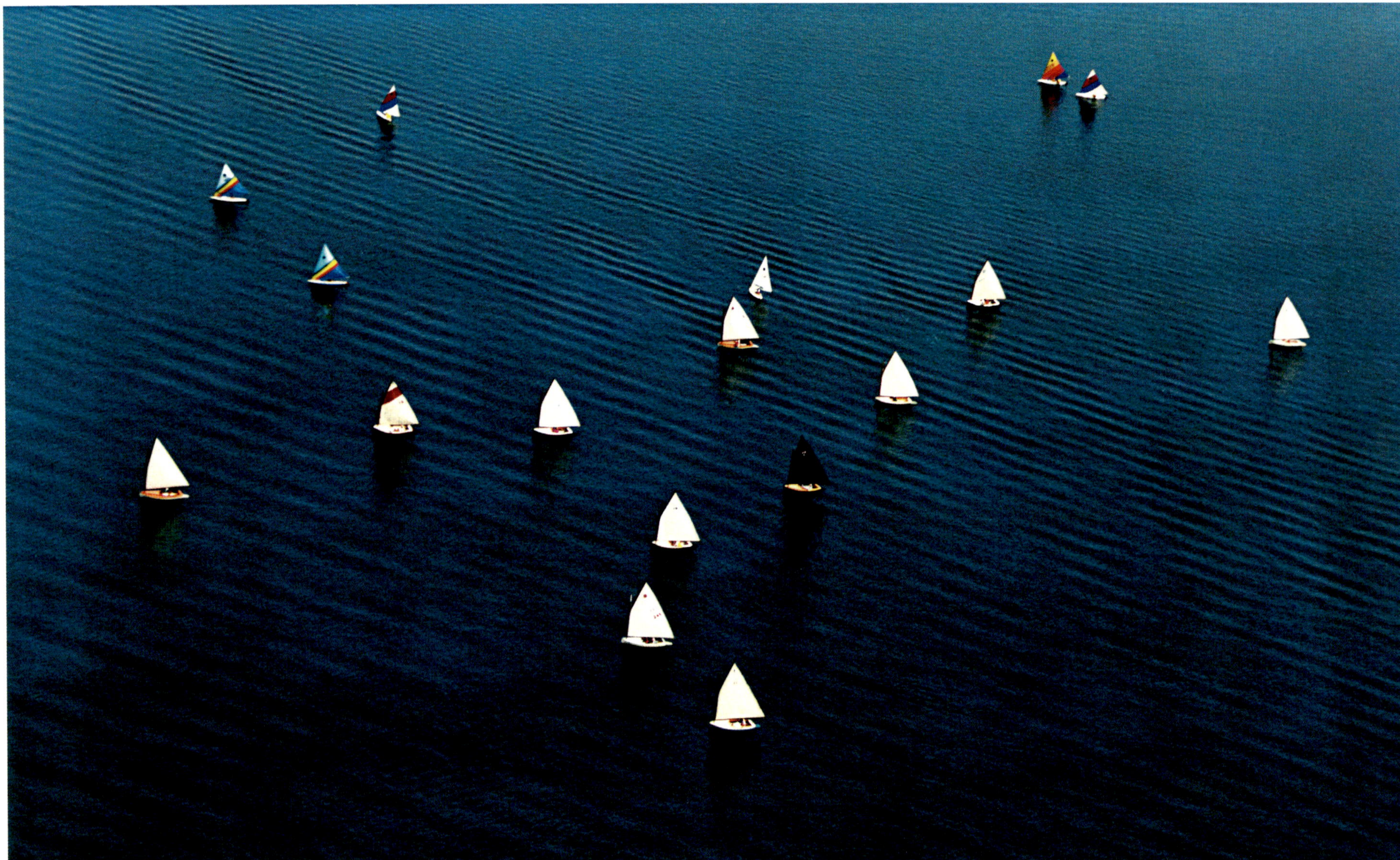

Regatta in Pleasant Bay.

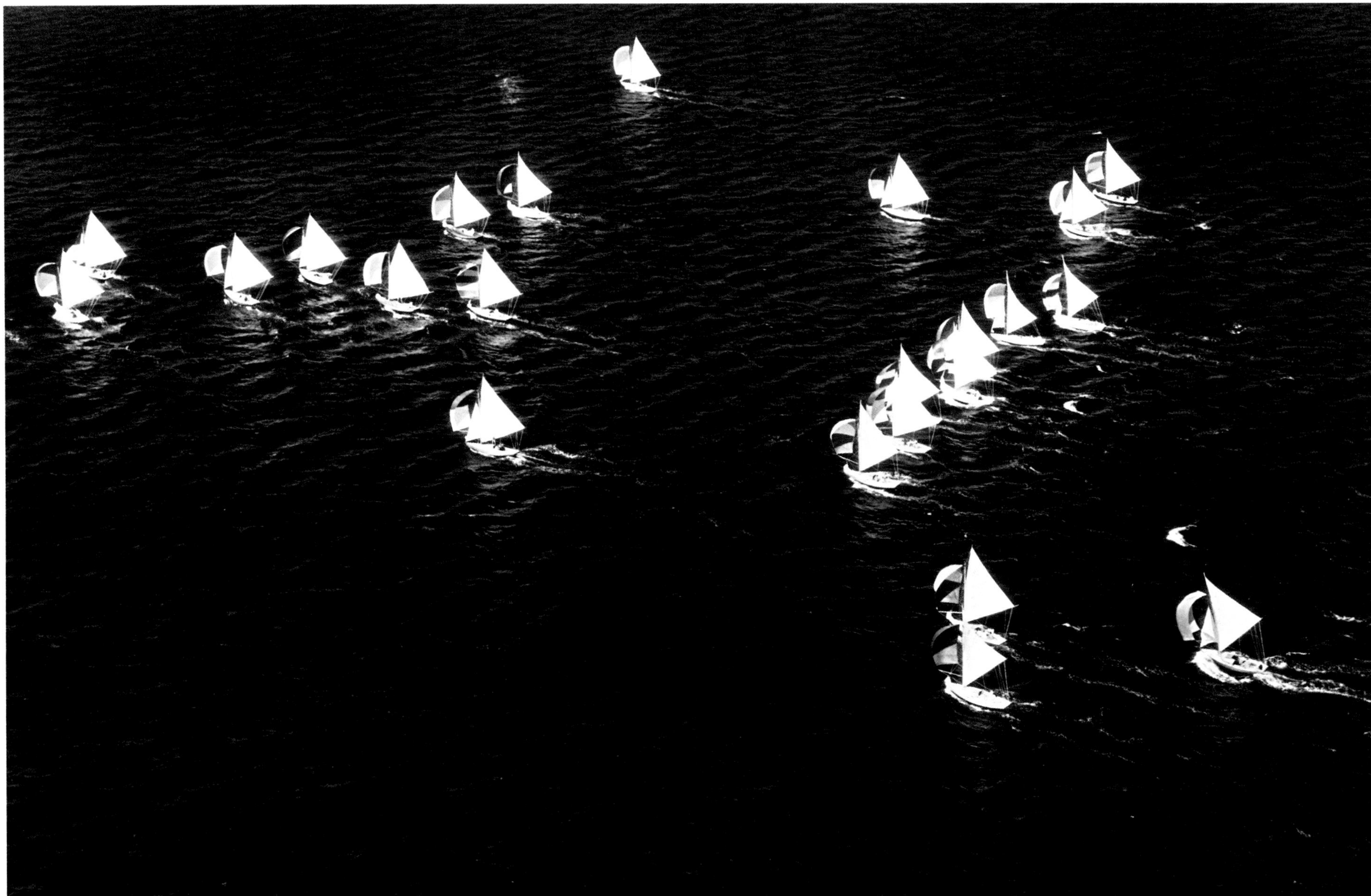

A regatta off Martha's Vineyard in 1966.

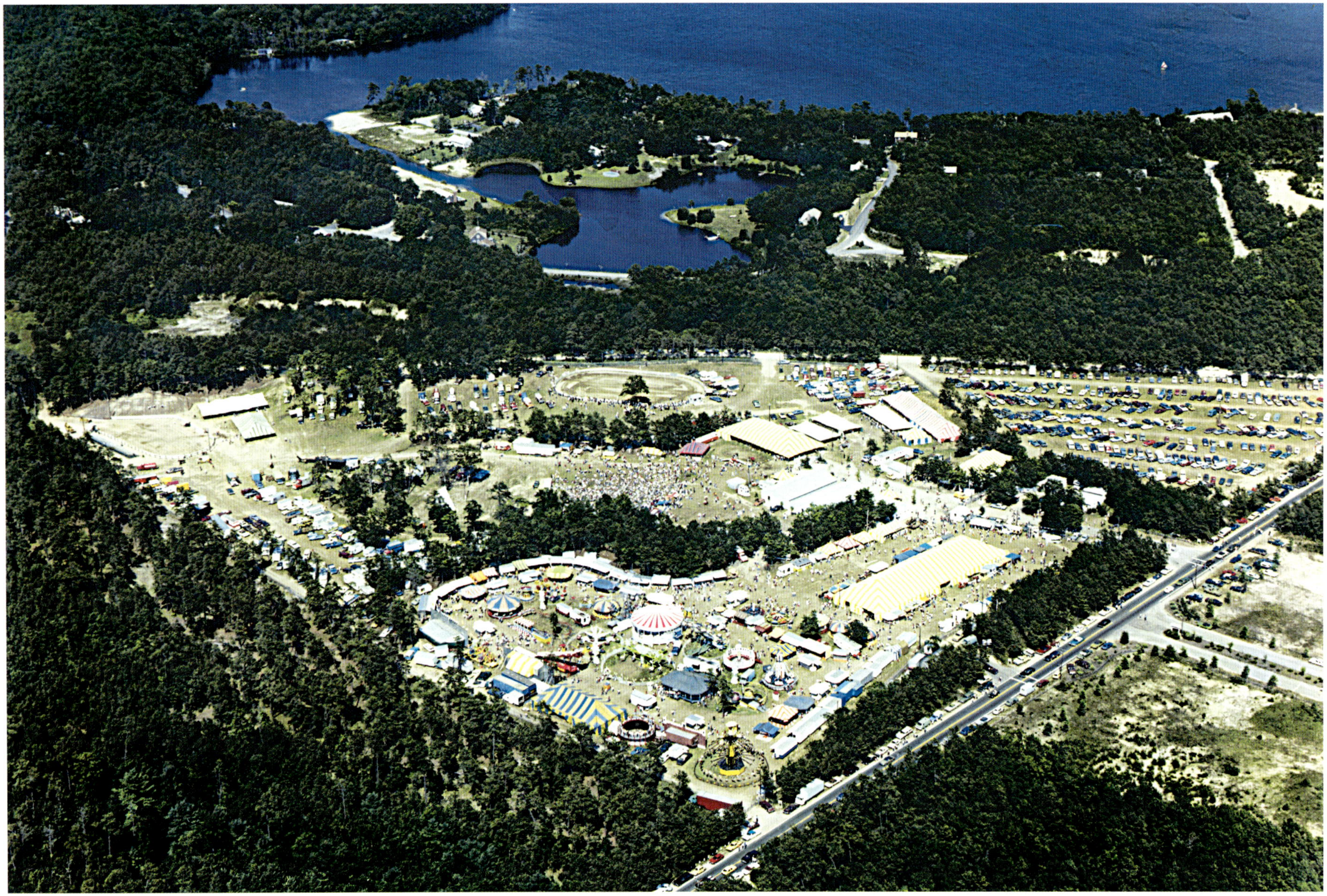

Barnstable County Fair. 1978.

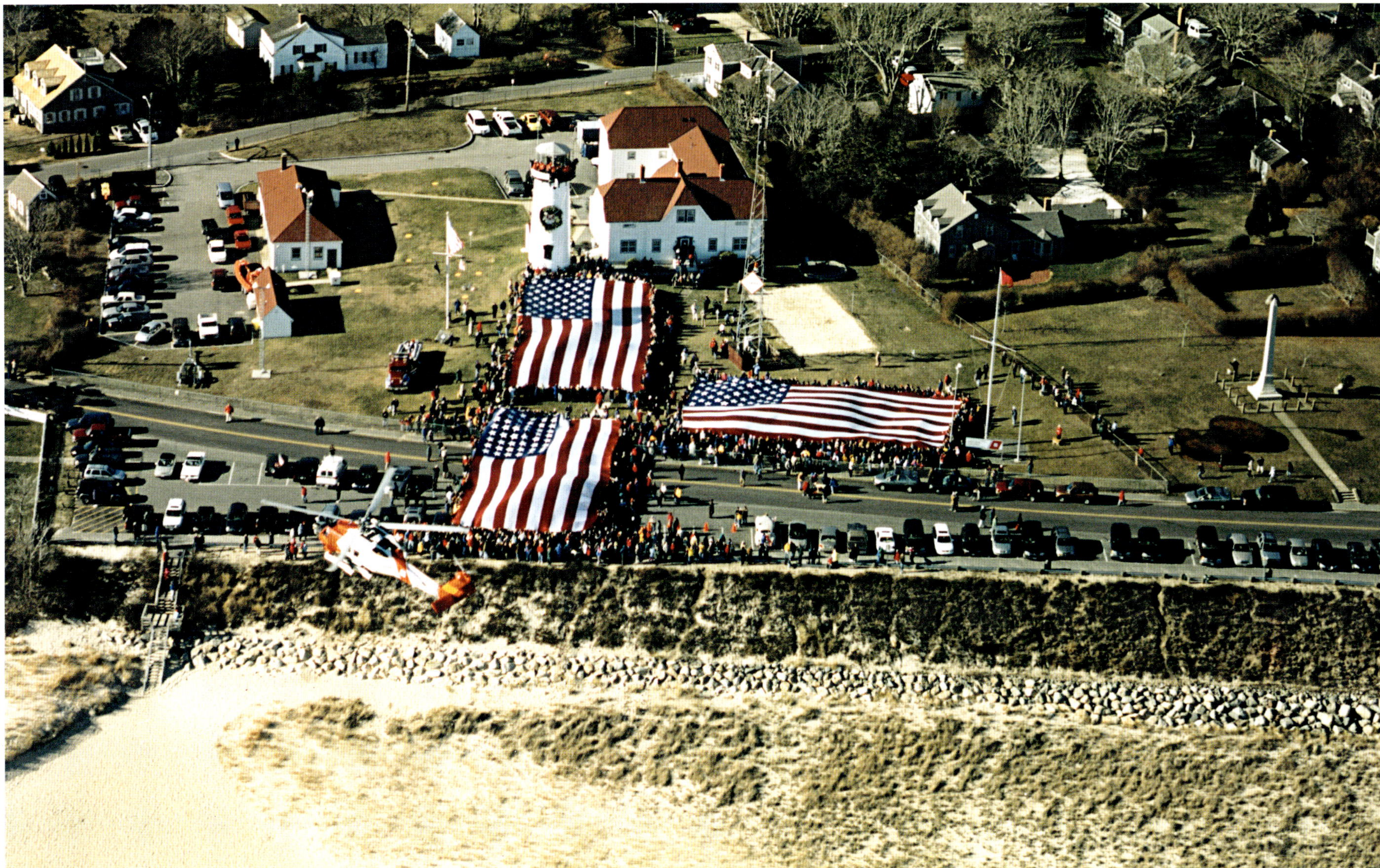

"First Night" Flag Celebration at Chatham Light, 2001.

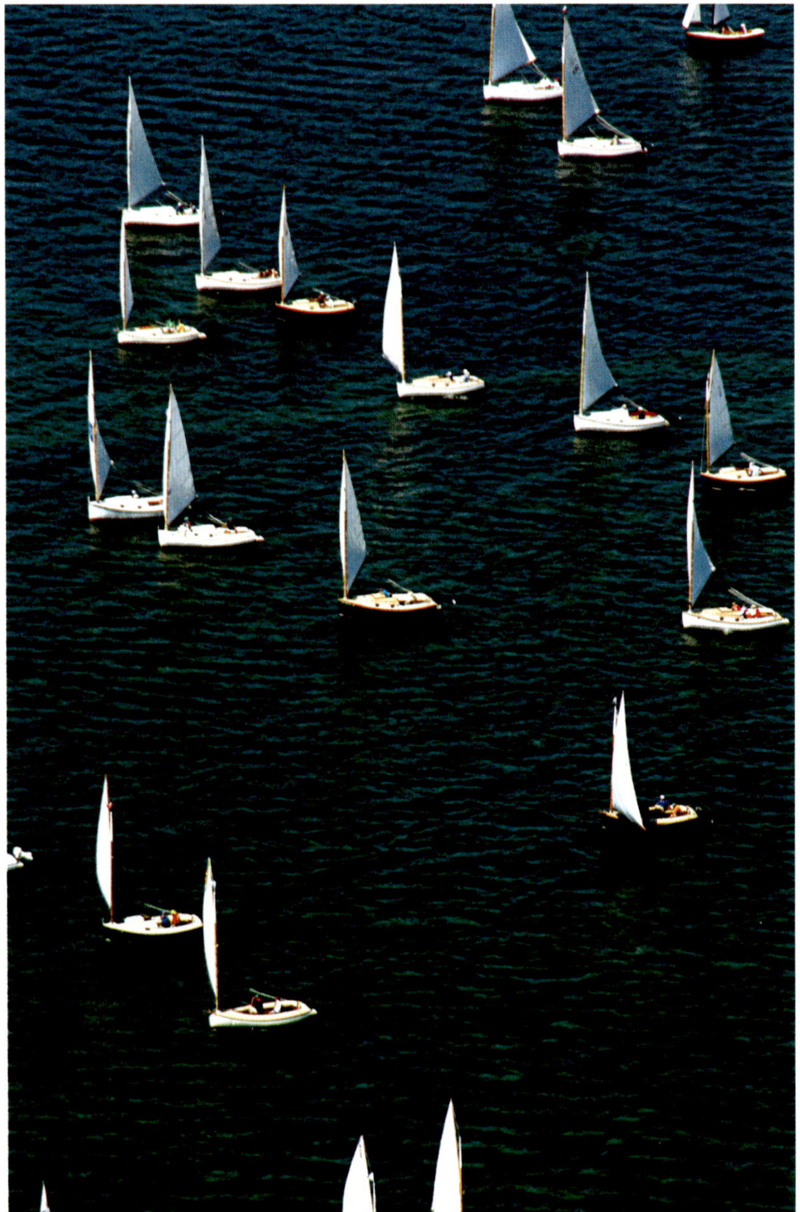

Boat Ballet in Pleasant Bay.

Cape Cod Baseball League in action. Wooden bats only!

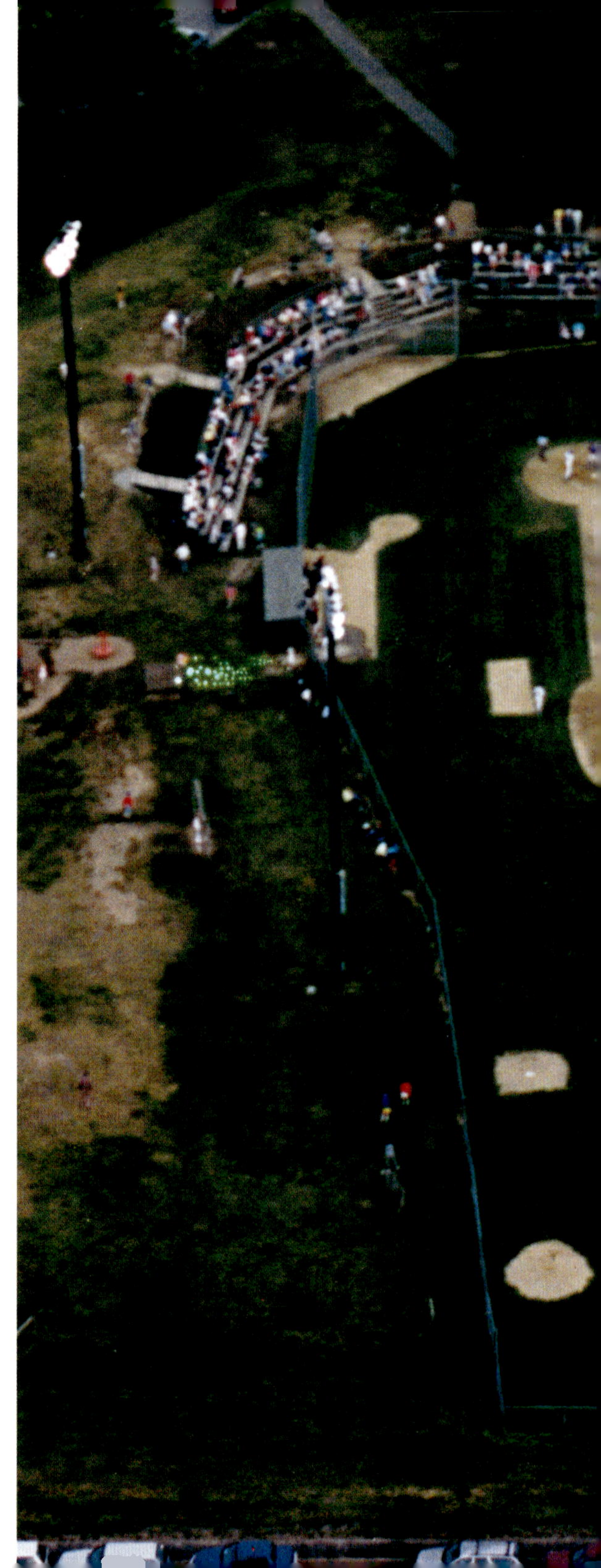

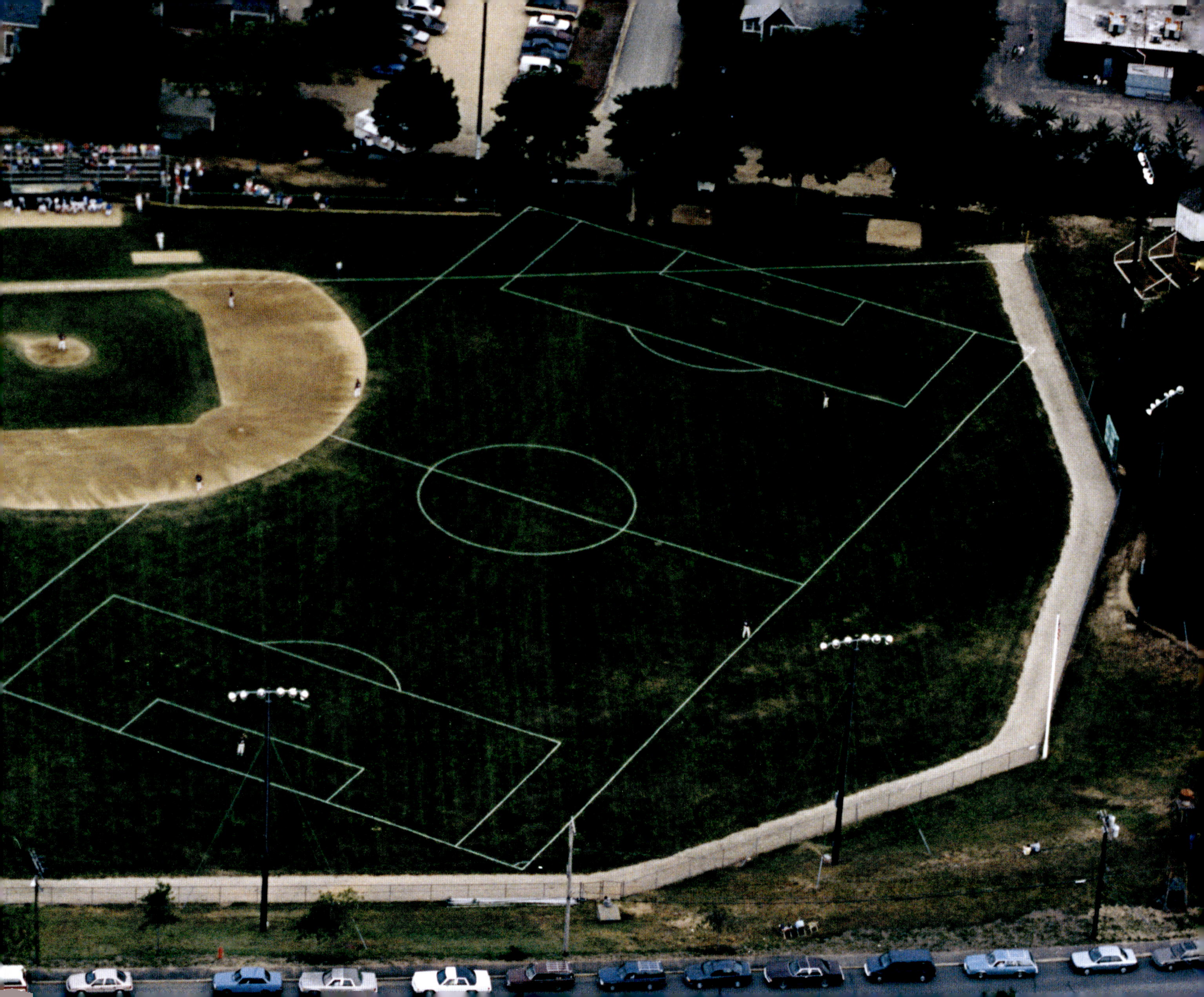

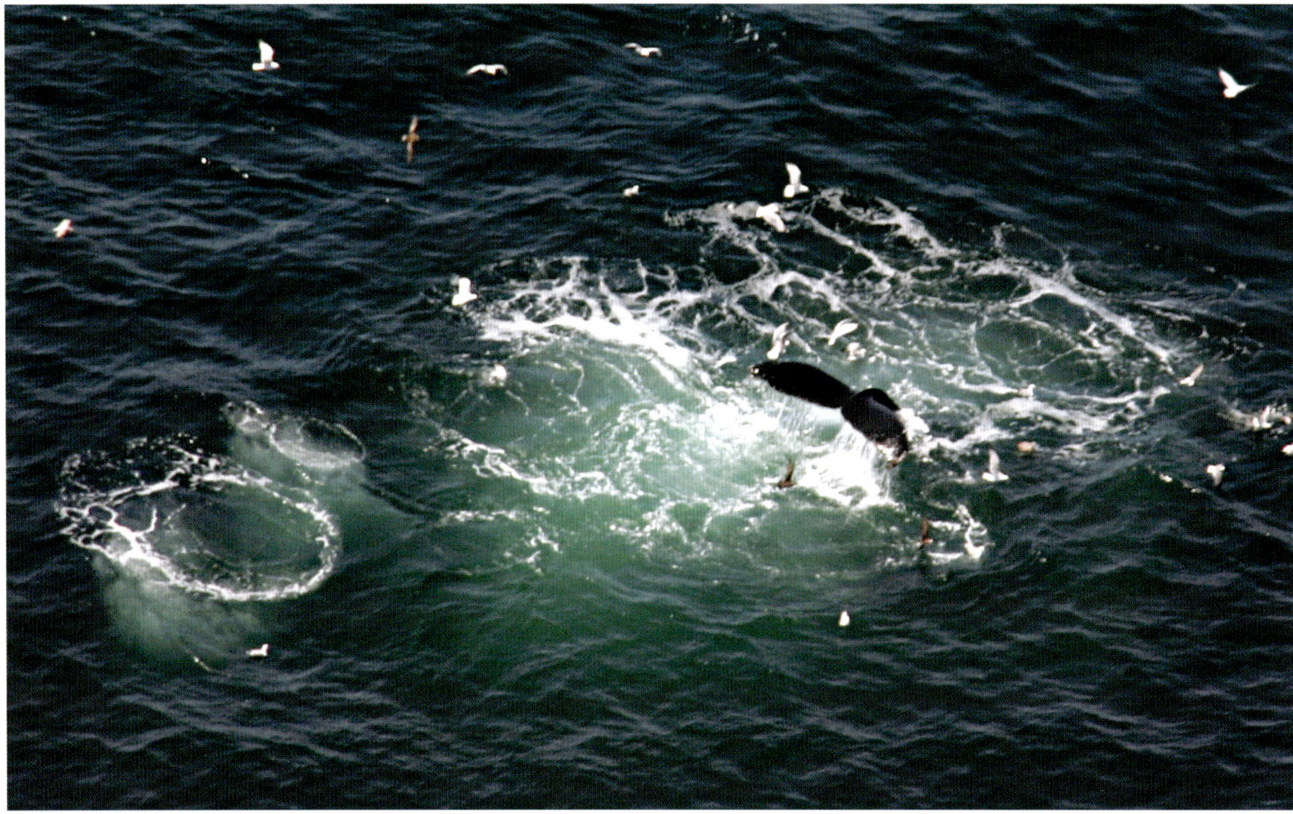

Whales feeding.

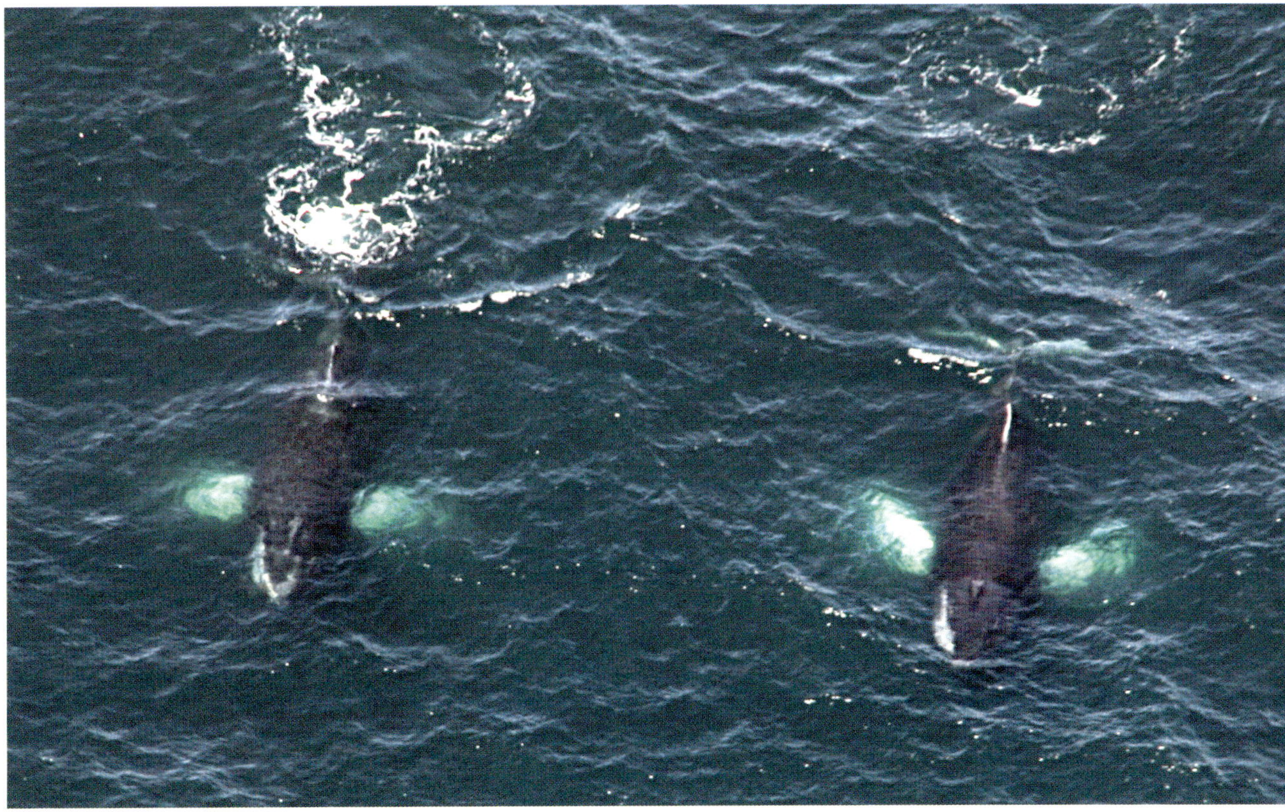

Whales side by side.

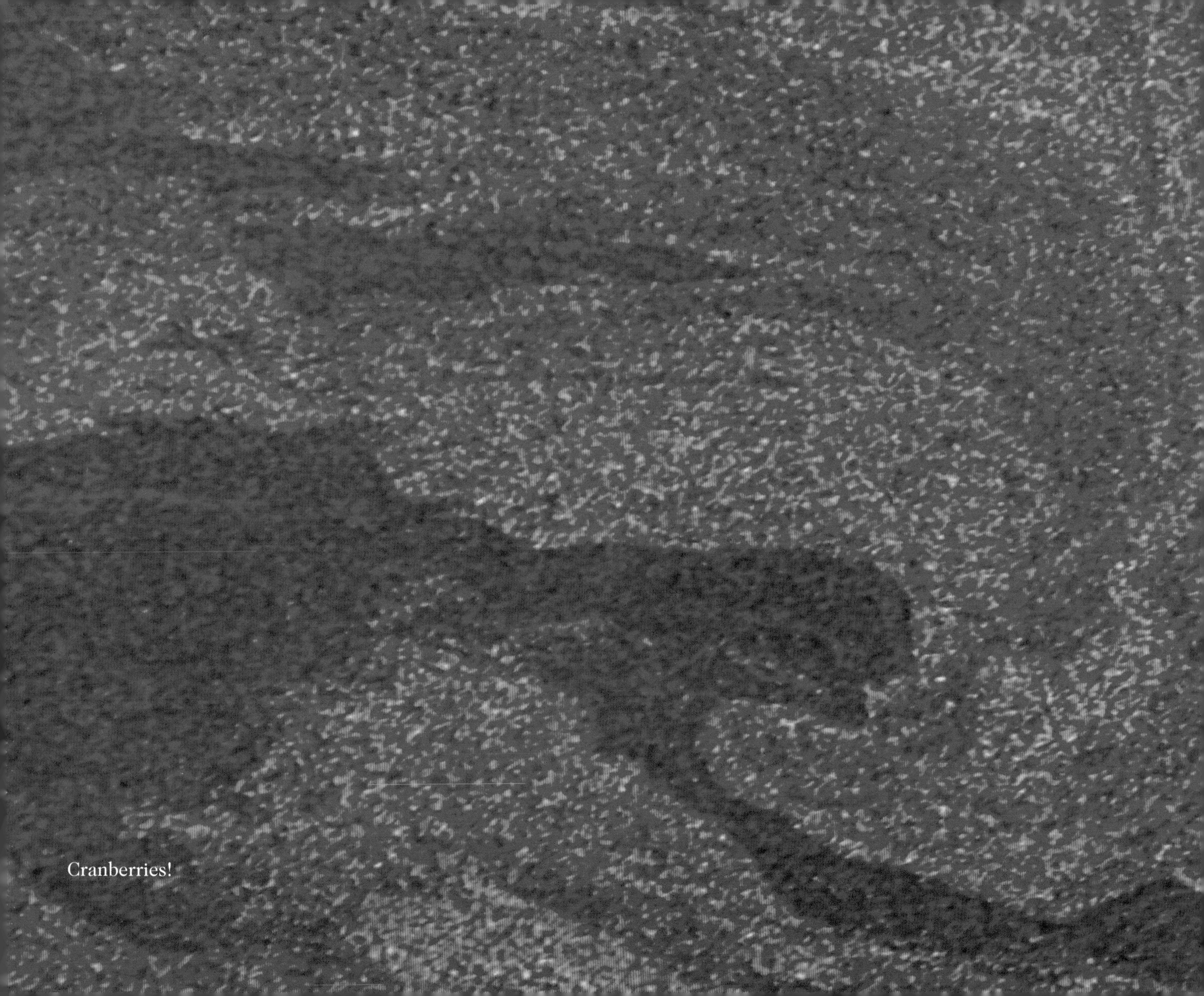

Cranberries!

Information about the photographs

Our Airviews encompass many forms of the photography medium. The black and white images are, for the most part, 5”x5” negatives taken by Dick Kelsey using a Kodak K-24 aerial camera. For those who don’t know, this heavy camera was usually mounted in the “belly” of the plane, but many times Dick hand-held his! The color images are taken with Pentax 6” x 7” cameras, a real workhorse, and now that we are in the digital world, a Canon EOS 20D has proved its worth. The Airviews are all dated by year, month and day. For example, 81-826-33c was taken in 1981, on August 26. The remaining numbers are for our negative file. Please note that any dates starting with a “0” are 21st century images! They, as well as all of our Airviews, can be ordered through our PhotoGallery in Chatham, Massachusetts, or our website: www.capecodphotos.com. Just mention the page reference in this book.

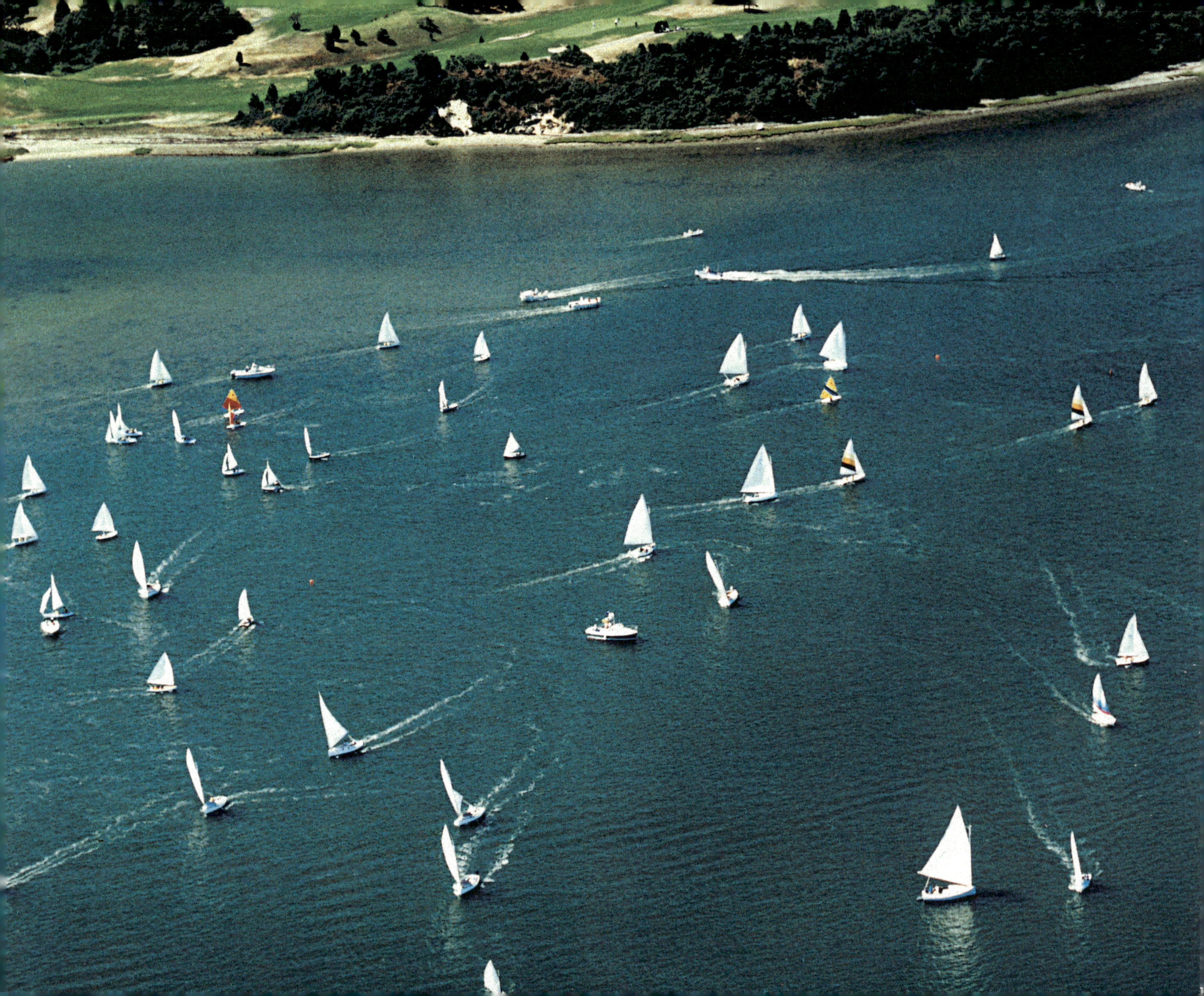